BUSINESS REVIEW BOOKS

Management

THIRD EDITION

Patrick J. Montana
Professor of Management
Frank G. Zarb School of Business
Hofstra University

Bruce H. Charnov
Associate Professor of Management
Chairperson, Management
and General Business Department
Frank G. Zarb School of Business
Hofstra University

BARRON'S

All inquiries should be addressed to:
Barron's Educational Series, Inc.
250 Wireless Boulevard
Hauppauge, New York 11788
http://www.barronseduc.com

ISBN-13: 978-0-7641-1276-8
ISBN-10: 0-7641-1276-7

Library of Congress Catalog Card No. 99-16327

Library of Congress Cataloging-in-Publication Data

Montana, Patrick J.
  Management / by Patrick J. Montana and Bruce H.
  Charnov.—3rd ed.
      p.   cm.—(Barron's business review series)
  Includes index.
  ISBN 0-7641-1276-7
  1. Management. I. Charnov, Bruce H. II. Title. III. Series.
HD31.M618   2000
658—dc21   99-16327

PRINTED IN CANADA
20 19 18 17 16 15 14 13 12 11

CONTENTS

PREFACE

Although there have always been good managers, management has been studied scientifically mainly by academics and practitioners since the beginning of the 20th century. It is not accidental that this growing interest in the understanding of management has been nurtured by and in turn benefitted the rising industrialism that has so changed and characterized the modern world.

Management, as defined in the dictionary, is "the act, art, or manner of managing, or handling, controlling, directing, etc.; skill in managing; executive ability." A modern manager might characterize it more as "the accomplishment of an organization's goals by the defining of goals, organization of work, motivation of others, staffing of the positions, the control of the labor, material, and evaluation of the completed effort." *Managers are managers because of what they do*—the task of this book is to describe and analyze functions of management so the reader will be able to describe the tasks of the modern executive.

Further, because our modern understanding of management did not develop full-blown but rather *evolved* since the beginning of the 20th century, the history of that development is presented in several different areas. This insertion of history was done with a great deal of forethought, for although one can practice management without the slightest knowledge of how that craft evolved, the authors feel that a knowledge of the past not only enhances an appreciation of the present but also helps the reader understand future trends.

This book describes in a traditionally sequential format the various functions of management. But since the modern manager must function within an increasingly complex global world, the environments of business (economic, technological, sociological, demographic, legislative, etc.) are described as they relate to the contemporary business organization. Finally, information has been provided concerning the future of a managerial career as well as executive skills of time management. The authors have also chosen illustrations of management in both the profit and nonprofit field.

Each chapter features Key Terms, several You Should Know portions, and Questions and Answers. This educational apparatus, which characterizes the *Barron's Business Review Series*, makes this book and others in the series a valuable tool for the student and manager alike.

Many individuals contribute to a successful project, and it's fitting to thank them for their contributions. No literary endeavor succeeds without a skilled editor who possesses a vision, exercises good judgment, and imposes a sense of discipline and deadline upon authors. Wendy Sleppin is such an editor and due far more thanks than expressed here. Thanks are also due to Miryam Esther (Charnov) Benovitz, Aharon Chayim (Roni) Charnov, and Jessica Lauren Charnov, who gladly accepted the sacrifice necessary for project completion. And this is especially for the next generation, Ariella Reva Benovitz. Connie L. Bueti also deserves thanks for her editorial advice, typing, and general assistance. Thanks also to Regine Franklin for her assistance in compiling the bibliography.

Bruce H. Charnov

Patrick J. Montana

1

WHAT IS MANAGEMENT: DEFINITION AND OVERVIEW

KEY TERMS

management working with and through other people to accomplish the objectives of both the organization and its members

management activities include planning, organizing, staffing, coordinating, motivating, leading, and controlling; getting results effectively through other people by process of delegation

technical activities the specialist functions of an individual, or those that derive from his/her vocational field

responsibility the duty or task to be performed

authority the power to act for someone else

accountability the obligation to be held responsible for what was expected or what happened that was unexpected

DEFINITION OF MANAGEMENT

Unfortunately in management, it is difficult to find standard definitions for many commonly used terms, yet a common vocabulary and a common understanding are vital to successful communication. As we go along in this book, we are going to develop a common vocabulary for managers, a vocabulary understood and agreed upon by most in the management field.

Perhaps the most important place to start is with an understanding of what management is. You will find many different definitions in various texts, all usually variations of the same themes. Over time, there has been and continues to be a shift in emphasis within the definitions. Let us think about this evolution for a minute by looking at two definitions.

In 1980, the President of the American Management Association (AMA) used this definition of management: "Management is getting things done through other people."

Now look at a current definition: "**Management** is working *with and through* other people to accomplish the *objectives* of both the organization and its members."

What are the differences between the two?

There are three key differences that should be highlighted. The more recent definition:

1. places greater emphasis on the human being in the organization.

2. focuses attention on the *results* to be accomplished, on objectives, rather than just things or activities

3. adds the concept that accomplishment of the members' personal objectives should be integrated with the accomplishment of organizational objectives

---

YOU SHOULD REMEMBER

Management is working with and through other people to accomplish the objectives of both the organization and its members.

THE MANAGERIAL ROLE
MANAGEMENT ACTIVITIES VS. TECHNICAL ACTIVITIES

In looking at the current definition, we come to the conclusion that management is both a science and an art. We also have to view the manager as an individual, to distinguish between the role as a manager and the role as a technician, following a vocational field. And when a person is a manager, he or she is doing the same thing no matter at what level in an organization. Every manager plans, organizes, staffs, coordinates, motivates, leads, and controls.

Planning is probably the most important activity in the manager's life. The manager may ask, "What is the objective of all my actions?" In the planning processes, it is very important to establish an objective in order to get a team together, determine duties and tasks, and begin the process of delegation. Only with established objectives can a manager effectively control and subsequently evaluate performance.

Figure 1-1 represents an organization—in this case a medium-sized business. Across the horizontal is measured 100 percent of time—all you have, whether 8 hours or 18 hours. On the top line is the president; the bottom line is the first-line supervisor, the lowest level manager. The line running from the lower left to the upper right creates a division between managerial activities and technical activities. The model says the first-line supervisor spends perhaps 30 percent of his/her time in managerial activities and 70 percent in technical activities. By the time the manager gets up to the presidential level, he/she is spending at least 90 percent of his/her time in managerial activities and only 10 percent (if any at all) in technical activities. If we were to put other levels of management in the model, we would see that as an individual advances in the organization, as management activities and demands increase, involvement in technical (or vocational) activities should decrease.

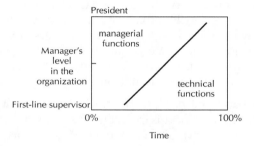

Figure 1–1. Managerial and technical activities at different levels of management.

To illustrate these concepts, let us take a look at a typical management situation. See if you can determine what is wrong here in terms of the managerial role.

CASE STUDY: TALKING WITH GEORGE

THE SCENE: The controller's office in a large corporation on a Monday morning. George, director of economic planning, has just submitted a report to his immediate supervisor, the controller.

CONTROLLER: Sit down, George, while I look this over.

GEORGE: (virtually collapsing into a chair before the desk) This is the first chance I've had to sit down in a week.

CONTROLLER: (after examining major aspects of the report carefully but briefly) This is fine, George, just what we need. But why

	couldn't it have been ready for the treasurer on Friday, as we had agreed?
GEORGE:	Frank became ill on Monday, that new employee's husband decided to accept a job in Des Moines. That makes three good employees I've lost in as many weeks. By the time I had a look at the first draft, it was already late and the draft was absolutely incomprehensible. Irving could have worked on it with me, but he has been scheduled for months to go on vacation to California as of last Wednesday, and all his plans were made and I couldn't ask him to delay leaving. So, hard as we tried, and God knows we slaved over this report, it was just impossible to finish it by Friday. As it was, I finished it up on Saturday and Sunday. I've worked like a dog on this project, and all I get are questions about why it wasn't ready sooner. There is very little appreciation around here for what goes into a report like that. The treasurer wants something, probably minor to him, and the word filters down to us until it is a major project. We go all out on it; then, no one gives a damn what we put into it. You can ask Phil; I was here until six o'clock Saturday working on that damn thing.
CONTROLLER:	I know you work hard, George. I have never suggested that you don't. This report is excellent. It's just what I wanted, but you shouldn't have done it. We have had this assignment for two weeks. We discussed it again ten days ago at my initiative. You never at any time during that period said it wouldn't be ready—until you came in here Friday morning asking me to phone the treasurer for an extension.
GEORGE:	He didn't really need it until tomorrow, anyhow. The board meeting isn't until then.
CONTROLLER:	But he asked us to have it ready by Friday, and we had plenty of time to do it. Why can't we schedule jobs and be sure they come out on time?
GEORGE:	[Repeats his previous explanation for the delay, putting added emphasis on his own hard work and on the amount of overtime he had devoted to the report (for which he received no extra compensation).]
CONTROLLER:	George, I don't want you to work harder. I don't want you to work overtime. I want you to organize your department so that jobs come out when they are scheduled.
GEORGE:	I don't know what you want. I work harder than anyone around here. (Again repeats explanation for the report's delay, with some elaboration and additions.)

CONTROLLER: Let's go to lunch and talk some more about this.

GEORGE: I can't go out for lunch. I don't have time. My desk is piled high with papers. I'll probably be here until eight o'clock tonight. You don't have any idea how much work goes through my office. I've got to get back to work. (Gets up and moves toward the door, muttering that he works harder than anyone else in the company and no one gives a damn. "Those people in investment go home right on the dot of five o'clock . . . .")

What might be some of the reasons that someone is involved more heavily in technical activities than he/she should be given his/her managerial level? Why, for example, might someone at management level C be functioning at a lower level (see Figure 1-2)?

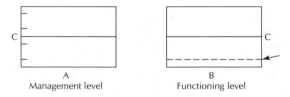

Figure 1–2. Contrast between managerial level and functioning level. A manager may be (A) in a midlevel management position (——) but be functioning (B) at a low-level management level (– – – –).

A typical list of reasons might include:

- small size of the unit
- technical nature of the tasks
- perceived need of the manager to stay current in the technical field
- subordinates not working to capacity
- comfort with the familiar
- expectations of the boss
- resource constraints

An important question for a manager to ask at this point is, "Which of these things are actually under my control and what can I do to change them?"

YOU SHOULD REMEMBER

As an individual advances in the organization and as management activities and demands increase, involvement in technical (or vocational) activities should decrease.

INTRODUCTION TO THE MANAGEMENT PROCESS

Let us go a little bit further now in thinking about the manager's role by looking at a critical incident of a case study.

Think about one question as you read it: Who is responsible for what has gone wrong?

> One of your workers, Joan, who is very bright and came to work for your organization with excellent recommendations, is not producing up to her capability. She has come to see you privately and has just told you that she is very dissatisfied with her job because it is not challenging. She also feels you do not give her enough freedom with her customers, and you continuously check up on all her work. She tells you that if you are not going to utilize her and give her an opportunity to prove herself, she is going to quit. After further discussion, she points out that she should make more money. She also indicates that she needs an assistant at all times.

If you determined that Joan's boss is responsible, you're correct. To understand the reasoning here we have to step back and review three key management concepts involved in the process of delegation: responsibility, authority, and accountability. Can a manager delegate responsibility to another level of management? Although there may be some disagreement here, most experts will agree that the answer is "no." A manager can, however, *share* responsibility through assigning responsibilities, or tasks, to others, but never giving up ultimate responsibility. Although a manager cannot delegate ultimate responsibility, he or she *can* delegate authority. And it is through the combination of sharing responsibility through assignment and delegating authority that a manager can hold other levels accountable for getting work done.

If we accept this, then, in our case incident, Joan's boss is ultimately responsible for the situation. What steps could he/she have taken to make sure that the problem was prevented, or at least alleviated? What we are interested in here is not specific actions, such as checking *each* item she produces carefully, but rather the *process* of ensuring that, say, a year from now, there is no longer a problem. Take ten minutes to list the steps you think Joan's boss should take to ensure that within a year there is no longer such a problem. In other words, is there a management process that could help prevent or alleviate these problems?

<u>Your Suggested Management Process</u>

_____

_____

_____

_____

_____

_____

_____

_____

You would have helped Joan's boss prevent the situation you saw in the case incident if your general outline of the management process included the following points:

1. define the problem

2. set objectives

3. assign responsibilities and delegate authority

4. allocate resources

5. design controls (such as work plans, milestone charts, or schedules)

6. monitor progress

7. solve problems along the way

8. appraise performance

These points and others—and their applicability to all management situations—will be discussed in later chapters.

MANAGEMENT SKILLS AND COMPETENCIES

Many skills are required to master the challenging nature of managerial work to meet the changing trends in management described in Chapter 25. The most important skills and competencies are those that allow managers to assist others in becoming more effective and productive in their work. Robert L. Katz classified the critical skills of managers into three categories:

technical (or operational), human, and conceptual (see Figure 1-3). Although all three skills are essential for managers, their relative importance tends to vary by level of managerial responsibility.

If we view the levels of managerial responsibility in the form of a triangle as depicted in Figure 1-3, we can then reverse the triangle and align it opposite the levels of management depicting how each of the three skills relates to the levels of management.

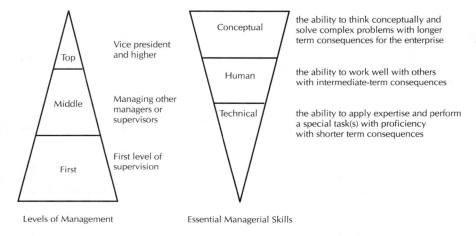

Levels of Management   Essential Managerial Skills

Figure 1–3. Levels of managerial responsibility—essential managerial skills.

Managerial competency is a skill that contributes to a high performance in a managerial job. In this regard, the American Assembly of Collegiate Schools of Business (AACSB) is urging business schools to assist practicing and potential managers in developing the following personal competencies for managerial success:

PERSONAL COMPETENCIES FOR MANAGERIAL SUCCESS

- *Leadership*—ability to influence others to perform tasks
- *Self-objectivity*—ability to evaluate oneself realistically
- *Analytical thinking*—ability to interpret and explain patterns in information
- *Behavioral flexibility*—ability to modify personal behavior to reach a goal
- *Oral communications*—ability to express ideas clearly in oral presentations

- *Written communication*—ability to express one's ideas clearly in writing

- *Personal impact*—ability to create a good impression and instill confidence

- *Resistance to stress*—ability to perform under stressful conditions

- *Tolerance for uncertainty*—ability to perform in ambiguous situations

---

YOU SHOULD REMEMBER

A manager gets results effectively through others by the process of delegation. Although a manager cannot delegate ultimate responsibility, he/she can delegate authority. It is through the combination of **sharing responsibility through assignment and delegating authority** that a manager can hold other levels (persons) accountable for getting things done.

KNOW THE CONCEPTS
DO YOU KNOW THE BASICS?

1. What is management?
2. How does the 1980 definition of management differ from the current definition?
3. What is the difference between management activities and technical activities?
4. What should happen as a manager moves up in an organization in terms of management activities vs. technical activities?
5. How would you explain the process of delegation to a new manager?

TERMS FOR STUDY

accountability
authority
delegation
management
management activities

management competencies
management skills
responsibility
technical activities

ANSWERS

KNOW THE BASICS

1. Management is working with and through other people to accomplish the objectives of both the organization and its members.

2. The current definition places greater emphasis on the human element in the organization; focuses on the results to be accomplished, i.e., objectives rather than activities; and adds the concept that the accomplishment of members' personal objectives should be integrated with the accomplishment of organizational objectives.

3. Management activities are those activities that involve getting results effectively through others by the process of delegation. Technical activities are the special function of an individual following a vocational field.

4. As management activities and demands increase, involvement in technical (or vocational) activities should decrease.

5. To understand the process of delegation (i.e., managing by getting results effectively through others), one must understand the concepts of responsibility, authority, and accountability. Although a manager cannot delegate ultimate responsibility, he/she can delegate authority. It is through the combination of sharing responsibility through assignment and delegating authority that a manager can hold other levels accountable for getting things done.

2

MANAGEMENT: HISTORY AND CONCEPTS

KEY TERMS

Classical Approach the earliest attempt to study management in a scientific manner, emphasizing worker efficiency achieved through the "one right way" to perform a task as determined by the expert who possesses a scientific understanding of the work achieved by methodic study

Behavioral Approach a school of management that emphasizes the improvement of worker efficiency through an understanding of the workers themselves as opposed to an understanding of the work

Management Science, also known as **Operations Research (OR)** approach, which dates from World War II, that maintains that worker productivity can be increased by the use of the scientific method combined with mathematical models of worker tasks

Contingency Approach asserts that the best management style will depend upon or is contingent on the leadership style of the leader in relation to the needs of the specific situation

Theory X and Theory Y terms coined by Douglas M. McGregor (1906–1964) to express the belief that management decision-making is based upon assumptions about human nature. A manager who believes in a Theory X view of human nature asserts that people are lazy, do not like work, will not accept responsibility, and require close managerial supervision. A Theory Y manager, however, believes that people enjoy work, seek challenge, accept responsibility, and will work well and willingly if fairly rewarded.

Theory Z or Japanese Management Theory stresses decision-making by means of group consensus and places highest emphasis on achievement of the group rather than the individual worker

efficiency, effectiveness, and productivity closely related terms used to describe individual and organizational effort. **Effectiveness,** according to famed management theorist Peter Drucker, refers to doing the "right thing." **Efficiency** refers to the effort required to do the right thing: the less effort, the greater efficiency. **Productivity** refers to the relationship between input and output. The more output derived from a given amount of input, the greater is the organizational productivity.

From the supervisors of the construction of the Great Wall of China to the advice given to Moses by his father-in-law Jethro (the first management consultant) in Exodus 18: 14–27, there have always been those who practiced effective management and gave management advice. However, only comparatively recently has a body of literature emerged that examines the dimensions of management and investigates it in a scientific manner. Attempts to view management in a comprehensive, coherent, and consistent manner constitute the development of management theory.

Some of the earliest writings regarding management date from the start of the Industrial Revolution—the 18th century in England and later spreading eastward into Europe and westward to America in the 19th century. Such early writers as **Charles Babbage** (1792–1871) were perceptive enough to assert that the emergence of an industrial world would require a systematic study of task management and standardization of work operations in order to adjust business, primarily the emerging area of light manufacturing, to a new and demanding reality. But just as the technology of Babbage's England of the 1800s was inadequate to construct his proposed "analytical engine" (in reality the first conceptual design for a mechanical computer), so too was the state of industrialization and management thought, so that his ideas were ignored until the "Father of Scientific Management," **Frederick W. Taylor** (1856–1915), rediscovered them. In *On the Economy of Machinery and Manufactures* (1835), Babbage asserted that jobs should be broken down into smaller, standardized tasks. Although this idea is one of the theoretical foundations of the modern assembly-line technology, it was ignored for over half a century.

The state of the emerging industrialization was such that managers did not see a need for a written theory of management. As was the rest of Europe, England was still the land of hereditary privilege, landed gentry, and status that derived from the possession of the intangible yet real state of being a "gentleman." Management and leadership abilities were not thought of as learnable skills but rather skills derived from one's heredity. There did not exist the need for a theory of management: leaders were born, not made. It is therefore not surprising that the ideas of men such as Babbage were ignored.

As industrialization increased and spread to other countries, the need for trained managers and a theory of management became apparent. The late 19th-century United States, in the midst of rapid economic expansion, needed a large number of workers to fuel industrial growth. The supply of workers drawn to America to meet this need was largely immigrant and unskilled, and this ethnically and culturally diverse immigrant workforce required a greater number of managers who were more highly skilled.

On May 26, 1886, **Henry R. Towne** (1844–1924), a leading industrialist, read a paper entitled "The Engineer as an Economist" at a regular meeting of the American Society of Mechanical Engineers. In this paper, Towne called for a scientific study of the "management of works" by engineers. This was the first call for a scientific approach to study management. Frederick W. Taylor and his colleagues in the United States and others in Europe took up the challenge and began to create what is now recognized as management theory.

The foundations of the various approaches to schools of management theory are found in a variety of disciplines, including economics, psychology, sociology, mathematics, philosophy, and industrial engineering. But management theory, even though it makes use of other scholarly areas and the observations of the practicing manager, has emerged as a separate area of study since the 1940s.

And while management theory began in the last part of the 19th century, it continues as a dynamic, evolving body of knowledge and practice that is truly international in scope.

YOU SHOULD REMEMBER

Prior to the 20th century most of the writing about management dealt with the practice of management, not the theory behind the practice. However, with industrial expansion, the changing nature of the workforce, and movement into mass production, there emerged a need for more managers and an understanding of the theoretical foundations of management. **Scientific Management** was founded by **Frederick W. Taylor** in America. His comprehensive approach to management theory is still practiced by many managers.

CLASSICAL SCHOOLS OF MANAGEMENT THEORY

The first management theory approach to emerge was that of **Scientific Management.** Created by engineers, scientists, and practicing managers concerned with the improvement of worker *efficiency* (the amount a worker produces in a given period of time), this approach assumed two major forms: management of work and management of organizations. Scientific Management emerged out of efforts to improve worker efficiency, which began in America with Frederick W. Taylor.

THE MANAGEMENT OF WORK

• *FREDERICK W. TAYLOR (1856–1915): FATHER OF SCIENTIFIC MANAGEMENT*

Frederick W. Taylor was an intense person, deeply committed to the study and understanding of work and the improvement of worker efficiency. His ideas, derived from years of experience at the Enterprise Hydraulic Works, the Midvale Steel Company (in 1878 he joined as a common laborer), Simonds Rolling Machine, and Bethlehem Steel companies, continue to influence *job design, work layout,* and *task scheduling* today. Taylor became an engineer, not at Harvard where his parents wanted him to go, but by attending the Stevens Institute of Technology at night.

Taylor believed that economic prosperity could only be achieved by maximal worker productivity, which, in turn, would be the product of making workers more efficient. Somewhat of an elitist, Taylor believed that this maximal efficiency could be achieved only by a specialist known as the "management scientist" and that one could not trust employees to work in the most efficient manner. He felt that workers would slack off in their efforts if left alone. (Based on his observations of the military, Taylor coined the term *soldiering* for "slacking off.") Taylor felt that maximum efficiency could only be achieved by redesigning work and by changing worker attitudes toward work. The redesigned task, designed to achieve maximum efficiency, was the *one right way* to do the job. Taylor felt that if workers and management could cooperate, there would be an improvement in society and in the workers' conditions. Taylor felt that this initiative could only come from the management scientist, a new kind of industrial leader.

Before Taylor's efforts, workers performed jobs according to hunches and intuition, what he called "rules of thumb." Taylor maintained that using such rules of thumb led to inefficiency and to inconsistent performance standards. There was no accepted standard of what constituted a "fair day's work for a fair day's pay." Management, because it lacked reliable performance standards by which to evaluate worker accomplishment, could never really know if it was being maximally efficient. Neither, Taylor asserted, could workers know if they were giving their best efforts. Taylor observed lathe operators, shovelers, metal cutters, pig iron handlers, and other workers. Taking thousands of measurements with a stopwatch, he minutely analyzed each job and broke each job down into its component tasks in a process he called *job fractionation*, thus creating time and motion studies. He called these component tasks the *basic work units* of a job. Taylor then took each basic work unit and tried to determine the most efficient way of doing it and the most efficient way of combining the work units into a total task. He called this most efficient manner of doing a job the one right way. Jobs that were analyzed and improved in this manner were often described as having been "Taylorized."

Making use of *time and motion studies* and a system known as *piece rate*, whereby workers were paid according to the amount produced, Taylor was able to improve worker efficiency dramatically. Although Taylor's incentive pay and more efficient manner of performing tasks resulted in greater wages for the workers, unions generally distrusted and sometimes resented his methods. The unions feared that the increased rate of work would result in earlier work completion and consequent worker layoffs. Unions generally resisted Taylor's innovations, but in America, management, impressed by the increases in worker productivity and reductions in costs, enthusiastically embraced his Scientific Management.

The influence of Taylor and his colleagues was felt throughout the first decades of the 20th century. Taylor himself was called to testify before Congressional committees in 1912–1914, and he influenced the way in which government viewed emerging industrial America.

YOU SHOULD REMEMBER

Frederick W. Taylor, considered the founder of **Scientific Management,** studied various jobs and, breaking them into smaller tasks, determined the most efficient way of accomplishing them. The hallmark of his approach to the understanding of work and improvement of worker efficiency was the scientifically determined **"one right way."**

- ## *FRANK (1868–1924) AND LILLIAN M. GILBRETH (1878–1972): INNOVATORS OF MOTION STUDIES*

Frank and Lillian Gilbreth were contemporaries and often rivals of Taylor and his later followers, even as they accepted his assertion of the "one right way" and the necessity of using the scientific method of observation and measurement to analyze work. The Gilbreths are considered pioneers in making use of *motion studies* to improve worker efficiency. Frank Gilbreth devised a classification scheme of seventeen motions used in jobs and used this classification to analyze worker actions. He coined the term *therbligs* (a slightly altered backward spelling of his name) to describe these seventeen actions. He would then observe, and sometimes film, a worker performing a task and analyze the therbligs involved. When he understood all the motions, he would seek to improve the efficiency of each action and reduce the number of motions required to accomplish the job—a process called *job simplification*.

Although Frank Gilbreth is the better known of the two, his wife Lillian also pioneered in the use of motion studies to improve worker productivity. (At least one publisher of a book coauthored by the Gilbreths refused to list her as an author and published the book under Frank's name alone, and when Lillian's thesis, "The Psychology of Management," was published, the publisher insisted that she be listed only as L. M. Gilbreth, with neither mention nor publicity that the author was a woman.) She applied the techniques of Scientific Management to the running of her household and is justly famous for the best selling literary chronicles of the Gilbreth's life with twelve children, *Cheaper by the Dozen* and *Chicken Every Sunday*.

• HENRY L. GANTT (1861–1919): INNOVATOR IN SCHEDULING AND REWARDING EMPLOYEES

Henry L. Gantt, an associate of Taylor at the Midvale and Bethlehem Steel companies, made significant contributions in the areas of scheduling and controlling of work as well as the rewarding of workers. He maintained that production inefficiency was, in large measure, the result of management's inability to formulate realistic standards. Since the pre-Scientific Management production standards were not realistic—either too high or, more often, too low—it was not surprising that worker and work scheduling inefficiency characterized many organizations.

Gantt maintained in the first two decades of the 20th century that management needed scientifically determined data in order to operate efficiently. Work standards should be determined by scientific observation and measurement, and only then may realistic work standards be set. Once the nature and amount of work to be accomplished were determined, the work could be effectively scheduled. Gantt's best-known contribution to management practice is the work scheduling chart that bears his name and is still widely used in industry. Figure 2-1 is an example of a *Gantt Chart*. The blocked-out sections show when each task listed on the left side is scheduled and how many weeks workers will take to complete the individual task.

Gantt maintained that workers would be more productive if there were some real incentive to exceed the normal levels of production that had been

Task	Weeks									
	1	2	3	4	5	6	7	8	9	10
Order parts	■									
Inspect parts		■								
Assembly of shell			■							
Subassembly of core				■	■					
Put core in shell						■				
Inspection of unit							■	■		
Affix labels									■	
Packaging										■
Shipping										■

Figure 2–1. Gantt Chart. This chart shows the assembly schedule in a thermos factory. The blocked-out sections show when each task listed on the left side is scheduled and how many weeks workers will take to complete the individual task.

determined scientifically. To motivate workers to go beyond the daily production quotas, he pioneered the use of a *production bonus*. In this way, Gantt differed significantly from Taylor, who had pioneered a piece rate system that paid each worker the same wage for each unit produced. Gantt offered not only the piece rate but also a bonus for producing above the expected daily quota. Both these systems of compensation—the piece rate and the production bonus—are used today. Taylor focused almost exclusively on the worker's task, but Gantt also directed attention to the worker's motivation, a topic that would be much discussed in the decades following Gantt's pioneering work and developed by such management theorists as Mayo, Herzberg, and Maslow.

• *MARY PARKER FOLLET (1868–1933): PIONEER IN CONFLICT RESOLUTION*

Mary Parker Follett, one of the few female classical management theorists, focused in the 1920s on how managers dealt with conflict. She felt that most managers choose a destructive way of dealing with conflict in the workplace. Her research and writings pointed to a *collaborative approach to problem solving* that advocated compromise. One of her favorite admonitions to management was "don't overmanage employees," a process that would come to be known as *micromanaging,* and she referred to this overmanagement as "bossism." She felt that workers could recognize the logic or "law of the situation" inherent in a management request and would comply. Management's task was to formulate requests in a logical manner but not to give too many orders. Her work forms the basis for modern problem solving and is receiving new recognition. Some writers have even asserted that if Frederick Taylor is the "father of Scientific Management," then Mary Parker Follet is the "mother."

YOU SHOULD REMEMBER

The **Gilbreths** pioneered the use of motion studies and **Henry L. Gantt** the use of work-scheduling techniques (the Gantt Chart). The techniques they developed are still used by management to improve worker efficiency. They and **Mary Parker Follet,** who advocated a collaborative approach to solving problems in the workplace, were major figures in the classical study of the management of work. They helped make the scientific approach to the improvement of worker efficiency accepted throughout American industry.

THE MANAGEMENT OF ORGANIZATIONS

Although Frederick W. Taylor and his colleagues focused on the individual worker and the improvement of production efficiency by means of the analysis of work, other classical management theorists were concerned about the management and design of the total organization. Organizations were growing in size and complexity in the first half of the 20th century, and there was a greater need to understand how the total organization could operate more effectively. The most famous developer of the management theory that centered upon the management of the organization was Henri Fayol.

• *HENRI FAYOL (1841–1925): DEVELOPER OF ADMINISTRATIVE THEORY*

Henri Fayol, trained as an engineer in France, achieved the senior executive position of managing director of a large French coal-mining company. His concern was the efficiency and effectiveness of the entire organization. Fayol sought to apply scientific principles to the management of the total organization; this focus has come to be known as **Administrative Theory.** His most famous book, *Administratim Industrielle et Generale* (1929), translated as *General and Industrial Management,* is still read and considered a classic in management. In this book Fayol made four major contributions to administrative theory:

1. He differentiated between the supervisory and managing levels, effectively giving more status and recognition to managing than to merely supervising workers. This distinction between the managing and operating levels of an organization did much to enhance the emerging status of the manager and help define the details of the modern hierarchical organizational design.

2. He defined what the managers did as the *functions of management*. These functions are still used to classify and evaluate management. This is regarded as a *functional definition of management*.

3. He developed general *principles of management* that are still used and being refined by contemporary managers. These themes offered practical advice on how to function as a manager.

4. He maintained that flexibility was needed in the application of his principles and also that new managers could *learn* how to manage. This marked a significant departure from the view that managers are born, not made and constitutes a hallmark of modern managerial theory and practice.

FUNCTIONS OF MANAGEMENT

Fayol asserted that the activity of management was characterized by five specific functions. These functions were what defined managers and added up, in short, to a functional definition of management. A person was to be considered a manager not because he or she had a title that said manager but because his/her work consisted of managerial functions: These functions, as observed by Fayol, were:

1. *Planning*. This function consists of forecasting future events and determining the most effective future activities for the company.

2. *Organizing*. This function consists of the ways in which the organizational structure is established and how authority and responsibility are given to managers, a task called *delegation*.

3. *Commanding*. This function concerns how managers direct employees. Fayol addressed such activities as effective communications, managerial behaviors, and the uses of rewards and punishments in discussing how a manager should command employees.

4. *Coordinating*. This function concerns activities designed to create a relationship among all the organization's efforts (individual tasks) to accomplish a common goal.

5. *Controlling*. This function concerns how managers evaluate performance within the organization in relationship to the plans and goals of that organization.

These functions are now taken for granted as one of the most significant ways of understanding management, but they were revolutionary when Fayol wrote about them. Each will be described in greater detail in later chapters in this book.

PRINCIPLES OF MANAGEMENT

Based on real-world observation, Fayol developed fourteen principles of management to guide the manager in resolving contemporary work problems. In asserting that managers could be guided by these principles, he took the view in his writings that managers needed certain skills and abilities and that these could be acquired by training. Fayol went on to urge that management training be taught in schools, not merely presented on an on-the-job basis. This suggestion that management skills be taught is the basis for *management training programs*. Although many good managers of his time made use of these principles, Fayol was the first to recognize their significance as an aggregate managerial tool and to present them in an understandable format.

Fayol's principles of management were:

1. *Division of labor.* Work is separated into its basic tasks and divided between individual workers or work groups that can specialize in the specific task, leading to *work specialization*.

2. *Authority.* Authority is the legitimate right to exercise power within the organization to obtain worker obedience. It is closely related to *responsibility*, which is the accountability for using authority. Authority and responsibility go together, and one without the other leads to managerial failure.

3. *Discipline.* Discipline is the application of punishment for failure to act in accord with the desires of those who possess legitimate authority in the organization.

4. *Unity of command.* Each worker should receive orders from only one manager, a simplified view of an organization that assures a minimum of conflict and promotes clarity of communication.

5. *Unity of direction.* The whole organization should have one common goal and seek to accomplish that goal in all its activities.

6. *Subordination of the individual.* The goal and interests of the organization are more important than and therefore take precedence over the personal goals and interests of the individual.

7. *Remuneration.* Each employee should receive compensation in accord with a general formula. The computation of amounts and forms of compensation should consider the following variables: cost-of-living, the general economic climate and specific business conditions, qualifications of the worker and the supply and demand for such workers, and the levels of productivity achieved.

8. *Centralization.* The importance of subordinates is reduced as organizational power and the responsibility for decision-making is concentrated in managers. Managers are responsible for decision-making and are ac-

countable for those decisions. Subordinates should be delegated responsibility with just enough authority to accomplish the assigned task. The opposite of centralization is decentralization.

9. *Scalar chain.* Managers in a company exist in a chain of command that is scalar, or hierarchical. Authority and responsibility are delegated down the chain of command and become less the lower one goes in the chain of command. Lower level managers have responsibility for informing those senior in the chain of command of current information regarding task accomplishment. This results in an organization that is "hierarchical."

10. *Order.* The resources of a company—its raw materials and workers—must be in the right place at the right time. This ordering of organizational resources ensures maximal efficiency.

11. *Equity.* Employees should feel they are being treated equally and fairly. The perception of equity will be accomplished by organizational rules that are reasonable and consistently applied to all workers.

12. *Stability of personnel.* Successful firms retain good managers, and this should be a goal of the organization. Skilled and successful personnel are a viable organizational resource, and organizational practices should encourage long-term commitment to the organization.

13. *Initiative.* Management should encourage individual employee initiative, which is defined as additional self-motivated work effort undertaken for the good of the organization.

14. *Esprit de corps.* Management should try to encourage harmony and common interests, resulting in good relations among employees.

YOU SHOULD REMEMBER

Henri Fayol is considered the **Father of Administrative Theory.** He focused on the management of the whole organization and defined the **functions of management,** which were **planning, organizing, commanding, coordinating,** and **controlling.** These functions are still used to describe the management position. Fayol is also famous for his **fourteen principles of management** and the belief that management skills could be learned.

EVALUATION OF THE CLASSICAL SCHOOLS

The developers of classical managerial theory met the needs of an expanding industrial world. By examining the *management of work*, individual worker productivity was improved and organizations could and did benefit, acquiring greater resources from the increased profitability and growth. Those who examined the *management of the organization* created a growing awareness of the nature of managerial functioning within the organization and enhanced the ability to manage the contemporary and increasingly complex organization. Managers were now attempting to determine the necessary skills for the managerial task and were experimenting with methods of teaching these skills.

The **Classical Approach** to management theory, formulated largely by those with an engineering background, had asserted that the key to worker efficiency and organizational productivity was efficient job design, use of appropriate incentives, and effective managerial functioning. This was perceived as a formal and impersonal approach to management and was resisted by many workers because it failed to take into account the human dimensions of an organization. However, the contributions of the Classical Theory of management still are used by successful managers.

THE BEHAVIORAL SCHOOL OF MANAGEMENT THEORY

The focus of the Classical Approach had been upon the work, but the **Behavioral Approach** stresses that effective management will come from an understanding of the worker. This assertion arose from experiments conducted by social scientists at the Hawthorne (Chicago) Works of the Western Electric Company between 1927 and 1932. These experiments, called the Hawthorne Experiments, have been justly famous for over half a century, not only for being the genesis of the *human relations movement* in business but also for the insight that they provided into worker behavior.

• *ELTON MAYO (1880–1949) AND THE HAWTHORNE EXPERIMENTS*

Elton Mayo was an Australian social scientist at the University of Pennsylvania when he was called in as a consultant to a Philadelphia textile plant. The management of this plant had previously engaged an efficiency engineer to perform scientific management studies in accord with the principles laid down by Frederick W. Taylor and his associates, and new work practices had been instituted, but to no avail. Not only had there been no improvement of worker efficiency and productivity, but personnel turnover in one department, called the mulespinning room, was over 250 percent each year.

The employees were very unhappy, and all attempts to apply scientific management had failed.

Mayo interviewed the workers in this troubled area of the company and observed two conditions, one obvious and one not so obvious. The workers complained of aching feet and legs related to the nature and pace of the work. This was an easily understood condition of fatigue and one to which Mayo reacted by suggesting to management that it offer more rest periods and a rest area containing cots for the workers. Management accepted these recommendations, implemented them, and saw an increase in productivity along with a decrease in the turnover rate. But while interviewing the workers Mayo had also listened to complaints of a more intangible nature. The workers complained of feeling depressed because they did not value their labor and felt a low personal esteem. Viewing their working conditions, Mayo termed the workers "solitaries" because there was little personal contact with others, no sense of belonging to a group, and no reliance upon others. He recognized that the lack of a feeling of belonging had effectively sabotaged the efforts of the management scientist. He later came to wonder if the improvements that had been realized after his consultation were not so much the result of the increased number of rest periods and presence of cots but of the changed feelings of the workers, as his interviews and expressed concern seemed to link them together as a group.

After the textile mill consultation Mayo became a faculty member at the Harvard University School of Business Administration. In April 1927, he joined colleagues in the Hawthorne Studies, which became the most famous and enduring research project in the human relations school of management, still being analyzed and discussed over 50 years later. These studies took place at the Hawthorne Works of the Western Electric Company located in a Chicago suburb and originally centered on the workers of the relay room. These workers—all women—were moved to an isolated location in the plant and subjected to different intensities of light in order to determine the best illumination to facilitate productivity. Two groups were created: one, the "control" group, worked under a lighting level that was held constant; the other worked under changing light conditions.

The results of these experiments greatly surprised the researchers. No matter how the light intensity changed, production increased. There did not seem to be a consistent relationship between lighting and productivity. Committed to discovering the reasons for increases in productivity, the scientists began intensive interviewing of all the workers. They discovered that workers increased productivity because:

- The test room was enjoyable to work in.

- The relationship between worker and supervisor was more relaxed for the worker group during the experimental period.

- The workers responded to the realization that they were taking part in a meaningful experiment. (Mayo and his colleagues termed this tendency of people to react differently—in this case, in a more productive manner—*because* they were being observed, the *Hawthorne Effect*.)

- The experience of participating in the experiment seemed to create an increased feeling of group identity and belonging.

Mayo and his colleagues concluded that factors other than the physical aspects of work had the power of improving production. These factors related to the interrelationships between workers and individual worker psychology and were termed, after much additional investigation, *human relations factors*. The Hawthorne Experiments highlighted the importance of worker social and psychological factors and the need not only to build a Taylor-like production-oriented manufacturing machine, but also to address the social values of the organization and its employees. The manager therefore must gain an understanding not only of the management science techniques of work analysis and productivity improvement but also of human relations skills.

YOU SHOULD REMEMBER

Elton Mayo, the founder of the **human relations movement,** discovered that experts seeking to improve worker efficiency had to take into account the human dimensions of work. The results of the **Hawthorne Experiments** revealed that work productivity was related to psychological and social variables as well as to the work itself. Mayo and his colleagues directed the attention of managers to the workers' feelings as a source of productivity improvement and managerial success.

• CHESTER BARNARD (1886–1961): THE ACCEPTANCE THEORY OF AUTHORITY

Another major contributor to the Behavioral School was **Chester Barnard,** a writer and working business executive (manager), eventually rising to the position of president of New Jersey Bell. In *The Functions of the Executive* (1938), he maintained that people form organizations to achieve common goals and stressed "cooperative effort" as a key to organizational success and managerial effectiveness. He also focused management's attention on motivation, decision-making, communication effectiveness, and the importance of objectives.

Barnard advanced the **Acceptance Theory of Authority,** which asserted that employees determine if a managerial order is legitimate and acceptable.

His research suggested that *only* orders that are considered acceptable in light of the individual's goals and personal interests will be accepted. Managerial effectiveness, then, was dependent upon the employee's acceptance of management's legitimacy. In a very real sense, Barnard had redefined the source of a manager's power—it was not the executive's position but the acceptance by the workers.

• *DOUGLAS M. McGREGOR (1906–1964): THEORY X AND THEORY Y*

Douglas M. McGregor observed that the different points of view embodied in the classical and the behavioral approaches to understanding worker conduct arose not merely from the different emphasis placed upon work and the worker but also from a profound difference in the way in which workers were viewed. Taylor and his colleagues, focusing on work and taking a pessimistic and somewhat traditional view of workers, asserted that the manager needed only to manipulate the working conditions and make effective use of rewards and punishments to foster worker productivity. Mayo and his colleagues, with their psychosocial focus (human relations) on the *worker*, were far more optimistic about the nature of the individual. McGregor characterized each of these philosophical views of the worker and labeled Taylor's **Theory X** and Mayo's **Theory Y.** The following table (see page 26) summarizes McGregor's characterization of Theory X and Theory Y.

McGregor's famous conceptualization of the different philosophical traditions regarding worker nature had the far-reaching effect of popularizing the insights gained by human relations researchers and practitioners. Theory Y, building upon an optimistic view of worker nature, advocated that managers address the psychological side of the worker and work by doing such things as:

- delegating authority to lower levels in the organization, thereby challenging workers to make decisions and expressing faith in their abilities

- making jobs more interesting for the worker

- increasing the level of responsibility inherent in each job

- innovating new rewards for worker performance that relate to a variety of worker psychological needs, not just money

- treating workers with respect and increasing the share of information regarding the work content, design, and results

McGregor summed up his observations in *The Human Side of Enterprise* (1960). This book had a profound impact on American management. Mayo studied one organization and reported on a prolonged period of in-depth

Theory X	Theory Y
Individuals dislike work and will avoid it if possible.	Workers do not inherently dislike work and will respond to good working conditions and attitudes.
Because individuals dislike work, they must be coerced, threatened, manipulated, directed, and controlled.	People will exercise self-motivation and direction to accomplish organizational goals to which they are personally committed.
The average person desires security, has little ambition, and will avoid assuming responsibility. Workers have to be directed and actually prefer to be told what to do.	The average person can learn to accept responsibility.
Few people are truly creative.	Most people are capable of being creative, exercising ingenuity, and being imaginative.
The limited intellectual capacities of common workers are adequately challenged by modern work design.	Individual capacities of the average worker are not fully used in the modern industrial environment.

and relatively narrowly focused experimentation, but McGregor painted his assertions with a broad social science brush. He did not suggest any specific courses of action for managers, but he did point to the need for a major philosophical reorientation by management as to how it viewed employees and work design.

YOU SHOULD REMEMBER

Douglas McGregor, in distinguishing between the pessimistic **Theory X** view of employees and the optimistic **Theory Y,** had a dramatic impact on management theory and practice. The Theory Y view advanced a humanistic approach that led to the introduction of work designs that better challenged workers, promoted personal growth, improved work performance, and facilitated productivity.

EVALUATION OF THE BEHAVIORAL APPROACH

The Behavioral Approach to the understanding of worker behavior and productivity improvement has had a powerful impact on U.S. management thought. It has provided many insights into organizational behavior and still continues as a major direction for those engaged in organization theory research. The Behavioral Approach has given rise to effective management skills training and development efforts in virtually every major American business. This has created a more sophisticated and effective style on the part of managers in dealing with human variables in the workplace.

MANAGEMENT SCIENCE APPROACH

"We have awakened a sleeping giant" was the comment of Fleet Admiral Isoroku Yamamoto, a senior Japanese Navy leader after the attack on Pearl Harbor, a comment that must be regarded as one of the most prescient observations in history. The vast American economic engine geared up for global war and adapted a civilian manufacturing sector to the rigors and requirements of wartime manufacturing. This manufacturing effort and the needs of a modern technological military for new management techniques to deal with operational problems of an increasingly complex nature flowing from the waging of the greatest war ever fought on this planet gave rise to the management approach known as **Management Science** or **Operations Research (OR).**

The government advisors and military experts who managed the war approached leading scientists and engineers to help in solving complex problems. These scientists, trained in the scientific method of inquiry and research and expert in the application of statistics and other mathematical techniques, brought their previous training to bear upon the problems presented to them as national priorities. Their approach to these managerial problems entailed two assumptions:

1. All problems that characterize a system can be solved by applying the scientific method.

2. These system problems can be solved by solving mathematical equations that represent the system.

The *scientific method* is an approach to problem solving that features the following methodological steps:

1. The management scientist *observes* the system within which a problem exists.

2. A *mathematical model* of the system, which describes the interrelationship between the variables that make up the system, is constructed.

3. The mathematical model is used to make *deductions* about how the actual system will act under certain assumed conditions.

4. The mathematical model is then tested by conducting *experiments* that examine if the system actually does act in a certain manner under the projected conditions.

The Operations Research (OR) groups were very successful in applying this methodology to determine the optimal solutions to complex wartime problems, and it was not surprising that this approach to managerial functioning, especially in the manufacturing sector, would be applied. As Operations Research was applied to an ever-increasing number of problems in the manufacturing sector, new techniques emerged and were refined by the management scientist.

• *HERBERT SIMON (1916–   ): INFORMATION PROCESSING AND EXECUTIVE DECISION-MAKING*

Management scientist **Herbert Simon** and his colleagues at Carnegie-Mellon University made major contributions to managerial effectiveness. Simon is best known for his research in decision-making and information processing. Before Simon, management theorists accepted the idea, known as the *economic man model of decision-making*, that executives had immediate access to perfect information and made the best decision to maximize organizational results. Simon found that executives rarely, if ever, had access to perfect information, valued data encountered early in the information search more than information gathered later, and made decisions that achieved not maximal but satisfactory results. He called this process *satisficing*. Simon replaced the economic man model of decision-making with the justly famous concept of *bounded rationality*, which narrowed the frame of decision-making to reflect the pragmatics and limitations of realistic managers. For this analysis of managerial decision-making, along with his life's work, Simon was honored with the 1978 Nobel Prize in Economics.

> # YOU SHOULD REMEMBER
>
> **Management Science,** also known as Operations Research (OR), is an approach to management that maintains that productivity can be improved and organizational effectiveness increased by means of the **scientific method** and the use of **mathematical models.**

EVALUATION OF MANAGEMENT SCIENCE APPROACH

The techniques of management science are widely applied in contemporary industry to improve worker productivity. Management science stresses a *systems approach* that views the total operating system and analyzes a problem within that system. The problem is seen to exist as it relates to the total system, and any proposed solution is evaluated as it relates to the same system. Any course of action that solves a production problem but that also causes more problems for the organization will probably be rejected.

Despite its success at solving complex production problems, Operations Research has been criticized for its focus on production and lack of focus on the worker and the human dimensions of the management function. Also, many problems in modern business, however complex, require an even wider perspective than that offered by a systemwide Operations Research Approach, which often fails to account for unanticipated opportunity or environmental threats. Finally, operations management skills of analysis and solution determination are often viewed as operational skills, not management skills. There is often a gap between the technical expertise of the management scientist and that same scientist's managerial skills. Management science solutions to production problems, which make sense on paper and in computer printouts, do not make the same sense on the factory floor. However, Operations Research has made and will continue to make a valuable contribution to management practice and its techniques have proven extremely useful.

THE CONTINGENCY APPROACH

The **Contingency Approach** to management asserts that there is no universally applicable approach to a management problem, but that the needs of the particular situation determine the best approach to the organizational problem. This approach arose out of the observation that the three earlier approaches to management—the Classical, the Behavioral, and the Operations Research—did not always lead to an acceptable solution. The Contingency Approach is *eclectic* in that a manager can make use of the techniques of other approaches to management if the applications of these various techniques or a combination of techniques is the best solution to the specific problem.

STEP-BY-STEP METHODOLOGY

The Contingency Approach is a methodology for determining the best possible solution to any organizational problem. It consists of the following step-by-step program for an organization to determine the best solution:

1. Perform a situational analysis, consisting of:

   a. analysis of the current *internal* condition of the organization.

   1) internal organizational strengths

   2) internal organizational weaknesses

   b. projection of the future *external* condition of the organization.

   1) external opportunities for the organization

   2) external threats to the organization

2. Based on the situational analysis, formulate a statement of the problem.

3. State the performance standards that meet the following requirements and the completion of which indicates that the problem has been solved. Performance standards are stated in the form of behavior that is:

   a. observable;

   b. measurable; and

   c. relevant to the goal.

4. Generate alternative solutions to the problem.

5. Evaluate the possible solutions in terms of their consequences to those involved in and with the organization called the organization's *stakeholders*.

6. Select the best alternative solution that solves the problem and causes the least number of detrimental side effects in the organization.

7. Implement a pilot test of the proposed solution and revise as indicated from practical experience.

8. Implement the solution.

9. Evaluate the solution.

10. Revise the process as necessary.

11. Begin again with a new situational analysis.

The Contingency Approach takes into account any limitations under which the organization must operate. For example, there may be the constraints of the current level of available technology. An organization may not have the appropriate level of technology or may not be able to afford to acquire the needed technology necessary to implement a particular alternative. Consideration of the company's level of technology will also take into account the interrelationships of all parts of the organization; any change in one area's technology will have an effect on the rest of the organization. And the impact upon the *total organization* must be considered in the evaluation of the consequences of a proposed solution.

The Contingency Approach also considers the human resources of an organization in evaluating the suitability of potential solutions. There must be an appropriate human resources support system, or the proposed solution may not work. Evaluation of the human resources component of an organization, also called a *human resources audit*, would include examining the level of worker competence, abilities, and skills.

Example Illustrating the Contingency Approach to Problem Solving

PROBLEM: The local McDonald's finds that its business is changing and that there are two concrete manifestations of change challenging it: (1) more people are eating out at fast-food establishments and (2) there are, with the changing demographics, fewer teenagers available to work for minimum wages in basically boring jobs.

Challenge 1 would suggest that McDonald's expand its business to take advantage of the opportunity for growth. The traditional response to more business—hiring more teenagers—is not an option, as Challenge 2 makes clear.

SOLUTION: The following are identified as potential solutions to this problem:

- ignore the market opportunities for growth and continue as now

- expand by buying more efficient machinery, thus reducing the need for employees

- spend more money to attract the disenchanted teenager

- explore other labor sources—for example, housewives, retirees, high school dropouts, the functionally illiterate, the physically challenged (previously called handicapped)

A true Contingency Approach would maintain that each of these options should be examined in terms of its consequences for the total organization and that the option with the best outcome be chosen. The best choice would be contingent upon the circumstances and projected outcomes. Just because one of the solutions worked in the past would not mean that such a solution would work now. A company would select the option or combination of options that (1) solved the identified problem and (2) created the least number of new problems.

YOU SHOULD REMEMBER

The **Contingency Approach** stresses that there is no one universal solution to management problems but that the correct solution will depend on the unique needs of the situation. This approach is **eclectic** and makes use of management techniques from many other approaches. It is distinguished by a problem-solving methodology that begins with a situational analysis and ends with the generation, evaluation, and recommendation of a potential solution to solve the managerial problem.

EVALUATION OF THE CONTINGENCY APPROACH

Unlike the previous three approaches to management, the **Contingency Approach** does not advocate a universally correct approach to solving management problems but maintains that different problems will require different solutions. The Contingency Approach is eclectic and allows the adherent to pick and choose from the available management techniques to solve the problem. This approach requires that the manager be flexible, not locked into any one solution or school of management. It allows a concern for the human dimension of the organization as well as the use of operations research techniques. Since this approach requires a manager to view the organization and its problems from a multifaceted point of view, it realistically reflects the complex nature of modern management.

Critics of the Contingency Approach stress the complexity of the approach and that it requires a manager of many abilities to use this approach effectively. Many managers will feel insecure since this approach does not have a set prescription for universal problem-solving but places the responsibility for solution generation upon the manager. There are those critics who also maintain that this approach lacks a coherent and consistent theoretical basis and is merely a methodology making use of other approaches. Although this may be true, it cannot be denied that, in the hands of a skilled and secure manager, the Contingency Approach becomes a powerful and flexible management tool.

THEORY Z: THE TECHNIQUES OF JAPANESE MANAGEMENT

Having observed the rise of Japanese industry to a position of significance in the world economic community after almost total destruction in World War II, U.S. management consultants and theorists turned to an examination of their conceptual foundations of management theory. William G. Ouchi dubbed the Japanese approach to management **Theory Z,** an obvious extension of McGregor's characterization of earlier approaches to management theory as Theory X and Theory Y. The Theory Z approach to management is pragmatically adapted from the style of management that emerged in Japan after the destruction of World War II and characterized as the "Japanese economic miracle."

BASIC TECHNIQUES

Theory Z has its philosophical roots in Japanese customs and culture and is far less a theoretical approach than a practical collection of management techniques that have been grouped together around the central focus of the work group.

This approach maintains that the most effective decision-making is that accomplished by the group rather than an individual manager. This style of decision-making is called *consensual decision-making* and assumes that the group decision-making process will result in better decisions for an organization because:

- the group has access to more data and personal experience

- members of the group will "buy into" the group decision

- the group decision-making process screens out extremely good and extremely bad information, resulting in a decision that will be better than the individual's decision

Theory Z also features an ideal of *lifetime employment* to build loyalty and ensure a constant workforce that is committed to the organization and the accomplishment of its goals. This management practice takes a long-term view of human resources utilization and development within the organization, and it stresses performance appraisals based on the accomplishment of long-term results. It should be noted, however, that economic difficulties and limitations (such as international competition) have led many Japanese companies to curtail, or even cease, the practice of lifetime employment.

The major manifestation of Theory Z in the U.S. workplace has been the introduction of *quality circles (QC)*. These are small groups of workers and management that meet on a regular basis during the regular workday and attempt to improve quality and help cut costs. Workers formulate problem statements from self-observation or in response to management-supplied data and then generate potential solutions. These solutions are subject to the group decision-making process and then are forwarded as official recommendations to higher management. Management's recommendations and action plans are then returned to the group to reinforce the group's dedication.

This approach requires the genuine support of management and is one of the techniques found in the *Quality of Worklife (QWL) Approach*. The overall approach, of which the quality circle is the most well-known technique, also features:

- greater worker involvement in decision-making

- improved and more frequent communication between workers and management

- self-control by workers over aspects of the workplace

These facets of QWL are *empowering* as they involve the worker in the managerial decision-making process.

In what must be regarded as the major organizational commitment to the managerial principles and practices that derive from Theory Z, the U.S. Navy has committed itself to a program called *Total Quality Management* or *Total Quality Leadership (TQM/TQL)*. The Navy, a hierarchical rank-structured organization characterized by a chain-of-command, seeks to involve every level in an appropriate manner in the management of the organization. Training individuals in quality circle techniques, including the use of statistics to understand data describing job performance, the Navy requires that problems be dealt with at the lowest appropriate organizational level. In this way, the Navy hopes to (1) manage the organization in the most effective manner and (2) solve problems at the lowest organizational level and, therefore, most efficiently. This process has been characterized as one of *power down*, and in a real sense it does exactly that by insisting that even the lowest organizational levels of personnel participate in managerial endeavor. In a military service distinguished by the latest in technological innovation, TQM/TQL balances the managerial reliance on technological superiority with a concomitant recognition that any organization, however distinguished by its use of the latest gadget or scientific discovery, ultimately consists of people.

YOU SHOULD REMEMBER

The Japanese approach to management, known as **Theory Z,** stresses **group consensus** and **achievement** and is embodied in two managerial techniques that have been adapted to the U.S. industrial setting: **Quality of Worklife (QWL)** and **quality circles (QC).** These techniques are often described as **participative management.**

EVALUATION OF THE THEORY Z/QWL APPROACH TO MANAGEMENT

The Theory Z/QWL approach to management is founded in Japanese historical and cultural experiences and adds a new dimension to American management. Less theoretical than some other theories of management, it is a pragmatic approach to management. Although quality circles have been credited with an initial increase in productivity where they have been introduced, their long-term benefit has not been documented. Furthermore, quality circles may be costly in terms of worker time commitment, and they presume high skill levels in communication abilities, goal formulation and prioritization, and interpersonal relationship techniques. If any of these skills are lacking, the quality circle will not achieve its goals. Furthermore, a successful QWL effort (including the QC) requires top management support. If this support is lacking, workers will perceive the entire endeavor as just another management attempt to placate workers with show that lacks real substance.

KNOW THE CONCEPTS
DO YOU KNOW THE BASICS?

1. Why did a formal theory of management not emerge before the end of the 19th century? Why did it emerge then?
2. What was the contribution of Frederick W. Taylor to the development of management theory?
3. How did Frank and Lillian Gilbreth contribute to the development of Scientific Management? What was a "therblig"?
4. How is a Gantt Chart used? How did Henry L. Gantt differ from Frederick W. Taylor in the area of incentives?

5. What management theory was created by Henri Fayol, and how did he, within this theory, define management?

6. Explain the significance of the Hawthorne Studies?

7. How does McGregor's Theory Y view of workers differ from the view of Frederick W. Taylor?

8. What are the main assumptions made by the management scientist?

9. Which management technique is always advocated by a Contingency Approach to management?

10. What is a quality circle, and how does it contribute to management?

NAMES TO KNOW

Charles Babbage
Chester Barnard
Henri Fayol
Mary Parker Follett
Henry L. Gantt

Frank and Lillian M. Gilbreth
Elton Mayo
Douglas M. McGregor
Herbert Simon
Frederick Taylor

TERMS FOR STUDY

Acceptance Theory of Authority
Administrative Theory
authority
Behavioral Approach
centralization
Classical Approach
collaborative approach to
    problem-solving
commanding
Contingency Approach
controlling
coordinating
delegation
division of labor
effectiveness
efficiency
functions of management

Gantt Chart
Hawthorne Effect
Hawthorne Experiments
human relations movement
job fractionation
management of organizations
management of work
Management Science
motion study
one right way
Operations Research
organizing
planning
principles of management
productivity
production bonus
quality circle
QWL

responsibility	Theory Y
scalar chain	Theory Z
Scientific Management	therblig
scientific method	TQM/TQL
situational analysis	unity of command
soldiering	unity of direction
Theory X	work specialization

ANSWERS
KNOW THE BASICS

1. Before the Industrial Revolution the general belief was that leaders are born, not made. It was difficult to speak of management theory in this environment when there was little acceptance of the belief that managers as leaders could be trained. By the end of the 19th century, industry was expanding and had become very complex, creating the need for a better understanding of management theory and the development of managerial techniques.

2. Frederick W. Taylor, considered the "Father of Scientific Management," made the first formal attempt to create a theory of management. Taylor advocated the application of the scientific method to work analysis and the development by the management scientist of the best way to do a task—the "one right way."

3. Frank and Lillian Gilbreth were pioneers in the use of motion studies to analyze jobs and to increase worker efficiency. "Therblig" was the term that Frank Gilbreth coined to describe the seventeen different motions that went into doing a job. By listing the therbligs, he could analyze job actions, seeking to gain efficiency.

4. A Gantt Chart is a management tool used to schedule work. Taylor advocated a piece rate to motivate workers to be productive; Gantt advocated the use of not only the piece rate for normal production but also a production bonus to motivate workers to produce above the expected norm.

5. Henri Fayol created Administrative Theory and defined management functionally. His five functions that characterized management were planning, organizing, commanding, coordinating, and controlling.

6. The Hawthorne Studies, performed between 1927 and 1932 by Elton Mayo and his colleagues from Harvard, examined the relationship between work conditions and worker productivity and showed that human relationships were more important than work conditions in facilitating increased productivity. These famous studies are considered the beginnings of the human relations movement.

7. Frederick W. Taylor and his colleagues in the Management Science movement maintained that workers did not want to work, were lazy and needed to be closely supervised, had to be threatened with punishment in order to be forced to produce, were not creative, and were fully challenged by work. McGregor's Theory Y view of workers maintains that they like work, welcome challenges, are capable of creativity, can learn to accept responsibility, and usually are not fully challenged by work. McGregor's view of the worker is much more optimistic than Taylor's rather pessimistic assessment.

8. Management Science assumes that (1) all problems that characterize a system can be solved by applying the scientific method and (2) these system problems can be solved by solving equations that represent the system.

9. None. The Contingency Approach to management asserts that there is no universally applicable technique or approach to a management problem. The needs of the particular situation will determine the best approach to the organizational problem.

10. A quality circle (QC) is a small group of workers and management representatives that meets on a regular basis during working hours to attempt to improve quality, cut costs, and enrich the quality of worklife (QWL). The members of a QC deal with problems and attempt to generate possible solutions, which are then presented to management for implementation.

3
MANAGEMENT: SOCIAL RESPONSIBILITY

KEY TERMS

social responsiveness the extent to which an organization is responsive to its perceived social obligations, generally a measure of business *effectiveness* and *efficiency* in pursuing actions that meet those social obligations

Social Obligation Approach an approach to social responsiveness that assumes that the main goals of a business are economic success, not the meeting of social obligations, and, therefore, business should merely meet the minimal social obligations imposed by current legislation

Social Responsibility Approach an approach to social responsiveness that assumes that the goals of business are not merely economic but also social and that business should devote economic resources to the accomplishment of social goals

Social Responsiveness Approach an approach to social responsiveness that assumes that business not only has economic and social goals but must also anticipate future social problems and act now to respond to those future problems

social audit the dynamic process by which an organization evaluates its level of social responsibility

The last few decades have seen an increasing concern with the social obligations of business, occasioned by the growing ecology and consumer movements, which focus on the relationship between business and society. Assertions that business should devote some of its economic resources to actions that benefit society have not always been kindly received. Business writers have differed not only about the appropriate level of corporate social action but also about whether a company has legitimate reasons for devoting *any* resources to social actions. This debate continues and has been crystallized in the writings and thoughts of two major writers, **Dr. Milton Friedman** (1931–), a Nobel Prize winner in Economics, and **Dr. Keith Davis** (1918–) of Arizona State University.

ARGUMENTS AGAINST SOCIAL RESPONSIBILITY FOR BUSINESS

The argument against social responsibility for business has been articulated most widely by the Nobel Prize-winning economist Milton Friedman. He asserts that the task of business is to maximize stockholder (owner) profit by the wise use of scarce organizational resources, as long as the activities of the business are within the letter of the law. Indeed, Friedman and his followers assert that business, through the actions of trade associations representing industrial groups (lobbying), can lawfully seek to influence laws affecting business operations. Many have accused Friedman and the advocates of his position of lacking both compassion for those in economic distress and a concern for social justice. This, however, is not the case. Friedman and his followers base the assertion that business should not assume *direct* social responsibility on both practical and theoretical grounds.

Theoretical Arguments Against Social Responsibility

1. This is the major function of the government; to link business with government will create too powerful a force in society and will ultimately compromise government's role in regulating business.

2. Business needs to measure performance, and social action programs often cannot measure success rates. There is often an inherent conflict between the way business works and the way social programs work.

3. The function of business is profit maximization, and to require that resources be devoted to social action programs violates this business goal since it reduces profits.

4. There is no reason to suppose that business leaders have the ability to determine what is in the social interest. Social scientists and government administrators often cannot agree among themselves about social interest goals. Why assume that business leaders can do a better job of defining the social interest?

Practical Arguments Against Social Responsibility

1. Managers have a fiduciary (trust) responsibility to stockholders to maximize equity value, and using business funds to accomplish social goals may be a violation of that responsibility, hence illegal.

2. The cost of social programs would be a burden to business and have to be passed along to consumers in the form of higher prices.

3. The public may want government to have social programs, but there is little support for business to have these programs.

4. There is no reason to suppose that business leaders have the specialized skills necessary to achieve social interest goals.

Friedman and his many followers argue that it is sufficient for business to seek maximum profit within the rules of society. They maintain that a company that successfully makes a profit benefits society by creating new jobs and paying high wages that improve the lives of its workers. Business can also improve the working conditions of its employees and will be contributing to public welfare by paying corporate income taxes. By allowing companies to concentrate their resources on actual business activities, not social responsibility, those resources are used most efficiently and effectively, and companies are able to successfully compete in the world marketplace. To divert corporate resources to social obligations, it is argued, would be to ensure inefficiency and perhaps to fatally handicap American business.

ARGUMENTS FOR SOCIAL RESPONSIBILITY FOR BUSINESS

Keith Davis advocates social responsibility in business. He argues that social responsibility goes hand in hand with social power, and since business is the most powerful force in contemporary life, it has the obligation to assume corresponding social responsibility. Society, in turn, having given power to business, can call business to account for the use of that power. Davis further asserts that business must be open to social representatives and expert analysis of social problems; society should pay attention to and value business' efforts in the area of social responsibility. Davis acknowledges that business efforts at social responsibility will be costly but maintains that such costs could legitimately be passed on to consumers in the form of higher prices. In a most revolutionary manner he goes on to assert that business, if it possesses the necessary expertise, has the obligation even to help solve social problems in which it is not *directly* involved. This obligation is for the general social good, for when society improves, business will benefit. In general, Davis views a business entity as a person. Can society expect any less of a business than it expects of an individual? The arguments of Davis and his followers for social responsibility of business are also theoretical and practical in nature.

Theoretical Arguments for Social Responsibility

1. It is theoretically in the best interest of business to improve the communities in which it is located and in which it does business. Improvement in community environments will ultimately benefit business.

2. Social responsibility programs help prevent small problems from becoming large. Ultimately this will be of benefit to society and business.

3. Being socially responsible is the ethical or "right" thing to do.

4. Demonstrating a responsiveness to social issues will help preclude government intervention in business.

5. The most widely held value system, the Judeo-Christian tradition, strongly encourages acts of charity and social concern.

Practical Arguments for Social Responsibility

1. Actions that demonstrate social responsiveness, if actualized within a model of sustainable economics, may actually be profitable to the company. For example, new machines that control pollution may be more efficient and cost-effective.

2. Being socially responsible improves the public relations image of the company as a good citizen.

3. If we do not do it ourselves, either public opinion or the government will require us to do so.

4. It may be good for the stockholders since such actions will earn public approval, lead to the company being viewed by professional financial analysts as less open to social criticism, and produce a higher stock price.

In each of these views regarding the desired degree of social responsiveness, there is agreement that business should perform all socially responsive actions *required by law*. The major difference is to be found in the levels of socially responsive actions that go beyond the legal requirements, and the difference in opinions regarding "going above and beyond the call of duty" has given rise to several different approaches to social responsibility.

YOU SHOULD REMEMBER

Milton Friedman has advanced the view that the only valid function of business is to maximize profits and equity value for stockholders. Business is not obligated to be socially responsive other than to conform to legally required actions. Business will help improve society by making profits and paying better wages to its workers.

Keith Davis maintains that since business has power in society, it should exercise its power to improve society and therefore has an obligation to show social responsiveness.

Both Friedman and Davis maintain that business should follow the law and perform acts of social responsiveness that are required.

DEGREES OF CORPORATE SOCIAL RESPONSIBILITY INVOLVEMENT

Social responsiveness is the extent to which an organization is responsive to perceived social obligations. Social responsiveness is measured by evaluating the *effectiveness* and *efficiency* of an organization in its efforts to pursue actions that meet social obligations. Reflecting the differences between a Milton Friedman "business has no social responsibility other than the law" view and a Keith Davis "business does have social responsibilities because it has been given social and economic power" view, business organizations have assumed different levels of social responsiveness. Three approaches have emerged: the *Social Obligation Approach*, the *Social Responsibility Approach*, and the *Social Responsiveness Approach*. These approaches represent a continuum of social responsiveness from the least involved to the most involved, as illustrated in Figure 3-1.

THE SOCIAL OBLIGATION APPROACH

The **Social Obligation Approach** assumes that the main goals of a business are economic in nature, primarily the maximizing of profits and stockholders' equity, not the meeting of social obligations. Therefore, followers of such an approach think that business should merely meet the *minimal social obligations* imposed by current legislation. A manager who takes the Social Obligation Approach will conform to the law and may seek to influence the formation of laws by making political contributions to candidates

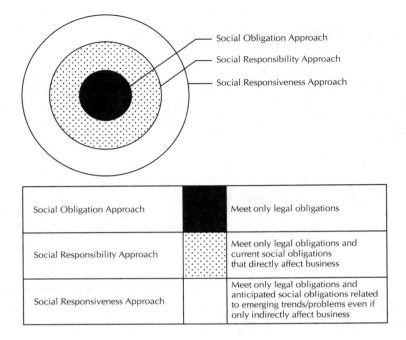

Social Obligation Approach		Meet only legal obligations
Social Responsibility Approach		Meet only legal obligations and current social obligations that directly affect business
Social Responsiveness Approach		Meet only legal obligations and anticipated social obligations related to emerging trends/problems even if only indirectly affect business

Figure 3–1. Levels of business social responsiveness.

for public office who share the same view or by lobbying lawmakers to create new laws or abolish existing ones. Managers who accept this approach maintain that business fulfills social obligation by maximizing profits and keeping workers employed. As long as they obey the law, these managers are accountable only to business owners (stockholders) for actions that expend organizational resources—not to society. Such managers select business actions that will result in the best economic outcome for the company, and/or that are required by law. Such managers may be very active in trade association efforts to oppose or change legislation and to limit business social responsibility. They will actively support political candidates advocating minimal government involvement in the affairs of business.

Managers who agree with the Social Obligation Approach may advocate contributions to charity by business, but only because such action benefits the company. Such charitable giving will be cited in public relations efforts and, it is hoped, earn the company a good reputation that ultimately influences consumer purchasing decisions or create a direct benefit for its employees. Otherwise, the social good deed of charity will be viewed as the responsibility of individuals, not of the business. In general this approach stresses that legal obligation or self-benefit is the only determinant for social responsibility—otherwise, such responsibility belongs to someone else, individuals or governmental agencies.

While the Social Obligation Approach has consistently been criticized by those who assert that mere compliance with legal obligation is insufficient, trends in legislation on the local, state, and federal levels have provided a frontal, pragmatic assault on managers and stockholders who would otherwise limit the business response to social problems. Businesses are now faced with a plethora of what might be called social responsibility laws—legal enactments that create new and imposing obligations on the contemporary business to limit pollution, create and maintain a safe workplace, avoid unfair anti-competitive business practices, treat workers equally, and report performance and personnel data to local, state, and federal regulatory agencies. Increasingly, failure to follow these growing bodies of laws may result in significant financial penalties assessed against both the individual manager and/or the organization, as well as potential criminal liability resulting in fines and possibly even a prison sentence. Those who would limit managerial response to legal requirements are now confronted with the necessity for an increasing awareness of changing social obligations and commitment of organizational resources.

YOU SHOULD REMEMBER

The **Social Obligation Approach** assumes that the **only** social responsibility **obligations** of business are those **required by law.** A company that believes in this approach will devote *only* the required organizational resources to meeting these social obligations but will undertake no voluntary efforts.

THE SOCIAL RESPONSIBILITY APPROACH

The **Social Responsibility Approach** assumes that business not only has economic goals but also social responsibilities. Managers who take this approach will make organizational decisions based not only on projected economic gain and legal compliance but also on criteria of social benefit. There is a willingness to expend some organizational resources for social welfare projects related to the needs of the larger community, although no course of action would be chosen that directly brought economic harm to the company. There is a concern for the maximization of profit and stockholders' equity, but also a willingness to consider those in the community who oversee social action programs. Social Responsibility Approach companies actively seek community approval for their social involvement and desire to be viewed as "good corporate citizens"; much corporate public relations effort will be directed to gaining this public recognition.

Managers in these companies will cooperate with communal social agencies in defining the dimensions of current social problems and discovering means by which business can help solve these problems. Employees are encouraged to participate in community social responsibility efforts, and such individual employee participation will often be recognized by company reward. Company policy will also encourage and support socially desirable individual action by such actions as matching the employee's charitable contribution with company funds.

When these companies discover that their actions have contributed to current social problems, they will practice *reactive adaptation*. This means that in cases in which the company's contributing role to the social problem is evident, the company will act to provide a remedy. This may include such actions as paying compensation to those injured by company-caused pollution or spending money to maintain the level of pollution control above that currently mandated by the community.

> An example of an organization that assumed social responsibility was seen in San Diego when the University of California decided to establish a branch campus. The university became aware that there were racial and religious quotas employed by a nearby expensive and exclusive housing development. Since many of the professors who would be teaching on the campus would be subjected to humiliation and rejection in their search for housing, the university administration decided to take direct action *even though there was no legal requirement to do so*. Local banks were contacted and told that no university department would do business with any financial institution denying mortgage financing to a university employee based upon discrimination. The university authorities went further and informed the local government that the branch campus would be located elsewhere in the state unless there was assurance that the housing area would be open to all financially qualified applicants regardless of race and religion. The local government officials gave this assurance, and the branch campus has become an outstanding educational institution.

> # YOU SHOULD REMEMBER
>
> The **Social Responsibility Approach** recognizes that business has both economic and social responsibilities. The economic responsibilities are profit maximization and stockholder equity increase. The social responsibilities are to deal with current social problems, but only to the extent that the economic welfare of the company is not affected negatively. This approach recognizes current social action groups and may even contribute to them while encouraging managers and employees to do likewise. This approach meets social problems by means of **reactive adaptation,** a process of reacting to problems.

THE SOCIAL RESPONSIVENESS APPROACH

The **Social Responsiveness Approach** assumes that business not only has economic *and* social goals but also *must* anticipate future social problems and act *now* to respond to these future problems. Of the three approaches described in this chapter, this is the most demanding of business:

1. Business is required to *anticipate* social problems and deal with them before they are evident.

2. In dealing with future social problems, business may have to make use of organization resources *now* for future social good, negatively impacting on profit maximization in the present.

A company subscribing to this approach believes that good corporate citizenship involves taking a very *proactive* role in society, of making use of the power given to business for the improvement of society. This will ultimately have a beneficial effect upon the company since it does business within that society. An example of this would be a company-funded drug education program in the public schools. The future gain is a healthier workforce even though a company may not be having any present problems with drugs in the workplace.

A socially responsive company actively seeks out community involvement and encourages its employees to do likewise. There is much effort devoted to being socially aware, particularly as such awareness relates to emerging areas of concern. Although the previously discussed Social Responsibility Approach sanctioned company and individual involvement in established social causes, the Social Responsiveness Approach gives approval to a wider view that actively embraces emerging charities and social action groups.

Since these emerging causes do not have wider social approval, they and the companies who support them may be viewed as "radical." One of the most well-known companies of this type is premium-brand ice cream maker Ben & Jerry's. Located in Waterbury, VT, this company is exceptionally well known for its environmental consciousness and beneficial involvement in the local community. It directly seeks to be a "force for positive change" locally and globally. In fact, when it was announced in January 2000 that an unidentified company had made an offer to purchase Ben & Jerry's, many of its franchise operators and independent dealers who carried its products banded together to publicly express concern. They were concerned that such a sale would compromise the company's unique culture and diminish its community involvement. The concerns of this group were prominently reported in *The New York Times* and thus widely noted.

This approach leads companies to take a stance of *proactive adaptation*. Future problems are anticipated and actions are taken to prevent the problems either from emerging or from becoming as significant as they might become. A company that seeks this approach will not only support currently existing laws but actively support the adoption of new legislation that meets anticipated social needs. The company may even make use of its unique research and development expertise to apply technology to meeting anticipated social needs. These companies may take the industry lead in developing new performance standards that are even more strict than those required by law, with the justification that these stricter standards benefit society, give the industry the reputation of being socially responsive, and may act to preclude government intervention and regulation. The courses of proactive adaptation may even be economically detrimental to the company but will be considered justified by recourse to the greater good of the society within which the company functions.

> A major railroad located in the Southeast exemplified the Social Responsiveness Approach in the late 1970s when it hired a kinesiologist, a scientist who studies motion, to analyze the motions found in each railroad job. The company wanted a classification in terms of muscle movements so that it could place physically challenged individuals in positions in which they could function and make a contribution to the railroad as productive employees. The classification system allowed the company to match such individuals with specific jobs. This was not then mandated by law but by the desire of the company to benefit all the constituencies involved: the company by acquiring valuable and dedicated employees; the physically challenged individuals by gaining employment; and the community by the addition of productive workers and taxpayers.

YOU SHOULD REMEMBER

The **Social Responsiveness Approach** stresses that business not only has economic and social responsibilities but also must anticipate *future* social problems and devote organizational resources to dealing with these future problems. This will be accomplished by **proactive adaptation,** anticipating future problems and dealing with them now. This includes problems that may not be directly relevant to the company but the solution of which will benefit the greater society. This is a very open approach and admits the responsibility of the managers to the business owners (stockholders) and also to society at large.

THE SOCIAL ACTIONS MANAGEMENT PROCESS

The process by which an organization manages its social actions, no matter which approach it takes, has two major facets: (1) the action phase and (2) an evaluative phase. The *action phase* consists of problem identification, the definition of successful performance criteria for a solution to the problem, generation and evaluation of alternative courses of action, alternative(s) selection and pilot plan implementation, full alternative implementation and program evaluation. The *evaluative phase* is the *social audit*, a formal appraisal of the overall organizational effort in the area of social responsibility.

THE ACTION PHASE

• *SITUATION ANALYSIS AND SETTING OF STANDARDS*

The first step in any corporate social action program is to perform a situation analysis with regard to the social condition. This consists of making a comparison between "what is" and "what should be." If there is a gap between the two, a social need has been identified.

Once a social need, or problem, has been identified, the next step is to define the performance standards by which you will know when the problem has been corrected. Ideally, these performance standards should be defined in terms of observable and measurable behavior, but this may prove impossible. Many social problems do not lend themselves to such a quantitative definition, and their proposed solutions will be stated in terms that are vague. This is less desirable but acceptable if it is the only way to define the direction in which a company wishes to go in the fulfillment of its social responsibility.

A company may decide that, as a social responsibility, it should contribute to the cultural advancement of the community in which it is located. A company will fulfill this social responsibility by acting as a corporate sponsor of a cultural event that benefits the community. Although money will be spent and the event held, it is extremely difficult to measure the actual impact on the larger community. There will be a general sense of cultural accomplishment but little if any hard data to measure goal accomplishment. (Gulf Oil has done this in its long-standing association with public television, specifically its sponsorship of *Masterpiece Theater.*)

• *ALTERNATIVE GENERATION AND SELECTION*

Only after a problem has been identified and performance standards stated for proposed solutions can alternative courses of action be generated. These proposed solutions may come from company employees, from the community, from government officials, and even from outside experts hired as consultants. Once a list of alternatives has been generated, they are evaluated based on three major criteria:

1. Does this option solve the problem?

2. Can the company afford this course of action?

3. What are the other consequences of this action?

If the answer is negative to any of these questions, that option will be rejected. It is obvious from question 2 that there may be no acceptable option for a company—some social problems are beyond the abilities, financial and otherwise, of companies to solve. Since most of the energy will be directed to question 3, this process is often referred to as *consequences analysis.*

Assuming that either a course of action or a combination of several proposed actions is chosen as the appropriate manner in which the company will fulfill its social responsibility, a pilot test will be run to see if there are any unanticipated difficulties. If need be, the programs can be revised and improved at this stage.

• *IMPLEMENTATION AND EVALUATION*

The final two steps are to fully implement the proposed social action program and, at some realistic point in time, to evaluate the program. This evaluation provides information that can be used in a new situational analysis, design of performance standards, generation alternatives, and so on. This information, called "feedback," is put back into the dynamic social action program design process.

The level of social responsiveness assumed by the company will strongly influence all steps in this process, limiting or widening the range of what will be defined as a problem, the range of proposed solutions, and program selection. A company subscribing to the Social Obligation Approach will maintain that most social problems are not within the range of concern of the company and that the only valid concern should be to meet legal obligation. But management subscribing to the Social Responsiveness Approach, dealing with anticipated social problems, will admit a much wider range of present and anticipated social problems into its concern.

Table 3-1 illustrates the typical behavior of each level of social concern during the action phase of a social action program.

YOU SHOULD REMEMBER

The steps in the **action phase** of a social action program are: perform situational analysis; set standards; generate alternative courses of action; and then determine appropriate action, implement it, and finally evaluate it. The organization selects actions that embody its basic philosophy toward social responsibility.

THE EVALUATION PHASE

Evaluation of a company's social responsiveness activities is accomplished by means of a *social audit*. This audit examines the total of organizational activities that relate to social responsiveness and is a formal assessment of organizational efficiency and effectiveness in meeting its perceived social program goals. It is obvious that some organizations, having a greater commitment to social programs, will have more involved efforts than less committed companies. A social audit does not focus on each individual program but on the *totality* of organizational efforts. Several major approaches to the social audit process have emerged: inventory approach, cost center approach, program management approach, and cost-benefit approach. An organization may frequently utilize the results of the social audit for reporting to local, state, and federal government authorities and agencies, as well as for beneficial public relations advertising.

Table 3–1 Responses to the Action Phase of a Social Action Program by Level of Social Responsiveness

Approach/ Level	Situational Analysis		Performance Standards	Alternatives Generation	Consequences Analysis	Program Evaluation
	What Is	Should Be				
Social Obligation Approach	Only recognize legal requirements Decisions based on profit/equity maximization	Conform to legal obligations	Meet legal obligations	Alternatives should only meet legal obligations	Accept alternatives that meet legal obligations or meet non-legal obligations	Has the company met its legal obligations?
Social Responsibility Approach	Recognize legal and social obligations Decisions based on profit/equity maximization and social goals	Conform to legal obligations and solve current social problems	Meet legal obligations Solve current social problems	Alternatives should meet legal requirements Alternatives to meet current social problems	Accept alternatives that meet legal obligations and solve current social problems	Has the company met its legal obligations? Has the company solved current social problems that affect it directly?
Social Responsiveness Approach	Recognize legal and social obligations Decisions based on profit/equity maximization and future social goals	Conform to legal obligations and anticipate future social problems	Meet legal obligations Prevent future social problems—meet emerging social needs	Alternatives should meet legal requirements Alternatives should solve anticipated future social problems	Accept alternatives that meet legal obligations and solve future social problems	Has the company met its legal obligations? Has the company solved future social problems that affect it even indirectly?

In the *inventory approach*, management supplies the general public with a listing (or "inventory") of its social program efforts during a specific time frame—at least on an annual basis. This may be a full public relations effort designed to gain a praiseworthy reputation for the company in the community or merely a section in the annual report to the stockholders and financial community. The strength of this method is that it does point to areas of social action within the community. Its weakness lies in the fact that it is a list, with generally no details about costs or successes, for example. It is therefore a *minimal approach* to the social audit.

The *cost center approach* is a more involved method in which there is not only a summary of the social programs conducted by the company but also an accounting of the costs for each program. Although this provides additional information, it fails to evaluate any program for efficiency and effectiveness. The public and management are not given an assessment of program success. A *program management approach* adds an assessment of organizational success in meeting corporate social responsibility goals. This program forces program managers into assessing levels of success but has been criticized for this assessment. It is maintained that some social programs do not have easily stated or measured goals, making assessment of success an extremely difficult task.

The *cost-benefit analysis* is the most involved social audit procedure. It seeks to evaluate social programs for their costs and the eventual benefits derived. This is the most difficult evaluation process since it assumes that one can define the goals in measurable terms, quantifying both the costs and the benefits, and compare the two. It has been criticized because of the inherent difficulties in social goal definition and benefit measurement.

Figure 3-2 illustrates the four approaches to the social audit.

YOU SHOULD REMEMBER

A **social audit** is the measurement of the social responsiveness actions taken by a business. It may range from a simple **inventory,** or list of social action projects, to a formal **cost-benefits analysis,** which seeks to estimate the cost and derived benefits from all social action projects undertaken in a given time frame. A social audit is complicated by the fact that it is often difficult to define and measure success in such programs.

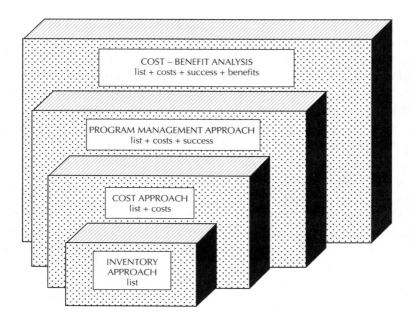

COST – BENEFIT ANALYSIS
list + costs + success + benefits

PROGRAM MANAGEMENT APPROACH
list + costs + success

COST APPROACH
list + costs

INVENTORY
APPROACH
list

Figure 3–2. Types of social audit.

AREAS OF SOCIAL CONCERN IN CURRENT MANAGEMENT PRACTICE

There are several significant areas of social concern that have drawn the attention of business since the 1970s and will continue to do so. These areas are air pollution, water pollution, solid waste pollution, noise and aesthetic pollution, minority responsibility, and employee safety. These areas are important for all businesses, even if they only assume a Social Obligation Approach to social responsibility. Each of these areas carries with it a legal obligation that must be addressed.

AIR POLLUTION

Since the early 1960s there has been a rising concern about air quality in the United States. The automobile is the major polluter, but industry has also been perceived as a significant offender. Mandated by legislation, business has adopted air cleaning technologies, primarily in the manufacturing sector, to reduce air pollution. These technologies include filters, gas washing processes, and electrostatic precipitators to reduce ash content. Major air quality legislation that creates social obligations for business are:

- Clean Air Act of 1963, focusing on multistate air pollution, which authorized the federal government to help states and local government create control programs and authorized *limited* federal action with regard to specific pollution problems

- Clean Air Act Amendments of 1965, also known as the Motor Vehicle Air Pollution Control Act, which created clean air standards for automotive exhaust systems that took effect for 1968 automobile models

- Air Quality Act of 1967, which authorized the federal government to establish air quality regions and to set clean air standards as well as mandate that local governments enact control programs or surrender jurisdiction to the national government

- National Environmental Policy Act of 1969, which mandated that all agencies of the federal government consider environmental factors when making significant decisions, including the preparation of an environmental impact statement (EIS), which details any impact on the environment, including quality of air

- Clean Air Act Amendments of 1970, which authorized the Environmental Protection Agency (EPA) to set nationwide air pollution standards and authorized private citizens to sue the EPA for enforcement against undiscovered offenders

- Clean Air Act Amendments of 1977, which postponed the implementation of automobile emission clean air standards, required air scrubbers for new coal-burning power plants, and required the EPA to establish a system to stop the deterioration of air quality in areas determined to be clean

- Clean Air Act Amendments of 1990, which further strengthened the government's legal authority to regulate air quality and business activities that have the potential to impact on that quality

WATER POLLUTION

With growing sophistication in physical chemistry and the detection of water pollutants in the food chain has come a public outcry. The general area of concern is the unsafe agricultural use of chemical pesticides that find their way into water and food systems and municipal sewage treatment. Each has resulted in serious contamination of water tables, and public pressure has resulted in requirements for industry and cities to clean up their use of water. Although business has responded with costly modifications to manufacturing systems, smaller companies have often found the cost unbearable.

The federal government first established the right to regulate water pollution with the Rivers and Harbors Act of 1886, as amended in 1899. This applied to "navigable waters," but this term is now applied to coastal and fresh-water "wetlands" and intrastate lakes and streams. Government authority also now extends to ocean dumping.

Although the Refuse Act of 1899, extended by legal interpretation to include industrial wastes, made it illegal to dump debris into navigable waters without a permit, it was not until the 1950s that federal legislation created new social obligations for business in the area of water quality. The major pieces of legislation were:

- Federal Water Pollution Control Act of 1956, which gave power to the federal government to award grants to the states to develop water pollution control programs and created federal authority to deal with specific and limited water pollution problems

- Water Quality Act of 1965, in which the federal government authorized the states to adopt water quality standards that were subject to federal approval

- Water Quality Improvement Act of 1970, which gave power to the federal government to provide for the cleanup of oil spills

- Federal Water Pollution Control Act Amendments of 1972, which gave authority to the EPA to set water quality standards and to regulate the pollution levels in industrial effluents, set up a mechanism to enforce the standards, and begin pollution control and standards research. These amendments also established the now-familiar goals of (1) ensuring that water would become or remain safe for recreational enjoyment; (2) protecting fish and wildlife; and (3) eliminating water discharge of pollutants. These amendments also set forth a specific timetable for remedial action.

- Safe Drinking Water Act of 1974, which set standards for the quality of drinking water.

- Water Quality Act of 1981, which extended the specific remedial action timetables of 1973, 1974, and 1977 with regard to drinking water.

HAZARDOUS AND SOLID WASTE POLLUTION

In the 1960s it was apparent to the general public that water pollution was not the only area of concern. There was also a recognition that landfills were reaching capacity and that other solutions had to be developed to deal with solid waste. In addition, popularization of advances in scientific knowledge of the changes that solid wastes underwent as they decayed, or failed to biodegrade—as in packaging and fast-food serving pieces made of plastic—led to a growing public concern that something had to be done concerning the management of solid wastes even if landfills were not closed. This began with the Solid Waste Disposal Act of 1965, which gave authority to the federal government to assist local governments in developing treatment programs and to conduct research, and it has extended to a major concern about radioactive wastes from nuclear power plants and disposal of hazardous chemicals. Major pieces of legislation are:

- Resource Recovery Act of 1970, which gave a federal subsidy to pilot resource recycling plants and mandated the development of a national solid waste control program

- Resource Conservation and Recovery Act of 1976, which directed the EPA to regulate all phases of hazardous waste management

- Surface Mining and Reclamation Act of 1976, which required restoration of reclaimed land from surface mining operations

Increasingly, in recognition of the fragility of the local ecosystem related to solid waste disposal, drinking water supplies, economic growth, and the straining of local disposal services and resources, state and local governments have enacted sanitation codes that impose new requirements on businesses. States, in particular, are creating solid waste management plans that take a wide approach, even as several affected states may band together to consider a larger regional view. An example of this is the New York State Solid Waste Management Plan that mandates the closing of landfills on Long Island for fear of contamination of the local aquifer, or water table, from where all drinking water comes in that area. This global approach, enforced by decisions of the New York court system, even requires the closing of solid waste landfills in local communities that do not affect the aquifer. Bottle deposit laws that require a deposit on soft drink containers, in an attempt to foster recycling, is another example of a global approach to solid waste management.

In addition, as science identifies hazardous substances that cause both long- and short-term maladies, governments at all levels have shown a willingness to require businesses to make provisions for adequate management and disposal. The Toxic Substances Control Act of 1976 regulates chemicals and substances known to be toxic (i.e., asbestos, PCBs, pesticides) and allows the EPA to regulate, even to the prohibition of use. The Resource Conservation and Recovery Act of 1976 (RCRA) requires the EPA to determine hazardous solid waste levels and to monitor and control via regulation the manufacture, use, storage, and disposal of hazardous solid waste.

State and federal environmental protection agencies actively encourage local reporting of hazardous incidents and vigorously investigate. The rising public concern can readily be seen in the outcry regarding disposal of medical wastes, and the industrial pollution of public beaches and recreational parks.

No business today can afford to ignore the rapidly evolving body of laws and regulations concerning waste disposal. Indeed, even individuals would be guilty of pollution by merely changing the oil in an automobile or lawn-mower, and accidentally pouring the oil into a stream or lake or even down the drain. Indeed, in 1980 Congress passed legislation called the Comprehensive Environmental Response, Compensation, and Liability Act, popularly known as CERCLA or "Superfund." This $1.6-billion allocation, financed by petroleum product taxes and levies on forty-two chemicals, provided for the cleanup of hazardous waste that could not be linked to a single polluter. This was amended in 1986 by the Superfund Amendments and Reauthorization Act (SARA) to first allow the EPA to react to an actual or threatened toxic release from a site and then to sue the polluter(s), the transporter(s) of pollution, and/or the owner(s) of the site.

NOISE AND AESTHETIC POLLUTION

Physiologists and physicians have now documented the loss of hearing produced by the levels of noise in many urban and industrial environments, from the subways in a large modern city to the factory floor. Many cities have passed local laws controlling the levels of permissible sound in public places, and the federal government enacted the Noise Control Act of 1972, which tasked the EPA with setting acceptable levels for major sources of noise and advising the Federal Aviation Administration regarding standards for airplane noise. These laws require business to take action to control noise by means of redesign efforts or by actually moving the sound generator, whether it is a machine or an entire factory.

The Occupational Safety and Health Administration (OSHA) sets acceptable levels of noise in the workplace to protect workers' hearing and control workplace noise pollution.

There is also growing concern in the area of aesthetic pollution, which is defined as anything that detracts from the beauty of nature or the essential character of an area. Although this is somewhat vague, it has been expressed on the community level by restrictive zoning, limitations on land usage, and an increasing willingness to limit growth and development by designating structures as "landmarks." Increasingly, proposed business uses for land and building construction plans have been rejected based on community reaction to their aesthetics—many communities now restrict building to those that are integrated with the already existing style. Virtually every community has risen in opposition to the construction of new landfills, incinerators, chemical waste disposal facilities, and prisons. Because of its potential impact upon business, aesthetic pollution concerns must be noted by modern managers.

THE HUMAN AREAS OF SOCIAL CONCERN

Since the Civil Rights Act of 1964, business has been responsible for minority affairs in the workplace. The rationale for requiring management to formulate, execute, and be held accountable for business practices in the workplace as they affect minorities is that this is an appropriate way to correct long-standing social wrongs done to those minorities. Such actions that correct social wrongs are of benefit to all: minorities, business, and society in general. Although a multitude of laws on the local and federal level regulate minority affairs in the workplace, business in general seeks to conform to the legally required practices of *affirmative action* and *equal opportunity*. These practices require that business not discriminate in hiring and promotion practices and actively advance minority employees to achieve a racial balance. It is readily evident that these requirements impose specific obligations upon business in the area of personnel practice and place legal limitations upon the way in which these practices can be accomplished.

The Occupational Safety and Health Act of 1971 empowered the federal government to set and enforce standards for worker safety and protection, such as the regulation of noise pollution mentioned previously. This arose because of growing worker and general public indignation at unsafe working conditions that resulted in thousands of worker deaths and hundreds of thousands of injuries each year. OSHA requirements include record-keeping and reporting of accidents, investigatory and enforcement powers, and the ultimate power to fine or even close a business that is judged to be unsafe and to have conditions that are hazardous to the health of workers. It is hard for most people to imagine how unsafe the workplace was a hundred years ago—it was not uncommon to find factory towns filled with widows and orphaned children of the young men who had been killed in industrial accidents. In fact, one of the earliest and ultimately most successful appeals of the labor union movement in the first decades of the 20th century was that unions could, by making collective demands on management, make the workplace safer. OSHA requirements for worker safety have done much to make the workplace a considerably safer environment. Management must consider OSHA requirements and current developments since this worker protection agency is continually doing research to develop new safety standards. For example, a current area of concern is the effect of prolonged use of the CRT (cathode ray tube) used in video display terminals upon computer operators.

Courts, in addition to state and local governments, have created new areas of managerial concern as existing laws, plus new ones being enacted, have been interpreted to mandate elimination from the workplace of sexual harassment or even the presence of a "hostile environment." This has been broadly interpreted to include unwanted sexual advances by one individual to another, or any sexual discrimination. Businesses are now being forced, under threat of legal penalty and individual managerial liability, to change what in many industries had been characterized as a "male-oriented" view.

But there is a more significant reason for businesses to eliminate sexual harassment and the environment that nurtures it. Since the end of World War II, women have entered college and business in increasing numbers, and currently comprise half of the workforce. They represent a major source of managerial talent and constitute a vital organizational resource. The business enterprise that ignores its female managers, and actively discourages the professional growth of women in its ranks, risks economic disaster and courts discrimination and harassment lawsuits. Also, there is a growing recognition that anyone, both men and women, can be the victim of harassment, and that the business organization suffers along with the harassed individuals in terms of reduced effectiveness of managerial effort and inefficient allocation of organizational management resources.

YOU SHOULD REMEMBER

Current areas of social concern include water, air, and noise pollution, as well as hazardous and solid waste pollution, and aesthetic forms of pollution. Human areas of social concern include minority affairs, sexual harassment, and employee safety. These areas are important to business because legislation imposes obligations upon companies and strongly influences the way in which business can be accomplished.

KNOW THE CONCEPTS
DO YOU KNOW THE BASICS?

1. Why does Dr. Milton Friedman feel that business should not be involved in social responsiveness other than to meet legal obligations?

2. On what basis does Dr. Keith Davis disagree with Dr. Milton Friedman and maintain that business does have social responsibility?

3. What is the Social Obligation Approach?

4. Describe the scope of concern found in the Social Responsibility Approach.

NAMES TO KNOW

Keith Davis   Milton Friedman

TERMS FOR STUDY

consequences analysis   reactive adaptation
cost-benefit analysis   social audit
cost center approach   Social Obligation Approach
inventory approach   Social Responsibility Approach
proactive adaptation   social responsiveness
program management approach   Social Responsiveness Approach

ANSWERS
KNOW THE BASICS

1. Dr. Milton Friedman maintains that the defined goals of business are economic, not social responsiveness. The responsibility of management is to maximize profit and stockholders' equity. Friedman maintains that there is no reason to assume that business possesses either the resources or the expertise to deal with social problems.

2. Dr. Keith Davis maintains that society has given business great power and that business should make use of this power to meet social responsibilities. Society will call business to account for the use of power, and if business does not voluntarily seek to fulfill social responsibility, society will compel it. Further, Dr. Davis argues that improvements in society will ultimately be of benefit to business.

3. The Social Obligation Approach maintains that the appropriate level of social responsiveness for a business is only that required by law.

4. The Social Responsibility Approach maintains that a company should meet all legal requirements and help solve current social problems that affect it directly.

4
MANAGEMENT AND THE ENVIRONMENTS OF BUSINESS

KEY TERMS

open systems model a view of an organization as dynamically and continually interacting with its environment as it takes input, acts on that input, and produces output

external environment those factors outside an organization that influence it and interact with one another; included are economic, political, sociological, and state-of-the-art technological factors

internal environment those factors inside an organization that constitute its resources; included are financial, physical, human, and current technology factors

corporate culture the total sum of the values, customs, traditions, and meanings that make a company unique, often called the character of an organization

business ethics a code used to guide business actions in which actions deemed unethical and therefore unacceptable, even though perhaps legal, are avoided because these actions go against the accepted moral standards of the time, place, and culture

---

Organizations exist within many environments that influence the way in which they can function. Management must often respond to environmental forces, such as the laws listed in the previous chapter, that compel management to control pollution and spend organizational resources for social responsibility programs. However, the legal environment is not the only external force affecting the organization. There are also economic, sociological, and technological forces that impact upon the modern business organization and must be taken into account by management.

In addition to these broad environmental factors that affect a business, there are several more specific forces within the external environment that have an immediate impact. These are the business shareholders, banks, unions, suppliers, and customers. A business must carefully relate to each of these essentials. These factors, which are external to the organization, are called the *external environment*. They influence not only the organization but also each other.

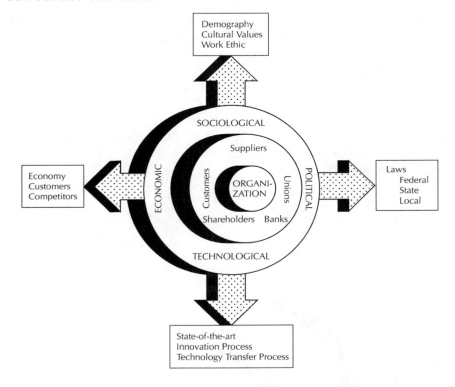

Figure 4–1. The external environments of business.

Figure 4-1 summarizes the external environment. The broad environmental factors are placed on the outer ring since they not only affect the organization in the center but also contain the more specific factors. The specific factors in the inner ring are more immediate to the organization. It is important to note that external factors are dynamic and constantly changing and management must recognize the need to respond to the changes. To ignore changing environments that affect your business is to risk the very survival of the company. Changing energy prices, rising union wage demands, rising or falling interest rates, and economic difficulties of a company's suppliers are examples of dynamic changes in external environments that can have a great impact on a business enterprise.

The *internal environment* consists of those factors inside an organization that constitute organizational resources, primarily financial, physical, human resources, and current technology factors. The level of technology inside an organization is different from the external technology level. The state-of-the-art technology may be computer-controlled manufacturing, but an individual company may still use and find manual control to be completely adequate for its needs. Thus the internal level of technology will not be as sophisticated as the external. The reverse may also be true. A company that is heavily committed to research and development may have invented technological processes not available in the external environment.

Figure 4-2 illustrates the internal environment of business. Note that the arrows now point into the organization because the factors listed are part of the internal environment.

Each of the internal and external factors will be discussed later in the chapter, but now it is valuable to place them in specific relationship to the dynamic process that characterizes the modern organization. This is called the *open systems model*.

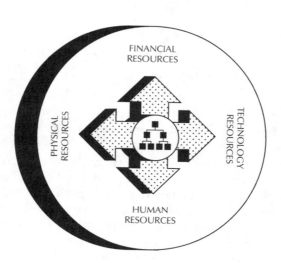

Figure 4–2. The internal environments of business.

YOU SHOULD REMEMBER

Organizations exist within a complex **external environment** that influences the manner in which business is done. The major factors of this external environment are economic, sociological, political, and technological factors. Within this external environment are factors that affect the organization in an immediate manner. These are a firm's shareholders, banks, suppliers, unions, and customers. The **internal environment** consists of the factors that are internal to the business. These are human, financial, technological, and physical resources.

OPEN SYSTEMS MODEL

An **Open Systems Model** views an organization as dynamic and continually interacting with its environment as it takes input, acts to transform that input, and produces output. This interaction is summarized in Figure 4-3.

The *input* of the organization is its productive resources, which are then manufactured or assembled (*transformed*) into the final goods or services, which are its *output*. Although Figure 4-3 shows a TV assembly line, it could also be a marketing research company producing research studies—whatever the company produces is its output. Ideally, the output will be of greater value than the input. If this is so, we can speak of the transformation

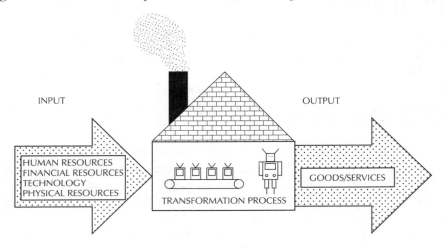

Figure 4-3. The open systems model.

process as one that is a *value added process*. The three possible situations faced by a company are:

Input > output The company is losing money since the input factors are of greater value than the output.

Input = output The company is just breaking even.

Output > input Since the value of the output is greater than the value of the input, the company is making a profit.

YOU SHOULD REMEMBER

True organizational productivity will be evident when the market value of an organization's **output** is greater than the **input** resources. The difference between output and input is called **gross profit.** The business organization that uses its limited resources with greater effectiveness and efficiency will have a greater gross profit.

THE EXTERNAL ENVIRONMENTS OF BUSINESS

The following are those forces external to the organization that influence the way in which it functions: sociological, political, economic, and technological.

SOCIOLOGICAL FACTORS

A sociological perspective of environment includes the demographic status and trends, the work ethic and personal values, and general cultural values. Each of these influences how management accomplishes its jobs. Each country has a unique social environment, and, as business becomes international, management must understand these unique environments. This is discussed in Chapter 24, which covers international management. Here, however, it will be useful to break the sociological area into three smaller perspectives.

• *DEMOGRAPHIC STATUS AND TRENDS*

Demography is the study of populations, and a demographic trend is a change in the population. Managers consult demographers to understand population trends and plan for the future because those trends can have a dramatic effect on business. For example, a manager planning to construct a new plant may find it useful to know the areas to which a large number of people are moving because a significant factor in site selection for a new factory is the availability of a labor supply. In another case, a fast-food restaurant chain that depends on high school students as workers would find demographic charts useful in predicting the future labor supply. In this way, demographics allows management to *anticipate* change, not merely *react* to it.

Three major demographic trends are emerging at the beginning of the 21st century. First, the workforce is becoming older. The U.S. Census Bureau estimates that by 2040, the population aged 65 to 74 will grow by 80 percent but that the 85-and-over group will increase by 240 percent! For example, in 1900 there were only 374,000 Americans 85 and older; in 2000 this number had increased to almost 4 million; and by 2040 it is estimated that there will be 13 million in that age group. By way of comparison, in 1995 there were 14 million college-age youth compared to 33.4 million elderly (age 65 and older); by 2040, this will be 20.4 million college-age youth to 75.2 million elderly. This means that there will be fewer working-age adults and an increasing number of retired workers (of course some will elect to continue working). This demographic trend, which will be a worldwide phenomenon, will impact companies and their workers. First, there may be a shortage of trained workers, and companies will have to compete to attract and retain qualified personnel. Additionally, fewer workers supporting more retirees vis-à-vis Social Security taxes may lead to considerably higher payroll taxes. In fact, some management writers have hypothesized that countries may look to immigration from less-developed countries to deal with labor shortages, resulting in a dramatically changed workforce makeup with much greater representation of minorities and more ethnic diversity.

Second, more women are entering the workforce. More than one-half of all women in the United States currently work either full- or part-time. Women are also going to college more and now are a majority of all students. They are shifting from traditional "female" studies (such as teaching, nursing, and home economics) into business and professional studies. All these trends suggest to the demographer that women will play a more significant role in U.S. business life.

Third, the population of the United States has, for a number of years, shifted from the Northeast to the southern states known as the Sun Belt. As noted in the preceding examples, population shifts can have a profound effect on the way in which business is done. Not only does such a shift signal a movement of potential labor, but it also means that markets for goods and services are shifting.

Finally, as work becomes more technical, there is a premium on education—the technologically competent workers make much more than those who lack such skills. The disparity in salary between the well educated and less educated will continue to grow. This also strongly suggests that learning and skills acquisition/maintenance will be, if not a lifelong preoccupation, at least a necessity for one's working life. Already many professions require continuing education as a prerequisite for practice.

• *WORK ETHIC AND PERSONAL VALUES*

The importance placed upon work by the individual is known as the **work ethic.** The traditional Puritan (also called the Protestant) work ethic assumed that work was good and godly and that the individual who did not work was a bum. Business organizations counted upon the desire to work in its employees, a work ethic expressed in dedication and company loyalty, and a commitment to getting the job done. However, the work ethic has changed, particularly in younger workers, and management increasingly must confront a new reality. It is obvious that the attitudes of the workers toward work will impact upon the organization as it recruits, trains, rewards, and retains employees. Additionally, as more foreign workers enter the workforce, bringing with them a more traditional work ethic derived from their original cultural traditions, managers will often encounter different work ethics in the same workforce.

Many managers have also noted a change in the **personal values** of today's workers. No more than 30 to 40 years ago the worker was loyal to the company and would accept any transfer to a new job. Now, however, some workers are turning down proposed transfers, citing a concern for lifestyle or quality of life. These have become real issues in the minds of many workers, and management is forced to respond. Companies have responded by enacting policies of flying not just the executive to the new proposed job site, but also the employee's family, in an attempt to convince the worker and all the family members to accept the new job. Another factor that now must be considered is the dual-career couple. As both husband and wife have jobs, the relocation of one occasions difficult decisions by the other.

Many workers also now voice concern not only about a job but also about the need for personal growth experiences. They want work environments that challenge and provide opportunities to grow personally and professionally. This has an impact upon job and incentive package design as management seeks to structure both the work environment and work itself to meet employee needs *and* get the job done while making a profit. One type of management response has been flexible work schedules known as "flextime." This allows the individual worker, within some organizational constraints, to arrange personal work patterns.

The realities of international competition and the derivative downsizing in industries that are not competitive has occasioned, on the part of many companies, a renewed dedication to hard work. This can readily be observed in the lengthening of the work day. While the concept of a 9 AM–5 PM work day had been widely if not universally accepted by the middle of this century, for many that is now a fond memory.

Previously, the individual who worked longer hours by toiling over the weekend or by taking work home came to be regarded as a "workaholic," and this behavior pattern was termed by mental health professionals and fellow workers as unhealthy. The dispensers of popular wisdom asserted that "all work and no play makes Jack a dull boy," so they prescribed recreational activity to rejuvenate the worker. The current trend, however, is for longer work hours in almost every industry, and the former workaholic is again coming to be characterized as the dedicated employee. Even the recreational activities now urged upon the employee in the health spa, gym, or company fitness facility are universally known as "workouts."

• *CULTURAL VALUES*

The word *culture* encompasses the values, customs, heritage, legal codes, educational traditions, social attitudes, political institutions and processes, and economic system. Management must consider the cultural values of an environment as it makes decisions. For example, if a company is located in a small town, bringing in high-powered managers to run the factory may produce a clash between the small town worker and the new management style and lead to difficulties with local authorities resulting in a negative impact on local operations.

Furthermore, as many business enterprises become international, they encounter radically different cultural settings. The role of the manager may be different in the United States than in other countries. In Japan, for example, a manager is the individual who builds a consensus among workers, not the fearless leader who imposes his or her will upon unwilling employees. A manager trying the American managerial style in Japan is doomed to fail. It must be noted that many American companies operate profitably in other cultural settings; the key to doing so is a knowledge of the important aspects of the foreign cultural setting and a willingness to adapt to that setting.

YOU SHOULD REMEMBER

Changes in the **sociological environment** can have a major impact upon managerial decision-making. Demographers study changes in population. They predict that the workforce is getting older, has less current experience, has a greater number of women than ever before, and is moving to the Sun Belt in ever-increasing numbers. Management must take these changes into account. Furthermore, as management plans for the company's future, cultural differences as well as the work ethic of employees should be considered. Research can help managers anticipate social change rather than merely react to those changes.

POLITICAL FACTORS

Laws are the primary way in which political factors affect a business. A business must respond to laws and regulations on the local, state, and federal levels. Many of these laws were summarized in the last chapter. All business transactions should conform to the legal requirements set forth in the Uniform Commercial Code (UCC), as well as other parts of federal laws and state commercial enactments. Additionally a business must respond to such laws as the National Labor Relations Act (NLRA) and its amendments and additions, which regulate union-management relations, and the Civil Rights Act of 1964 and its additions and amendments, which regulate equal opportunity and affirmative action. This list of legal requirements is not exhaustive but is meant to show that business *must* respond to the legal environment as management decisions are made.

This section, however, is the "political factors" section because it is in the political arena that business seeks to influence the legal process. A business may be affiliated with other like-minded companies in a trade association and seek to influence or "lobby" for change in the laws. Examples of trade associations are the National Association of Manufacturers, the American Bar Association, and the American Medical Association. Businesses must also relate to federal, state, and local regulatory agencies charged with overseeing the conduct of certain kinds of enterprise. Some of the more prominent federal agencies are the Civil Aeronautics Board (CAB) and the Federal Aviation Agency (FAA), which are charged with overseeing the aviation industry; the Securities and Exchange Commission (SEC), which regulates the securities industry (stock markets, bonds, and financial offerings); the Food and Drug Administration (FDA), which regulates the drug industry; and the Federal Communications Commission (FCC), which regulates the broadcast industries and awards radio and television licenses. As we saw in the last chapter, the Environmental Protection Agency has been charged with protecting the environment and the Occupational Safety and Health Administration oversees worker safety issues. It is obvious that governmental regulation, on the local level or on the federal level, can influence and sometimes constrain management decision-making.

YOU SHOULD REMEMBER

All businesses operate within several external environments, the most important of which is **political and legal.** To help ensure commercial success, all managers must be aware of the current status of and proposed changes in these environments. To ignore changes in the political arena or legal codes is to court disaster.

ECONOMIC FACTORS

As has been seen in discussing the open systems model of a business enterprise, the organization makes use of resources (input factors) to produce goods and services (output). All this takes place within the general economic environment, which affects each of these factors. Managers must consider the state of the economy in making business decisions, and, increasingly, even the international economy must be factored into managerial planning and decision-making. Those aspects that must be considered are the economy itself, the customers of a firm, and its competitors.

• *THE ECONOMY*

Aspects of that economy, such as inflation, interest rates, and rates of unemployment, must be considered by management as it makes decisions. A widely accepted measure of the general economy is the **gross national product (GNP).** This is the total market value of all final goods and services produced by American companies within a year. The GNP measures the productive resources of a country. It does not include such payments as Social Security, which are not the result of genuine production but a transfer of money from one area of society (the government) to another (recipients). As such, Social Security checks are referred to as *transfer payments* and are not included in the GNP. While the GNP includes all international business done by American companies, the sum of all domestic business is the **gross domestic product,** known as the **GDP.**

The value of the GNP is that it is used to compute per capita productivity, a basic measure of the standard of living in a country. This is derived, as shown in Figure 4-4, by dividing the total productive resources of a country (GNP) by its population.

The greater the productive resources for each person in a country, the better the achieved standard of living. However, per capita productivity, an average measure, does not mean that every individual has such a standard of living. There continues to be a great disparity between the rich, the middle class, and those living in poverty in contemporary America. It is for that reason that economists and social scientists often develop less precise but more informative models to measure the true quality of life in a country. The number of toilets, television sets, radios, computers, square feet of living space per individual, automobiles, infant mortality rates, average lifespan, number of medical doctors per one million people, and average number of calories consumed per day have all been advanced as better measures of the quality of life than the usually cited per capita productivity.

The standard of living figure helps to compare the quality of life of different countries. It also provides a basic measure of the economic strength of a given society, as well as a comparative measure by which a country can evaluate its economic progress. Management makes use of the GNP to estimate economic opportunity for new product opportunities, for example. If an economy is doing well, signaled by a strong GNP, there will be increased opportunity. If the economy is not doing well, as it was not during the Great Depression beginning in 1929, there will be an absence of economic opportunities. Management's assessment of the economic environment will influence subsequent decisions.

It is also obvious that current business will not be like that of the 1980s, a decade that was characterized by entrepreneurial activity funded by high-priced financing called "junk bonds." These bonds, sold by companies to raise the capital necessary to fund acquisitions, had little real value backing them up to ensure repayment. Thus, as the risk of a bond was mirrored by the interest rate it promised to pay, these bonds were sold on the basis of high interest rates to entice people to buy. Often, however, the businesses built with such financing were incapable of producing enough income to pay the bondholders the promised interest rates to "service the debt."

$$\text{Standard of living} = \frac{\text{GNP}}{\text{Population}}$$

Figure 4–4. Standard of living computation.

This inability was periodically heightened by downturns in the economy and the resultant decline in business profits. Well-established businesses and renowned entrepreneurs suffered declines in their fortunes as a result of crushing debt loads because of junk bond financing.

Also, a record number of consumers sought the legal protection of the bankruptcy court as a solution to their financial difficulties. Whether because of poor use of credit, the loss of one's job from business downsizing or relocation, or unanticipated business reversals, individuals found themselves in economic difficulty. Rising bankruptcy rates resulted in the growing concern to protect the seller. Thus bankruptcy rules were tightened in the 1990s to make such legal relief from debt harder to obtain.

The result is that business is more cautious and now finds an extremely wary customer. Managers recognize that the business decision-making process is complex and necessitates a broad knowledge of the latest developments in the dynamic environments of business plus more accurate assessments of financial risks and rewards.

• *COMPETITORS AND SUPPLIERS*

An essential task of management is to acquire raw materials, which are necessary input into the transformation process. These raw materials may be common and thus easily obtained, or they may be very rare and not easily obtained. Management must act to ensure that there is a steady and reliable supply. This will entail establishing a relationship with suppliers and an effective inventory policy that meets the needs of the specific company. If there are many potential suppliers, there will be much competition among them and the needed raw materials will be secured at the best price, but if there are few potential suppliers, a company desiring them may have to pay "top dollar." The number of possible suppliers will influence the price of raw materials and will also influence management pricing policy.

Competitors also influence management decision-making. If there is great competition in the marketplace, a company must be price competitive. If it is the leading company, it may set the standard price in the marketing arena and be known as a *price leader*. If it is not a dominant force in the marketing arena, it may have to follow other companies in setting a product price. In this case it will be a *price follower*. In either case, the amount and quality of competition in the marketplace will directly influence the strategic and operational (day-to-day) decisions of management.

The advent and dramatic growth of doing business by means of the *Internet* vastly increases competition as those seeking supplies of raw materials, and those wishing to expand markets, can now readily obtain worldwide exposure by creating a web site. Competition is increased when instantaneous price comparisons are possible; suppliers will have to compete with the lowest cost providers.

• *CUSTOMERS*

The final facet of the external economic dimension is a firm's customers. This is perhaps the easiest to understand, for it is obvious that a company *must* consider its customers as managerial decisions are made. The goal of this decision-making process is to better and more profitably reach the customer. These decisions become crucial, for even with the greatest of products or services offered, a firm will not prosper if it cannot deliver these goods and services to the customer. Consumers seek to have a product at the correct place, at the right time, and in the right form. We speak of these aspects as *place utility, time utility,* and *form utility.* If a company fails to deliver on any of these forms of utility, it risks failure. It is apparent, then, that the delivery of goods and services that embody these forms of utility will influence managerial decision-making.

Management seeks to know the identity of the customer, and as much as possible about that customer, who is called the *target market.* Information about the customer is gained by market research into, for example, the customer's personal statistics (*demographic profile*), buying behaviors (*consumer behavior*), or general lifestyle (*psychographic profile*). And information gathering regarding consumer behavior and purchasing decisions has gone "high tech" with **shopper registration cards.** These cards must be presented at every purchase, whereupon the cashiers enter customer purchasing behaviors directly into a database which facilitates sophisticated analysis of consumer decision-making and leads directly to better business planning. A business that fails to keep in touch with its market will be unable to respond to emerging opportunities and will fail to respond to changes in that markeplace. A business that fails to keep in touch with its market will probably fail.

YOU SHOULD REMEMBER

The **open systems** model of a business assumes that a company will have both input and output, a continual and dynamic relationship with the **political and economic environment.** Management must study the economy, the company's suppliers, competitors, and customers as well as current political factors in order to make effective managerial decisions. Products must have **place, form,** and **time utility** to succeed in the marketplace.

TECHNOLOGICAL FACTORS

The final factor in the external environment is that of technology. It has the most dramatic effect on business, as changes in this external environment are often quickly felt by a company. A company may be thoroughly committed to a form of technology and have made major capital investments in machines and human training, only to see a new, more innovative and cost-effective technology emerge. As seen by the unprecedented speed of growth of the Internet in the last five years of the 20th century, markets can change almost overnight, much to the distress of the companies that fail to adjust to changing technology. Indeed, to ignore changes in technology may constitute a fatal managerial flaw, leading to a company's demise. Consider the impact of the scientific calculator on the slide rule business. Some of you may never have seen a slide rule, yet they were used in math and common in the classroom through the 1960s. What about the impact of the automobile on the horse and buggy? There are three major areas of the technological environment that management must consider as decisions are made. These are the source of new technology, called the *process of innovation*, the way in which new technology is introduced into a company, called the *process of technology transfer,* and the current state-of-the-art technology and its application within the company. Each of these will be briefly discussed.

• *PROCESS OF INNOVATION*

The source of new technology is generally the *research and development* efforts *(R&D)* of private industry, the government, and academic researchers. A company may decide to fund R&D internally and then make use of the developed technology. Even if the technology is not applicable to the current industry, it can be licensed to other companies. Technological discoveries can be initially patented for 17 years and renewed for an additional term, which gives the inventor an exclusive right to make use of the technology or invention, or to license it for use by others for a fee.

If the source of the innovation is in the past or even in current technology levels, it is said to be an *evolutionary technological innovation* since it evolved from what came before. If, however, it does not build on past technology but represents a significant shift from the past, it can be said to be a *revolutionary technological innovation*. Adding a computer chip to the iron to turn it off if left unattended would be evolutionary—both the iron and the computer chip existed before they were combined into a new product. But since the discovery of the transistor in 1948 by William Shockley, John Bardeen, and Walter Brattain at the Bell Telephone Laboratories, for which they shared a Nobel Prize, was not based upon the previous vacuum tube technology that prevailed at that time, it could be considered truly a revolutionary technological innovation. And what a revolutionary technology! One need only consider that prior to the transistor, many electronic devices were based on vacuum tube technology. After the invention of the transistor, comparatively few modern electronic consumer devices use such tubes. That the transistor led directly to the near destruction of the vacuum tube industry amply illustrates the power of revolutionary technology.

The task facing management is to anticipate the source of innovative technology. A company can fund R&D itself, join with other companies in a joint R&D venture in which all will share in the derived technology, or purchase rights to a new technology from its inventors. Funding R&D can be very expensive, with little prospect of immediate return, but R&D efforts can give a company a proprietary right to the technology. Purchasing the right to make use of technology developed by others may be less expensive than R&D in the short run but may not confer a proprietary right.

If a company believes that technological innovation will be *evolutionary*, it will look to the leaders in that technology to develop new products and processes. If a company believes that technological innovation will be *revolutionary*, however, it may wish to seek out the research efforts of smaller companies, specialized research companies, and university researchers. Many companies are now, in fact, entering into agreements in which they agree to fund university research efforts in order to gain rights to subsequent discoveries. This is, however, controversial.

• *TECHNOLOGY TRANSFER PROCESS*

Once a new technology has been discovered or acquired by a licensing agreement, the major issue becomes how to effectively introduce it into an established technological environment. People have an investment in maintaining the current situation, the *status quo*. Most workers will therefore resist new technology until they are shown how such technology will make them more productive or their work life easier. The more radical and innovative the technology, the greater will be the resistance. This relationship between innovation and resistance is shown in Figure 4-5.

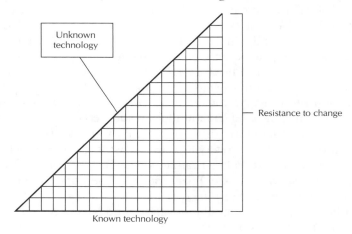

Figure 4–5. Resistance to change as a function of the known-unknown ratio.

People will accept what is perceived as nonthreatening and advantageous or helpful to them, and one of the ways in which management can successfully introduce new technology is to show the worker how such technology will be of personal benefit. Another useful technique is to introduce the new technology gradually. This is called *incremental innovation* and involves introducing the new technology in smaller steps or increments. Each change in technology is then less distant from the known technology and will be resisted less. As soon as workers are comfortable with the newly introduced technology, it is no longer the unknown. Management can then move on to more innovation. This incremental approach to the introduction of new technology is represented in Figure 4-6.

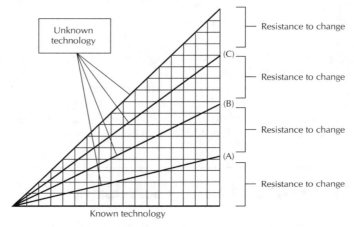

Figure 4–6. Variable resistance to change ratios as a function of incremental change introduction.

In the example shown in Figure 4-6 from the 1980s when personal business computers were first introduced, management wanted to replace manual typewriters with individual personal computers. This would be a very radical change, so management decided to introduce this change gradually. Change A, the first increment, was to introduce electronic typewriters. When clerical employees were familiar with electronic typewriters, then management introduced Change B, electronic typewriters with 90-character memory. Change C was the introduction of floppy disk memory typewriters that have little computer functioning but make use of computer disks. The final change was the introduction of individual personal computers.

• *STATE-OF-THE-ART TECHNOLOGY*

State-of-the-art is used to refer to the latest technology. Management is often faced with the question of whether to upgrade current levels of technology to the state-of-the-art. Companies that have the latest technology often claim with great pride that they are state-of-the-art, and in fact many achieve significant savings in manufacturing by making use of this newly acquired technology. There are several important questions with which management must deal, however, before deciding to purchase the latest technological marvel.

- Does the company need the state-of-the-art? Perhaps some other form of technology will meet all the company's needs? Computer ribbons are made using sewing machine technology that is over 50 years old.

- Can the company afford the new technology? That new machine may be wonderful and do everything but make the morning coffee, but can we afford it? Will the benefits derived be worth more than its cost? Will the new technology pay for itself in production costs savings?

- Can the new technology be successfully introduced into the current labor force or will that labor force need retraining? Does the company have the necessary resources (time, money) for such training? Will the workers accept it, or will they resist? Can that resistance be overcome, or is the company going to lose valuable employees who cannot adapt to the new technology?

YOU SHOULD REMEMBER

Every company exists within a **technological environment** and management must decide (1) the appropriate level of technology for the company and (2) how new levels of technology will be introduced. One effective way to introduce new technology is to incrementalize the changes to minimize resistance to change.

When considering the introduction of new technology, management will want to consider the financial cost and the cost in human terms. Some workers cannot adapt to new technology and will be the casualties of change. Progress, in the form of new technologies, may exact a human price in the form of lost jobs.

THE INTERNAL ENVIRONMENTS OF BUSINESS

The elements within the organization that are available to be used in the accomplishment of its goals are organizational resources. These are physical, human, technological, and financial resources. Although these terms sound like those we previously used in describing the *external* environment, there may be a significant difference between these resources as they occur in the general environment and specifically within the organization. Each is briefly discussed.

FINANCIAL RESOURCES

All organizations require **financial resources** to provide for ongoing operations and to fund growth. If it is very profitable, the money earned can be kept within the organization and used to fund the desired growth. These funds are called *retained earnings* (since they are retained in the organization, not paid out as dividends to stockholders); this is the cheapest way to fund business growth. This source of funds is often inadequate to fund the desired level of growth so other sources must be utilized. In order to secure needed financial resources, management can look outside the organization for sources of funds. There are two general sources for business: debt capital and equity capital.

Debt capital is that money lent to the organization for business use. Bank loans, lines of credit, and corporate bonds are forms of debt owed by a business that borrows the funds to the banks and bondholders who lend it. Interest is the money paid to either the bank or the individual bondholder for the use of the money. The interest is expensive in the short run, but debt capital is often the cheapest source of funds in the long run. Once it is paid off, more money can be borrowed. However, when a company sells stock it is giving up ownership—this is called *equity capital*. Once stock is sold the company has no obligation to repurchase it. A company generally has no obligation to pay dividends. Because the stock need not be repurchased nor dividends be paid, equity capital is the cheapest source of funds in the short run. Since the company gives up ownership, however, and once sold the stock is gone forever (unless repurchased), equity capital is the most expensive long-term way for a business to raise capital.

From a managerial planning perspective, the task is to match use of funds with their source. Short-term use (e.g., to acquire seasonal merchandise for sale) should be funded from short-term debt (e.g., a business loan), which then can be quickly repaid when the seasonal merchandise is sold. If a company sold its stock (i.e., equity) to fund seasonal merchandise, it would exhaust its equity for a use better served by short-term loans.

In general, the major financial tasks confronting management are to acquire necessary funds by some combination of retained earnings, debt capital, and equity capital and allocate the acquired financial resources for organizational use. The accounting profession, through its records and accounting procedures, provides management with a financial perspective on how the funds are being used. Accounting data provide an executive with a powerful managerial tool for controlling the financial affairs of an enterprise.

PHYSICAL RESOURCES

The **physical resources** of a company include plant and manufacturing equipment and distributing facilities and raw materials inventories. As noted in the section dealing with suppliers, the task of management is to ensure that plants are located in areas in which the local values are conducive to the manufacturing enterprise and there is an adequate local supply of labor. This is of increasing importance as younger workers, especially those with technical skills, have relocated to the southwestern states. Adequate and reliable supplies of raw materials must also be acquired. The availability of raw materials and the local values of the community in which the plant is located will exert an influence upon managerial decision-making. Management periodically evaluates the manner in which the physical resources of an organization are acquired and utilized. These resources are ultimately the tools used by management to improve productivity and ensure profitability.

HUMAN RESOURCES

The people who work in an organization are its **human resources.** They meet the needs of the organization to acquire the necessary skills to conduct an efficient and effective business. Four main tasks confront management in the area of human resources. The first of these is to acquire the necessary workers. The various ways in which a company can do this are detailed in Chapter 12, which deals with human resources management. The second task is to place the correct employees in the right jobs. This may require extensive employee training. It is the managerial function of staffing and is discussed in detail in Chapter 12. The third task confronting a manager in the human resources area is to motivate effective human performance leading to acceptable levels of worker productivity. This is a very complex task, as complex as the workers themselves, and Chapter 13 is devoted to an in-depth discussion of motivation. The final task that must be accomplished by a manager is to evaluate employee performance; some of the methods available to management are presented in Chapter 15.

TECHNOLOGICAL RESOURCES

Technological resources refers to the level of applied technology within the firm. As previously noted, the level within a firm may be considerably different from the state-of-the-art level available in the external environment. Management must decide the appropriate level for the company in terms of its goals and the appropriate level of skill for the firm's human resources necessary to operate the technology applied. A firm may not need the latest technology to operate effectively, but if a higher level of skill is necessary to operate the new technology, the firm must either train current employees in the new skills or hire new workers who already have the additional skills training. This training can be gained within the organization in company-sponsored classes, or in the external environment at institutions of learning and vocational training. Increasingly, such training is available via the Internet, by means of what is called "distance learning." As previously noted, if current workers cannot be retrained to master new technology, they may become casualties of technological advance.

YOU SHOULD REMEMBER

The **internal environment** of a company consists of the organizational resources available to accomplish its goals. These are **human, technological, financial,** and **physical resources.** The task of management is to acquire these resources and make efficient and effective use of them within the organization. In this task, the management of each company is in competition with all other companies. Organizational resources are therefore scarce, and management success depends on how well these resources are both acquired and used.

CORPORATE CULTURE: BUSINESS CLIMATE AND MANAGEMENT ETHICS

An important aspect of the internal environment of a company is its **corporate culture,** the total sum of the values, customs, traditions, and meanings that make a company unique. It is also often called the character of an organization. Although it is difficult to measure corporate culture, it is not as difficult to characterize it. A 100-year-old bank located in the financial district of New York City will have a conservative character, and a trendy computer company located in California's Silicon Valley will have a liberal character.

Corporate culture embodies the vision of the company founders and the early heroes of the business enterprise. Often found in a mythology that embellishes the actual accomplishments of these individuals, these early values serve to guide and influence current management. One need only think of the image of the inventor-hero Thomas Edison toiling late into the night to understand much of the dedication of the current employees of the company he founded, General Electric, or the image of the postal carrier who allows neither rain nor sleet nor hail nor dark of night to prevent delivering the mail. The dedication of an Edison and the perseverance of the early mail carrier continue to influence and inspire workers today. These values have been called the "core values of a corporate culture."

When workers join a new company, they usually receive an official orientation. This orientation ranges from a simple oral briefing, a mimeographed handout, or a printed company handbook to formal classes. Part of that orientation may be a retelling of the early days of the company and the deeds of its heroes. This is not merely a sharing of the company's "war stories" but a transmission of the essential values prized within the company. Orientation sets forth the philosophy, values, and actions expected of company employees.

Managers are also influenced by ethical standards that mandate conduct both within and without the organization. Some actions are deemed illegal by codes of law, but other actions, although legal, are considered unethical. Unethical actions are those that go against the accepted moral standards of the time and place, and this brings up an important point. Ethical standards are the product of their time and place and may change with the passage of time and with a change in locale. That which is acceptable in one place may be completely unacceptable in another, and conduct that was allowed a few decades ago may now be forbidden. Political bribes and managerial payoffs, acceptable and expected in certain parts of the world, are unacceptable in the United States today. For decades, the privacy of the average U.S. worker was not important. Now it is expected that such privacy will be respected, and an employer who routinely violates a worker's privacy encounters great ethical and ultimately legal difficulties!

The values of a corporate culture also influence the ethical standards within an organization. A corporation that values winning in the business arena may encourage and approve of "winning at any cost" behavior by its managers. The ruthless manager who embodies this philosophy, even if he or she has great personnel turnover and is hated by employees, will be rewarded by the corporation. Another company, however, may not approve of "winning at any cost" and declare such managerial behaviors unethical and unacceptable.

Industries have established codes of ethical conduct. These are often formally stated, internally (to the industry) enforced codes of conduct that serve to direct business behavior within a specific industry. The American Association of Advertising Agencies, the American Medical Association, the American Bar Association, and thousands of other industry associations have codes of conduct and ethics that guide business behavior. The actions of management are influenced by such ethical codes of conduct. Should managers violate the accepted code of ethics, dire consequences may result. Thus if a lawyer violates the local canons of ethics, he or she may be expelled from the local bar association and even lose his or her license to practice law.

YOU SHOULD REMEMBER

Management behavior is influenced by the **corporate culture,** the total sum of the values, customs, traditions, and meanings that make a company unique, often called the character of an organization. **Managerial ethics** refers to the standards of acceptable conduct embodied in industry and company codes. Some of the behaviors specified in the ethical codes *may* be legal, but they are not accepted within a company or an industry. Codes of ethics influence management conduct.

KNOW THE CONCEPTS
DO YOU KNOW THE BASICS?

1. What is the external environment, and why is it important to management?
2. What factors make up the internal environment?
3. What are the elements of the open systems model of business?
4. Under what conditions will the transformation process be considered a value added process?
5. Why should management pay attention to population trends?
6. How well do you think an American manager will do in Japan if he or she tries to make use of U.S. management techniques? Why?
7. What are the concepts of place, time, and form utility? Why are they important for management?
8. What is the difference between evolutionary technological innovation and revolutionary technological innovation?
9. If management is considering introducing a great change, how can it do so with minimal employee resistance?
10. What is corporate culture, and why is it important for management?

TERMS FOR STUDY

business ethics	debt capital
consumer behavior	demographic profile
consumer ethics	demography
corporate culture	economic factors

equity capital
evolutionary technological
  innovation
external environment
form utility
GNP
input
internal environment
open systems model
organizational resources
output
place utility
political factors
price follower
price leader
process of innovation

process of technology transfer
R&D
retained earnings
revolutionary technological
  innovation
sociological factors
staffing
standard of living
state-of-the-art
target market
technological factors
time utility
transfer payments
transformation process
value added process
work ethic

ANSWERS
KNOW THE BASICS

1. The external environment consists of those factors outside an organization, primarily economic, political, sociological, and state-of-the-art technological factors, that affect and influence the organization. These factors are important for management because they influence managerial decision-making.

2. The internal environment is made up of those resources that are internal to an organization and available to be used in the transformation process. They are human, financial, physical, and technological resources.

3. The open systems model consists of input, transformation processes, and output. It expresses a dynamic view of an organization interrelated with its environment.

4. A transformation process will be considered value added if the value of the output is greater than the value of the input factors.

5. Management should note and evaluate population trends because these trends influence not only the sources of future labor but also future markets for the company's goods and services.

6. An American manager in Japan who attempts to make use of U.S. management techniques will probably meet with very limited, if any, success. There are cultural differences between the United States and Japan, and one of the ways these differences are expressed is in the manner in which management works.

7. Consumers want goods in a useful form, at a suitable time, and at the right place. A product that is in the correct place and form at the right time is said to have time, form, and place utility. If a company's products lack any of these forms of utility, they will fail in the marketplace.

8. Evolutionary technological innovation is based upon past technology and invention. Revolutionary technological innovation is that innovation that is not based upon past achievement but is more radical in nature. Revolutionary technological innovation is far more difficult to assimilate in a business environment than is evolutionary.

9. Management can minimize employee resistance by introducing the proposed technological change in small increments. This is called an incremental approach to change.

10. Corporate culture is the sum total of the values, customs, traditions, and meanings that make a company unique, often called the character of an organization. It is important for managers because the values of a company, embodied in the myths of its founders, influence current employee behavior and managerial decision-making.

5

MANAGEMENT DECISION-MAKING: TYPES AND STYLES

KEY TERMS

decision-making process the sequence of events taken by management to solve managerial problems, a systematic process that follows a sequence of problem identification, alternative solution generation, consequences analysis, solution selection and implementation, evaluation, and feedback

linear thinking a simplistic approach to problem-solving that assumes that each problem has a single solution, the solution will only affect the problem, not the rest of the organization, and, once implemented, a solution will remain valid and should be evaluated only on how well it solves the problem

systems thinking a more contemporary and complex approach to problem-solving that assumes that problems are complex and related to a situation and that solutions not only solve the problem but will also impact the rest of the organization and should be evaluated for how well they solve the problem (intended results) *and* affect the total organization (unintended results); further assumes that neither problems nor solutions remain constant— situations change, problems change, and new solutions are constantly necessary

programmed decisions those problems that are well understood, highly structured, routine, and repetitive and that lend themselves to systematic procedures and rules

nonprogrammed decisions those problems that are not well understood, not highly structured, tend to be unique, and do not lend themselves to routine or systematic procedures

Analysis of the managerial function reveals that virtually every manager, no matter what his or her official title, makes decisions during the course of business. This points to *decision-making* as the common function of managers, and some writers have used the term "decision-maker" in place of manager. The *decision-making process* is the sequence of events taken by management to solve business problems, a systematic process that follows a sequence of problem identification, alternative solution generation, consequences analysis, solution selection and implementation, evaluation, and feedback. We have briefly examined this managerial decision-making process in Chapter 3 in describing the social action phase of social responsibility and examine this process in greater detail in this chapter. First, however, we must clarify the ways in which management thinks about decisions, the general types of decisions, preferred styles of decision-making, the organizational levels at which the various kinds of business decisions are made, and the conditions that influence managerial decision-making.

WAYS OF THINKING ABOUT BUSINESS DECISION-MAKING
LINEAR THINKING

As contemporary business has become more complex, there has been a growing consensus that effective decision-making must take the complex nature of business into account. The most simplistic approach, however, to the solution of business problems exemplifies **linear thinking.** This assumes that each problem has a single solution, the solution will only affect the problem area, not the rest of the organization, and, once implemented, a solution will remain valid and should be evaluated only for how well it solves the problem. Problems are conceived of as *discrete,* singular, and unique. The way in which most fast-food restaurants deal with hiring and retention of counter or table personnel shows evidence of linear thinking. In the past, most fast-food restaurants hired teenagers and experienced 150–300 percent turnover—the average duration of employment was just under 4 months. A linear thinking approach to personnel has suggested in the past to managers that the solution to the turnover problem is "hire more teenagers." The abundance of teenagers made this *look* like an effective solution. But when the demographic picture changed and there were fewer available teenagers, it became apparent that this simplistic solution no longer worked. Now management must consider many potential solutions—higher pay, making jobs more interesting, hiring retirees, hiring the physically challenged, offering better benefits, and others. These solutions will impact and interact with other aspects of the organization: benefits and compensation, the need for different managers and supervisory structures, employee training, and so on. As long as the problem was seen in a simplistic and linear manner, neither the range of solutions nor the impact of these solutions upon the whole organization was considered.

Although there is allure for managers in the very simplicity of a linear thinking solution, it often does not prove an effective way of dealing with organizational problems. In the rapidly changing environments of modern business, there are at least three major difficulties with this approach to problem-solving.

- Since the solution affects not only the problem area but also the rest of the organization, the results of the solution may not be anticipated. Parts of the organization not considered in the original problem-solving efforts may be affected by the solution and react in unanticipated ways. A manager may get more than was originally bargained for.

- Even if the results of a solution are only those desired and intended, the focus on a single problem area ignores the interrelationships among organizational elements and may lead to a simplistic solution that does not solve the larger problem.

- Linear thinking assumes that problems, once defined, and solutions, once implemented, are always valid and ignores the rapidly changing nature of the environments of business.

Such difficulties have led many business thinkers and practitioners to take a different approach to business decision-making. This new approach is called systems thinking.

SYSTEMS THINKING

Systems thinking is a more contemporary and encompassing approach to problem-solving that assumes that problems are complex and related to a situation, that solutions not only solve the problem but will also impact on the rest of the organization and should be evaluated on how well they solve the problem (intended results) *and* affect the total organization (unintended results), and further, that neither problems nor solutions remain constant—situations change, problems evolve, and new solutions are constantly necessary.

A systems thinking approach does not view problems as discrete but sees them as related to all aspects of an organization. Organizations are composed of interrelated systems and processes, and any change in one organizational aspect affects all others. A *systems thinker* would therefore consider the interrelationships among the systems and processes of the organization *before* implementing a solution. That solution will be evaluated on the basis of *all* results produced, as cited earlier. Further, there is the recognition that not only do circumstances change, requiring new solutions, but solutions themselves also function to change circumstances. It is therefore necessary, after implementing any solution, to evaluate the effect of that solution and provide feedback to the organization as it begins anew the problem-solving process. Problem-solving is therefore a dynamic process as new solutions create new realities and those new circumstances require new solutions.

YOU SHOULD REMEMBER

Linear thinking stresses that problems have only one solution and do not affect the rest of the organization, and, once a solution is found, that it remains constantly valid. **Systems thinking,** however, asserts that problems are complex, have more than one cause and more than one solution, and are interrelated to the rest of the organization. The solution selection process under systems thinking features an evaluation of the effects of any solution on the whole organization, not just the problem area. Systems thinking also maintains that problems and their subsequent solutions are not constant, but constantly changing. Both must be continually re-examined—problem-solving is a dynamic process.

TYPES OF MANAGERIAL DECISIONS

Whether a manager takes a linear thinking or systems thinking approach to business problems, there are two major kinds of problems confronted, and the nature of the problems will influence the methods applied to reach satisfactory solutions. These are programmed and nonprogrammed decisions.

PROGRAMMED DECISIONS

Programmed decisions characterize those problems that are well understood, highly structured, routine, and repetitive and that lend themselves to systematic procedures and rules. Each time one of these decisions is made is similar to every other time. The checking out of a book from a library or the processing of a hospital insurance claim are examples of programmed decisions because they are repetitive and routine. Much effort may have gone into the solving of these problems the first time they were encountered in the enterprise. As they were solved for the first time, there was probably much thought given to how the solutions could be routinized. When a process is produced that will give an acceptable result each time, management has created an *algorithm*, a mathematical concept applied to management. An algorithm is "repetitive calculation," in this instance a repetitive process by which an acceptable solution will always be found. Once implemented, such solution-generating processes become SOP—standard operating procedures.

Programmed decisions, since they are well structured and understood, may lend themselves to linear thinking, but this will only be so if the programmed decisions are simple problems. A programmed decision, however routine and well understood, may be quite complex and require a true systems approach when first encountered. This implies that a systems approach will be necessary *the first time the problem is solved*, but the result of this problem-solving approach will be an algorithmic solution that can then be applied every time the same problem recurs. The computer is particularly well suited to algorithmic processing since it possesses the ability to make error-free complex calculations each time.

The latest application of algorithmic decision-making to a programmed decision is *artificial intelligence*, which is a multidisciplinary application of computer science, philosophy, and psychology. After understanding how an individual approaches a well-understood problem, artificial intelligence (AI) seeks to duplicate human reasoning and action. The goal of AI is to improve decision-making by enhancing consistency by applying decision-making rules as an employee would do. Thus by defining decision-making rules based on mathematical modeling of expert decision-making, that expertise is preserved (even when the expert no longer has the job) and passed to others. An example of such an AI *expert system* would be a customer service computer-generated voice rotary consisting of a series of "if . . . then" alternatives. Each positive answer leads to a specific alternative, the "then," and the consumer eventually arrives at a satisfactory resolution of the problem initially presented. These systems may be either rule-based and operate by reference to a series of expert rules or case-based, where, having been presented with a problem, a computer searches through a database of past cases for the case that most closely resembles the current situation.

NONPROGRAMMED DECISIONS

Nonprogrammed decisions are those problems that are not well understood, not highly structured, tend to be unique, and do not lend themselves to routine or systematic procedures. The key to understanding these decisions is to remember that they happen infrequently, and because they happen so rarely, there is little precedent for decision-making. A merger is an example of the kind of event that requires management decision-making and happens so rarely that neither standardized nor routine decisions are available.

Nonprogrammed decisions rely heavily on the decision-making abilities of managers since there is no routine solution available. Management will make use of data from past problems and performance, examining historical analogy—how others in the past have solved similar problems. Managers look for principles and solutions that *may* apply in the current situation but must be ever mindful that past solutions and problem-solving methodologies *may not apply* now. There may well be something in the past problem that was unique or special to that problem that makes deriving a solution for the current problem impossible. Additionally, managers may review how similarly situated companies are currently solving similar problems to discern ways of dealing with the difficulties currently facing their organization.

YOU SHOULD REMEMBER

A **programmed decision** can be applied when the problem is routine, well structured and understood, and repetitive. A **nonprogrammed decision** can best be used when the problem is not well structured or understood and is neither routine nor repetitive.

Managers, particularly at higher organizational levels, make many nonprogrammed decisions during the course of defining the goals of the enterprise and running its daily activities. Because nonprogrammed decisions are so important to business and so common to the managerial position, a manager's effectiveness and future promise to the business will often be judged according to the quality of his or her decision-making. Businesses have created training programs in decision-making to help train managers because they make so many nonprogrammed decisions. Many managers elect to seek advanced educational degrees in business, and much of this education teaches problem analysis and decision-making. One of the most popular ways of developing analytic abilities and managerial decision-making is the case study. The case study is a written history of a business problem and the manner in which management solved it. A good case study does not pretend to teach a unique solution, although it may be valuable to see how that solution worked in a specific situation. The greatest benefit to be derived from a case study is to learn how a decision was made and a solution selected. The decision-making methodology can then be applied to other problems.

LEVELS OF DECISION-MAKING IN AN ORGANIZATION

Just as there are different kinds of business decision-making, there are different levels of decision-making within a business. These are the strategic, administrative, and operational levels of decision-making in an organization.

STRATEGIC DECISION-MAKING

Strategic decisions are those that determine the goals of the entire business organization, its purpose and direction. These are discussed in depth in Chapter 8, but it should be noted here that the strategic decision-making function is largely the task of top management. Top management has the "big picture" of all the elements of a complex business enterprise, and it must be able to *integrate* all aspects of a business into a coherent whole. The decisions made at this level also determine how the business will relate to external environments. Because strategic policies affect the entire business, they can best and must be made at the highest level within an organization. These policies and goals are not very specific because they must be applied to all levels and departments in a company. Strategic decisions are usually nonprogrammed in nature. The *general* decision to produce a breakfast cereal or to enter a new market are examples of strategic decisions.

ADMINISTRATIVE DECISION-MAKING

Administrative decisions are those made on a lower level than the previously discussed strategic decisions. They are usually made by midlevel management, such as divisional or departmental managers. These decisions concern the development of tactics to accomplish the strategic goals defined by top management. Although top management's strategic decisions are nonspecific because they are applied to all departments within the organization, administrative decisions express corporate goals in a *specific* departmental manner. Administrative decisions are therefore more specific and concrete than strategic decisions and more action oriented. The decision to produce a specific kind of cereal, in this case a fruit-and-fiber breakfast cereal, is an example of this kind of administrative decision.

OPERATIONAL DECISION-MAKING

Operational decisions are made on the lowest or supervisory level within the company and concern the course of daily operations. These decisions determine the manner in which operations are conducted—operations designed to accomplish the tactical decisions made by mid-management. These decisions concern the most effective and efficient way to accomplish the goals stated on the administrative level. Setting a production schedule and determining the appropriate level of raw materials inventory are examples of operational decisions. In our continuing example of the breakfast cereal, an operational decision would be to produce each week 10,000 boxes holding 12 ounces.

Figure 5-1 is a graphic representation of the levels of decision-making shown for each part of the organization.

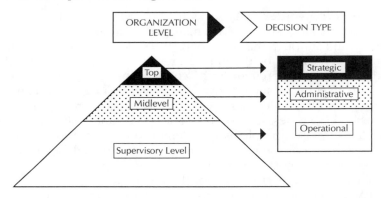

Figure 5–1. Levels of decision-making in an organization.

YOU SHOULD REMEMBER

Different organizational levels will make different kinds of decisions. Top management will be responsible for determining the **strategic goals** of a company while midlevel managers will make **tactical** or **administrative** decisions. The lowest organizational level of management, the supervisor, will make **operational** decisions. In every instance of managerial decision-making, success will depend upon the manager's analytic abilities.

STYLES OF DECISION-MAKING

Just as there are different kinds of decisions, there are different kinds of decision-making styles. The corporate culture that was discussed in the last chapter will influence the acceptable decision-making style in the company.

One style may be more acceptable than others, and decision-makers who show the desired style will be rewarded and promoted to even higher business positions. The task of the new manager is to determine the most effective decision-making style. This can be done by observing the styles of established executives in the specific company. A manager whose style of decision-making is different from that of the company will often encounter great difficulty in having his or her managerial decisions accepted.

THE "SMOOTHER" OR PROBLEM AVOIDER

The **problem avoider (PA)** seeks to preserve the status quo and acts to keep from making changes. This manager functions to maintain current conditions, and although this may not be the *stated* goal of managerial decisions and actions, it will be the practical result. When confronted with difficulty, the PA will either reconcile the conflicts in the reported data with a rationale that seeks to "smooth over" any conflict or ignore it completely. Thus the PA is often called a smoother. This manager may not recognize problems in the business environment and will be able to come up with rationales for supposed problems that demonstrate that they are not really problems at all. He or she may appear blind to business difficulties and will be the person who most resists business changes, even when the changes are obviously for the best interest of the company.

The PA, in the desire to preserve the status quo and avoid making changes, will give great effort and value to intensive preplanning studies. These studies will present and justify organizational efforts designed to minimize change. Problem avoiders are good people to keep an organization on a calm and even course, and this *may be* the most effective decision-making style in industrial environments in which there is little need for change. However, if the business is conducted in a dynamic, changing environment, a more active approach will almost always be more effective for problem-solving. Such a manager will be known as a problem solver.

THE PROBLEM SOLVER

The **problem solver** is the most common managerial style. Most managers expect to be confronted with problems and to solve those problems in the normal course of doing business. There is no hesitation to make changes when there is an indication that such changes are good and necessary. There is no prior commitment to make changes, however, until it has been determined by means of research and scientific analysis of the data that changes are necessary. It is recognized that change without necessity is gratuitous, a waste of organizational resources. Such gratuitous changes serve to foster an illusion of progress while merely confusing everyone. As was seen in the previous chapter, change is made more acceptable when those affected by the changes understand the *reasons* for those changes.

The problem solver accepts that modern business operates under conditions of risk and uncertainty. This means that business is often in a very turbulent environment with the imperative to adapt to changing circumstances. Businesses that fail to adapt suffer decline, cease to be productive and profitable, and may eventually die. It has been observed that the marketplace is unforgiving of a business that fails to change when confronted with the necessity to do so. The problem solver accepts the risk and makes decisions that help deal with the uncertainty. These managers deal with problems as they arise and do not seek to preserve the status quo unless the current situation is better than any possible change.

The only criticism we may advance of the problem solver is that this kind of manager is preoccupied with the current problems. This person is generally always in a primarily *reactive mode*, reacting to problems as they arise. Often these problems could be better dealt with if they had been anticipated—when they were smaller and more efficiently managed. The problem solver rarely anticipates problems but is very effective in dealing with them once they have become known.

THE PROBLEM SEEKER

The **problem seeker,** as the name implies, actively seeks out problems and attempts to deal with them before they emerge as major difficulties for a business. This manager is enthusiastically involved with future planning and the creation of contingencies. The problem seeker not only recognizes the need for change but also believes that the best way to deal with change is to anticipate it, not merely react to current needs. This kind of managerial decision-maker makes use of data analysis, not merely to understand the present, but also to project the future. The problem seeker is a corporate champion of research and will devote many hours of dedicated work trying to understand the implications of research data for the company's future.

Although this preoccupation with the future of the company may seem to lead to a neglect of current needs and situations, the problem seeker has a vital role in planning the future of the company. There are two major points in favor of the decision-making style of the problem seeker: (1) It is often easier and more efficient to deal with small problems before they become big ones. (2) It is not enough for a company to change; it must change in the right direction to survive in the rapidly changing contemporary environments of business. The problem seeker is a major corporate resource in planning for the future, but it is obvious that a company must be able to change *both* in response to current problems *and* in response to anticipated future problems.

One of the major distinguishing features of these three types of decision-makers is the ability to deal with conditions of risk and uncertainty. The problem avoider seeks to minimize risk and eliminate uncertainty by promoting the status quo, a totally known condition. The problem solver recognizes the need to risk change and function in an environment of uncertainty in which there are unknown conditions and the possibility of unanticipated results. The problem seeker accepts the greatest amount of risk and uncertainty in actively seeking to deal with problems *before* they have emerged and become known. We now turn to a general description of the different levels and types of risk and uncertainty to better understand the conditions under which managerial decisions are made.

YOU SHOULD REMEMBER

Decision-making within the contemporary business organization involves all the problem-solving styles. The **problem avoider, problem solver,** and **problem seeker** *each* have a role to play within the same company. Although one particular style may be more effective than the others in a specific situation, all organizations are confronted with a complex variety of challenges that will require a *variety* of problem-solving styles.

DECISION-MAKING UNDER DIFFERENT CONDITIONS
CONDITIONS OF CERTAINTY

Under **conditions of certainty** all decision variables and the results of each potential course of action or solution are known in advance. A manager can approach the decision-making secure in the knowledge that there will be no unanticipated results. In this sense, decisions made under conditions of certainty are *programmed decisions*. An example of these conditions is the relationship between the manufacturing of television sets and inventory levels of parts. There is no uncertainty—the higher the level of manufacturing, the lower the level of inventory of parts used in the manufacturing. A decision to increase production leads directly to a reduction in inventory level. A manager making the decision to increase production knows the impact on inventory *exactly*. Since all results are known before making a decision, many managers prefer to make decisions under conditions of certainty. This is possible only in the most simple situations. There is rarely knowledge of all possible results, and management usually encounters a degree of risk.

CONDITIONS OF RISK

Risk is defined as a condition in which the results of any decision or course of action are not definitely known but will probably fall within a known range. One describes risk in terms of probability; that is, the "probability of a specific outcome is a fraction between 0 and 1, and if the probability of the specific outcome is 1, it is completely known; if the probability is 0, it is completely unknown." Since under conditions of risk the probability is neither completely known nor completely unknown, it is described as a fraction between the two extremes. If the probability of a batter in a major league baseball game getting a hit is .2 (note that this is point two, or *two-tenths*), it means that this batter will generally get a hit 20 times out of every 100 he bats. The odds, or probability, of getting a hit in any one time at bat is 20/100, or 1 of 5, or 20 percent. Each of these becomes an expression of the risk involved in the event. Techniques used to make decisions under conditions of probability or risk are listed at the end of this chapter, and in-depth examples are provided in Chapter 20.

An example of making decisions under conditions of risk would be to introduce a redesigned automobile model into the market. There may be a .20 probability of sales of 20,000 cars the first year, a .50 probability of 30,000 sales the first year, and a .30 probability of 25,000 sales the first year. Since there are past sales data on how last year's design for this car did, there is a basis for estimating the probability of success for the new design. Note, however, two aspects of this description: (1) Although the actual results of the decision to introduce a new car model are not known, the *general limits* of possible probabilities and results are known, and (2) all the probabilities add up to 1. *When the probabilities are known*, even though the actual results are not, it is possible to use various techniques to estimate the most favorable decision outcome. The techniques for decision-making under conditions of risk are discussed later in this chapter.

This example supposed that we had past data and could estimate the probabilities of specific outcomes, but suppose the new car was something never seen before, a totally new concept for which there were no previous sales data. In this case it would not even be possible to estimate probabilities. In situations in which there is *no reliable estimate of probabilities or the potential decision results are unclear or not known*, we have conditions of uncertainty.

CONDITIONS OF UNCERTAINTY

When a manager cannot predict the outcome of a managerial decision, or if the outcome can be predicted but the probability of that outcome actually happening cannot be predicted, a **condition of uncertainty** exists. The inability to predict outcome or assign probability may be due to the following factors: (1) too many variables in the situation; (2) few variables in the situation but not enough knowledge about the variables; or (3) both too many variables and not enough knowledge about them. The assignment of probability becomes impossible under these conditions. This is the situation set forth at the end of the last section in which a totally new car was to be introduced into the marketplace. Although the potential results of such a new product introduction are known (failure or success), the probabilities of each possible result are not known. There is no past data upon which to make a prediction. This is why introductions of completely new products are *very uncertain* events and vast sums of money are lost each year if such managerial actions do not succeed. The single failure of a "new product launch" does not automatically doom a manager's career (although *many* such failures may destroy a career). Because of the great uncertainty in this management decision-making process, it is understood that some new products, however well conceived, designed, and produced, will fail.

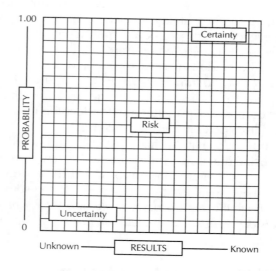

Figure 5–2. Probability of predicting results of decision-making under conditions of uncertainty, risk, and certainty.

YOU SHOULD REMEMBER

Managerial decisions made when the potential results of the decisions *and* the probabilities of occurrence of the results are known are made under conditions of **certainty.** Decisions made when the potential results are not totally known and probabilities must be assigned are made under conditions of **risk.** When neither the results nor the probabilities of occurrence of the results are fully known, management is making decisions under conditions of **uncertainty. As uncertainty increases, so does the possibility of failure.**

STEPS IN THE DECISION-MAKING PROCESS

The first step in the managerial decision-making process is an examination of the current situation to determine if a problem actually exists. This is accomplished by performing a "situational analysis." Once a statement of goals is determined, alternatives are considered and evaluated, performance standards set, and pilot testing begun.

SITUATIONAL ANALYSIS

The current situation, determined from an examination of available data, is the "what is." It is not always obvious since, as evidenced by the discussion concerning the problem avoider, there are managers who have a stake in the status quo and will resist change. These managers may not see the current situation in an unbiased manner, and their perceptions cannot be relied upon to determine an accurate analysis of "what is." One of the ways in which management can accomplish an accurate analysis of the current situation is to make use of an external consultant. Since outside experts theoretically have no stake in the status quo, they should be able to give an accurate appraisal of the current company situation.

Managers often find it useful, in executing a **situational analysis,** to focus on the internal organization conditions, the external factors that bear upon the business, and the relationship between the two. The internal analysis, called an *organizational audit*, consists of listing the organization's strengths and weaknesses. The strengths, what the business does well, are referred to as its "core competencies." But it is not enough to view an organization internally; the situational analysis also requires an understanding of the external reality, the opportunities and threats that are on the horizon. This external analysis is called the *environmental scan*. Internal audit and environmental scan are collectively referred to as the *SWOT analysis (Strengths, Weaknesses, Opportunities, and Threats)*. Both are necessary for the situational analysis because if an external opportunity exists, there must be an organizational ability to take advantage of that opportunity. If the business is internally weak where such an external opportunity requires strength, the business must either develop that necessary strength, hire experts who bring the necessary skills and abilities to bear, or be unable to pursue the opportunity.

Even so, this may be difficult. What is a realistic goal for the company? If a future goal statement is unrealistic, it will give false directions to the company's management. Goals that are not realistic do not motivate management—they only misguide and cause misallocation of organizational resources. Some indication of future directions for management may be gained by examining past company performance and the performance of other companies in the industry. Both of these are indications of what is *possible*, and management is free to build upon past performance in formulating new goals. The new goals will at least be built upon the foundation of past performance.

If there is a gap between the "what is" (current situation) and the "what should be" (desired future), an organizational need is demonstrated and the "what should be" becomes an organizational goal statement. The next step is to formulate performance standards.

SETTING PERFORMANCE STANDARDS

If the end result of situational analysis is an organizational goal statement, how will a manager know if the goal has been accomplished? Only by having **performance standards** can management know if it has been successful in goal accomplishment. These performance standards must be (1) realistic, (2) behaviorally based, (3) observable, and (4) quantifiable.

Some managers resist the creation of performance standards precisely because they create *accountability*. When performance can be measured against standards, managers can be held accountable for that performance and the use of organizational resources. Once performance standards have been stated, managers can turn to the generation of alternative courses of action.

It must be recognized that accountability does impact not only the individual manager but also the entire organization, with potentially devastating results. The publicly held corporation that reports its earnings quarterly risks financial disaster should it fail to meet its projected return. In a real sense, the stock market holds the entire business organization to account for its performance, and the marketplace is littered with the remains of corporations that lost a significant portion of their equity value (defined here in limited form as the value of their publicly held stock) based on a single quarter's financial results. Thus, there is a premium placed upon an organization's ability to set performance standards accurately and realistically. It has often been observed, in consideration of this "quarterly results" accountability, that it is a uniquely American phenomenon; in countries such as Japan, the evaluation of organizational performance flows from annual performance or an even longer time frame. In addition, the American emphasis upon a short-term performance evaluation of business organizations leads to short-term decision-making with concomitant payoffs. Organizational decision-making that involves a longer term commitment of resources and similarly longer term payoffs—as with esoteric research and development projects—is often discouraged.

GENERATION OF ALTERNATIVES

There are always at least two courses of action that management can take—do something or do nothing. The alternative of doing nothing may in fact prove to be the best action decision *if* the other potential course of action either does not accomplish the organization goal or creates significant new problems in the process. Under the heading of "doing something," management may creatively generate all sorts of alternatives.

Brainstorming is a technique that is often used with a small group of employees to generate a large number of alternatives in a short period of time. In brainstorming, every participant in a group is confronted with a business problem and then calls out potential solutions. No criticism is voiced during the alternative generation phase because this would interrupt the generation of potential solutions. The ideas are recorded on a chart or chalkboard. When the participants have exhausted their imaginations, each potential solution is evaluated in detail by the group. After evaluation it may be that doing nothing is actually the best course of action. How can management know which is the best course of action or combination of actions to accomplish the organizational goal? The selection of an action alternative is made based on a comparative analysis of the consequences of each action.

CONSEQUENCES EVALUATION

Each proposed alternative action has consequences if implemented and can be evaluated based upon these consequences. An alternative is selected based upon the best possible consequence or outcome. In performing this consequences evaluation, management must ask three questions: (1) Does this alternative achieve the organizational goal? (2) Are there any undesirable consequences or side effects? (3) Can the organization afford this alternative? A negative answer to any of these questions is a strong indication that this alternative is unacceptable. This process is detailed in Figure 5-3.

Note that if the answer is *no* to any question, the process stops and the alternative is rejected.

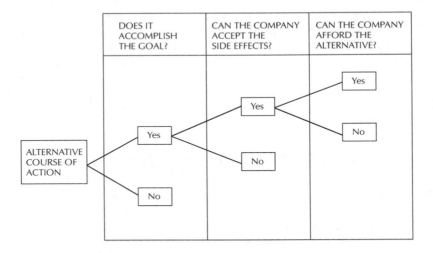

Figure 5–3. Process of evaluating the consequences of selecting an alternative.

PILOT-TESTING AND FULL IMPLEMENTATION

Once an alternative or combination of alternatives is chosen, the alternative(s) must be **pilot-tested.** Management should not proceed to full implementation of the alternative without testing it out on a small scale, unless there is great need to do so. This is because what looks good on paper may not act as predicted in a large-scale application. Thus a pilot test offers the final chance to modify the action plan based upon information derived from the small-scale test. This information, which is used to modify the action plan, is called *feedback*.

After the pilot test and action plan modification, the selected course of action is fully implemented. After a sufficient period of time the accomplishment of the organizational goal can be measured and evaluated. If the plan does not seem to be working on the larger scale as intended, it can be modified, again based on feedback.

The decision-making process, complete with a feedback loop, is shown in Figure 5-4.

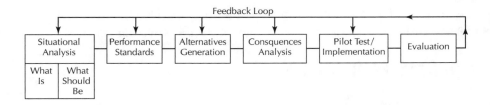

Figure 5–4. Steps in the process of decision-making.

YOU SHOULD REMEMBER

Although the decision-making process may be different from company to company, it will involve a general format. The first step is to identify the problem and this is done by means of a **situational analysis** that compares the current situation with the desired one. If there is a difference, a problem has been documented. The next step is to define the **performance standards** by which management will know that the problem has been solved. This creates accountability. **Potential solutions** to the problem are identified, but a recommendation for implementation cannot be made until the **consequences** of each option are evaluated. Once a solution has been selected it will be **pilot-tested.** Information derived from the pilot test, called **feedback,** will be used to make adjustments before full implementation of the selected solution to the problem.

KNOW THE CONCEPTS
DO YOU KNOW THE BASICS?

1. What is the decision-making process?
2. Describe linear thinking?
3. What is systems thinking?
4. How do programmed and nonprogrammed decisions differ?
5. What is the relationship between organization level and types of decisions?
6. Which type of manager will show the most enthusiasm for organizational change?
7. What is the difference between the conditions of certainty and risk?

8. Under what conditions is a new venture most likely to fail? Why?

9. What are the steps in the managerial decision-making process?

TERMS FOR STUDY

administrative decision	performance standards
algorithm	pilot testing
anticipatory mode	problem avoider
brainstorming	problem seeker
case study	problem solver
certainty	programmed decision
decision-making process	reactive mode
feedback	risk
linear thinking	strategic decision
nonprogrammed decision	systems thinking
operational decision	uncertainty

ANSWERS
KNOW THE BASICS

1. The decision-making process is the sequence of events taken by management to solve managerial problems. It is a systematic process that follows a sequence of problem identification, alternative solutions generation, consequences analysis, solution selection and implementation, evaluation, and feedback.

2. Linear thinking is a simplistic approach to problem-solving that assumes that each problem has a single solution; the solution will affect only the problem, not the rest of the organization; and, once implemented, a solution will remain valid and should be evaluated only for how well it solves the problem.

3. Systems thinking is a more contemporary and complex approach to problem-solving that assumes that problems are complex and related to a situation and that solutions not only solve the problem but also impact on the rest of the organization and should be evaluated on how well they solve the problem (intended results) *and* affect the total organization.

4. Programmed decisions are those problems that are well understood, highly structured, routine, and repetitive and that lend themselves to systematic procedures and rules. Nonprogrammed decisions, however, are those problems that are not well understood and not highly structured, tend to be unique, and do not lend themselves to routine or systematic procedures.

5. Top management is responsible for making strategic decisions that set the course of business. Midlevel management makes administrative decisions. Supervisory-level managers make operational decisions.

6. The problem seeker actively seeks out problems before they emerge and will anticipate their significance. This manager will enthusiastically devote corporate resources to solving these problems before they can assume major significance. This manager anticipates rather than merely reacts.

7. A condition of certainty is when both the results of a decision and the probability of its occurrence are known to the manager. A condition of risk exists when the results of a manager's decision are not definitely known but will probably fall within a known range.

8. A new business venture will be most likely to fail under conditions of uncertainty in which neither the results of management's decisions nor the probabilities of occurrence of those results are known. This condition makes effective decision-making difficult.

9. Situation analysis, performance standards design, alternatives generation, consequences analysis, pilot test and implementation, evaluation, and program revision via feedback are the steps in the decision-making process.

6
AN OVERVIEW OF THE FUNCTIONS OF MANAGEMENT

KEY TERMS

goal a long-range aim for a specific period

objective a result expected by the end of the budget cycle

standard of performance a statement of what will occur when a responsibility is carried out well

hierarchy of objectives a managerial concept that enables the different levels or magnitudes of decision-making within an organizational structure to be viewed in terms of a hierarchy of objectives to be achieved

budget period the time period for which the budget is compiled in an organization and against which the manager is evaluated; may be 6 months, annual, or even an 18-month rolling budget period

---

THE MANAGEMENT PROCESS

In Chapter 1, you were introduced to management and the managerial role. We defined management, distinguished between managerial and technical activities, and, using the case of Joan and her boss, developed some steps that a manager might take to ensure that the intended results are achieved.

Thinking about the problem of Joan's boss was an introduction to thinking about problems in a similar way, the first step in developing a *system* that you can use to get the results you want.

First, let us step back and look at the broad picture, the **management process** that applies to any organization. It does not matter whether you are currently managing yourself or a department, a division, or the whole organization. The management process outlined here will work for you.

THE MANAGEMENT PROCESS

I. PLANNING
   A. Strategic planning
      1. Setting goals
   B. Operational planning
      1. Defining objectives
      2. Designing the organization in the best way to achieve the goals and objectives
      3. Assigning responsibilities
      4. Allocating resources
      5. Designing organizational controls (timetables and measures of the organization's performance as a whole)

II. CONTROLLING
   A. Management control (ensuring efficient and effective use of resources)
      1. Developing individual standards
      2. Designing project controls (such as work plans and milestone charts)
      3. Motivating
      4. Monitoring
      5. Reviewing progress
      6. Solving problems
      7. Coaching and counseling
      8. Performance appraisal
   B. Operational control (ensuring that specific tasks are carried out efficiently and effectively)
      1. Scheduling
      2. Establishing procedures

III. EVALUATION AND FEEDBACK TO THE NEXT CYCLE

We are now going to run through this process step by step. You will notice in Figure 6-1 a circle. This represents the cyclic nature of the process or, in other words, that the activities or steps an organization takes should go on continuously, usually moving through one cycle during a budget period or other designated period.

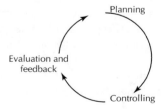

Figure 6–1. Cyclic nature of the management process.

PLANNING

One of a manager's most important jobs is **planning.** There are many kinds of planning, and planning can be defined in a number of different ways. We say we are planning when we list activities for the day or when we think about the family vacation next year. In terms of management activity, however, what we mean by planning can be broken down very specifically.

There are two major kinds of planning in management: strategic planning and operational planning.

• *STRATEGIC PLANNING*

The major outcome of **strategic planning,** after gathering all necessary information, is the setting of goals for the organization. In state government, for example, strategic planning is the domain of the highest levels, the governor and cabinet and the legislature. They produce goals for managers to work toward.

A *goal* is a long-range aim for a specific period. Unlike an aspiration or a hope, a goal is always specific and realistic. A familiar example is that of the Kennedy Administration, which in the early 1960s set a long-range goal to be accomplished in a specific time period: to have a man on the moon by 1970. Note that the goal was long-range over the course of the 1960s and there was a specific time by which it had to be accomplished, 1970. Long-range goals set through strategic planning are translated into activities that will ensure reaching the goal through operational planning.

• *OPERATIONAL PLANNING*

Strategic planning takes place at the highest levels; other managers are involved with **operational planning.** The first step in operational planning is defining objectives.

An *objective* is a result expected by the end of the budget (or other designated) cycle. At the beginning of the cycle we indicate a specific result we want to occur by the end of that cycle.

After strategic planning, the definition of objectives is the critical step in the management process. It tells us where we are going; without knowing where we are going we cannot possibly know how to get there.

After the objectives have been defined, the manager must design the organization in the best way to achieve the goals and objectives. In general, private industry allows greater flexibility in periodically reshuffling an organization to achieve specific goals. In the nonprofit sector (for example, in government), there is less flexibility, although in some cases personnel shifts or changes that do not violate legislative staffing mandates or authorizations can be made.

The next step in operational planning is assigning responsibilities. The manager breaks down the objective into pieces and hands out responsibility for those pieces to various units or individuals. When all the assigned responsibilities are fulfilled, they should equal the successful accomplishment of their objective. The manager must then allocate to the various units or individuals the resources necessary to get the job done.

Finally, the manager must be aware of problems that may occur along the way to prevent meeting the objectives. Timetables, schedules, performance standards, and other techniques serve as major checkpoints to trigger action if necessary to keep things on course. The manager thus sets up ways to check the progress of the unit as a whole toward its objective.

CONTROLLING

Once planning is complete, management concentrates on the business of **controlling,** making sure on a day-to-day basis that the objective will be met. It is first necessary to ensure the efficient and effective use of the resources dedicated to achieve the objectives—the most critical resource being the human resource. This is management control.

• *MANAGEMENT CONTROL*

The first task in **management control** is to develop individual *standards of performance*, statements of what will occur when a subordinate fulfills his or her responsibilities well. You remember that after objectives were defined, responsibilities were assigned to units or individuals and that when the responsibilities were successfully carried out and added together they equaled the successful achievement of the objectives. Now standards of performance are developed for each responsibility assigned. All achieved responsibilities added together will equal the accomplishment of the objective. This is an important relationship among objectives, responsibilities, and standards of performance.

After individual standards are developed, specific project controls, such as work plans and milestone charts, should be designed. Whereas the controls developed under operational planning were measures of progress toward achieving the unit's objective, the controls designed here as part of the controlling process are measures of the progress toward fulfilling the responsibilities assigned as components of that objective. In other words, we are going further down the line and becoming more specific.

In the course of the budget cycle, with standards of performance and project controls as tools, the manager must motivate people to meet their standards, monitor and review their progress, problem solve, and coach and counsel when necessary, that is, steps 3–7 of the outline. At the end of the cycle the manager must appraise individual performance in terms of the standards that were developed at the beginning of the cycle.

• *OPERATIONAL CONTROL*

Another key component in the controlling activity is **operational control.** This is the nitty-gritty function of ensuring that specific tasks are carried out efficiently and effectively. It is the detailed scheduling and procedures that become routine activities. We need not be concerned with this now. It is only mentioned to give a complete picture of the management process.

EVALUATION AND FEEDBACK

The last major activity in the management process is to evaluate how well the organization has done in achieving its objectives and then to prepare to begin the entire process all over again.

YOU SHOULD REMEMBER

There are three major activities in the cyclic management process: **planning, controlling,** and **evaluation and feedback.** Once we have the goals set through strategic planning, we define objectives, assign responsibilities, and set up organizational controls for each budget cycle. We then enter into the day-to-day process of ensuring that we meet our objectives. This is controlling. The type of control with which we are most concerned is **management control,** ensuring the efficient and effective use of resources devoted to achieving the objective. We are particularly concerned with the **human resource.** In controlling, we develop individual standards of performance with our subordinates, set up specific project controls, motivate our employees to fulfill their responsibilities, monitor and review progress, solve problems along the way, coach and counsel when necessary, and, finally, appraise individual performance.

At the end of the cycle we evaluate how well we did in achieving our objectives and prepare to begin the cycle again.

A SYSTEM FOR MANAGING FOR RESULTS

Right now we will take from this comprehensive management process a system to help us get the results we want. There will be four components to that system, recognizable from the process outline. What may not be so obvious is that they are the critical links which support the whole process:

- defining objectives

- assigning responsibilities

- developing standards of performance

- appraising performance

Just as the whole management process is a cycle, so also is this system within a unit. The system for managing for results is illustrated in Figure 6-2. At the beginning of the budget period, objectives are defined for the unit, responsibilities are assigned, and standards of performance are developed with the aid of subordinates. At the end of the period, performance is rated against standards and the cycle begins again.

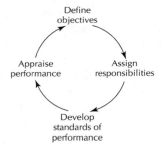

Figure 6–2. A system for managing for results.

To help you start thinking concretely about all of this, refer to Figure 6-3 (see page 112), a graphic presentation of the *hierarchy of objectives*. Assume these are units in your organization, and see how a results-oriented system works in your unit and relates to the units above and below yours. Say that you are *D*. Your boss, *A*, at the beginning of the budget period, has consulted with you and your coworkers, *B* and *C*, and has defined an objective for the organizational unit, which is made up of him/herself, you, *B*, and *C*. Actually, he or she has undoubtedly defined several objectives for the unit, but let us work with only one objective for the time being.

After defining the unit's objective, *A* assigns responsibilities for parts of that objective to you and parts to *B* and *C*. If you and *B* and *C* fulfill your responsibilities, with the direction of *A*, the unit's objective will be met. *A* will want to develop with you, and with *B* and *C* separately, standards of performance that will indicate when you have each fulfilled your responsibilities, when you have done your job well. Thus, if all the standards for you, *B*, and *C* are met, the unit's objective should be met.

At the end of the budget period, *A* will sit down separately with you, *B*, and *C* to discuss your performance, how well you did in achieving your standards of performance.

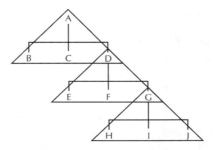

Figure 6–3. Hierarchy of objectives.

As *D*, you have your own triangle, your own unit. You have been given a responsibility by *A* for which you are accountable. You meet that responsibility by effectively and efficiently managing your unit. Within your unit, you are now in the same position that *A* was within that unit. You must define an objective for your team. The objective you define will ensure that the responsibility given to you by *A* will be fulfilled. In other words, you will translate that responsibility into an objective for your unit. You will assign responsibilities to *E*, *F*, and *G* and develop standards of performance with each of them. When *E*, *F*, and *G* have met their standards, your unit will have met its objective, and you, in turn, will have met your standards, fulfilling your responsibility as assigned by *A* and doing your part to ensure that the objectives of *A*'s unit are met. In other words, you will be simultaneously acting as "president" of your own unit, defining objectives, assigning responsibilities, developing standards of performance, and having responsibility assigned to you with standards to be met.

Just as you appraise the success of your subordinates in meeting their standards, you will be appraised by your boss.

Now, *G* is in the same position you are in—remember, each triangle in itself will fulfill organizational theory, different levels or magnitudes in the decision. This is the idea behind the hierarchy of objectives.

In private business, increased productivity may mean more sophisticated machinery that produces more of product *x* at a lower cost and at a higher quality as illustrated in Figure 6-4.

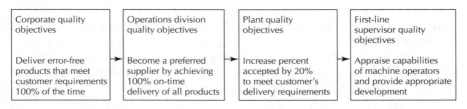

Corporate quality objectives	Operations division quality objectives	Plant quality objectives	First-line supervisor quality objectives
Deliver error-free products that meet customer requirements 100% of the time	Become a preferred supplier by achieving 100% on-time delivery of all products	Increase percent accepted by 20% to meet customer's delivery requirements	Appraise capabilities of machine operators and provide appropriate development

Figure 6–4. A sample hierarchy of objectives for total quality management.

In the nonprofit sector, however, productivity has to mean *people*—people accomplishing more. Human beings, for the most part, are the only resource we have to fall back on. In fact, private industry, in spite of its frequently sophisticated technology, has come to a similar conclusion.

Thus, we saw in Chapter 1 the emphasis in the definition of management shifting over time, shifting toward recognition of the need to recognize the goals and objectives of members of the organization as well as the objectives of the organization itself.

Well, where do we stand in terms of the productivity of employees? Psychologist William James did some research at Harvard 75 years ago that told us that we are sitting on top of a great untapped resource. He found that employees in many instances could work at 20 to 30 percent of their ability and still maintain their jobs—in other words, not be fired; startling, but perhaps not beyond our own experience. A manager's job is to tap that 70 to 80 percent of unused effort.

Some of the reasons for this unused ability can only be explained on the basis of individual circumstances, but there is another piece of research that gives us a clue to where we can take some action across the board. In the 1930s, Rensis Likert at the University of Michigan performed an experiment. He took a large group of supervisors, put them in one room, and then took their subordinates and put them in another. He asked the supervisors individually what they expected from their subordinates and recorded their answers. Then he asked the subordinates what they thought their supervisors expected of them. He then linked up the responses of each supervisor with those of the subordinates. The result? In 85 percent of the cases there was a major disparity between what the supervisor expected and what the subordinate *thought* was expected of him.

Well, you say, that was 1930. We've come a long way since then with sophisticated management theory and techniques. In 1999, some up-and-coming young researcher decided to repeat the experiment. What do you think were the results? Right, no substantial change; there was approximately an 85 percent disparity between what supervisors expected and what their subordinates thought was expected of them.

THE PSYCHOLOGICAL CONTRACT

It is important to remember at this point that individuals join organizations for certain reasons such as good pay and chance for promotion, and that organizations expect certain things from the employee for paying him or her well and offering opportunities for promotion, such as performance and creativity. This unwritten understanding of expectations is known as the **psychological contract.** It is important to keep the psychological contract in mind when contemplating any change in an organization because when individual or organizational expectations are violated problems can develop for management.

What about the consequences of a situation in which the employee's expectations are out of line with the expectations of the organization? When the employee and the manager operate on two different sets of expectations with the result that the employee eventually feels violated? In this situation, the employee may do one of three things:

1. send signals that expectations must be brought into line

2. become alienated

3. sever the relationship; in other words, quit the job

Consequently, what forms may alienation take in terms of job performance? Some possible answers are:

- employee is disruptive

- employee shows no initiative or interest in the organization

- employee is unwilling to change

- employee cannot be motivated

- employee will use only part of his or her abilities

We're saying, then, that this business of knowing your employees' expectations and having them know yours, with some negotiation to get the two in line, is important. It can have a commanding impact on individual performance and, thus, the performance of your units as a whole.

Not clearly communicating your expectations can have disastrous results on the motivation and productivity of your employees, too. If you do not take the initiative to clearly define what you expect, do not think that your employees will not make their own assumptions, leaving both sides wide open for frustration and disappointment later.

At the heart of managing for results, then, is defining expectations. That's what we're going to be doing as we break down further the functions of management: learn how to define and communicate our expectations through objectives and standards of performance.

YOU SHOULD REMEMBER

At the beginning of the budget period, you define objectives for your unit, assign responsibilities, and develop with your subordinates standards of performance. At the end of the period, you appraise performance against the mutually developed standards and prepare to begin the cycle again.

The **hierarchy of objectives** is an interesting managerial concept that enables you to view the different levels or magnitudes of decision within an organization in terms of a hierarchy of objectives to be achieved.

KNOW THE CONCEPTS
DO YOU KNOW THE BASICS?

1. What are the major activities in the management process?
2. What is the significance of the circle in the management process?
3. What are the two major kinds of planning in management?
4. What are the key steps in the two major kinds of planning?
5. What is so important about assigning responsibilities?
6. Explain the significance of the controlling function?
7. What are the two basic types of control?
8. Why is it important to develop standards of performance?
9. What are the major components of the system for managing for results?

TERMS FOR STUDY

appraisal of performance	objective
controlling	operational control
evaluation and feedback	operational planning
goal	planning
hierarchy of objectives	psychological contract
management control	standard of performance
management process	strategic planning
managing for results	

ANSWERS

KNOW THE BASICS

1. There are three major activities: planning, controlling, and evaluation and feedback.

2. The circle represents the cyclic nature of the process; in other words, these are the activities or steps an organization should go through continuously, usually moving through one cycle during a budget or other designated period.

3. The two major kinds of planning are strategic planning and operational planning.

4. The major outcome of strategic planning is the setting of goals for the organization. The key steps in operational planning are defining objectives and assigning responsibilities.

5. When we assign responsibilities, we essentially break down our objectives and hand out responsibility for those pieces to various units or individuals. When the assigned responsibilities are fulfilled and added up, they should equal the successful accomplishment of our objectives.

6. Controlling enables us to make sure on a day-to-day basis that our objectives will be met.

7. The two basic types of control are management control (ensuring efficient and effective use of resources) and operational control (the detailed scheduling and procedures that become routine functions).

8. Standards of performance are the conditions that should exist when responsibilities are carried out well. Standards of performance are developed for each responsibility assigned. It follows that standards of performance successfully added together will equal the achievement of the assigned responsibility. All achieved responsibilities added together will equal the accomplishment of the objective.

9. The major components of the system for managing for results are defining objectives, assigning responsibilities, developing standards of performance, and appraising performance.

7
PLANNING

KEY TERMS

planning the process of determining organizational goals and how to achieve them

strategic planning planning for the direction of an organization and all its components. It addresses the mission of the organization in terms of its main business. Outputs of strategic planning include broad, general guidelines for selecting business areas or markets to enter or withdraw from.

long-range planning analyzes alternatives to achieving the mission; outputs are usually targets of opportunity within the industry or market

operational planning or day-to-day planning, addresses specific timetables and measurable targets

IMPORTANCE OF PLANNING

Let's begin with an illustrative dialogue from Lewis Carroll's *Alice in Wonderland:*

Alice: Would you tell me, please, which way I should go from here?
Cheshire Cat: That depends a good deal on where you want to go.
Alice: I don't care where.
Cheshire Cat: Then it doesn't matter which way you go.

The organization choosing the "I don't care where" approach may find itself at the mercy of multiple forces in the marketplace. Competition may overwhelm it; new ideas may replace the product; new marketing methods may make its distribution systems obsolete. The organization may never reach its goals.

Planning involves (1) choosing a destination, (2) evaluating alternative routes, and (3) deciding on the specific course to reach the chosen destination. Planning is an extremely important element of each manager's job, whether from the corporate view or from his or her personal, day-to-day set of responsibilities. The cost of an error as a result of the old "seat-of-the-pants" decision-making method is, in today's complex economy, too expensive. Planning forces managers to sit down and think through issues and alternatives.

YOU SHOULD REMEMBER

Planning can be described as (1) choosing a destination, (2) evaluating alternative routes, and (3) deciding the specific course. Planning is a discipline that can help managers think through the issues and problems and design alternatives to address the issues and overcome the problems.

THE PLANNING FRAMEWORK

Planning in an organization can be viewed from three different perspectives: *strategic, long-range,* and *operational.*

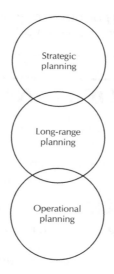

Strategic planning

Long-range planning

Operational planning

Figure 7–1. Hierarchy of planning.

STRATEGIC PLANNING

In the **strategic planning** arena, the basic question is, in what business is the entity or organization (more commonly known as, "What would we like to do when we grow up?"). Some examples illustrate this type of planning.

- A company was, at one time, in the business of making printing presses. On reflection, members of the board of directors and the senior vice presidents saw opportunities for that company to be in the information communication business; this expanded their market dramatically in a targeted area.

- An organization of farmers saw themselves in the business of raising vegetables, fruits, and cattle. On looking at industry opportunities, however, they saw possibilities of being in the convenience food business. This forced a view of consumer need and packaging and processing for the end user.

- A retail and catalog store changed its view from selling goods to selling goods and services. It now also focuses on the consumer's need for insurance, travel, credit card, and brokerage services, all provided by this same organization.

- A hospital focused, at one time, on providing medical services to an inpatient population. Recognizing that it really wanted to be a medical center with significant teaching and research capabilities in addition to its patient care capability, this hospital decided to pursue becoming a medical center and sought an educational affiliation with a school of medicine.

- A small company was manufacturing lawn mowers. The mowers were the best in the industry. Another company began catching up on the technology. Soon, the first lawn mower manufacturer was losing sales. Thinking about the business, this owner saw opportunities, not as a lawn mower manufacturer, but as a manufacturer of motors for additional motorized tools. Thus, the marketplace was introduced to weed wackers, garden tillers, and hedge trimmers, and an expanded market for the manufacturer.

To further describe strategic planning, let's take a look at some of its attributes:

Time frame. Usually long, over five years.

Basic question. What business are we in? Should we broaden or shrink our business?

Process. probably several top executives, perhaps members of the board of directors; heavy use of staff personnel and management consultants; use of gap analysis (see Chapter 8).

Complexity. Many variables, because the external environment and the internal environment must be assessed; strengths, weaknesses, and opportunities are reviewed.

Degree of structure. Very little structure, or a structure developed specifically for each organization. Strategic planning tends to be viewed differently by each organization depending on the culture, philosophy, and personnel within the organization.

Output. A very general statement that broadly sets in writing the agreements reached in the planning process; sometimes called the *Mission Statement,* it states the basic purpose of the organization and what businesses it will concentrate in.

In summary, this level of planning looks at the most general questions, scans the external environment to ensure that the approach is realistic, and states a broad, general direction for the organization. This direction is written and can be communicated to internal and external constituencies.

YOU SHOULD REMEMBER

Strategic planning has a long lead time and looks at the future in terms of the organization's mission.

LONG-RANGE PLANNING

Let's make a simple analogy to show the relationships among the levels of planning. You have taken a map of the United States and have scanned its entirety, looking for a city you would like to live in. You pick Chicago; this may be regarded as analogous to stating your mission—strategic planning. Stating the mission, however, is by itself not going to get you there. Issues about getting to Chicago, such as the amount of time and money available and types of transportation, must be developed and analyzed; choices must be made about which alternative would be most suitable and what level of resource expenditure is appropriate. This is analogous to the **long-range planning** that must be done by each organization if it is to reach its mission. Similarly, there is a third level of planning—*operational planning*—which in our example of a trip to Chicago would entail developing a more detailed plan with specific trip plans, time frames, and schedules. Additionally, if you yourself were making this trip, you would make plans to ensure that your car is ready, your clothing packed, and your personal schedule arranged for the trip. Each of these levels of planning contributes to achievement of the overall mission.

In an organizational setting, the attributes of long-range planning can be stated as follows:

Time frame. Shorter than strategic planning; usually one to five years.

Basic question. What are the major components of our business? Are there specific areas of concentration during this time frame?

Process. Top executives who participated in formulating the strategic plan must be involved; additionally, chief division managers or those senior line officers responsible for the organization are involved. The corporate mission is reviewed, and all long-range plans fall under this umbrella.

Complexity. Although complex, there are fewer variables than in strategic planning since the mission has been stated. A variety of data sources, such as financial returns, market conditions, and organizational resources, are considered. External data are re-reviewed.

Degree of structure. Some structure, in terms of existing policies and the current organizational assets (people, facilities, and way of doing business), exists.

Output. Called by many names (e.g., strategic guidelines, long-range plan, targets of opportunity, the five-year plan), this level of planning results in written guidelines generally covering at least the following areas:

- *Basic areas of the business.* What products or services are planned?

- *Financial objectives*, including such areas as sales growth, profit growth, expected return on investment, and financing sources.

- *Market opportunities* in terms of segments of the target population as well as geography.

- *Management organization.* This involves asking difficult questions about labor and the ability to carry out the plan.

- *Physical facilities.* To carry out a plan, additional (or fewer) facilities may be needed. This question must be assessed in conjunction with financial objectives.

- *Time frame for next review.* Long-range planning should be reviewed periodically, at least every two years, or more frequently if major unanticipated changes occur. These may include major changes in a law or regulation (e.g., the AT&T court decision) or a competitive product being introduced (e.g., the introduction of the Polaroid Land camera).

This middle level of planning can be viewed as the bridge between strategic planning and day-to-day operational planning.

YOU SHOULD REMEMBER

Long-range planning has a shorter time frame than strategic planning and looks more specifically at such variables as market conditions, financial objectives, and the resources necessary to accomplish the mission. All long-range planning is done within the framework of the strategic plan.

OPERATIONAL PLANNING

Returning to the Chicago planning example, the operational plan would be specific enough to get you to Chicago according to the schedule and within the resources that had been decided upon. In an organizational setting, **operational planning** ensures that the right combinations of resources are available at the right time to produce the good or service for the target customer. Its attributes can be stated as follows:

Time frame. Generally one year or less; could be monthly.

Basic question. What specific tasks must be done to achieve the results stated in the long-range plan?

Process. Generally headed by senior division chiefs who participated in the long-range planning process, this process involves executives in each unit or division. These will also be the people responsible for achieving the plan's targets.

Complexity. Generally, more specific variables are included in the operational plan. These may include such areas as a time-related market forecast for each product, along with a budget for each product; amounts of resource necessary for production of each product are also included.

Degree of structure. Of the three levels of planning, this is the most structured since systems for business planning tend to exist in organizations. Budgeting and financial forecasting are examples of these systems.

Output. The operational plan takes into account:

- Assumptions for the period. Are there any labor stoppages, material shortages, or changes in costs of resources?

- In-house changes that need to be made. Do new facilities need to be acquired? Are inside labor and policies in need of change?

- Production and timetables. How much product or service will be produced, and in what time frame?

- Responsibilities. Who is the person with responsibility for each of the major elements?

- Budget. What is the operational and/or sales budget?

The operational plan differs from organization to organization but in all cases provides enough documentation and data to be reviewed by the corporation from a marketing and financial viewpoint and to be integrated into the overall corporate operational plan.

The example of a firm undergoing a restructuring in Figure 7-2 shows how a clear hierarchy of strategic and operational plans integrates and directs actions in organizations. Good strategic plans set the stage for operational plans, which, in turn, serve the strategic plans by identifying the activities and resources needed to accomplish them.*

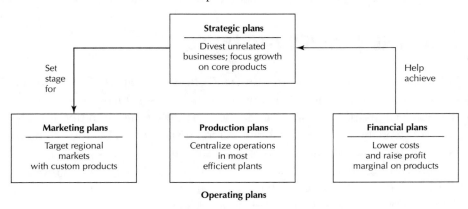

Figure 7–2. How strategic and operational plans should support each other.

---

* John R. Schermerhorn, *Management*, John Wiley & Sons, New York, 6th ed., 1999, p. 141.

YOU SHOULD REMEMBER

Operational planning has an even shorter time frame than long-range planning. It is the day-to-day planning that addresses specific timetables, tasks, and measurable targets and involves managers in each unit who will be responsible for achieving the plan's targets.

In general, there are three levels of planning, each with some overlap, but each providing a different level of detail and time framework. No two organizations' planning philosophies or processes are alike, but each organization and each individual manager, either by design or default, does planning.

THE PLANNING FUNCTION

Planning in an organization is done on a corporate level and on lower individual levels with each manager planning for his or her unit.

ON THE CORPORATE LEVEL

Each level of planning requires time and effort on the part of the manager or executive. Planning also demands data and analyses. Busy line executives may have an insatiable desire for data but very little time for in-depth analyses. These analyses in the corporate planning sphere can be and are often performed by a corporate planning department or function.

The planning department can also facilitate each of the planning processes by ensuring that appropriate data and analyses are available in a timely fashion. For example, at the strategic level, data on the external environment—new technology, pending legislation, licensure of a competitor, potential sources of competition, long-term market and economic trends—can be made available to the planning task force. Data on, say, next month's planned production would be inappropriate for the strategic planning effort but may be appropriate in assisting departmental managers in their planning efforts.

The corporate planners do not actually do the planning, nor do they take any credit for the planning. They coordinate, facilitate, and provide staff support for line executives.

ON EACH MANAGER'S LEVEL

In addition to corporate planning, each manager plans in his or her day-to-day job. Planning is not the responsibility only of the division chief, plant manager, or head of department. Each manager must think ahead and estimate time, people, capital, and raw material resources necessary for providing the production of the goods and/or services for which he or she is responsible. Several planning tools can assist in this process. Among them are *scheduling techniques,* such as Gantt Charts; the *critical path method (CPM)* of analyzing the events and time frames that are potential bottlenecks to achievement of the desired result; the *project evaluation and review technique (PERT),* which displays all tasks and time frames from start to finish; *project management,* which allows a manager to phase a project from idea to implementation; and simulation models depicting various options or *"what ifs."*

YOU SHOULD REMEMBER

Planning is every manager's job as well as a corporate function. A corporate planning department may gather data, analyze it, and make it available to line executives and all managers who do the day-to-day planning to phase a project from idea to implementation. Many tools and techniques exist to assist in planning.

Example

Let us now consider a case history and use it to illustrate the planning actually done in an organization—the planning process, levels of involvement, and actual outputs.

BACKGROUND

The Helene Fuld School of Nursing of Joint Diseases North General Hospital of New York (HFS of N) is located in East Harlem in New York City. The School's main business is training licensed practical nurses (LPNs), with one year work experience, to become registered nurses (RNs). The RNs who graduate from Helene Fuld School of Nursing attain an Associate Degree (AA). In the nursing field, many schools and universities offer a bachelor's degree in nursing.

For many years, HFS of N always had a more than adequate supply of qualified students. It was one of two similar schools in its market area; numbers of enrollments and graduates were stable from year to year. In the last two years several events occurred:
• Another, similar school became operational in the same market area.

• Another school was planning to become operational.

• Regulations governing the specific duties of the LPN changed. This decreased the incentives for hospitals to hire LPNs and thus was a potential force in decreasing the future supply of LPNs who might be interested in the program at HFS of N.

• The future reimbursement of hospitals for LPNs and student nurses was being discussed at the state regulatory level. The possibility existed that reimbursement would be decreased and hospitals would not find it attractive to hire student nurses, thus effectively eliminating a valuable training environment for the school.

• There appeared to be a growing trend for hospitals to employ Bachelor's Degree RNs as opposed to Associate Degree RNs.

The HFS of N Board was interested in gaining a better understanding of business directions for the School.

THE PLAN FOR PLANNING

A strategic plan, or planning process, does not simply occur by decision of the chief executive officer or the board. Planning takes time and effort. In order to be successful, the planning process also needs to be planned for. Using the concepts described in this chapter, Helene Fuld School of Nursing developed a plan for planning, outlining the various categories important to the School (program; organization and management; finances; resources, equipment, and facilities) from the three levels of planning. Note that data and analyses of both the external and internal environments are important parts of the planning process (see Figure 7-3 on page 128).

For strategic and long-range planning, the entire organization did not have to be involved. However, enough overlap among the levels was important. The organization for planning was developed to incorporate this principle and to ensure consistency and communication. This is shown in Figure 7-4 on page 129.

Note the heavy use of staff in this process. Typical tasks of staff were:

• Gathering data that were sometimes very obscure, analyzing data on, for example, numbers of LPNs currently in the market area who might choose HFS of N.

• Documenting the results of the Planning Committee meetings to ensure consistency of information.

• Developing fast-paced and accurate agendas in preparation for Planning Committee meetings. The objective was to have the correct data and analyses prepared for decision making by busy members of the Planning Committee of the Board.

THE PLANNING PROCESS AND RESULTS

After approximately a year of bimonthly meetings, the Mission Statement was developed and presented to the full Board; it was approved in its entirety and is shown as Figure 7-5 on pages 130–131.

Additionally, the Planning Committee examined and discussed external and internal environmental data and analyses and arrived at statements regarding the School at each of the three levels of planning. Examples of these statements are shown in Figure 7-5. Note the increase in specificity as one moves from the strategic or mission statement level to the operational or specific action plan level.

A CONTINUUM

Planning continues in the sense of reviewing the mission, evaluating threats and opportunities in the environment, and reviewing specific actions for each year. The planning itself provides a context, consistency, and method of communicating data and decisions to each level of the organization.

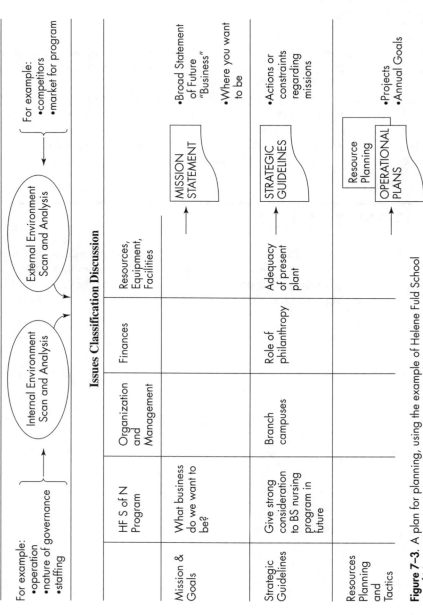

Figure 7-3. A plan for planning, using the example of Helene Fuld School of Nursing.

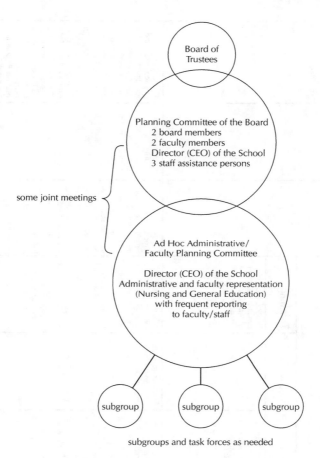

some joint meetings

Board of
Trustees

Planning Committee of the Board
2 board members
2 faculty members
Director (CEO) of the School
3 staff assistance persons

Ad Hoc Administrative/
Faculty Planning Committee

Director (CEO) of the School
Administrative and faculty representation
(Nursing and General Education)
with frequent reporting
to faculty/staff

subgroup   subgroup   subgroup

subgroups and task forces as needed

Figure 7–4. Organizing for planning.

| | Program | | | | | Organization Governance Management | Finances | Resources, Equipment, Facilities |
	Curriculum	Outcomes	Students	Faculty	Teaching			
Mission and Institutional Goals	To enhance education, and to improve nursing practice through monitoring of:							
	Provide educational opportunity for advancement in the profession.	See paragraph 2 of mission statement	Continue to serve students from diverse racial, ethnic, and socio-economic backgrounds and those who might otherwise be excluded from career advancement.		Provide broadest possible spectrum of learning opportunities by using the vast resources of New York City.			
Institutional Objectives (Strategic Guidelines)	Maintain current program. Continue ongoing curriculum review	Continue to evaluate students' reaction to and success in the program.	Continue to draw from diverse demographic groups. Increase efforts directed toward retention of *full-* and *part-time* students. Extend evaluation process well beyond graduation.	Continue to recruit and retain high-quality faculty.	Maintain and evaluate clinical affiliations. Explore new *clinical* facilities. Establish Computer Assisted Instructions. Introduce students to outside resources of NYC with particular emphasis on those in the Harlem Community	Review Organizational Structure. Increase awareness of threats through environmental scans; check threats from new competition. Maintain an active and concerned Board. Initiate public relations efforts to gain students and to raise $$.	Maintain financial integrity. Pursue new sources of income.	To maintain the physical plant and facilities appropriate to the current needs of the students. Continue present agreement with J NGH to provide for ongoing maintenance needs. Provide new and expanded facilities to meet the future needs of nursing education. Continue as a part of the Hospital Campus and participate in the hospital rebuilding program.

Specific Objectives & Action Plan							
Maintain active Curriculum Comm. Monitor current curriculum and program to meet NLN and State requirements. Encourage faculty to attend professional meetings.	Continue existing evaluation process. Stu-Fac eval. Course eval. End of prog. eval Follow-up and grad supervisor eval. Board results. Faculty observation. Institute 5-year follow-up eval.	Recruit new students through . . . Increase retention of students by. . .	Provide attractive benefits: Medical Pension Tuition reimbursement Prof. meeting reimbursement Faculty development programs Faculty evaluations Students Peers Dean	Use computers for: CAI Create assignments that require use of outside resources: Sydenham Clinic Harlem Hospital Museo del Barrio Schomburg Center Join Metro Library System Libraries of CUNY	Report annually on state of competitors & other threats. Expand the Board with a critical eye toward getting members with expertise, backgrounds and skills useful to HESN. Form a recruitment committee. Maintain an active Board. Acquire computers for data base management.	Maintain Helene Fuld Health Trust scholarship and other grants.	1. Maintain premises by performing necessary ongoing repairs. 2. Expand conference rooms and classroom space by reacquiring 416 & 6th fl. 3. Explore feasibility of expanding available laboratory space by using laboratories in the Research building. 4. Provide CAT work areas by using Learning Center and reacquiring rm. 308. 5. Maintain up-to-date library collection and resources to support nursing and general education courses by maintaining current Learning Ctr. procedures for review and purchase of materials. 6. Participate in the planning of the New Hospital Campus.

Figure 7-5. Results of a year of bi-monthly meetings—the Mission Statement.

The following statement, part of the complete Mission Statement, summarizes the goals of the School that are detailed in Figure 7-5.

HELENE FULD SCHOOL OF NURSING

Mission and Goals

The Helene Fuld School of Nursing is an independent single-purpose institution. Its mission is to provide the opportunity, through a career-ladder approach, for men and women to enhance their education and improve their nursing practice. The school endeavors to produce high-quality and technically adaptable nurses who are able to function effectively in a changing society.

The school aims to teach its students the value of intellectual skills and to help them develop the capability of making choices based on knowledge and unbiased evaluations; to advance the students' knowledge of the profession and their proficiency in technical skills; to encourage personal growth, resourcefulness, a heightened sense of responsibility, and a concern for people; to educate the students to recognize and appreciate diverse cultural value systems through studies in the liberal arts; to familiarize the students with resources for future learning so that they can adapt to the increasing complexity of professional responsibilities; and to promote learning as a lifelong commitment.

The school strives to provide continued leadership in nontraditional nursing education with an emphasis on educating Licensed Practical Nurses to advance to the Associate Degree Registered Nurse level; to offer opportunities to men and women of diverse racial, ethnic, and socioeconomic backgrounds and to those who might otherwise have been excluded from career advancement; to prepare graduates who benefit from their increased level of expertise; and to provide the base for further professional education.

The Helene Fuld School of Nursing continually seeks to provide its students with the broadest possible spectrum of learning opportunities by using the vast resources of New York City. The school is dedicated to serving its students, the profession of nursing, and the Harlem community of which it is an integral part.

Although there is no single model for a successful business plan, there is general agreement that a plan should have an executive summary, cover certain business fundamentals, be well-organized with headings, be easy to read, and be no more than about 20 pages in length. The basic items that should be included in a business plan are summarized next.*

---

* Marcia H. Pounds, "Business Plan Sets Course for Growth," *Columbus Dispatch*, March 16, 1998, p. 9.

What to Include in a Business Plan

- *Executive summary*—overview of business purpose and highlight of key elements of the plan
- *Industry analysis*—nature of the industry, including economic trends, important legal or regulatory issues, and potential risks
- *Company description*—mission, owners, and legal form
- *Products and services description*—major goods or services, with special focus on uniqueness vis-à-vis competition
- *Market description*—size of market, competitor strengths and weaknesses, five-year sales goals
- *Marketing strategy*—product characteristics, distribution, promotion, pricing, and market research
- *Operations description*—manufacturing or service methods, supplies and suppliers, and control procedures
- *Staffing description*—management and staffing skills needed and available, compensation and human resource management systems
- *Financial projection*—cash flow projections one to five years
- *Capital needs*—amount of funds needed to run the business, amount available, amount requested from new sources

---

YOU SHOULD REMEMBER

Planning is tailored for each organization. Although the basic concepts are the same, each organization's culture and philosophy will result in a slightly different set of priorities. Levels of involvement and a consistent method of communication are critical to success, as is heavy use of staff in the planning process.

KNOW THE CONCEPTS
DO YOU KNOW THE BASICS?

1. What are the three levels of planning?

2. Once a plan is developed, it is generally carried out exactly as developed. True or false?

3. Name some tools or techniques that may assist the manager in planning.

4. Planning is done by senior managers in an organization; the middle-level manager does not get involved in planning. True or false?

5. What outputs typically result from each level of planning?

6. Define planning as a management function.

TERMS FOR STUDY

corporate planning	strategic planning
long-range planning	tools for planning
operational planning	

ANSWERS
KNOW THE BASICS

1. The three levels of planning can be termed strategic, long-range, and operational.

2. False. Plans are reviewed periodically to ensure a fit with the environment. Operational plans are usually reviewed and/or revised most frequently, such as monthly or yearly, but strategic plans may be reviewed and/or revised only every several years.

3. Some commonly used planning techniques or tools include Gantt Charts, critical path methods, the project evaluation and review technique, and project management and simulation models.

4. This statement is partly true and partly false. It is true that planning is done by senior managers; most typically strategic planning involves a small number of very senior executives, such as the president and members of the Board. Long-range planning may involve division chiefs. The statement that middle-level managers do not get involved in planning is false. Operational planning typically does involve middle-level management. Additionally, it is important to remember that planning is a crucial part of every manager's job.

5. The output of strategic planning is usually a mission statement, which expresses in very general terms the basic business of the organization. The output of long-range planning is a statement of guidelines regarding how the mission will be achieved. Operational planning output is usually a one-year (or less) plan for deployment of resources within the long-range and strategic planning framework.

6. Planning, simply defined, is the process of defining an organization (that is, what business we are in); determining where it wants to go (that is, choosing a destination); and addressing the alternatives to that end (that is, deciding the specific course).

8
PLANNING: STRATEGY FORMULATION

KEY TERMS

goal a long-range aim

managerial strategy the long-term goals and objectives of the enterprise, the allocation of resources, and the adoption of appropriate courses of action (to carry out these goals)

long-range objectives objectives that extend beyond the current budget cycle of the organization

policies general broad guidelines to action that relate to goal attainment

organizational purpose the reason the business is in existence. It is the current and future business and can be viewed as the primary objective of the organization

The process of planning or determining managerial strategy and goal setting can be broken down into five major components:

1. Identifying what the organization *might do.* This can be determined from the environment, largely in terms of the market opportunity.

2. Appraising what the organization *can do* in terms of its resources and competences.

3. Deciding what the organization *wants to do* in terms of the personal values and aspirations of its key executives.

4. Determining what the organization *should do* in terms of its acknowledged obligations to segments of society other than stockholders.

5. Matching the opportunities, capabilities, values, and obligations to society at an acceptable level of risk in the pursuit of organizational goals.

The first four components of strategy are much easier than reconciling their implications in a final choice of purpose. The limitations of strategy principally involve the inherent difficulties of conceiving a viable pattern of goals and policies and implementing them wisely. The strategic decision is concerned with the long-term development of the enterprise.

Organizational objectives, strategies, and policies are not mutually exclusive components of the managerial process but are highly interdependent and inseparable. One cannot talk about attaining objectives without hearing the policy guidelines to follow. Similarly, a program strategy cannot be determined without first knowing the objectives to be pursued and the policies to be followed. Unfortunately, many semantic differences exist with reference to the meanings of the terms "objective," "strategy," and "policy." The managerial process, however, hinges upon predetermined organizational goals. The goal-setting process should begin at the top with a clear statement of the organization's purpose and should cascade down through the hierarchy. The MBO process described in Chapter 9 is an example of such a system at work, and represents a practical way of implementing strategy through operational objectives.

Figure 8-1 describes two major responsibilities in the strategic management process. The first is *strategy formulation.* This involves assessing existing strategies, organization, and environment to develop new strategies and strategic plans capable of delivering future competitive advantage. The second strategic management responsibility is *strategy implementation.* Once strategies are created, they must be acted upon successfully to achieve the desired results.*

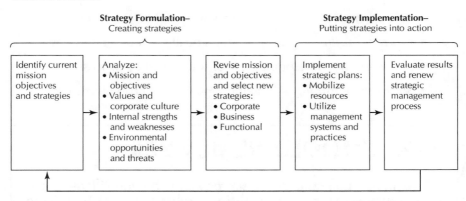

Figure 8–1. The strategic management process—strategy formulation and strategy implementation.

---

* Schermerhorn, *Management,* pp. 159–160.

Peter Drucker associates this process with a set of five strategic questions.*

1. What is our business mission?

2. Who are our customers?

3. What do our customers consider value?

4. What have been our results?

5. What is our plan?

Any and all strategies should, in turn, offer clear and demonstrable opportunities to accomplish operating objectives. According to Peter Drucker, the operating objectives of a business might include the following:

Benefits of Strategy

- *Profitability—* producing at a net profit in business
- *Market share—* gaining and holding a specific share of a product market
- *Human talent—* recruiting and maintaining a high-quality work-force
- *Financial health—* acquiring financial capital and earning positive returns
- *Cost efficiency—* using resources well to operate at low cost
- *Product quality—* producing high-quality goods or services
- *Innovation—* developing new products and/or processes
- *Social responsibility—* making a positive contribution to society

---

YOU SHOULD REMEMBER

Five major components of strategy can be identified—determining **opportunity, capabilities, values,** and **obligations** and then matching these factors in a final statement of **purpose.** Objectives, strategies, and policies are not mutually exclusive components of the managerial process but are highly interdependent and inseparable.

---

* Peter F. Drucker, "Five Questions," *Executive Excellence,* November 6, 1994, pp. 6–7.

GAP ANALYSIS—AN APPROACH TO PROVISIONAL PLANNING

IDENTIFYING A PLANNING GAP

A practical way to determine managerial strategy is to apply the **gap analysis approach** to strategic planning. This approach asks the following questions: Where are we today in terms of our strategy planning? Where are we going? Where do we want to go? How are we going to get there? Figure 8-2 illustrates this approach.

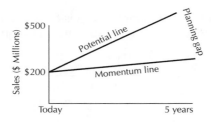

Figure 8–2. Gap analysis. A planning gap exists between the momentum of the organization—where it is going—and its potential—where it wants to go.

In planning terms, this diagram points out that if we are a $200 million company today in terms of sales and we did nothing more than continue to stay in our current line of business, our momentum might carry us to be a $220 million company in five years.

On the other hand, we could be a $500 million company in five years if we realize our potential by taking certain steps in provisional planning to fill the so-called **planning gap.**

FILLING THE PLANNING GAP

How do we fill this planning gap? There are four ways:

1. Improve our current operations.

2. Develop new products or services.

3. Develop new markets.

4. Diversify.

Look at Figure 8-3.

Figure 8-3. Filling the planning gap. The gap between momentum and potential can be filled by improving current operations, by developing new products and markets, and by diversifying.

Another way to view filling the planning gap is from the *product market matrix* of the business. Figure 8-4 illustrates this technique.

	Markets	
	Present	New
Present	Momentum	New Market Development
New	New Product Development	Diversification

(Products on vertical axis)

Figure 8-4. Filling the planning gap by analyzing the product market matrix.

However, in the real world many organizations have a product market matrix that shows much more attention given to the present.

Most of the organization's efforts are devoted to the present products in the present market, or maintaining their momentum. The trick is to plan to obtain a better balance among the four areas in order to realize the potential for the organization. Or, in other words, the organization must still develop an approach to fill the planning gap in terms of new products or markets or through diversification.

YOU SHOULD REMEMBER

Gap analysis is a planning approach for determining where we are today, where do we want to go, and how are we going to get there. The ways to close the planning gap are to improve current operations, to develop new products or new markets, or to diversify.

SWOT—AN APPROACH TO ASSESSING ORGANIZATIONAL PREPAREDNESS

An interesting approach to filling the gap has been called the **SOFT** or **SWOT Approach** to provisional planning by getting at planning issues for the business. In this approach, the strengths (S), opportunities (O), faults (F) or weaknesses (W), and threats (T) of or to a company are analyzed.

Basically, this approach takes inventory of executive judgment in an organization by gathering planning issues through selective interviewing of executives. It is based on the assumption that the goals and objectives of an enterprise are best found in the minds of its key executives. Therefore, if one can get at these issues, one would have a comprehensive understanding of the nature of the business in terms of its strengths, opportunities, faults or weaknesses, and threats.

INTERVIEW EXECUTIVES

The approach that we have followed successfully to identify the readiness of an organization to deal with a problem is to take inventory of key executive and employee judgments about the planning issues through **interviewing.**

The first step is to develop a list of key executives and employees in whom you have confidence and who know your organization. Arrange to interview them individually. A workable format for gathering planning issues from these executives and employees is the following:

1. Explain the purpose of the interview. A strategic planning program is being considered, and you need their views about the favorable and unfavorable elements that would affect such a program.

2. For purposes of classifying responses of all interviewees, use a SWOT order arbitrarily, and ask all interviewees to be as candid as possible.

3. Assure all interviewees that their responses will be strictly confidential and that none of the assessments will be directly attributable to an individual.

4. Use a form, such as the Provisional Planning Issue Form in this chapter, to record each issue raised during the interview. This will provide you with an organizational tool for sorting out those aspects of a strategic planning program that are specific to your organization.

GATHER INFORMATION

In beginning the interview, ask these questions:

From a total company standpoint, what do you see as good or satisfactory in our present operations?

What is the basis for your opinions?

Do you have any references, sources, or facts to support your remarks?

Record briefly all the points that each interviewee sees as good or satisfactory in the present operation of the organization—these are the strengths of the business as they are seen in their eyes. Next, ask what is seen as not so good, or bad, in present operations. Record these issues. Then, ask and record what is seen as future opportunity. Finally, ask each interviewee what he or she sees as threats to future operations.

YOU SHOULD REMEMBER

The **SWOT approach** is an approach to provisional planning that assesses the organization's strengths, weaknesses, opportunities, and threats, usually through data gathered by interviewing selected executives.

USE THE PROVISIONAL PLANNING ISSUE FORM

After you have begun to elicit responses, carefully guide the interviewees to complete a form for each issue raised. The constraining effect on an open interview will be balanced by your having a well-organized database from which to develop a strategic planning program.

PROVISIONAL PLANNING ISSUE FORM

Title: _____

Present appraised as:
Strength ☐
Weakness ☐

Future appraised as:
Opportunity ☐
Threat ☐

Description of statement of issue

References, sources, or facts

Ranges of possible action and resource requirements

ORGANIZE DATA

Once you have gathered information on all the issues, the next step is to rearrange them into logical planning units. The premise for assembling planning issues can be visualized by looking at the SWOT matrix (Figure 8-5). What your respondents see as good in your present operations are the strengths of the business; what they see as bad are the weaknesses. What they see as good in terms of future operations are the opportunities; what they see as bad are the threats. Your objective is to determine what must be done to safeguard the strengths in present operations; what must be done to fix the cause of, or overcome, the weaknesses of present operations; and what must be done to take advantage of the opportunities in the future to avert the threats to future operations.

What is	Present Operations	Future Operations
Good	Strengths	Opportunities
Bad	Weaknesses	Threats

Figure 8–5. SWOT matrix.

Other points gathered during your interviews with the selected key executives or employees may fall into logical planning families of marketing, finance, administration, and so forth.

These planning issues, which have been grouped into logical planning families, are best visualized along the links of what we call the *strategy chain.* The links in the chain will usually be determined by the nature of your business and the number of planning families you gather. Generally speaking, they fall into the categories illustrated in Figure 8-6.

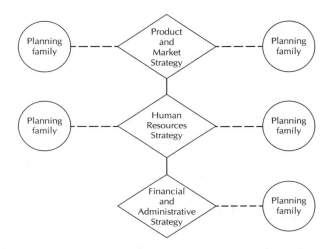

Figure 8-6. A strategy chain.

PROVIDE FEEDBACK

After all the issues have been grouped into logical planning families, it is a good idea for you to present **feedback** to the executives and employees interviewed. Since they were involved in the data-gathering process, they will appreciate the feedback that you give them because they will better understand what you are trying to do. Moreover, they will become committed to seeing the process work, since it is based on data they provided.

Their feedback will also help you decide which specific issues should be given priority for planning purposes. Once the priorities have been assessed by this group, as well as you, let us say, as head of the planning staff, you are in a better position to know the direction your business should take. The Planning Issue Evaluation Form will guide you in establishing priorities.

PLANNING ISSUE EVALUATION FORM

Issue title: ——————— Issue no.: ———————

Description of issue

Priority assessment (rate: high, medium, or low)

Cost to solve and test	Estimated value of benefits	Saving in executives' time
Ease of execution	Degree of urgency	Remarks

Priority 1 ——————— 2 ——————————— 3 ———————

The probability is that most of the high-priority subjects will be assigned to one or several of the individuals you interviewed. Again, it is highly recommended that this be done because these executives were involved in the process from the beginning, understand the nature of the data compiled—for they had the opportunity to assess it—and now would be presented with a collection or an assemblage of planning issues for solution. They should, therefore, be more committed to finding a solution to the assignment for the benefit of your organization.

For example, an information technology (IT) department needs to determine the strengths and weaknesses of its people and its technology. It also needs to make sure the IT strategy complements the company's business goals. The department head needs to ask: What is each staff member good at? What are they not good at?

Dell Computer Corporation is a great example of how an IT company can use a SWOT analysis to carve out a strong business strategy, according to

PROVISIONAL PLAN ASSIGNMENT

Ref. no. _____
Short title _____
_____
_____

Assignee: _____

Control: _____

Summary of assignment: _____
_____
_____

Resource schedule:

Date	Description	Plan & allocation

Results expected:

Date	Description (qualitative and quantitative)

Method of control: _____
_____

References: _____
_____

Collett.* Dell recognized that its strength was selling directly to consumers and keeping its costs lower than those of other hardware vendors. As for weaknesses, the company acknowledged that it lacked solid dealer relationships. Identifying opportunities was an easier task. Dell looked at the marketplace and saw that customers increasingly valued convenience and one-stop shopping and that they knew what they wanted to purchase. Dell also

---

* Source: Stacy Collett, "The SWOT Analysis," *Computerworld*, July 19, 1999, vol. 33, no. 29, p. 58.

saw the Internet as a powerful marketing tool. On the threats side, Dell realized that competitors like IBM and Compaq Computer Corporation had stronger brand names, which put Dell in a weaker position with dealers. Dell put together a business strategy that included mass customization and just-in-time manufacturing (letting customers design their own computers and custom-building systems). Dell also stuck with its direct sales plan and offered sales on the Internet.

CRITERIA FOR EVALUATING MANAGEMENT STRATEGY

Once solutions to these planning families are determined, the key executive group, with the assistance, if available, of a corporate planner, should reconcile the implications of the provisional plan assignments in a final choice of purpose, strategy, and goals as well as a viable pattern of objectives and policies of implementing them.

Last, but not least, top management should ask some key questions in terms of evaluating the strategy. Typical questions are as follows:

- Does the strategy explore fully the environmental opportunity?

- Is the strategy consistent with corporate competence and resources, both present and projected?

- Is the strategy appropriate to the personal values and aspirations of the key managers?

- Is the strategy appropriate to the desired level of contribution to society?

- Are the major provisions of the strategy and the major policies of which it is comprised internally consistent?

- Does the strategy constitute a clear stimulus to organizational effort and commitment?

Finally, management should continually evaluate and review its strategy in terms of the market response to the strategies, and reformulate the strategy as appropriate.

A FRAMEWORK FOR EVALUATING MANAGERIAL EFFECTIVENESS

Although it was developed as an intelligent approach to organizing by McKinsey & Co., a leading consulting firm with wide-ranging experiences in strategic analysis, the McKinsey 7-S Framework can be used for examining the "fits" with managerial strategy. These fits fall into seven broad areas: (1) strategy; (2) structure; (3) shared values, attitudes, and philosophy; (4) approach to staffing the organization and its overall "people orientation"; (5) administrative systems, practices, and procedures used to run the organization on a day-to-day basis, including the reward structure, formal and informal policies, budgeting and programs, training, and financial controls; (6) the organization's skills, capabilities, and core competencies; and (7) style of management (how they allocate their time and attention), symbolic actions, their leadership skills, the way the top management team comes across to the rest of the organization. McKinsey has diagrammed these seven elements into what it calls the McKinsey 7-S Framework (the seven S's are strategy, structure, shared values, staff, systems, skills, and style—so labeled to promote recall), shown in Figure 8-7.

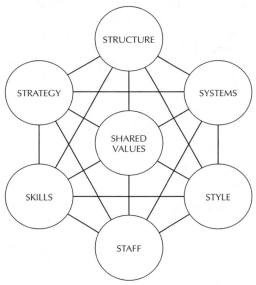

Figure 8–7. McKinsey 7-S Framework©.

*Source: Figure from *In Search of Excellence* by Thomas J. Peters and Robert H. Waterman, Jr. Copyright© 1982 by Thomas J. Peters and Robert H. Waterman, Jr. Reprinted by permission of HarperCollins Publishers.

KNOW THE CONCEPTS
DO YOU KNOW THE BASICS?

1. What are the five major components of strategy?

2. What is the strategic decision concerned with?

3. What is the gap analysis approach to strategic planning?

4. What is the planning gap?

5. What are the ways in which a company can fill the planning gap?

6. What is the SWOT approach?

7. What is the end result or objective of using the SWOT matrix?

8. Why is it a good idea to give feedback to the executives and employees involved in the SWOT approach of gathering planning issues?

9. What is the purpose of the strategy chain?

10. What are some key questions to ask in evaluating managerial strategy?

TERMS FOR STUDY

gap analysis
goal
long-range objectives
managerial strategy
McKinsey 7-S Framework
momentum line
organizational purpose
operational objectives
planning family
planning gap

planning issue
policies
product/market matrix
provisional plan
strategic planning
strategy chain
strategy formulation
strategy implementation
SWOT analysis

ANSWERS
KNOW THE BASICS

1. Identifying what the organization might do; appraising what it can do; figuring out what it wants to do; determining what it should do; and, last, matching these four components at an acceptable level of risk in the pursuit of organizational goals.

2. It is concerned with the long-term development of the enterprise.

3. Basically, it is an approach that asks the following questions: Where are we today in terms of our business or strategic planning? Where are we going? Where do we want to go? How are we going to get there?

4. It is the distance between a company's momentum line and the potential line.

5. A company can fill a planning gap by improving current operations through new product development, through new market development, and through diversification.

6. It is an approach for assessing an organization's preparedness for strategic planning through the gathering of planning issues that in essence identify the strengths, weaknesses, opportunities, and threats to the business.

7. Your objective is to determine what must be done to safeguard the strengths in your present operations; what must be done to overcome the weaknesses; what must be done to take advantage of the opportunities in the future; and what must be done to avert threats to future operations.

8. Since they were involved in the data-gathering process, they will appreciate the feedback because they will better understand what you are trying to do. Moreover, they will become committed to seeing the process work.

9. It enables you to align logical groups of planning families for solution. Generally speaking, these planning families will fall into key functional areas of the business—namely, marketing, finance, human resources, and so on.

10. Some typical questions are as follows: Does the strategy explain fully the environmental opportunity? Is it consistent with corporate competence and resources? Is it appropriate to the personal values of its key managers? Does the strategy constitute a stimulus to organizational effort and commitment?

9
PLANNING: STRATEGY IMPLEMENTATION

KEY TERMS

management by objectives a systematic and organized approach that allows management to focus on achievable goals and to attain the best possible results from available resources

performance contract the agreement made between manager and subordinate on the responsibilities and standards for the subordinate during a given budget cycle

routine objectives those objectives that are ongoing, that continue from year to year

innovative objectives those objectives that involve solving a special problem, starting a new project, or similar nonrecurrent assignments

improvement objectives those objectives that require improving one's performance over that of past years

Before we begin to discuss objectives, let's just take a moment to quickly review the material in Chapters 1 and 6.

First, we established a common definition of management: working with and through other people to accomplish the objectives of both the organization and its members. We said that this definition reflected the changing emphasis in management that:

- focused greater emphasis on individual employees as human beings.

- stressed results, rather than only activities.

- introduced the concept of managing the objectives or expectations of the organization's members as well as those of the organization itself.

We then looked at the managerial role in terms of the necessity of reducing our technical or vocational activities in favor of increasing management activities as one moved up in the organization. We also explained (or suggested) why our management activities are sometimes sacrificed to technical demands.

In further defining the management role, we briefly reviewed the concepts of responsibility, authority, and accountability.

We then stepped back and looked at the broad perspective of a common management process and identified a specific system to use in our units to successfully manage for results.

This system had four components, which recycled every budget period. For purposes of review, the system cycle appears in Figure 9-1.

We also talked about the hierarchy of objectives and the relationship of one unit's objectives to the units above and below it.

Finally, we discussed the importance of managing expectations to the motivation and productivity of our unit.

In essence, this review comprises the basic elements for an effective management by objectives system.

Figure 9–1. Cyclic nature of a management system.

TYPES OF OBJECTIVES

There are three basic **types of objectives:**

- routine objectives
- innovative objectives
- improvement objectives

This classification is offered to give you a sense of what some objectives may look like and the differences between them.

It is important to note the inclusion of "routine" as one of the types of objectives. Frequently, it is easy for us to focus on the new and the different—the improvement and the innovation—in our objectives while losing sight of the ongoing responsibilities and the obligation to continue performing them satisfactorily. If we do not express our expectations explicitly in these areas, our employees are likely to focus their energies largely on those expectations we *do* explicitly express. Providing our unit with objectives for the routine ensures that we maintain our current level of service while moving on to innovation and improvement.

CRITERIA FOR EVALUATING OBJECTIVES

There are also six tests that all our objectives must pass. The tests could be called criteria for writing and/or evaluating a valid objective. Objectives must:

- be focused on a *result*, not an activity.
- be consistent.
- be specific.
- be measurable.
- be related to time.
- be attainable.

You will be putting your own objectives to the test of these criteria in a while, so let's look at such a test in a government unit.

In an article that appeared in the *Harvard Business Review* (March/April, 1973), entitled "MBO Goes to Work in the Public Sector," an example appeared of an objective-setting meeting between Elliot Richardson, then Secretary of HEW, and one of his agency heads. Richardson was testing the objective that the agency head had proposed. Take a minute or two to review this objective-setting meeting.

AN OBJECTIVE-SETTING MEETING AT HEW

Here is a typical dialogue between former HEW Secretary Elliot L. Richardson and an agency head as they formulated an objective.

Agency head: One of our agency's most important initiatives this year will be to focus our efforts in the area of alcoholism and to treat an additional 10,000 alcoholics. Given last year's funding of 41 alcoholism treatment centers and the direction of other resources at the state and local level, we feel that this is an achievable objective.

Secretary: Are these 41 centers operating independently or are they linked to other service organizations in their communities? In other words, are we treating the whole problem of alcoholism, including its employment, mental health and welfare aspects, or are we just treating the "symptoms" of alcoholism?

Agency head: A program requirement for getting funds is that the services involved must be linked in an integrated fashion with these other resources.

Secretary: I am not interested in just looking at the number of alcoholics that are treated. Our goal ought to be the actual rehabilitation of these patients. Do you have data to enable you to restate the objective in terms of that goal?

Agency head: As a matter of fact, Mr. Secretary, we have developed a management information and evaluation system in which each grantee will be providing quarterly data on the number of alcoholics treated, as well as on the number of alcoholics who are actually rehabilitated.

Secretary: How do you define "rehabilitated?"

Agency head: If they are gainfully employed one year after treatment, we regard them as being rehabilitated.

Secretary: Please revise this objective, then, to enable us to track the progress on how effective these programs really are in treating the disease of alcoholism and in rehabilitating alcoholics.

What is Secretary Richardson trying to do when he asks, "Do you have data to enable you to restate the objective in terms of that goal?" He's trying to make sure that the final objective will be *measurable*. Why is he asking, "How do you define rehabilitation?" He wants to make sure that the objective will be *specific* enough so that they will know when it is achieved. Finally, what is the main purpose behind Richardson's questioning? He's trying to get the agency head to focus on the *result, not the activity*. This is probably the most important criterion for an objective. An objective is a statement of the *result* we expect to be achieved during a budget cycle.

How many times do we hear objectives such as the following:

- Train X number of people.

- Treat X number of alcoholics.

- Counsel X number of job applicants.

What is the purpose of these activities, the outcome we're looking for? That is the valid objective.

As well as being the most important criterion, focusing on the result (rather than the activity) can also be one of the more difficult to apply. Frequently, we start with a statement of an objective and then go through several versions or modifications to really get at the result we're after.

Adding to the difficulty of the task is the phenomenon called "one man's result is another man's activity." This means that, at one level of the organization, an objective statement may be a valid statement of the result expected at *that* level of the organization, whereas if the same objective were stated

one level *higher,* it would be considered an activity rather than a valid statement of a result to be achieved. An example should help clarify how this
can occur.

> The Director of Volunteer Services in the Department of Mental
> Health set as an objective for his unit:
> Ensure that there are at least five certified volunteer mental health
> aides in each community mental health center in the state by Febru-
> ary 28, 200__.
> In his unit is the Chief of Volunteer Training, who set the following
> objective for his own unit:
> Provide the training required for certification as a mental health aide
> to at least five volunteers in each community mental health center
> in the state by February 28, 200__.
> At his level in the organization, training services for certification is
> the result that the Chief of Volunteer Training legitimately can be
> expected to produce. To his superior, however, the Director of Vol-
> unteer Services, training is an activity that contributes to achieving
> the result expected of him, which is to have at least five certified
> volunteers at each center. An activity for the Director at his level of
> the organization is for the Chief, at a lower level, a result.

Thus, we see that the result criterion will be applied differently at each
level of the organization. The focus is on the result that can be expected
at a given level of the organization.

YOU SHOULD REMEMBER

There are three types of objectives: **routine, innovative,** and
improvement objectives. There are six tests that all objectives
must pass. The objective should be **consistent, specific, measurable, related to time, attainable,** and, most importantly,
focused and expressed as a **result,** not an activity.

WRITING OBJECTIVES—PRACTICE

The rest of this section puts into practice all that has been said about objectives.

Try to write three objectives for your unit. Included in the three should
be at least one *routine* objective, one *innovative* objective, and one *improvement* objective. After you have developed the objectives, ask yourself
the following questions:

Is this objective *specific* enough for people to understand what is expected?

Is it *consistent* with the goals of my organization, my responsibilities, and my other objectives?

Is it *related to time*?

Is it *attainable*?

And finally, or perhaps you should ask yourself this first, is it a *result*, not an activity?

Do not hesitate to modify or rewrite completely. It is the rare person who writes a perfect objective on the first attempt.

THREE OBJECTIVES FOR MY UNIT

Objective   Type

1. _____ _____

 _____

 _____

 _____

 _____

 _____

2. _____ _____

 _____

 _____

 _____

 _____

3. _____ _____

 _____

_____

_____

_____

_____

POTENTIAL EXCEPTION TO THE "RESULT RATHER THAN ACTIVITY" CRITERION FOR WRITING OBJECTIVES

There are a few limited circumstances in which an objective cannot be stated in terms of the true result desired because it would be impossible to measure the result in a direct way. An example of this is a State Council on the Arts, the mission of which is to increase appreciation of the arts in the State. The result looked for in each budget cycle, or the objective, is increased appreciation, but how can we accurately measure appreciation? In this case, surrogates for the result must be stated as the objectives. For example, you could set objectives for the number of people attending State-sponsored programs or the number of children exposed to the arts through State-sponsored school programs.

Remember, this situation arises rarely; in most cases a measurable result can be found.

PERFORMANCE CONTRACT

We've been taking a role as unit leader in our testing objectives activities. Now, let's get back to our dual role of having to define responsibilities and standards for our own job with our superior while having to help our subordinates define their key responsibilities and standards for their jobs. (Develop an imaginary superior and subordinate if you do not have one at this stage of your life and career.)

Earlier, we mentioned managing expectations and the concept of the psychological contract. We also explored the consequences of violating the employee's expectations. Through defining objectives, we've taken one step in ensuring that expectations are defined and clear by letting the employee know where his or her team is headed. Now it's time to define and communicate with the employee what the budget cycle holds for him or her personally—to mutually agree on the expectations for him or her. We do this through the **performance contract**.

In the performance contract, we put in writing our expectations (the manager's and the employee's) and commitments for the coming period. We do not leave it to chance or assumptions based on different perspectives. There are two parts to the performance contract: *statements of key responsibilities* and *standards of performance* for each of those responsibilities.

YOU SHOULD REMEMBER

The **performance contract** is the agreement between manager and subordinate on the responsibilities and standards for the subordinate for the budget period. There are two parts to the performance contract: **statements of key responsibilties** and **standards of performance** for each of those responsibilities.

STATEMENT OF RESPONSIBILITIES

The key responsibilities of your job probably remain fairly constant from year to year, with the changing objectives of your unit reflected in the more flexible standards of performance. Also keep in mind the relationships among objectives, responsibilities, and standards of performance.

Focus for a few minutes on defining responsibilities for our own jobs. Take 10–20 minutes to write **statements of responsibility** for your job. Remember, this is not to be a laundry list of all your tasks, but rather four to six statements of *critical* responsibility into which all those tasks fit in some way and for which you will be held accountable.

As with objectives, the types of statements you make will differ somewhat depending on your level in the organization. For example, a Commissioner of Personnel might draw up the following responsibility statements:

- Manage the Personnel Department effectively and efficiently to achieve its objectives.

- Keep the Governor informed of all critical personnel issues.

- Act as the agent of the State in all contract negotiations with the employee's bargaining unit.

- Serve as the representative of management on the State's Labor Relations Board.

A first-line supervisor in the classification section in the same Commissioner's department might draw up this statement of responsibilities:

- Plan and coordinate the work of six classification technicians.

- Hire, fire, and train all personnel assigned to the unit.

- Classify all new positions in State government.

- Carry out reclassification analyses.

- Develop objectives for the unit and standards of performance for all individuals in the unit for each budget cycle.

Notice that, at the Commissioner's level, there is a responsibility statement for managing the Personnel Department. The other responsibility statements relate to tasks for which he personally will be accountable in addition to the managing of his unit. The first-line supervisor, on the other hand, has no tasks outside of managing the unit.

A statement that the Commissioner used, "to manage the unit effectively and efficiently to achieve its objectives," is too broad to clearly communicate the responsibilities of the first-line supervisor. The statement must be further broken down into the several critical responsibilities involved in managing the unit.

The degree of specificity or detail of responsibility statements will depend on the level of the position in the organization. The higher the position, the broader the responsibility statements will be.

• *WRITING STATEMENTS OF RESPONSIBILITY*

Use this space to practice writing a few critical responsibilities for a job you have now or for a past job. If you have never worked before, formulate some responsibility statements for yourself in terms of career and life planning.

RESPONSIBILITY STATEMENTS

1. _____

_____

_____

_____

2. _____

_____

_____

_____

3. _____

_____

_____

_____

4. _____

_____

_____

_____

5. _____

_____

_____

_____

6. _____

_____

_____

_____

The responsibility statements you have just written will serve as the basis for developing standards of performance later, so be sure you refer to them.

YOU SHOULD REMEMBER

The **statement of responsibilities** lists those responsibilities for which you will be held accountable. The degree of specificity in the statement depends on the level in the organization: the higher the position, the broader the responsibility statements.

STANDARDS OF PERFORMANCE

Standards of performance are statements of the results expected when a job is completed.

• *TYPES OF STANDARDS*

Table 9-1 lists the types of objective standards and the ways of expressing them. Subjective standards include personal preference, bias, prejudice, intangible criticisms, and so forth.

Table 9–1 Objective Standards

Types	Ways to Express
Engineered	Positive
Historical	Negative
Comparative	Zero

OBJECTIVE STANDARDS

Types of Objective Standards

There are three types of standards: engineered, historical, and comparative. These three differ according to whether the standard is based on the results the organization needs, the results that have been produced previously, or the results others are achieving.

The *engineered standard* is essentially a statement of the results each of your subordinates must achieve so that you can achieve your objective.

The *historical standard* is based on results produced in the past. Comparing today's results with yesterday's results determines tomorrow's results.

The *comparative standard* is based on the results others are producing.

Ways of Expressing Objective Standards

Each of the three types of standards can be expressed in three different ways: positively, negatively, or zero.

All *positive standards* are statements of the results you know you want—for example, "The Licensing Division will produce 1000 licenses per week."

Negative standards express the results you *don't* want when you don't know exactly what results you do want. For example, "No more than 0.3 percent of data cards keypunched will be rejected because of errors."

The *zero standard* is used when you don't want something to happen at all—for example, "There will be no taxpayer complaints because of unobtainable service."

SUBJECTIVE STANDARDS

So far we have described only measurable or *objective* standards, standards that are based on measurable results. There are also *subjective* standards, which are based on the personal preference of the manager rather than on any specific, measurable results to be achieved. Although subjective standards generally should not exist, it is unrealistic to say that they do not or that subordinates are not often judged by them. Therefore, whenever they do exist, the subordinate has every right to know what they are.

You should bear in mind that since subjective standards are not really job related, they are not *valid* and can give us potential grievances and personnel problems.

• *CRITERIA FOR EVALUATING PERFORMANCE STANDARDS*

Let's move along now to a discussion of the criteria for writing valid standards of performance, so that you'll be ready to start writing some of your own.

There are four criteria for **performance standards.** A performance standard should:

- apply to a single job responsibility.
- be specific.
- contain a target date for achievement.
- be attainable.

These are familiar criteria to us by now, since they resemble fairly closely the criteria we talked about for objectives. In other words, you should be thinking in much the same terms when you write standards as when you wrote objectives.

YOU SHOULD REMEMBER

Standards of performance are statements of the results that will exist when a job is well done. They may be **objective** or **subjective.** The four criteria for performance standards are that they apply to a single job responsibility, are specific, contain a target date for attainment, and are attainable.

We're hearing that word *results* again. Thus, I'd like to propose the fifth criterion for performance standards: to the extent possible, a standard of performance should be stated in terms of the *result* expected, rather than in terms of an activity to be carried out.

There is a primary reason for this addition, which we mentioned earlier in our discussion of objectives. When you communicate to employees the outcome you expect, you allow them the freedom to be creative and imaginative in reaching that outcome. On the other hand, if you tell employees the activity they are to perform, you are constraining their flexibility and imagination. You are giving them no latitude to use their own judgment.

Let's use an example:

> To prepare twenty disadvantaged individuals so that they will pass the civil service entry-level clerical examination by June 30, 200__.

This is a standard stated in the form of a result that we expect—twenty people sufficiently prepared to pass the examination.

Let's see what would happen if we put this in the form of an activity.

> To conduct weekly classes in clerical skills for twenty disadvantaged individuals so that they will pass the civil service entry-level clerical examination by June 30, 200__.

Would you care to point out what has happened here? As you probably figured out, the training director has been constrained in being able to use his or her judgment of how to bring skill levels up to test standards. The director no longer has the option of on-the-job training or monthly sessions but must hold clerical classes each week and all twenty candidates have to attend, whether or not that is the best route for them.

So we see that in terms of allowing our subordinates, or ourselves, the freedom to be creative, stating a standard in terms of *results,* rather than *activities,* is the best way.

This is not a cut-and-dried issue, however. There are situations in which an activity is really what we want—we really want something done a particular way for whatever reason. We want a report on the fifteenth of each month so that we can keep informed to report to our superiors, even though the critical outcome we're looking for is, say, the number of people placed by the end of the year, not the report. As long as we incorporate in our standards the outcomes we expect, allowing subordinates the freedom to decide how those outcomes are reached, we can if necessary add activity standards that we believe are important as well. These might be called substandards or secondary standards, so that we don't detract attention from our primary standards, the outcomes we expect.

• *WRITING STANDARDS OF PERFORMANCE*

Part of your assignment now is to write a set of standards for one of the job responsibilities you defined earlier in this chapter. The number of standards you develop will depend on the nature of the responsibility you select to work with. You will have to develop as many standards as it takes to define the results that will occur when that responsibility is carried out well. If you try to focus primarily on results, the list will be substantially shorter than if you concern yourself with activities.

Before you choose a responsibility for which to develop standards, take another look at the statements you wrote. Are they an accurate and complete portrayal of your major areas of responsibility? Don't hesitate to adjust them after a fresh look.

Up to this point, we've tried to develop some tools to use in writing our standards, describing the types of standards, the ways standards can be expressed, and the criteria for writing a valid standard. Before you venture forth, however, let me bring to your attention something called "the fuzzies," the words we use constantly that don't really mean anything, much less communicate what we really expect. They are words and phrases that sneak into our communication without our really thinking about it. That's the problem—we don't think about defining what we mean.

Let us give you a few examples:

- do better

- do more

- improve the situation

- as much as possible

In different situations and to different people these all mean different things.

Take a quick look at a situation in which some standards of performance are obviously at issue. As you read the following case situation dialogue, jot down any "fuzzies" you find.

THE NEW ELEMENTARY SCHOOL PRINCIPAL
CHARACTERS
Ed   Superintendent of Instruction
Susan   Elementary School Principal
John   Third Grade Teacher
(Ed is in Susan's office. Their conversation is in progress.)

Ed: Susan, this is a rough way to treat a new elementary school principal, but I have no choice. I've got a problem, and I'm dumping it in your lap.

Susan: I have a feeling I know what you're going to say. It's about the reading problem in the third grade.

Ed: Exactly. We've been getting complaints from the fourth-grade teachers. We've got to make some dramatic improvements about the reading abilities of John's former third-grade students. I'd like to solve the problem now, before his current class moves on.

Susan: I've been aware of some rough edges but—well, frankly, I was hoping to have enough time to gradually straighten things out.

Ed: We can't take the time, Susan. I've been checking through the records, and it doesn't look good. Look, understand, I blame the slackness on Bill, your predecessor. He was a good principal, but pretty easygoing in some areas—and John's third-grade class was one. He seemed to permit John to do things just good enough to get by.

Susan: And the level of "just good enough" gradually declined.

Ed: Exactly.

Susan: Well, I'm already pushing all my teachers for better work. That may be the reason this problem surfaced now. And maybe what I should be doing is talking to them individually. Maybe we can find some faster ways to sharpen everyone's performance, including John's.

Ed: OK, fine. Get going on it right away. I want to make some inroads into this thing.

How's your list? Long? List a few examples here.

_____

_____

_____

_____

So, with a warning to beware of the fuzzies when you take a first cut at a set of standards for one of your responsibilities, let's practice writing standards.

By the end of the last section, we developed our skills in setting valid objectives and in defining key responsibilities and were well on the way to writing valid standards of performance. Now, we'll make sure our skill in writing standards is solid, and then we'll step back to look at the whole idea of the *negotiation* of objectives and performance contracts. Our objective is that by the end of this section you will be able to establish performance contracts with subordinates.

Remember that a *performance contract* is a mutually agreed upon document that defines the expectations of both manager and employee for the employee's performance during the budget cycle. The expectations are defined through statements of responsibility for the employee's position and standards of performance for the employee.

You had a chance to work on the standards part of a performance contract. Let's support your work by practicing some standards for a job other than your own.

You have just hired a new Executive Secretary. You have defined these primary responsibilities for the job:

- Maintain a filing system for the Director.

- Screen and refer all incoming mail to the unit.

- Transcribe and edit the Director's correspondence.

- Maintain the Director's appointment schedule.

Develop a standard of performance for each of these responsibilities. As you work, keep in mind the five criteria for a valid standard. Remember, the standards must:

- be related to one job responsibility.

- be specific.

- have a target date for achievement.

- be attainable.

- to the extent possible, be a result rather than an activity.

This last is particularly important, because we're going to say that this secretary has had a lot of experience and that you've hired him or her for the ability to use judgment and initiative. Be careful; activity-stated standards may constrain his or her initiative, resulting in a lack of job satisfaction. Think about the *purpose* of each responsibility. This will help you think about the real result or outcome you're looking for when the job is well done.

RESPONSIBILITY/STANDARD SHEET

Responsibility 1: Maintain a filing system for the Director
Standard 1:
(fill in)

_____

_____

_____

Responsibility 2:   Screen and refer all incoming mail to the unit
Standard 2:   _____

_____

_____

_____

Responsibility 3:   Transcribe and edit the Director's
Standard 3:   correspondence _____

_____

_____

_____

Responsibility 4:   Maintain the Director's appointment schedule
Standard 4:   _____

_____

_____

_____

What do you think of the standards when compared with the criteria? The real problem areas are likely to be over the result versus activity issue, what this exercise is designed to bring out. The kinds of standards you should be looking for or guarding against for the four responsibilities are as follows:

Responsibility 1: Maintain a Filing System for the Director

Think first about the purpose of a filing system. A major purpose is to have ready access to information when it is needed. Since you're interested in maintaining this ready access, an appropriate result-oriented standard might be:

> To be able to retrieve any information from the files within three minutes.

This tells the secretary that you want quick access to all information; how he or she goes about making sure that happens is left to individual judgment and initiative.

Perhaps if your company has a requirement for purging files, you need to include an additional standard that would have to be stated as an activity:

> To have purged all files of material five years old or older by March of the budget cycle.

You probably developed some standards that are activity statements alone, such as:

> Have all material in file box filed by 5:00 PM of each day.

Another standard likely to appear, which does attempt to get at the expected result, is:

> Have no more than X number of documents misfiled per month.

The problem here is, how are you going to know if this is the case? The only time you'll know if something is misfiled is when it cannot be found rapidly. This obviously leads us back to our original result statement, which raised the issue of rapid access, something we can recognize and measure. Always question the purpose of the responsibility. It must lead to a result statement of the standard.

Responsibility 2: Screen and Refer Incoming Mail to the Unit

It is a little easier to identify a result-oriented standard for this responsibility. Obviously, what you desire here is that the mail get to the person who can best respond to it, within a reasonable period of time. You will know this isn't happening when you get complaints. A result-stated standard thus might be:

> To receive no more than one complaint a month regarding either misdirected mail or delayed mail.

Watch for constraining standards, such as:

> Have all incoming mail screened and referred within one hour of receipt.

Responsibility 3: Transcribe and Edit the Director's Correspondence

This should also be fairly straightforward. A result you may be interested in is that:

> No more than X number of letters be returned, because of secretarial error, for retyping per month.

Be careful of getting into detailed standards that are difficult to keep track of or identify, such as:

> No more than X number of misspelled words per week, or X number of grammatical errors, or X number of typographical errors.

What you're basically interested in is how many have to be redone because of secretarial error of whatever type.

As Director, you may also be concerned that your correspondence get out promptly, so you might add the standard:

All correspondence is returned for the Director's signature within eight business hours of receipt by the secretary.

Responsibility 4: Maintain the Director's Appointment Schedule
This is another for which it is easy to become distracted by activities; for example,

Ask the Director each morning if he or she has made any appointments of which you are unaware.

Again, think about the outcome you're really after, such as:

There will be no conflicts in scheduling. Or, make no more than one appointment per month for the Director for something that should have been handled by someone else.

Remember, though, some activity-stated standards may be appropriate. For example, if the Director really wants his/her appointment calendar for the day on his/her desk by 8:30 AM, he or she should make this a standard so that the secretary knows what to expect.

YOU SHOULD REMEMBER

This exercise has highlighted two important points to keep in mind when developing standards. First, work to get at the **result** you're after so that you do not unnecessarily constrain the judgment and initiative of your subordinates.

Second, make sure that the *performance* measured against the *standard* is **something you can keep track of.** A standard is useless if you cannot determine accurately whether performance has come up to the standard. (For example, the filing standard that said no more than X documents should be misfiled. Frequently, misfilings go undiscovered for months or longer.)

NEGOTIATING THE PERFORMANCE CONTRACT

You have practiced the skills necessary for writing objectives for your unit and for writing the responsibilities and standards that make up the performance contract between a manager and a subordinate. On several occasions, we alluded to another skill that is critical to your management system—the skill of **negotiating agreement.**

In talking about both the psychological contract and the performance contract, we talked about *mutual* agreement on expectations in our achievement of both the organization's objectives *and* the objectives of its members. Finally, the superior's role is to help an individual relate targets for the ensuing period to the realities of the organization. All this implies a process of negotiating agreement. The process a manager would use to implement a results-oriented management system in a unit follows:

1. The manager of the unit receives agreement and commitment from subordinates on the objectives for the unit.

2. The subordinates write in draft form their understanding of the key responsibilities of their jobs.

3. The manager reviews these drafts to assess the correspondence between his/her perceptions and those of his/her subordinates.

4. The manager meets with his/her subordinates individually to close any gaps in perception.

5. The subordinates draft standards of performance for their key responsibilities.

6. The manager reviews these to see how congruent his/her expectations are with those of his/her subordinates.

7. The manager meets with his/her subordinates individually to negotiate final standards that will reflect the expectations of both parties.

TECHNIQUES OF NEGOTIATING

We can use three techniques in this process to assist superiors and subordinates to reach agreement:

1. Open questions

2. Reflection

3. Directed questions

Although they cannot be used in any predetermined pattern, some or all might be used depending upon the situation. They are all tried and true methods; experience has shown that they actually work in most situations. Used correctly, they reduce the risk of rejection and increase the probability of agreement.

• *OPEN QUESTIONS*

These are questions that cannot be answered "yes" or "no." They are questions that invite a true expression of opinion and feelings regardless of whether they are favorable or unfavorable to your point of view. An example is, "How do you feel about _____?" Open questions show your interest in the other person; make the other person more comfortable and secure; and draw out the other person, allowing you to learn more about that individual and what's on his or her mind. His/Her answers tell you about the real blocks to acceptance so that you can design your approach accordingly.

• *REFLECTION*

This is the repetition or rephrasing in your own words of what the person is trying to say or seems to feel. The first essential to reflection is *careful listening,* and the second is *selectivity.* You must then select the most important idea or feeling from what the person has said and put it into your own words. Reflection does several things in engineering agreement. It is a good way of avoiding argument because it enables you to respond without either rejecting or accepting what the person has said. Moreover, the sharing of feelings tends to create a "climate for agreement," and therefore it encourages people to express themselves further or to clarify something they had said.

• *DIRECTED QUESTIONS*

These are questions that request expansion or further explanation of a particular point. Generally speaking, you should use directed questions after you have had a complete expression of opinions and feelings so that you understand the other person's point of view as well as possible. Directed questions keep two-way communication going and have the following advantages. They give you more information about the person's thinking about points for which you need such information. They tend to make the other person more favorable to your position because the area of agreement is explored and therefore the area of disagreement will seem less important. Finally, they enable the person to be convinced by concentrating on the positive factors.

Roger Fisher, William Ury, and Bruce Patton offer a method for negotiation based on years of real-world research conducted by the Harvard Negotiation Project.* Here are four major components:

1. Separate the people from the problem.
   People often start in the wrong place by relying on their own fears or their past relationships with others to define a problem that requires negotiation. Learning to understand the other's position is not the same as agreeing with the person. Start with discussion surrounding perceptions and look for opportunities to act consistently with each other's perceptions and values.

---

* "Negotiating Agreement Without Giving In," *Trustee*, Chicago, 1998, vol. 51, no. 8, p.22.

2. Focus on interest, not positions.

People often act on the wrong information by pushing their own position and fighting the other's position. Ask why positions are what they are. What interests explain the starting positions? Make a list of the multiple interests that are underneath or behind a bargaining position, starting with the basic human needs of security, economic well-being, a sense of belonging, recognition, and control over one's life.

3. Invent options for mutual gain.

People who stop being creative about the negotiation process often do not recognize potentially good solutions. Separate invention from decisions. Use a facilitated brainstorming session of several people. Do not be afraid to recycle ideas and bounce back and forth between what is "wrong" and "what might be done."

4. Insist on using objective criteria.

People often overlook the fact that there are usually basic conflicts in the interests held by the parties involved. Doing the first three steps well means that you are now in a position to negotiate. Framing each issue in the negotiation as a joint search for objective criteria makes mutually optimal solutions possible and demonstrable.

Up to this point, we have taken ourselves all the way through standards of performance in our system for managing for results.

• *PERFORMANCE APPRAISAL*

Although there are many basic forms of performance appraisal, such as graphic rating scales, checklists, essay appraisals, critical incident logs, and various employee ranking methods, MBO (Management by Objectives), as described in this chapter, is a preferred alternative to resolving the problem of basing performance appraisals on subjective data. MBO is appropriate particularly for managers and professionals since appraisal is based on mutually determined and agreed upon standards of performance.

Some general guidelines for conducting a performance appraisal under an MBO system follow under the subtopic, The Appraisal Process.

THE APPRAISAL PROCESS

Prepare for the Performance Appraisal Interview. Two weeks before the appraisal interview, notify the employee of the date of the interview and ask the employee to submit to you a list of major accomplishments for the budget cycle. The purpose of asking for this information is that it provides the following:

1. Gives the employee an opportunity to formally state achievements.

2. Gives the manager the opportunity in the interview to reinforce the employee on things that the employee thinks are important.

3. Forewarns the manager on what areas might be a source of pride to the employee.

Compare the standards of performance for the cycle with actual performance. Select one or two areas that need improvement or change to be discussed in the interview. Review with your superior the appraisal of the employee's success in meeting standards. This latter step provides the following: Gives the manager a chance to check perceptions before giving feedback to the employee.

THE APPRAISAL INTERVIEW
The setting should offer:

1. complete privacy.

2. sufficient time, with no interruptions.

To get off to a good start:

1. make the employee comfortable.

2. explain the purpose of the interview.

Reinforce the employee for things done well and give the opportunity to discuss how he or she did it.
To discuss the one or two major areas that need improvement:

1. save the little things for day-to-day interactions.

2. give specific examples of what you mean, rather than making general evaluative statements.

3. don't overwhelm the employee.

Agree on a development plan for the employee.
Remember throughout to:

1. be open and honest.

2. show sincere interest.

3. listen to the emotional content of what the employee says as well as the informational content.

4. use the three techniques of open questions, reflection, and directed questions to draw the employee out and put you on common ground.

Follow up on the development plan and prepare to begin the next cycle.

YOU SHOULD REMEMBER

The process of implementing a results-oriented management process consists of **seven steps** and implies a process of **negotiating agreement.**

The three techniques that you can use to assist you in negotiating agreement with others are: **open questions, reflection,** and **directed questions.**

KNOW THE CONCEPTS
DO YOU KNOW THE BASICS?

1. What are the basic elements for an effective "management by objectives" system?

2. What are the basic types of objectives, and why are they important?

3. What are the criteria for writing valid objectives?

4. Are there any potential exceptions to the "result" rather than "activity" criterion for writing objectives?

5. What is the significance of the performance contract, and what does it consist of?

6. What are the types of objective standards and the ways of expressing them?

7. What are the four criteria for performance standards?

8. What are the fuzzies?

9. What does the process of negotiating agreement mean?

10. What techniques can be used in the process of negotiating agreement to implement a results-oriented management system?

TERMS FOR STUDY

comparative standards
directed questions
engineered standards
fuzzies
historical standards
improvement objectives
innovative objectives
key responsibilities
management by objectives (MBO)

negotiating agreement
objective standards
open questions
performance contract
reflection
routine objectives
standards of performance
subjective standards

ANSWERS
KNOW THE BASICS

1. The process starts with defining objectives, assigning responsibilities, and developing standards of performance and ends with redefining objectives for the next budget period.

2. The three basic types of objectives are routine, innovative, and improvement. By providing your unit with routine objectives you ensure that you maintain the current level of service while moving on to innovation and improvement with the two other types of objectives.

3. These criteria are that the objective should be focused on a *result*, not an *activity;* and should be consistent; specific; measurable; related to time; and attainable.

4. In a few limited circumstances an objective cannot be stated in terms of the true result desired because it would be impossible to measure the result in any sound way.

5. In the performance contract we put in writing our expectations (the manager's and the subordinate's) and commitments for the coming budget period. We do not leave it to chance or assumptions based on different perspectives. There are two parts to the performance contract: statements of key responsibilities and standards of performance for each of those responsibilities.

6. There are three types of objective standards: engineered, historical, and comparative. They can be expressed in a positive, negative, or zero manner. Sometimes personal preference, bias, or prejudice enters into setting standards and the standards become subjective.

7. A performance standard should apply to a single responsibility, be specific and attainable, and contain a target date for achievement. To the extent possible, a standard of performance should be stated in terms of the result expected rather than in terms of an activity to be carried out.

8. The fuzzies are words we use constantly that don't really mean anything, much less communicate what we really expect.

9. Negotiating agreement means that the supervisor should help the subordinate relate his or her targets for the ensuring budget period to the realities of the organization to obtain mutual agreement or expectations.

10. Three techniques to assist superiors and subordinates to reach agreement are open questions, reflection, and directed questions.

10
BASIC CONCEPTS OF ORGANIZING

The process of organizing is essentially the same for all types of businesses. Once objectives and plans have been formulated, management must develop an orderly way to bring together the physical and human resources that are essential to accomplish the goals of the enterprise. This task is referred to as the organizing function of management.

In studying the structure of a company, it is also important to keep in mind the definition of organization: the entity that makes it possible for a group or team to work together more effectively than they might work alone in order to achieve goals.

No single individual can be expert in every specialty of the organization or do everything. Therefore, the manager must analyze the strengths and weaknesses of the team, balance their talents, and add competencies where necessary. It is also important that people know their responsibilities, the authority they have, and what they are trying to accomplish. In our total effort we should also keep in mind the relationships among the functions of management: planning, organizing, staffing, motivating, leading, and controlling.

WHY ORGANIZE?

We organize for the purpose of reaching our goals and objectives. These goals and objectives, of course, should be marketing oriented. A business exists for the purpose of serving customer needs and wants. Therefore, the structure of the business should take its primary direction from the marketplace. Tell me what business you're in or wish to be in, and I will tell you how to structure your business. This is a sound principle for organizing. It is based on an organization's plan or strategy and the concept that structure follows strategy. Strategy comes primarily from the product or market scope of the business.

Although marketing is to be in the forefront in organizing a business, we must make certain that the other functions do not suffer. The market plan alone, without supporting elements, is of little value.

There should be little argument at this point that planning is the first function of management, it is necessary to organize. If we do not have a plan, we cannot really establish objectives; if we have no objective, we have no reason to organize. In other words, if we do not know where we're going, we do not know how to organize to get there. Planning and organizing are the integrated responsibilities of the manager. Because an organization typically has a growth plan, it should be recognized that structure should be developed over the long term and is subject to change. Sometimes the impact of change is not recognized, yet it is one of the reasons that planning and organizing are so intimately related, each an integral part of the other. Planning helps to quickly evaluate the impact of change when crises occur. Organizing in accordance with your plan or strategy and making use of the formal (i.e., official organizational structure, consisting of responsibility, authority, and accountability), as well as the informal organization, which consists of informal relationships deriving mainly from politics, power, and status, also helps us manage change effectively.

YOU SHOULD REMEMBER

We organize for one purpose—reaching our goals and objectives. These objectives should come from the marketplace, that is, to satisfy a customer need or want. Structure follows strategy is a sound concept for organizing. The primary function of management that supports organizing is planning.

BASIC CONCEPTS

Organization is a process that takes place as a form of planning. It is not an end in itself. We go into business, not to have an organization, but to serve a purpose—basically to satisfy some customer need or want. We then develop a plan to achieve that purpose and create an organization structure to implement that plan.

The basic concepts in organizing are analyzing, identifying, and defining the work to be performed to accomplish the objectives of the enterprise. If this process is done properly, it will result in some logical grouping of work and a means for individuals to cooperate effectively in achieving objectives.

In organizing, we must first agree on the work to be performed. This is known as *unity of purpose* in organizational terms. Second, we must decide what has to be done to achieve that purpose; what functions must be performed, who will carry them out, and what authority they will have to accomplish the work. This aspect is known as *division of labor*. Third, the type, number, and experience of individuals who will implement the work must be determined. This is *staffing* and is the subject matter of Chapter 12. Finally, we develop the *structure or organization framework* that will provide for effective teamwork in terms of reporting relationships—chain of command and flow of information. Moreover, management should make a strong commitment to make the organization work in terms of getting things done effectively through others, our working definition of management. The organizational structure is the vehicle to make this happen. As managers we should work within the structure, for we are what we do. If we do not practice what we preach in terms of sound management principles, our employees will find ways to bypass the structure and therefore the organization may not be as effective as it might be.

Figure 10-1 shows the key role organizing plays in the management process.

Figure 10–1. Organizing viewed in relationship to the other management functions.

The way in which the various parts of an organization are formally arranged is referred to as the Organization Chart.

What Can You Learn from an Organizational Chart:

- *Levels of management*— vertical layers of management
- *Supervisory relationships*— lines showing who reports to whom
- *Major subunits*— positions reporting to a common manager
- *Division of work*— positions and titles
- *Communication channel*— formal communication flows

YOU SHOULD REMEMBER

Organization is not an end in itself. It is a process that takes place as a form of planning. The basic concepts in organizing are analyzing, identifying, and defining the work to be performed to accomplish the objectives of the enterprise. A **unit of purpose,** a **division of labor,** and a **staff** and an **organizational framework** must be developed.

GUIDELINES FOR ORGANIZING

Some guidelines that should be followed in all companies in terms of organizing are as follows:

1. Be aware of the impact of change on people as well as on structure. As you change your strategy or plan, your policies, practices, programs, pro-

cedures, and so forth may also be affected. Hence, changes will also have to be made within many parts of the organization. Involve your people in any change so that they will understand its impact and how it affects them. Consequently, they will be more committed to make the change succeed.

2. Keep your structure lean and simple. Try not to develop too many levels for approval and review. Also, avoid whenever possible overburdening or underburdening any one individual or group with tasks and responsibilities. The *span of control*, the number of subordinates the manager can effectively supervise, is a subject for much discussion. If a manager can finish his or her own work and still develop, counsel, motivate, and control twelve people effectively, then the span of control is 12.

3. Once the ideal structure has been developed, fit your people to it as well as possible. In other words, approach your structure from a "need" rather than from a "personnel available" point of view.

4. You cannot report to two people at the same time about the same work and satisfy either of them. This principle is known as the *unity of command*. In the early days of organization, this principle was easy to follow. Today it is more difficult, with the upsurge in the numbers of staff positions and as organizations have grown in size and complexity. Yet as a principle or guideline for organizing, it should be followed whenever possible.

5. Write down a description of the work. This is the *principle of definition*. Some people find position descriptions to be an unnecessary hassle. They claim that their people know what to do; they know the work. What's all this paperwork for? If you feel this way and you don't have position descriptions in your organization, try a brief experiment. Write down the work (responsibility) and authority that you think one of your employees is accountable for. Ask that person to do the same. Then compare the two. In most cases, the results will read like two different jobs.

YOU SHOULD REMEMBER

In organizing, be aware of the impact of change on people and structure; keep the structure lean and simple; fit people as well as possible to the ideal structure; have people report to one boss; and write down the definition of work to be performed (the **position description**).

KNOW THE CONCEPTS
DO YOU KNOW THE BASICS?

1. What is involved in the organizing function of management?
2. Why do we organize?
3. Why is planning the first management function that is necessary to organize?
4. What is meant by "structure follows strategy?"
5. What are the basic concepts in organizing?
6. What is unity of purpose in organizational terms?
7. What is meant by division of labor?
8. What is meant by structure?
9. What are some guidelines for organizing?
10. What is meant by the unity of command principle?

TERMS FOR STUDY

definition	span of control
division of labor	staffing
formal organization	strategy
informal organization	structure
organization	unity of command
organizing	unity of purpose

ANSWERS
KNOW THE BASICS

1. Organizing is the process of developing an orderly way for bringing together the physical and human resources that are essential to accomplish the goals of the enterprise.
2. We organize for the single purpose of reaching our goals and objectives.
3. If we do not have a plan, we cannot really establish objectives, and if we have no objective, we have no reason to organize. In other words, if we do not know where we're going, we do not know how to organize to get there.
4. "Structure follows strategy" means that your structure or organization should be developed from your plan or strategy, which comes from the

product or market scope of the business and is oriented toward serving specific customer needs and wants or product or market segments.

5. The basic concepts involve analyzing, identifying, and defining the work to be performed to accomplish the objectives of the enterprise.

6. Unity of purpose is agreement on the work to be performed.

7. Division of labor is the division of work and functions into smaller activities.

8. Structure is the organizational framework that will provide for effective teamwork in terms of reporting relationships and ensuring the flow of information.

9. Guidelines for organizing include the following: be aware of the impact of change on people as well as on structure; keep your structure lean and simple; fit your people to the ideal structure as well as possible; and write down the description of the work.

10. The unity of command principle means you cannot report to two people at the same time about the same work and satisfy either of them; it also means that an employee should have one and only one immediate boss.

11

ORGANIZATIONAL STRUCTURES: CONCEPTS AND FORMATS

When two or more people work together to achieve a group result, it is an *organization*. After the objectives of an organization are established, the functions that must be performed are determined. Personnel requirements are assessed and the physical resources needed to accomplish the objectives determined. These elements must then be coordinated into a structural design that will help achieve the objectives. Finally, appropriate responsibilities are assigned.

Determining the functions to be performed involves consideration of division of labor; this is usually accomplished by a process of departmentalization.

DEPARTMENTALIZATION

Grouping people and jobs into manageable work units to achieve the objectives of the enterprise in the most efficient and effective manner is **departmentalization.** A variety of means can be utilized for this purpose. The primary forms of departmentalization are by function, process, product, market, division, customer, geographic area, and even matrix (also called project organization). In many organizations, a combination of these forms is used.

FUNCTIONAL STRUCTURE

Perhaps the oldest and most common method of grouping related functions is by specialized **function,** such as marketing, finance, and production (or operations). Sometimes this form of departmentalization may create problems if individuals with specialized functions become more concerned with their own specialized area than with the overall business. An example of departmentalization by function appears in Figure 11-1.

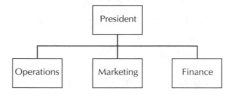

Figure 11–1. Functional organization.

DIVISIONAL STRUCTURE

A second organizational structural alternative is **divisional,** if it groups people who do not work in the same product or process, serve similar customers, and/or are located in the same area or geographical region. Divisional structures attempt to avoid problems common to functional structure and are popular among organizations with diverse operations that extend across many products or services, geographical areas, customers, or work processes.

PROCESS

Departmentalization can also take place by **process.** This type of departmentalization, which often exists in manufacturing companies, is illustrated in Figure 11-2.

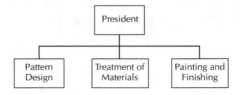

Figure 11–2. Process organization.

PRODUCT

Whenever specialized knowledge of certain products or services is needed, departmentalization by **product** may be best. This usually occurs in large diversified companies. This form of departmentalization is illustrated in Figure 11-3.

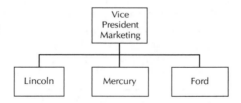

Figure 11–3. Product organization.

MARKET

When a need exists to provide better service to different types of markets, departmentalization by **market** may be the appropriate form. An example of a business serving nonprofit markets, which uses the market form of departmentalization, is shown in Figure 11-4.

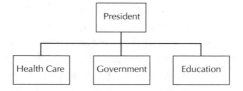

Figure 11–4. Market organization.

CUSTOMER

Sometimes key or major customers warrant departmentalization by **customer.** This is often the case in banks. See Figure 11-5.

Figure 11–5. Customer organization.

GEOGRAPHIC AREA

When organizations are spread throughout the world or have territories in many parts of a country, departmentalization by **geographic area** may provide better service to customers and be more cost effective. A typical example for this form of departmentalization is shown in Figure 11-6.

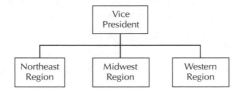

Figure 11–6. Geographic organization.

MATRIX (PROJECT ORGANIZATION)

A **matrix** organization combines functional and divisional approaches to emphasize project or program teams. In effect, it is an attempt to gain the advantages of the two structures by using permanent cross-functional teams to integrate functional expertise with a divisional focus. Workers in a matrix structure belong to at least two formal groups at the same time. They also report to two bosses—one within the functional area and the other within the team or division. Matrix structures are also found in multinational corporations, where they offer the flexibility to deal with regional differences as well as multiple product, project, or program needs.

Departmentalization by matrix, or project, has received considerable use in recent years, particularly in such industries as aerospace (e.g., NASA). In this method, personnel with different backgrounds and experiences that bear on the project are assembled and given the specific project to be accomplished within a certain time period. When the project is completed, these specialized personnel return to their regular work assignments. An example of this form is illustrated in Figure 11-7; it often takes the shape of a diamond.

Figure 11–7. Matrix/project organization.

COMBINATION APPROACH

Many organizations, particularly large, physically dispersed, and diversified organizations, utilize several different forms of departmentalization. Figure 11-8 is an organizational chart showing the use of several forms of departmentalization.

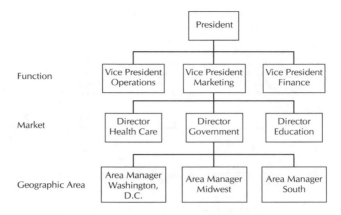

Figure 11–8. Combination organization.

OTHER DEVELOPMENTS IN ORGANIZATIONAL STRUCTURES

TEAM ORGANIZATION

In organizations that operate with team structures, both permanent and temporary teams are used extensively to accommodate tasks. Cross-functional teams bring together members from different functional departments or areas of work responsibility. Organizations such as General Electric, Ford, and Intel are trying to utilize teams as basic building blocks of new organizational structures as a way of changing more traditional *vertical* structures in favor of more *horizontal* ones.

As illustrated in Figure 11-9, a team structure involves teams of various types working together as needed to solve problems either on a part-time or full-time basis.

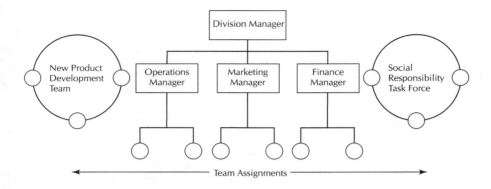

Figure 11–9. Team organization.

VIRTUAL ORGANIZATION (BOUNDARYLESS)

These are network organizations that utilize the latest communications and information technology while engaging in a shifting variety of strategic alliances and business contracts that sustain operations without the cost of *owning* all supportive functions. These organizations operate with the support of extensive computer networks and, in so doing, are able to work across large geographical distances with a minimum number of full-time employees.

As we move into the new millennium, organizing trends are toward shorter chains of command, using more cross-functional teams, task forces, and horizontal structures as well as wider spans of control as empowerment gains prominence.

YOU SHOULD REMEMBER

Determining the functions to be performed in an organization involves consideration of division of labor; this is usually accomplished by a process of **departmentalization.** The primary forms of departmentalization are by function, division, process, product, market, customer, geographical area, matrix (project), or some combination of these forms.

DELEGATION—THE ART OF MANAGING

As shown earlier, the process of managing begins with the establishment of objectives. Once the objectives have been established, the functions that must be accomplished are considered. Then the work to be performed or the responsibilities to be assigned are determined. This means that it is necessary to know the personnel and physical resources needed to accomplish the objectives of the enterprise. Thus, when the functions, personnel, and other resources are grouped together by some means of departmentalization into a logical framework or organizational structure, the process of **delegation** begins.

Delegation is the process that makes management possible. Why? Because management is the process of getting results accomplished through others.

DELEGATION PROCESS, AUTHORITY, AND ACCOUNTABILITY

At the moment a job becomes too complex, too diverse, or too voluminous for one person, the need for delegation arises. In its simplest form, imagine the sole administrator with objectives and limited time and no subordinates with which to accomplish them. Resources permitting, the manager can create a new job, hire an employee, and assign the accomplishment of the objectives to the new employee.

To meet these responsibilities, the new employee must also have the authority to achieve them. Thus, **authority** is delegated along with the responsibility. The manager, however, is still ultimately responsible. By assigning some of his or her responsibilities, the manager transfers or creates **accountability.** If the employee does not exercise the responsibility properly, the manager can always withdraw the authority. Delegation without control is *abdication.*

In practice, the process of management works in conjunction with the process of delegation. Since management is the process of getting results through others, delegation facilitates that process by assigning responsibilities, delegating authority, and exacting accountability by employees.

The delegation process works as follows. The manager has certain defined objectives (i.e., results) to accomplish at the end of the budget period. He or she assigns the responsibilities (i.e., duties to be performed) to key employees, along with the commensurate authority to go with those responsibilities. Thus, the accomplishment of the assigned responsibilities should equal the defined objectives.

The manager then develops standards of performance with each key employee (i.e., the conditions that should exist when a job is done well). These standards should be developed mutually to be effective. In essence, these standards of performance become the accountability of each employee for the budget period. The successful accomplishment of the standards of performance should equal the assigned responsibilities. The process continues with the appraisal of key subordinates rated against the agreed-upon standards of performance and closes with evaluation and feedback to the beginning of the next budget cycle, when the process begins all over again. See Figure 11-10.

Defining Objectives

Appraising Performance

Assigning Responsibilities

Developing Standards

Figure 11-10. The key links in the management process.

RISKS IN DELEGATION

The sheer volume of management responsibilities necessitates delegation. There is somewhat of a paradox in this situation, however, because delegation involves taking **risks.** Among the risks of delegation are loss of control, reverse delegation, and even loss of a job.

• *LOSS OF CONTROL*

In giving over authority to another, the manager loses some control over the proper completion of a project. The manager who has lived by the adage "If you want it done right, do it yourself" may find it difficult to delegate tasks for which he or she will ultimately be held accountable.

The key to successful delegation is assigning the right responsibilities to the right person. Of course, one never knows who the right persons are until one meets and works with them, but it must realistically be assumed that a given organization, department, or section employs at least some competent, willing, and responsible individuals. This assumption does not address itself to the fact that it is nearly impossible today for the manager to be technically superior to all employees. A staff that is not utilized effectively because of a manager's failure to delegate is a major loss to an organization and a waste of human resources.

• *REVERSE DELEGATION*

An important consideration for the manager who tries to do everybody's job is that he or she does so at the expense of the job for which he/she was hired—managing. An interesting analogy that underscores the value of delegation for management's sake is the "monkey-on-the-back" analogy, which claims that managers spend far more time with their employees than they even faintly realize. This habit especially occurs when a problem is brought to the manager's attention. In encounters with employees, the manager's use of simple phrases, such as "send me a memo on that," or "let me think about that and I'll let you know," or "just let me know what I can do," causes the "monkey" (problem) to jump onto the manager's back.

The manager assumes the responsibility for handling the task that was delegated to the employee in the first place, and when the employee reaches an impasse, the manager takes the next step. This is **reverse delegation,** and many employees are adept at it. Naturally, there will be situations in which the next step is justified, but unless the manager wants endless lines at the office door, he or she should avoid the casual and repeated use of those phrases that permit employee problems to ride on the manager's back. In fact, this principle of delegation is that accountability to a superior cannot be delegated.

A solution to this problem is to encourage initiative in employees. Employees should not have to wait until told to do something; nor should they have to ask. They should practice the completion of assigned tasks. By keeping the responsibility where it belongs, the manager will increase discretionary time to manage and can still handle system-imposed tasks. To develop initiative in employees early is one of the ways to develop a new generation of capable managers.

• *LOSS OF JOB*

The foregoing discussion brings to mind another risk in delegation from management's viewpoint. Is it possible to delegate one's self right out of a job? Suppose a subordinate develops so much initiative that he or she becomes superior to the boss. This is a threatening problem for the manager. The employee would be very happy if his or her development resulted in promotion, but what if the promotion means the manager's job.

Consensus among theorists suggests that the employee should be given the opportunity to perform to as high a level of responsibility as possible if this improves the group's performance. The manager should then endeavor to reward that person accordingly, even if it means helping that person to land a better job outside the organization. To neglect and waste the talents of any individual is as criminal as the misuse of company funds or equipment.

In practice, we have all heard stories from individuals who feel more competent than their managers. Thus it would seem that the best safeguard a manager has in preserving his or her position is to be a good manager and to prepare for his or her own advancement.

TECHNIQUES OF DELEGATION

The art of delegation often depends on a given situation. Plans change and people differ, but this does not imply that the employee should have to be notified on a daily basis of what is needed. Nor does it imply that there are not some generally accepted techniques that can facilitate the process of delegation, as discussed next. More suggestions are detailed in the list of do's and don'ts.

• *DEFINITION OF RESPONSIBILITIES AND AUTHORITY*

A clear definition of responsibilities and the authority to accomplish them constitute the foundation of the art of delegation. Whenever possible, these responsibilities should be stated in writing. The employee should also have a good idea of how the job fits into the total picture and why it is important. The manager should also encourage questions and be completely approachable. This practice, in combination with exhibiting confidence and trust by allowing subordinates to pursue goals without undue reporting, constant checking, and other exaggerated forms of control, will create a supportive climate and help to build an effective working relationship.

• *PERFORMANCE RATING*

Once the employee understands the job, that person should be made aware of how performance will be measured. This step in the management process has already been mentioned.

By and large, and within reason, managers receive the type and level of job performance they expect or informally accept over a period of time. In fact, low expectations tend to breed low performance and the opposite is true of high expectations. The failure to confront lower than desired levels of performance is tantamount to acknowledging them as acceptable; high expectations mean setting challenging but achievable goals. The focus should be on results that are motivating and attainable.

The manager should establish a system for setting objectives and set up a procedure for periodically reporting progress toward these objectives. Consideration of less-experienced employees demands more frequent consultation and, possibly, reporting. The manager who is committed to delegating authority should avoid switching back and forth in delegation, thereby causing only confusion and stagnation among employees.

• *AWARENESS OF LIMITATIONS*

It may seem self-evident, but delegation cannot be used when the individual does not welcome additional responsibility. Knowing who wants greater responsibility or promotion is as important as knowing who is qualified for a job. It is often difficult for successful executives, who owe their success to a driving desire for greater responsibility and recognition, to understand others who seem to lack that motivation.

In essence, the manager-employee relationship is one of interdependence. A major goal of delegation is to reduce dependence on the manager, but the manager incurs a certain responsibility to the employee in delegation. The manager is responsible for helping the employee discover how best to develop his or her abilities in order to meet future responsibilities.

Managers can develop employees through the art of delegation and should practice this art judiciously. With effective delegation, a manager can multiply his or her effectiveness and, through others, achieve the results expected.

PARITY OF AUTHORITY AND RESPONSIBILITY

An important principle of organization as well as management is that authority should equal responsibility. This principle is known as the **parity of authority and responsibility** and ensures that work will be performed with a minimum amount of frustration on the part of personnel. By not delegating authority equal to responsibility, a manager will create employee dissatisfaction and generally waste energies and resources.

SCALAR PRINCIPLE

This concept is generally referred to as the *chain of command*. It means that there should be a clear definition of authority in the organization and that this authority flows, one link at a time, through the chain of command from the top to the bottom of the organization. Communication in the organization is through channels. Following this principle generally results in clarification of relationships, less confusion, and improved decision-making.

YOU SHOULD REMEMBER

Delegation is the process that makes management possible because management is the process of getting results accomplished through others. Understanding the process of delegation involves employing the principles of **responsibility, authority,** and **accountability,** as well as understanding the concept of the **chain of command (scalar principle).**

DELEGATION DO'S AND DON'TS
Do's

- Delegate as simply and directly as possible. Give precise instructions.

- Illustrate how each delegation applies to organizational goals.

- Mutually develop standards of performance.

- Clarify expected results.

- Anticipate the questions your employees may have, and answer them in order.

- Discuss recurring problems.

- Seek employee ideas about how to do the job.

- Accentuate the positive rather than the negative. Be supportive. Exhibit trust.

- Recognize superior performance.

- Keep your promises.

Don'ts

- Do not threaten your staff. Effective delegation depends more on leadership skills than on position power.

- Do not assume a condescending attitude.

- Do not merely give answers. Show an employee how to do something and why it is done that way.

- Do not overreact to problems.

- Refrain from criticizing an employee in front of others.

- Avoid excessive checks on progress.

CENTRALIZATION VERSUS DECENTRALIZATION

The issues of **centralization** and **decentralization** involve the principle of delegation of authority. When a limited amount of authority is delegated in an organization, it is usually characterized as *centralized*. When a significant amount of authority is delegated to lower levels in the organization, the business is characterized as *decentralized*. Centralization and decentralization are opposites, and there are different degrees of each. In a highly centralized organization, employees at lower levels have a limited range of decision-making authority. The scope of authority to make decisions in decentralized organizations, by way of contrast, is very broad for lower level employees (see Figure 11-11).

Figure 11-11. Scope of authority delegations and resulting centralization/decentralization.

One cannot classify all forms of centralization as effective or ineffective. The same applies to decentralization. Each form has its advantages and disadvantages and is affected by a number of factors. For example, the size and complexity of the enterprise can affect the delegation of authority. If an organization is extremely large and diversified, the limitations of expertise will generally lead to decentralization of authority to the heads of these different businesses. If speed and adaptability to change are characteristic of the business, it tends toward decentralization. Geographic dispersion also favors decentralization of authority. On the other hand, some organizations have excellent and speedy communications systems that tend to favor the centralization of authority. In situations in which adequate personnel are unavailable, the organization tends to centralized authority.

ADVANTAGES OF CENTRALIZATION

1. Closer control of operations.

2. Uniformity of policies, practices, and procedures.

3. Better use of centralized, specialized experts.

ADVANTAGES OF DECENTRALIZATION

1. Faster decision-making without resort to higher level consultation.

2. Excellent training experience for promotion to higher level management.

3. Decisions better adapted to local conditions.

YOU SHOULD REMEMBER

The issues of centralization and decentralization involve the principle of delegation of authority. In **centralization,** a limited amount of authority is delegated; in **decentralization,** a significant amount of authority is delegated to lower levels. Each form has its advantages and disadvantages and is affected by a number of factors, such as size of organization and the amount of geographic dispersion.

ORGANIZATIONAL STRUCTURES

The primary formal relationships for organizing, as discussed earlier, are responsibility, authority, and accountability. They enable us to bring together functions, people, and other resources for the purpose of achieving objectives. The framework for organizing these formal relationships is known as the **organizational structure.** It provides the means for clarifying and communicating the lines of responsibility, authority, and accountability.

MAJOR TYPES OF ORGANIZATIONAL STRUCTURE

Although there are a number of variations of organizational structure, we shall discuss line and staff organizations and committee organization here.

• *LINE ORGANIZATION*

The **line organization** is the simplest organizational structure. It is the "doing" organization, in that the work of all organizational units is directly involved in producing and marketing the organization's goods and services. There are direct vertical links between the different levels of the scalar chain. Since there is a clear authority structure, this form of organization promotes greater decision-making and is simple in form to understand.

On the other hand, managers may be overburdened when they have too many duties. Figure 11-12 illustrates a simple line organization.

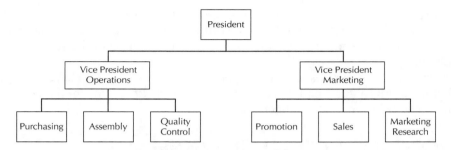

Figure 11-12. Line organization.

• *LINE AND STAFF ORGANIZATION*

When staff specialists are added to a line organization to "advise," "serve," or "support" the line in some manner, we have a **line and staff organization.** These specialists contribute to the effectiveness and efficiency of the organization. Their authority is generally limited to making recommendations to the line organization. Sometimes this creates conflict. However, such conflict can be reduced by having staff specialists obtain some line experience, which will tend to make them better understand the problems facing the line managers they support. Such functions as human resources management and research and development are typical staff functions. Figure 11-13 provides an example of such a structure.

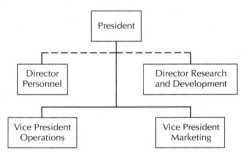

Figure 11-13. Line and staff organization.

• *COMMITTEE ORGANIZATION*

When a group of people is formally appointed to consider or decide certain matters, this type of structure is a **committee.** Committees can be permanent (standing) or temporary and usually supplement line and staff functions. Sometimes ad hoc or temporary committees are set up to deal with a specific problem. Once this committee makes its recommendations, it is dissolved. On the other hand, permanent committees usually act in an advisory capacity to certain organizational units or managers. For example, committees are used to a large extent in universities. They may report to a dean or department chair. Certain committees, called plural committees, have the authority to order, not just to recommend. These committees are usually reserved for a very high level, such as the board of directors. An example is an executive committee of the board for compensation or for succession planning.

Although committees have a number of advantages, they also have a number of disadvantages, particularly being excessively time consuming. Hence they should be managed effectively.

ORGANIZATIONAL STRUCTURE AND ENVIRONMENT AND TECHNOLOGY

Most studies that have been conducted on the relationship between organizational structure and the environment have concluded that the best organizational structure is contingent to some degree on the conditions in the environment. Several studies have also shown a relationship between technology and structure. In fact, these researchers even suggest that technology itself determines structure. These studies and others have lead to a **Contingency Approach** to **organizational structure.**

CONTINGENCY APPROACH

This approach indicates that the most appropriate organizational structure depends not only on the organizational objectives but also on the situation, which includes the environment, the technology employed, the rate and pace of change, the managerial style, the size of the organization, and other dynamic forces.

By the year 2000, the period of change resulted in organizational change, with many of the old hierarchies being replaced with flat structures, cross-functional teams, and empowered and highly skilled employees making their own decisions, all made possible by developments in information technology and communications.

Communications within organizations will continue to evolve utilizing information technology-based office automation, as well as the latest technology offered by the Internet and video conferencing. The increasing use of this technology will make where managers are based less important, and the emphasis in the management of human resources will be switched to measurement by performance and away from the traditional need to be in the office from 9 AM to 5 PM each day. Management information systems will enable managers and other staff to view high-level information in multiple dimensions for faster decision-making.*

---

* Margaret May, "Preparing Organizations to Manage the Future," *Management Accounting*, London, February 1997, vol. 75, no. 2, pp. 28–32.

INVESTIGATING COMPETITIVE ADVANTAGE: THE VALUE CHAIN

Few strategists and organizational planners have the ability to view the organization as a whole and recognize opportunities for creating **competitive advantage.** That is why the traditional method of surveying strengths and weaknesses divides the organization into smaller, more manageable subsystems and why the resource-based view looks for competitive opportunities in light of the firm's unique competencies and resources. Once potential strengths and opportunities have been translated in terms of resources and competencies, it is important to investigate deeper relationships and determine how and where these factors actually add value. An interesting illustration is reported in Exhibit 1 relating to the value of academic medical centers as engines for economic development within the community.

Exhibit 1
Value Added, Economic Development, and Academic Medical Centers*

Why should a state support academic medical centers? Because of their unique research and teaching mission and the patient mix, costs are almost always higher than at other hospitals. The quality of their services may or may not be better than that of competitors.

In addition to patient care, academic medical centers can be valuable aids for economic development. Three academic medical centers in Virginia, for example, have reported that they spend $2.7 billion each year on goods and services, employ 26,520 people, and create an additional 31,591 jobs among private sector firms that sell goods and services to the centers. The resulting impact is significant:

1. One dollar in every $84 in the state can be traced to academic medical centers.

2. State government receives more than $116 million in tax revenue as a direct result of the centers' operations.

3. Visiting clinicians, patients, and students inject another $103.8 million into the state's economy.

4. Patients from outside Virginia who came to the state for specialized care spend $30.6 million on nonhealth-related goods and services.

5. In 1995, biomedical research conducted at the medical centers brought in more than $160 million in research funds.

*Source: "Academic Medicine," *Hospitals and Health Networks.* 70, no. 6, March 20, 1996, p. 14.

The report, based on a study by Tripp, Umback, and Associates of Pittsburgh, indicated that academic medical centers are good investments and add considerable value to the state's economic development activities.

YOU SHOULD REMEMBER

The framework for organizing the formal relationships of responsibility, authority, and accountability is known as the **organizational structure.** There are a number of variations of organizational structure, including line, line and staff, and committee.

Most studies of organizational structure indicate a relationship to the environment as well as to the technology employed. Consequently, a **Contingency Approach** to organizational structure has developed, which indicates that a number of dynamic forces can and do affect structure.

KNOW THE CONCEPTS
DO YOU KNOW THE BASICS?

1. What is departmentalization?

2. What are the primary forms of departmentalization?

3. Describe a matrix form of departmentalization.

4. Why is delegation the art of managing?

5. Describe how the process of delegation works.

6. What is meant by the parity of authority and responsibility?

7. What is the scalar principle?

8. In the organizational context, what is meant by centralization versus decentralization?

9. How do you differ between line and staff in organizational terms?

10. What is committee organization, and what forms can it take?

TERMS FOR STUDY

centralization
committee organization
Contingency Approach
cross-functional teams
decentralization
delegation
departmentalization
empowerment
environment
information technology
line organization

matrix organization
parity of responsibility and
   authority
project organization
reverse delegation
scalar principle (chain of
   command)
staff organization
team organization
technology
virtual organization

ANSWERS
KNOW THE BASICS

1. Departmentalization is the process in which related functions are grouped into manageable units to achieve the objective of the enterprise in the most efficient and effective manner.

2. The primary forms of departmentalization are by function, division, process, product, market, customer, geographic area, and matrix (also called project organization). In many organizations, a combination of these forms is used.

3. Departmentalization by matrix (or project) involves bringing together personnel with different backgrounds and experience that bear on a project and giving them a certain time period to complete it. Once the project is completed, these specialized personnel return to their regular work assignments.

4. Delegation is the art of managing because it makes management possible, and management is the process as well as the art and skill of getting results accomplished through other people.

5. The delegation process works as follows. The manager has certain defined objectives (i.e., results) to accomplish at the end of a budget period. He or she assigns the responsibilities (i.e., duties to be performed) to key employees, along with the commensurate authority to go with those responsibilities. The accomplishment of the assigned responsibilities should equal the defined objectives. The manager then develops standards of performance with each key employee (i.e., the conditions that should exist when a job is done well). These standards should be mutually developed to be effective. In essence, these standards of performance become the accountability of each employee for the budget

period. The successful accomplishment of the standards of performance should equal the assigned responsibilities. The process continues with the appraisal of the key subordinates against the agreed-upon standards of performance and closes with evaluation and feedback to the beginning of the next budget cycle, when the process begins all over again.

6. It means that authority should equal responsibility.

7. The scalar principle means that there should be a clear definition of authority in the organization and that this authority flows, one link at a time, through the chain of command.

8. The issues of centralization and decentralization involve the principle of delegation of authority. When a limited amount of authority is delegated in an organization, it is usually characterized as centralized. When a significant amount of authority is delegated to lower levels in the organization, the business is characterized as decentralized.

9. The line is the simplest organizational structure. It is the "doing" organization, in that the work of all organizational units is directly involved in producing and marketing the organization's goods and services. When staff specialists are added to a line organization to "advise," "serve," or "support" the line in some manner, we have a line and staff organization. Staff authority is generally limited to making recommendations to the line and contributing to the effectiveness and efficiency of the organization.

10. When a group of people is formally appointed to consider or decide certain matters, this type of structure is a committee. Committees can be permanent (standing) or temporary and usually supplement the line and staff functions.

12

STAFFING: HUMAN RESOURCES MANAGEMENT

KEY TERMS

BFOQ (bona fide occupational qualification) the selection criteria used to hire a new employee; criteria that refer to job-related aspects and that do not violate the laws against discrimination

career path a planned progression of jobs within an organization, each of which develops business or technical skills necessary for the next higher level position

compensation a system for fairly and equitably rewarding each employee. Generally, compensation can be viewed as *cash* (i.e., salary) and *non-cash* (i.e., the value of all other benefits such as sick leave, vacation, health and welfare benefits, tuition payments, social security payments).

development the human resource function that emphasizes the development of skills in employees so that they may better perform their current job and enhance their abilities to perform additional, more difficult, or higher level jobs in the organization in the future

Human Resource Management the term generally applied to those activities concerning the management of people. It includes the typical personnel functions, such as recruitment, selection, compensation, training, development, research and audit, and separation. It may also include other functions such as overseeing programs of Affirmative Action, Equal Employment Opportunity, Safety, Industrial Health, and Performance Appraisal.

> **Labor Relations** a management function that addresses rules, regulations, and procedures regarding how employee behavior and performance are managed
>
> **recruitment and selection** the process by which a new employee or new employees are attracted to the organization and are chosen to fill specific positions
>
> **research and audit** activities undertaken to assess Human Resource Management's efficiency and effectiveness. Research and audit studies form a factual basis for decisions about future human resource programs as well as ensure compliance with current regulations.
>
> **separation** the functional term describing the manner in which an employee leaves the organization
>
> **task specialization** or **division of labor** the belief that productivity results for employees specializing in specific jobs and developing the skills necessary to perform those jobs; advanced by Charles Babbage and used by Henry Ford to create the modern industrial assembly line

Managing human resources is quite different from, let's say, managing the production of widgets in an assembly line. To produce the widgets, one must order x number of widget-producing resources, each of which is assumed to be identical, and can be reordered by specifying the lot number or reorder number. Unlike the widget resources, human resources cannot be so easily categorized, or reordered, or processed through an assembly line.

Each person brings a different talent, level of expectation, contribution, and sometimes problem to the organization. Organizations cannot purchase human resources *en masse*, nor can a day's work be used twice; a day's work lost is a day's work lost and can only be replaced by another human resource doing that particular job. A day's low productivity is an even worse situation, since the person is costing resources but not turning out the fullest level of production. Although the organization can discharge the person under certain conditions, the person can leave the organization at any time; thus the organization must continually strive to maintain a positive environment to encourage each individual to continually do his or her most productive work. This benefits both the person and the organization.

HISTORY OF HUMAN RESOURCES FUNCTION

EMERGENCE OF AN INDUSTRIAL ECONOMY

Let's take a brief look at the history and background of the human resources function in the United States. During the late 1800s, the country witnessed a movement from an agrarian, home-work economy to that of an emerging industrial economy. There was a basic shift from self-employment to working for steel mills, railroads, or other large factories. By 1870 the Industrial Revolution was well under way. This "new" mode of working involved participating in only one portion of the finished product as opposed to the "old" mode of being responsible for the total product, whether that product was house cleaning, raising vegetables, or forging a cast iron part for a buggy. This "new" work environment forced a division of labor and a need for management of people in an organizational setting. As these phenomena occurred, specialists developed in such areas as hiring and plant safety.

The period 1900 to the 1940s saw the growth and development of large, factory-type organizations and their personnel programs, the enactment of many key laws, and the emergence of social science principles to guide Human Resource Management. One of the most important contributors to management in this era was the founder of "Scientific Management," Frederick W. Taylor, who in 1911 authored *Principles of Scientific Management.* Taylor was an industrial engineer and a strong advocate of management's responsibility to plan and the worker's responsibility to execute the work. Taylor introduced such methods as time and motion studies, incentive wages, and measures of technical efficiency. As Taylor stated in his book *Shop Management,* "Each man must learn how to give up his own particular way of doing things, adjust his methods to the many new standards, and grow accustomed to receiving and obeying directions covering details, large and small, which in the past may have been left to this individual's judgment." This type of philosophy is, in part, responsible for one of the most popular slogans of the time: "The right man in the right job."

The 1920s were a decade in which several new developments occurred in the Human Resource Management field. During World War I, the U.S. Army began to use tests to recruit and select officers. On-the-job training programs began. One of the most famous studies began in 1927 at the Hawthorne plant of the Western Electric Company. These pioneering studies were conducted by Elton Mayo and his associates. The purpose of the studies was to determine the effect of physical factors (such as hours of work and periods of rest) on productivity. The findings of the study were that informal factors (such as social environment and informal work groups) could have an equal or greater impact on productivity. From the human resource perspective, this study formed an important basis for social programs, such as Recreation, Employee Benefits, and Counseling.

BEGINNINGS OF LABOR ORGANIZATIONS

The major influences of the 1930s were undoubtedly the Depression and the emergence of labor organizations. Human Resource Management programs, previously initiated in the 1920s, were now in a retrenchment phase as management emphasis shifted more toward increased productivity and worker emphasis shifted toward job security. In 1935, the National Labor Relations Act, usually called the Wagner Act, was passed. This act, often referred to as the Magna Carta of labor, recognized unions as being authorized representatives of employees and forced employers to bargain collectively with unions. Thus began a new facet of Human Resource Management: the need to negotiate with unions as intermediaries between workers and management. In 1938, the Fair Labor Standards Act was passed. This act set a federal minimum wage and stated the conditions under which overtime must be paid.

PROLIFERATION OF LAWS INFLUENCING THE WORKPLACE

The post-World War 1940s through the 1970s saw a proliferation of federal laws influencing and guiding managerial discretion in the human resources arena. Of importance are:

- 1946—Employment Act of 1946, stating the national goal of full employment.

- 1947—Labor Management Relations Act, as amended, placing some restrictions on union activities.

- 1962—Manpower Training and Development Act, providing special funds for the unskilled.

- 1963—Equal Pay Amendment to the Fair Labor Standards Act, prohibiting pay differences based on sex.

- 1964—Civil Rights Act, prohibiting discrimination based on race, color, or national origin.

- 1967—Age Discrimination in Employment Act, prohibiting discrimination based on age and protecting workers between the ages of 40 and 65.

- 1970—Occupational Safety and Health Act (OSHA), establishing health and safety standards and modes of enforcement.

- 1972—Equal Employment Opportunity Act, providing Affirmative Action programs.

- 1973—Rehabilitation Act of 1973, requiring employers to take affirmative action to hire handicapped persons (now referred to as physically challenged persons).

- 1973—Comprehensive Employment and Training Act (CETA), providing funds primarily for the hard-core unemployed.

- 1974—Employee Retirement Income Security Act (ERISA), regulating private pension systems.

- 1978—Amendment to Age Discrimination Act, extending protection to ages 40 to 70.

- 1982—Job Training Partnership Act, allocating billions of dollars to private industry councils to implement training for the hard-core unemployed. These councils, under private industry control, were designed to train people for long-lasting jobs in contrast to the typical CETA job, which lasted only 18 months. This act signaled the death of CETA.

- 1983—Civil Rights Act of 1983, prohibiting deprivation of any rights, privileges, or immunities secured by the Constitution and other laws, and allowing civil suits to recover for such deprivation. Although this must, according to the statute, involve a public official, the statute is being broadly interpreted and has been used to limit the kinds of laws for which management can lobby as well as the awarding of damages for discrimination in both the public and private sectors.

- 1992—Americans with Disabilities Act, providing for mandated accommodation for the physically challenged in terms of accessibility and prohibition of employment discrimination. This has had a profound impact upon employees, customers, and employment practices. With a gradual phase-in application to businesses of increasingly smaller size, it will eventually impact upon all business planning.

These laws have had a significant influence on the ways in which organizations manage their recruitment, selection, compensation, development, and separation programs. As a manager, one must ensure compliance with these laws in managing people.

In addition to these laws a considerable body of case law has developed affecting almost all aspects of employment. Case law is most extensive in the areas of sex discrimination, age, seniority, testing, personal history, and preferential selection.

It must also be noted that many pieces of legislation are "enabling" in that they create enforcement agencies that have defined regulatory powers and that promulgate rules and regulations binding upon businesses with penalties for noncompliance. This necessitates major efforts on the part of business to avoid violations. An example from the preceding list is the Equal Employment Opportunity Act that led to the Equal Employment Opportunity Commission (EEOC), and that has created a vast and sometimes perplexing body of rules and regulations governing conduct in the workplace. It has further been given enforcement powers to ensure compliance. Thus, one of the most valuable functions of a trade or professional association, in addition to lobbying for new laws and rules, is to monitor and evaluate legislators and rule- and regulation-makers to gauge the impact of such new legal requirements and to assist businesses in meeting their obligations. It must be noted that liability for violation of laws regulating conduct in the workplace has increasingly been assessed not only against organizations, but against individual managers who are being called to account personally for their conduct. And given that both individual and organizational discriminatory actions result in well-publicized negative publicity in the national media, it is clear that discrimination can seriously tarnish a business's reputation.

One can only speculate about the future, but several trends are becoming apparent. First, there are no indications that federal regulations regarding Human Resource Management will decrease; recent court decisions, for example, have maintained Affirmative Action and equal opportunity law provisions. Second, glancing back to the pre-World War II types of Human Resource Management, one sees personnel departments which tended to dictate policy to the organization. Today, and even more likely so tomorrow, Human Resource Management is regarded as part of every manager's job. Evidence of this trend can be found in, for example, the amount of on-the-job training for new managers in the art of communicating, motivating, and managing subordinates. Third, one must acknowledge the changing nature of the workforce. In the recent past, "the right person for the right job" may have meant a lifetime in the same job or industry; today career changes are much more common. Flexibility is important as more people adopt alternative lifestyles, work sharing, and part-time work; time for parenting and child care, in particular, have become important components of workforce expectations. Lastly, the workforce itself is changing, with increased numbers of minorities and an increase in the median age of the population. Each of these trends has an impact on the available supply of potential employees, on the human resource programs that each organization will choose to sponsor, on the records that must be kept to document compliance, and on how each manager will manage his/her human resources.

> # YOU SHOULD REMEMBER
>
> **Human Resource Management** in the United States has evolved over the last century from narrow aspects such as hiring and firing to a broader view of employees as complex persons with a variety of needs. Managers today take the broader view in managing human resources.

FUNCTIONS OF HUMAN RESOURCES MANAGEMENT
PLANNING

Human resources planning stresses the interrelationships between jobs within an organization. A *career path* is a progression of jobs linked together, each of which furnishes skills and/or experience necessary for advancement to the next job. The interrelationship between the jobs is the main difference between a business position that is part of the career path and the business position that does not qualify the individual for advancement. The contemporary organization contains both career paths and jobs that are not part of any career path. **Human resources planning** aids management in the design of career paths as well as successful recruitment for personnel to take positions in the career path. The gamut, then, of human resources planning runs from career path or job design to recruitment, appraisal, and rewards systems design and implementation. Human resource planning, however, is differentiated from personnel administration in that it views all these elements as interrelated parts of a dynamic total organizational system. The previous chapter dealing with organizational behavioral controls already covered performance appraisal systems, and the rest of this chapter discusses the central issues related to the organizational management of human resources.

As previously stated, a career path is composed of sequential jobs that are interrelated and that lead to higher positions within the organization. An example of a *vertical career path* is shown in Figure 12-1. A new employee entering the organization begins with the secretarial position. This position is held for at least six months before the individual may move up the career path to the next job, that of senior secretary. A worker who advances after the minimum required time in this position is considered an employee on the *fast track*. If an employee were found not suitable for advancement after the maximum time allowed for the position, in this case two years, the organization might conclude that this was not an ambitious individual.

As an employee advances up the career path, here symbolized by a stair-step arrangement, new skills are acquired and greater knowledge of the business gained. By requiring a minimum number of years in each position or *time in grade*, the company accomplishes two advantageous goals: (1) it ensures that employees have enough time to gain the skills necessary for advancement and (2) it allows time for improved interpersonal and leadership skills by virtue of increased maturity and experience.

Figure 12-1 illustrates a five-step career path, and the office manager level is the highest possible job attainable on this particular career path. Two points are important here: (1) if an employee wanted to advance beyond the office manager level, he or she would have to move to a completely different career path and (2) just because an employee begins on this career path, there is no assurance that he or she will advance to the highest possible level. Many employees' careers stall or even stop at a lower level, a phenomenon known as *career plateauing*. There is nothing wrong with this; an organization cannot promote everyone, and competent individuals are needed at all levels. Further, a career may plateau because of factors beyond the employee's control. A stalled career is not necessarily an indication of employee failure. When faced with a plateaued career, an employee has several options. He or she may (1) ask for a transfer to a different career path in the same organization, (2) quit and seek a job with a different company where there are promotion opportunities, or (3) accept that the career has plateaued and continue in the same job.

In human resources planning, specialists assess the personnel needs of the company and create the necessary career paths. Career paths are created to facilitate the accomplishment of organizational goals, and if a career path ceases to serve the organization's needs, it may be eliminated. The example shown is a *vertical career path* in which the jobs are placed in a hierarchical arrangement. There is also a *horizontal career path*. An example of this, taken from the advertising industry, is shown in Figure 12-2. In this career path, the employee is expected to complete the internship experience, consisting of time spent in the marketing research, copywriting, account executive, and marketing services areas, *before* being promoted to the position

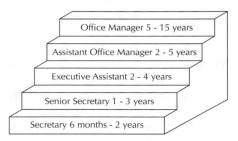

Office Manager 5 - 15 years

Assistant Office Manager 2 - 5 years

Executive Assistant 2 - 4 years

Senior Secretary 1 - 3 years

Secretary 6 months - 2 years

Figure 12–1. Career path from secretary to office manager—a vertical career path.

of assistant vice president. The jobs exist in a horizontal arrangement, and the employee can enter the internship experience at any job. These jobs are not interdependent and, therefore, do not exist in a sequential arrangement. The career advancement to assistant vice president will take place only after the internship is completed but can occur after the completion of any of the individual jobs, provided that the other components of the internship have been completed.

The career path differs from the job in that the former obviously leads to higher positions within the organization and the latter does not. Not every career path leads to the top of a business organization; in general, although there are exceptions, career paths that feature significant line positions tend to lead to the top run of organizational management. Keeping in mind the many exceptions, the career paths to the top of a manufacturing organization would be production and operations, marketing and sales, legal, and financial. Staff career paths, such as personnel and human resources, advertising, and public affairs, do not generally lead to the top organizational level.

One of the most popular questions asked during a job interview tests the job candidate's knowledge of the relationship between the job being sought and its career path. The individual will be asked, "Where do you think you'll be in five years?" This question actually asks, "How much do you know about the career path? How far along that career path do you expect to be in five years?" Even though the interview is usually for a specific job, that job may be part of a career path. The enterprise conducting the interview must judge the suitability of the job applicant for the specific position and for the higher positions in the career path. An applicant may be acceptable for a specific job but be judged unacceptable for the career path of which the job is a part. This job candidate will probably be rejected.

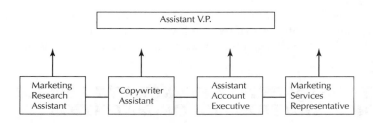

Figure 12–2. Horizontal career path.

YOU SHOULD REMEMBER

A **career path** consists of a series of jobs existing in either a **vertical hierarchy** of interdependent sequential jobs, or a **horizontal arrangement** of jobs that are not sequentially interdependent but must be completed before moving to the next higher position in the organization. Organizations are made up of both career paths and jobs that are not part of career paths. If an individual has risen to a level within a career path and then fails to rise further, the career of this manager is described as **plateaued.**

RECRUITMENT

Each manager will undoubtedly need, at some point in his or her career, to recruit and select subordinates. This section discusses alternatives for recruiting personnel—within the organization or outside the organization—that are within current laws and regulations.

There are many alternatives for recruitment. Among the most common are recruiting people from within the organization and from outside the organization.

• *TECHNIQUES FOR RECRUITING PEOPLE WITHIN THE ORGANIZATION*

At times a manager may want to select people from within the organization for new positions. There are several ways to do this:

Job Posting. Many employers periodically (perhaps once or twice a week) list positions available. These lists are posted in heavy traffic places like the cafeteria, where they are highly visible, or sometimes they are published in employee publications. This gives an opportunity for current employees to apply for a position. Additionally, current employees may refer their colleagues or friends for a position.

Search of Existing Files. An organization may have an existing database of skills and interests of its employees as a source. Periodic review of these files may reveal employees well suited to a new position in the company.

• *TECHNIQUES FOR RECRUITING PEOPLE FROM OUTSIDE THE ORGANIZATION*

Advertising. This is a common technique for recruitment, but must be thought out carefully, since advertisements are fairly costly and must portray, in an honest way, the particulars of the position. Most advertisements will state "Equal Employment Opportunity Employer." Advertisements can be placed in a local newspaper, a national newspaper, or in a specialty publication, such as *The Tool Engineer*, for a highly specialized person.

Use of Employment Agencies. There are both public (supported by tax revenues) and private (supported by fees paid for each placement) employment agencies. Since private agencies are supported by fees, they tend to provide more specific services to the client. These private agencies may include search services and/or management consulting services.

Referrals by Current Employees. Employees' friends, family, and colleagues can be an important source of referrals. When people to fill a particular occupation (e.g., nurses, secretaries, data processing professionals) are in short supply, some organizations develop incentives for employees to refer others.

Other Organizations. Colleges, universities, labor unions, and professional organizations can also be valuable sources of recruitment.

Other. Other recruitment possibilities include Internet-based job references/resume services, casual or unsolicited applications, and temporary help agencies.

SELECTION

Selection is the process by which the job applicants are screened and interviewed and a hiring decision made. Figure 12-3 illustrates the sequential steps that comprise the selection process. There is no one way to facilitate the employee selection process, and much depends upon the nature of the job itself. As can be seen in this figure, after the initial reception and screening of the prospective employee a company may require some form of employment testing. A typing test given to prospective secretaries and clerical employees is an example of this kind of skills testing. In fact, with regard to a secretary, the employment testing may be sufficient to make the hiring decision, in which case no other employment process steps would be necessary. Some jobs, however, most notably those at the midmanagement level and above, may not require any employment testing but do require some of the other steps.

The next stage in the employment selection process is usually some sort of interview, and because this is such a widespread practice, it is discussed in depth in the next section. References may be checked, a background information search accomplished, and a medical examination completed before either an interview with a supervisor or the actual hiring decision (in which case there may not have been any supervisory interview). The decid-

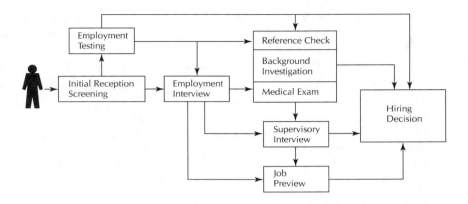

Figure 12–3. Employee selection process.

ing factor about the actual performance of any of these functions in the employee selection process is, "What is required by the job?"

In the selection process, management must take great care to avoid any form of discrimination, for this can be punished by law. A hiring decision must be based upon criteria that are *job-related*. Such factors as sex, religion, race, political affiliation, age, place of origin, or marital status cannot be used in the selection process; they are not job-related and would be declared illegal according to the *Equal Economic Opportunity* (EEO) guidelines. Any criterion used in employee selection must be a *bona fide occupational qualification* (BFOQ), that is, job-related. For example, the EEOC has ruled that airlines cannot refuse employment to a male as an airline attendant even though most flight attendants are women. Being a female is not a requirement of the job, and therefore cannot be used as a selection criterion. Additionally, being a woman does not automatically disqualify a woman from becoming a member of the fire department. Any pre-employment test must measure a BFOQ if that test influences the selection decision. Because interviews are so commonly used in the selection process, a more in-depth discussion is in order.

• *INTERVIEW*

It is generally acknowledged that the **interview** should allow management to determine three things: (1) Does the prospective employee have the necessary qualifications for the job under consideration? If technical skills are involved, some sort of skills testing may be incorporated within the initial interview or scheduled immediately after. (2) Does the prospective employee possess the necessary motivation both to perform the job and to remain employed for a sufficiently long period of time to justify the expense of hiring and training? And finally, (3) Does the prospective employee "fit" with the existing company culture? Often, after the formal interview, a prospective employee will be taken out to lunch or dinner by a small group of current employees. Many a job has been lost because the individual was not aware that the group meal was a different kind of interview, albeit in a more relaxed, informal, social setting.

Interviews, of whatever form, offer a great opportunity for both the prospective employee and employer to look each other over. Just as the individual is interviewed by the company, so also is the company interviewed by the individual. Therein is one of the major difficulties associated with interviews. Both parties are on their best behavior, and neither may be showing a realistic view. Individuals present themselves in the best of light, and the company may speak glowingly of the job.

The strength of the interview, however, is found in the communication theory that is discussed in Chapter 17. The personal interview allows an appraisal based not only upon verbal messages but also upon body language. The individual who sounded so confident in the letter and over the phone may communicate nervousness and lack of ability in the personal interview.

Before conducting an employment interview, the manager should:

1. Determine the questions to be asked or information to be gathered. This should be the same for all job candidates to ensure that they can be compared. Interviews should be standardized in content and consistent.

2. If the interviewer is not a good speaker, these questions should be practiced before peers. Rehearsal can only help.

3. Determine the timing: a good interview takes between thirty and sixty minutes. Interviews generally cannot be scheduled effectively without a sufficient interval between them to allow the interviewer to digest the previous candidate and prepare for the next.

4. Review the necessary qualifications for the job.

5. After the initial conversation, designed to put the candidate at ease, the questions should be job-related.

6. At no time should the candidate be asked questions that either violate or appear to violate the EEO guidelines. No questions concerning race, religion, marital status, political affiliation, age, sexual orientation, or national origin are acceptable. *Questions should be job-related.*

7. Before conducting the interview, the manager will find it useful to review the personnel application form that has been filled in by the applicant. If this form is correctly structured, it should reveal much information about the candidate.

YOU SHOULD REMEMBER

The **job interview** is the major selection device used by a business to determine the fit between the organization and the prospective employee. Job interviews demand a great deal of preparation, and those employees tasked with conducting an interview need to be trained and possess a high level of communication skills.

Within these guidelines there are three general formats for the employee selection interview. These are the structured interview, the unstructured interview, and the stress interview.

• *STRUCTURED INTERVIEW*

The **structured interview,** also called the **patterned interview,** makes use of predetermined questions. The predetermination of questions ensures that every interview will be in a standardized format and will gather comparable employee data. This helps prevent illegal questioning and promotes interview consistency. The questions are gathered together in an *interview protocol*, which is then used for each interview. Four different kinds of questions may be asked: (1) *job-knowledge questions* seek to ascertain if the candidate possesses knowledge essential to the job performance; (2) *job-simulation questions* ask the candidate to simulate some aspect of job performance to determine if he or she knows not only the theoretical knowledge necessary for the job (Question 1), but also facets of the actual task performance; (3) *situational questions* test how the applicant would act in a specific situation—this may relate to an actual job situation or may be to determine how the individual would respond in a general situation; and (4) *work willingness* questions attempting to determine the candidate's availability and motivation to work.

• *UNSTRUCTURED INTERVIEW*

The **unstructured interview,** unlike the structured interview, may have an interview protocol that contains general, open-ended questions or no protocol at all. This form of interview is much more free form and features general job-related questions. It is not unusual for such an interview to begin with such general questions as "Broadly describe your career goals" or even "Tell me something about yourself." Whereas each structured interview is approximately the same, unstructured interviews are likely to be unique. To ensure a minimal degree of comparability between job candidates, many interviewers combine both the structured and unstructured interview formats.

• STRESS INTERVIEW

During the **stress interview,** the job candidate is deliberately placed under a great deal of stress. This is contrived by the setting, often with either very bright or obviously inadequate lighting, by two or more interviewers acting in concert to prevent the candidate from being at ease (they may alternate questions and perhaps stand far apart to create the necessity of dividing individual attention), with argumentative, often provocative questions. The rationale for the stress interview is that the candidate is, under pressure, less likely to present a facade—the real person will be revealed. Managers also believe it is valuable to know how someone will perform under stress conditions.

There are two major criticisms of the stress interview: (1) Performance under stress is rarely job-related, so the data derived from such an interview are of little value in determining who will be the best employee. (2) The stress interview, in addition to not yielding relevant job performance information, may actually dissuade a prospective employee from continuing to apply for the job; it will "turn them off." Additionally, even if the person accepts the job, they may harbor resentment against the interviewers. In rare cases, a stress interview may lead to a complaint with the EEOC or other agencies for discrimination.

Selection Process

DO

- Read the person's application or resume carefully before the interview.

- Put the interviewee at ease; ask him or her to sit down.

- Describe the position and the organization honestly; have a position description available, if possible.

- Ask questions that cannot be answered by "yes" or "no." Ask the interviewee to explain his/her answers.

- Feel free to ask for references and to check them out.

DON'T

- Ask about the interviewee's marital status, maiden name, ethnic background, age, religious preference, sexual orientation, or armed services discharge. These are some of the questions generally not legal under current law.

- Give a quick, five-minute interview. This person may be working with you (hopefully) for a long period of time.

- Insist that the applicant take your special pre-employment test. It may be against the law.

Once a new employee is hired, the manager must be sure that the new employee passes a physical, if necessary, and that the start date and salary are firmly agreed upon.

YOU SHOULD REMEMBER

Hiring and selection is the first step toward a productive relationship with an employee. Taking the time to interview thoroughly and fairly can result in a long-term, motivated employee.

COMPENSATION

Compensation systems are important to all employees. In general, these can be categorized into two types: *cash,* which refers to wages and/or salaries, and *non-cash,* which includes all the other benefits employees receive.

• *CASH COMPENSATION*

Cash compensation typically includes any one or more of the following:

- *Salary*—the money received for one's work over a period of time. Generally, salaried people are not paid overtime and are paid the same salary each pay period.

- *Hourly wages*—money received for working the base number of hours each week. Any hours worked above the base number (can be 35, or 37.5, or 40 hours) are paid at overtime rates in accordance with the provisions of the Fair Labor Standards Act of 1938.

- *Incentive or piecework wage*—this is paid based on the number of units produced. Usually a base hourly wage is paid and the incentive or piece rate is paid on top of that. It is to the worker's advantage to produce as many pieces as possible since monetary rewards increase as production increases.

- *Bonus*—a one-time payment to employees based on the total organization's performance during a specified period of time, or in some cases, based on individual employee performance during a period of time.

• *NON-CASH COMPENSATION*

Although not generally regarded as important in past years, **non-cash compensation,** especially in the form of health care insurance, is becoming an important factor in attracting and retaining qualified employees. Recent articles have shown a growing concern about the rising cost of all insurances. Managers should show employees the value of their organization's non-cash compensation programs.

General areas of non-cash compensation include:

- health care insurance (hospital, major medical, dental, drug, optical, hearing aid, etc.)
- legal assistance counseling programs
- day care provisions for employees' children
- paid time off such as sick days, vacation, maternity, paternity, condolence days, personal days
- tuition assistance programs
- Employee Health and Employee Assistance Programs
- special awards and employee recognition programs
- social security, state disability and unemployment benefits contributions
- pension contributions (401K plans)

Non-cash compensation may amount to anywhere from 20 to 40 percent of each dollar spent on salary. In other words, for each dollar in pay, an additional twenty to thirty cents is spent on the same employee for non-cash benefits.

YOU SHOULD REMEMBER

Compensation is of two types: **cash,** including salary, hourly wages, and bonus; and **non-cash,** including health care insurance, pension contributions, tuition and legal assistance programs, and other programs.

• *FACTORS THAT AFFECT COMPENSATION*

Factors that affect compensation that must be considered by management include supply and demand, labor unions, a company's ability to pay and its productivity, and government regulation.

SUPPLY AND DEMAND

All companies within a geographic area, national or regional, are in competition for a finite supply of labor. Often this competition is not noticeable because the pool of available labor is large and there are many applicants for every advertised job vacancy. If the job is highly technical and specialized or requires a great deal of education or previous experience (for example, patent lawyers, chemists, petroleum geologists, systems engineers, computer network designers, physicians, or tool-and-die makers), a company may have a great deal of difficulty in finding qualified personnel. In this case, the competition for the few qualified personnel is fierce and the company must offer an increased level of compensation to attract and retain applicants. This increased compensation rate, reflecting the current **supply and demand** of labor, is generally termed the *going rate*.

Because supply and demand influence the cost of acquiring and retaining human resources, management is faced with the task of measuring, analyzing, and, if possible, anticipating the changing supply and demand for labor. This is not an easy task, but there are some general guidelines. If the economy is prosperous and companies are growing and expanding, there is great competition for the available labor supply. In such an expanding economy, management must pay "top dollar" to acquire and retain workers. If the economy is experiencing a depression and companies let workers go to adjust to market conditions, there is an increased supply of labor. The wage rate generally falls and businesses that are hiring may be able to pick and choose from those seeking work.

Management must continually be attentive to the changing supply and demand factors in the labor arena. Useful information can be gathered by managers by means of:

- speaking to managerial peers at other companies.

- listening to worker comments about wage rates at other firms.

- analyzing wage rates in help-wanted advertisements and in trade or professional journals.

- participating in and contributing to industrywide wage and salary surveys conducted by industry groups, trade associations, and government agencies.

LABOR UNIONS

Labor unions have traditionally exerted powerful control over workers in certain industries. Wage and benefit determination was often the product of successful concerted action by workers in the forms of strikes and labor actions designed to influence management. Local unions banded together to form a "national" union whose various locals could support action by other local union chapters. Union membership, though, has been steadily declining as the accomplishments of past union leadership have become the entitlements of a new generation of workers who take such benefits for granted, together with the specific migration of many traditionally unionized jobs to foreign countries where labor costs are significantly less. Union membership, formerly one out of every four workers in America, is now down to less than 10 percent. However, where they do exist, unions continue to have a major impact upon wage and benefit rates.

Even if a company is not unionized, its workers are influenced by the prevailing union wage rate for comparable jobs. Nonunionized employees may well demand compensation similar to that received by their union counterparts, and it is important that management pay attention to what is happening within union ranks.

A COMPANY'S ABILITY TO PAY AND ITS PRODUCTIVITY

A company that is profitable is able to pay higher wages than a company that is not profitable. The successful company is able to pay the going rate, but employees of the less successful company may not be able to command such wages even if they perform similar jobs. Since the latter company does not have the ability to pay the going rate, its employees may leave to seek jobs with more successful firms. If a firm has the ability, it may wish to consider paying a wage higher than the going rate to promote greater employee loyalty.

A company's **ability to pay** is usually directly related to its level of **productivity.** This concept was evident in the earlier-cited open systems model. This is shown again in Figure 12-4, which is a simplified version of the earlier Figure 4-3. If an organization is truly productive, this is evident in the results of the transformation process. In Chapter 4 this transformation process was described as a valued added process, since the output is ideally worth more than the input factors. The value of the output is determined by the marketplace, that is, a product is worth what someone else is willing to pay for it. Companies fit one of the following situations:

Input > output   company losing money
Input = output   company breaking even
Input < output   company making money

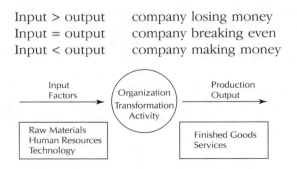

Figure 12-4. Open systems model of an organization.

The difference in the last example between input and output is called *gross profit*. Productivity is measured as the relationship between the value of the input factors and the output production of goods or services. This is shown in the following manner:

$$\frac{\text{Output}}{\text{Input}} = \text{Return on assets or investment}$$

The return on assets or investment is greater than one (indicating profitability) only if the value of the production output is greater than the input factors. Only a genuinely productive organization can afford to pay competitive wages. Productivity not only influences the potential for paying competitive wages, but it can also prove an effective managerial tool for motivating employees. Managers, relating wages to productivity levels, can make workers understand that only by increasing productivity can the wage level rise.

GOVERNMENT REGULATION

Government regulation, one of the major facets of the external legal environment previously discussed in Chapters 3 and 4, often has a direct effect on compensation. Legislators, responding to both the injustices of the past on the part of ruthless employers and the demands of the labor electorate for higher standards of living, have passed laws that influence the wages paid to workers. Laws mandating a minimum level of wages and setting forth a standard work week (Fair Labor Standards Act of 1938 as amended), requiring equal pay for equal work (Equal Pay Act of 1963 as amended), and setting wage levels for companies that contract to provide goods or services to the federal government (Walsh-Healey and Davis-Bacon Acts) directly impact worker wage levels.

• MANAGEMENT, COMPENSATION, AND THE LAW

Compensation package design is a major function of the human resources function within the business organization, providing management with valuable and useful tools for the motivation of employees. Since decisions regarding compensation, either base salary or wages or variable incentives, involve employee ranking, there is always the possibility of abuse to the detriment of individual workers. It is not surprising that antidiscrimination legislation has been extended to cover the incentive decision process. Management must consider the legal requirements to ensure that its compensation package can function effectively as an employee motivator.

Title VII of the Civil Rights Act of 1964, as amended, prohibits discrimination based upon criteria that are not job-related, principally race, color, religion, sex, or national origin. This antidiscrimination legislation covers companies with fifteen or more employees, unions, local governments, and employment agencies. Discrimination of two general forms is prohibited:

- *Disparate treatment.* An employer cannot treat workers differently, a legal principle that effectively outlaws different standards for pay or promotion for different groups.

- *Disparate impact.* Employment practices that have a substantially different impact on different groups (ethnic, worker, sexual, political, national, and others) are outlawed.

Disparate impact is the more subtle of these two forms of discrimination, and the Human Resources Management staff must constantly guard against it. This practice was outlawed in the famous court decision of *Griggs versus Duke Power*, in which pre-employment tests used by the company were found to eliminate a disproportionate number of African Americans. The court ruled that the pre-employment tests were illegal because (1) they were not job-related and (2) the tests discriminated against African Americans. The company was not exonerated because the discrimination was unintentional. Management is held responsible for its actions, however unintentional. This subtlety of the concept of *disparate treatment* can be seen in this famous example in that *no specific individual act of discrimination was shown to have taken place.* The discrimination was to be found in the *impact* of the screening practices upon a specific group.

TRAINING AND DEVELOPMENT

In breaking down the Human Resources Management function into its many components—including listing **training** and **development** as one of the major ones—there is an absence of the term "education." Yet, an understanding of the key differences among training, education, and development is important in order to appreciate the relationships and meanings of these activities and their relevance in developing human resources.

One interesting approach is to think about the focus and evaluation of each of these activities. The focus of training is on the present job held by an individual. Evaluation of training is on the job. The focus of education is on a future job for which the individual is being prepared and the evaluation consequently will be on that future job. The focus of development, on the other hand, is on future organizational activities and evaluation is almost impossible.

All three activities are part of the Human Resources Development (HRD) concept, which means a series of organized activities conducted within a specified time, and designed to produce some type of behavioral change. Keeping this concept in mind, and the differences among the activities involved in it, should provide a better understanding of the on-the-job methods of development and off-the-job methods that follow.

The development of employees can take place in many ways, some formal and some very informal. This section outlines some on-the-job development methods and others that take place off the job.

• *ON-THE-JOB METHODS OF DEVELOPMENT*

Employees can be trained and develop new skills through several on-the-job techiques.

- *Orientation for new employees.* This can be formal, such as an all-day program sponsored by the employer, or informal, such as a manager spending a half hour with each new employee. If there is no orientation program, the new employee will, by default, develop his or her own, which may be more time consuming and less factual than a formal program.

- *Apprenticeship training.* Used widely in the trades, apprenticeship programs provide an opportunity for a person to work at less than the regular wage and to learn under the aegis of a skilled tradesperson.

- *Internships, residencies, assistantships, clerkships, and fellowships.* These offer paid opportunities to work in an area under a controlled educational setting. Specific schooling may be required in order to be considered for these programs; for example, completion of medical school is necessary before an internship at a particular hospital can occur.

- *On-the-job rotation.* Many companies rotate their personnel, especially their managers, every two or three years so that managers can gain a broad understanding of the entire organization.

- *Coaching.* Managers must coach and counsel subordinates. (A manager should also expect to receive this type of advice from his or her senior manager.) Coaching may be formal—for example, based on a Performance Appraisal Review (see Chapter 15)—or informal, such as a lunchtime discussion where ideas for changed performance are discussed.

- *Departmental staff meetings.* These can be powerful tools, when conducted appropriately, to develop staff. A manager might choose to hold weekly or bi-weekly staff meetings where staff members can present status reports on each of their projects or activities. This can help develop presentation skills, keep the staff informed about the department's activity, and create peer pressure on any members who may need to increase their production. A part of the staff meeting might be devoted to a short presentation or discussion of a new magazine article or pending legislation or regulation in your field or any other topic which can "stretch" the interests of manager and subordinates.

- *Company-sponsored courses.* Companies frequently sponsor on-site courses taught by inside or outside experts. The purpose of these courses is to bring managers together for a common learning experience; the application of the learning experience on the job is expected to increase productivity and/or enable the employee to assume greater duties.

- ## *OFF-THE-JOB TRAINING*

  - *Off-site seminars.* Attendance at an off-site seminar may have several purposes: learning; communicating with peers in the same profession or industry; and, perhaps, a reward for performance.

  - *Tuition assistance or reimbursement programs.* Many companies offer tuition aid for courses that are related to the employee's job.

Development activities generally are aimed at increasing job knowledge and improving interpersonal skills and understanding of the organization. Multiple techniques may be involved, including simulation exercises, videotaped presentations, in-basket exercises, job instruction training, case studies, and lectures.

YOU SHOULD REMEMBER

There are many avenues to assist employees in developing their skills. Since each person is unique and at a particular stage in his/her career, it is important to select the development method or methods appropriate at the time to the organization and to the person. **On-the-job** methods may include apprenticeship, coaching, job rotation, and staff meetings. **Off-the-job** methods may include off-site seminars and tuition reimbursement programs.

LABOR RELATIONS

Up to now, the chapter has assumed that management has a "free rein" in terms of the policies and procedures that cover employees. However, with the advent of unions and collective bargaining activities, a variety of "rules" may set some parameters as to how management actually manages employees.

Labor unions and unionism began growing soon after the passage of the National Labor Relations Act in the mid-1930s. From national memberships of slightly less than 15 percent of the workforce in 1935, unions grew to almost 25 percent of the U.S. workforce in the late 1940s. Since that time membership has been on a steady decline; unions now represent less than

10 percent of the total U.S. workforce (declining from 20.1 to 15.5 percent between 1983 and 1994, a relatively short and recent time frame).

Some of the reasons for this decline include changes in the nature of American industry: "smokestack" industries are being replaced with "service" industries where high-tech and white-collar workers are typically more resistant to joining labor unions; in recent years, unions have made "give backs" to management and have not been gaining the significant wage increases of the 1960s and 1970s; and older, less efficient U.S. industries are being replaced by more efficient, lower cost foreign competition.

Labor unions are organizations of workers formed to advance their members' interests. They are legal representatives of employees and, when officially recognized through an employee election, are empowered by federal law to bargain collectively and/or negotiate with management to determine the conditions under which employees will work. The result of this collective bargaining process or negotiation is a contract, which is a written agreement covering two basic areas:

- Working conditions, such as wages, hours, seniority, and time off; and the status of the union, that is, it is recognized as the bargaining agent and dues may be collected from employees covered by the contract.

- Rules and procedures for settling questions or disputes over the interpretation and/or application of the terms of the agreement.

It is the second of these two areas which is of great importance to the person responsible for managing people. In many labor contracts, there are very specific provisions about how to resolve disputes; these are generally referred to as Grievance Procedures.

• GRIEVANCE PROCEDURES

Although historically arising out of the labor union movement, **grievance procedures** today may apply to nonunion employees as well. Some companies and organizations have no unions at all, but do have grievance procedures for their employees. As examples, a grievance may arise when an employee feels that he or she has been passed over unfairly for a promotion or a raise or is being asked to perform a job which is inappropriate.

Grievances can be described generally as disagreements arising from changes in working conditions or from decisions made by lower level managers. There are as many specific grievance procedures as there are organizations and unions. There are, however, several concepts common to all:

- *Documentation.* "If it isn't written down, it doesn't exist." In any grievance procedure, specific evidence of the unfair treatment is key. Diaries, incident reports, and written material on prior warnings provide important data on the facts of the case.

- *Steps or tiers.* Every grievance procedure starts with a meeting of the grievant and the person supervising him or her. If unresolved, another step is required—perhaps a meeting with the department manager. Most grievance procedures have at least two steps—many have up to five steps.

- *Involvement of persons outside the grievant's department.* If the grievance cannot be resolved at the supervisory or managerial level, it is typically referred to a human resource professional, perhaps the Labor Relations Manager or the Personnel Manager. Grievances that are not resolved at this level may be referred to other areas inside or outside the organization.

- *Time requirements.* A grievance procedure usually specifies the time within which a hearing must be held or a response given. For example, Step 1 may require that the initial meeting between supervisor and employee be held within five working days after the employee has presented the supervisor with the written grievance request.

A TYPICAL GRIEVANCE

Step 1. The employee requests a grievance by presenting a written grievance request to the immediate supervisor. A meeting to air the facts must be held within the specified number of days. In most cases, the employee may bring a representative (e.g., union steward) to that meeting.

Step 2. The grievance might be referred to the department manager. The manager and supervisor, along with the grievant and representative, meet again and a written response is forwarded within the required time.

Step 3. If the grievance remains unresolved, the Labor Relations person or function is officially notified. A meeting, similar to that in Step 2, is held and all parties are present. If there is no resolution at this level, the grievance could go:

   (a) higher in the management structure of the organization or company. Some organizations refer grievances to the President, whose decision is final.

   (b) outside the organization for mediation and/or arbitration.

Mediation is a process whereby a neutral outside person (a mediator) is called in to talk with both sides in order to arrive at a solution that each party finds acceptable. If both parties accept the recommendations, the grievance is considered settled. The mediator's recommendations, however, are *not binding* and the grievance may still remain unresolved.

Arbitration is a process whereby a neutral outside person (an arbitrator) is called in to review the facts of the case, hold a hearing if necessary, and prepare a written determination as to the outcome of the case. Each party must agree in advance to use arbitration; the parties generally agree in advance also as to who will pay for the arbitrator. The decision of the arbitrator is *final;* no appeals can be made by either side. This is called "binding arbitration."

YOU SHOULD REMEMBER

Labor unionism began in the United States in the mid-1930s, grew to a peak in the late 1940s and has been declining steadily since then. The **collective bargaining agreement** stipulates the working conditions, status of the union, and ways to resolve disputes between management and employees. A widely used dispute resolution mechanism is the **grievance procedure,** which may apply to both union and nonunion employees.

RESEARCH AND AUDIT

Research and audit activities assess the efficiency and effectiveness of Human Resource Management. They are perhaps more difficult to apply in the human resources field than in the physical science field because each person is a unique, complex individual. However, there are some widely used research methods:

Historical studies. Much useful information can be derived from historical studies. For example, a manager who needs to analyze turnover, or absenteeism, or lateness could look at the historical records by variable (e.g., day of the week, position classification, section, amount or length of absence or lateness). From these data, the manager may be able to derive observations and, most importantly, make changes for future improvements.

Surveys. Surveys are usually questionnaires or structured interviews addressed to a specific audience.

Controlled experiments. These are relatively rare in a general management setting. Usually, controlled experiments contain hypotheses, are designed with specific sampling techniques in mind, have a test group and a control group, and have pre- and post-measurements.

Audits can also be very useful tools in measuring the effectiveness of Human Resource Management. Audits are systematic surveys and analyses of any or all human resource functions, with results and recommendations presented to management. Audits usually make a judgment about the adequacy of the program and contain suggestions for improvements in the future. Audits may be conducted companywide or may be departmental.

YOU SHOULD REMEMBER

Gathering and evaluating factual data on human resources is an important mechanism for charting future management paths. Although this takes time and effort, it may form the basis for otherwise unobserved opportunities to better management.

SEPARATIONS

At some point, everyone, including the Chairman of the Board, leaves an organization. An understanding of the various types of **separations,** or conditions under which employees leave the organization, can help you categorize each separation appropriately:

- *Resignations.* Resignations are the easiest separations to manage. The employee gives notice, in writing, to the manager, that he or she intends to leave on a specific date. A rule of thumb for the amount of notice is that the notice should be equal to the year's vacation eligibility, that is, if an employee is normally eligible for two weeks vacation per year, the notice period should be two weeks or more. Resignations may be for many reasons, each concerning itself with what that particular employee is choosing for the next part of his/her career. Resignations, in this sense, are always voluntary—that is, at the employee's request.

- *Retirement.* Retirement separations may be planned ahead since one's age does not change. As a matter of course, a manager may want to ask for a listing of employees by age so that the manager and the employees can plan for retirements. Retirement may be *voluntary*, that is, a person may elect to retire within the eligibility provisions of the organization's retirement benefit plan—or retirement may be *mandatory*—that is, attainment of an age threshold at which retirement is required by the organization. Under federal law, employees may not be required to retire solely based on age except for specific circumstances.

- *Reductions in force (RIF).* Reductions in force take place in many industries from time to time. These may be *voluntary*, with special programs such as severance pay, continuation of benefits for a period, and outplacement services to encourage employees to leave. Or reductions may be *involuntary*, such as an across-the-board layoff or a reorganization leading to fewer positions. In layoff situations, people are generally eligible for unemployment insurance.

- *Discharge.* Discharge, sometimes called *termination, separation for cause, or firing*, is always *involuntary*, and is the most serious penalty exacted of an employee. It may imply a significant breach of work rules or may be derived from actual work performance. However, studies have consistently shown that almost half of all terminations have little relationship to job performance, but are grounded in personality differences between managers and employees.

  If a discharge is based on poor performance, management must take positive steps to ensure that such deficient performance is thoroughly documented. A business that discharges an employee upon claims of poor performance, but lacks the documentation of such a lackluster worker, may well be liable to a successful suit for worker discrimination, perhaps even unlawful discharge. Such documentation is usually stressful for all involved and may, on occasion, worsen relations between the manager and employee, not to mention other employees in the immediate work environment. The manager may want an immediate solution to the problem of a poor employee, while fellow workers in the shop may feel that the poor worker is letting them down by not performing up to expected standards. The employee discharged on this basis is usually ineligible for continuing fringe benefits and unemployment insurance, and may even be evicted from the job by being escorted off the business premises.

YOU SHOULD REMEMBER

Separations may be voluntary or involuntary. In separating employees on an involuntary basis, management is well advised to document each situation very carefully.

KNOW THE CONCEPTS
DO YOU KNOW THE BASICS?

1. Define a career path.
2. What is career plateauing?
3. What is a horizontal career path?
4. Name the seven most common methods of recruiting new employees.
5. Compensation systems are generally viewed from two perspectives. Name them.
6. What are the environmental factors that affect compensation?
7. Why should a manager in a nonunion company pay attention to wages paid in a unionized company?
8. Which type of separation normally requires the most documentation?
9. Why are personnel audits important to Human Resources Management?
10. What is the difference between an hourly wage and an incentive wage?
11. Discrimination in employment is banned, based on what factors?
12. Name the four basic concepts common to all grievance procedures.

TERMS FOR STUDY

arbitration	labor relations
audits	mediation
BFOQ	non-cash compensation
career path	pay equity
career plateau	recruitment
cash compensation	salary
collective bargaining agreements	seniority-based system
discrimination prohibitions	stress interview
disparate impact	structured (patterned) interview
disparate treatment	time in grade
division of labor	unstructured interview
grievance procedure	value added process
horizontal career path	variable (incentive) pay
incentive wages	vertical career path
internal recruitment	wages

ANSWERS
KNOW THE BASICS

1. A career path is a progression of jobs linked together, each of which furnishes the skills and/or experience necessary for advancement to the next job. The interrelationship between the jobs is the main difference between a business position that is part of the career path and the business position that does not qualify the individual for advancement.

2. Even though an employee begins on a career path, there is no assurance that he or she will advance to the highest possible level. Many an employee's career stalls or even stops at a lower level, a phenomenon known as career plateauing.

3. A horizontal career path is a series of jobs that are not interdependent, exist on the same organizational level, may be completed in any order, and must all be completed before the employee is suitable or eligible to be promoted to the next higher organizational level.

4. The seven most common methods of recruiting new employees are job posting, search of existing files, advertising, employment agencies, referrals by current employees, other organizations, and Internet-based job reference/resume services.

5. Compensation systems can be viewed as "Cash" and "Non-Cash."

6. Factors that affect compensation that must be considered by management include supply and demand, labor unions, a company's ability to pay and its productivity, and government regulation.

7. A manager in a nonunion company should pay attention to unionized wage rates because its workers will be influenced by the prevailing union wage rate for comparable jobs. Nonunionized employees may well demand compensation similar to that paid their union counterparts, and it is important that management pay attention to what is happening within the union ranks.

8. Any involuntary separation requires complete documentation. In a reduction in force, for example, the least senior employees are usually the first to be laid off. Accurate records must be kept to ensure fairness in the layoff procedure or process. Discharge, a second type of involuntary termination, requires specific documentation as to the reason the employee is being separated so as to prevent future lawsuits charging that the discharge was unfair.

9. Audits are systematic surveys of any or all human resource functions with data reporting, results and recommendations presented to management. They ensure compliance with regulations such as Affirmative Action and present suggestions for future improvements.

10. The hourly wage is paid for each hour actually worked by the employee regardless of production during that hour. The incentive wage is paid based on number of units produced regardless of hours put in.

11. An employer may not discriminate in employment based on race, age, color, national origin, or sex. These factors are described in the 1963 Equal Pay Act, the 1964 Civil Rights Act, and the 1967 Age Discrimination in Employment Act.

12. The four basic concepts common to all grievance procedures are documentation, steps or tiers, involvement of persons outside the grievant's department, and time requirements.

13
MOTIVATION: THEORY AND PRACTICE

KEY TERMS

motivation the process of stimulating an individual to take action that will accomplish a desired goal

need hierarchy the five different levels of individual needs identified by Abraham H. Maslow in his theory of motivation—namely, physiological, safety, social, esteem or ego, and self-actualization

two-factor, or motivation-hygiene, theory a theory of motivation identified by Frederick Herzberg which states that all work-related factors can be grouped into one of two categories: *hygiene maintenance factors*, which will not produce motivation but can prevent it, and *motivator factors*, which can encourage motivation

job satisfaction an individual's general attitude and feeling about his or her job

expectancy theory a theory of motivation developed by Victor Vroom which attempts to explain behavior in terms of an individual's goals and his or her expectations of achieving those goals

---

Motivation theory and practice has been with us for a long time. Highly motivated individuals can bring about substantial increases in productivity and job satisfaction and substantial decreases in absenteeism, tardiness, grievances, and so forth. Therefore, it is important for us to understand some of the basic theories of motivation as well as to be able to apply some of these theories.

In the motivation process, unfulfilled needs create tension, which produces motives that cause behavior or activity aimed at satisfying the human need to reduce the tension. This process is illustrated in Figure 13-1. **Motivation** then can be described as a process of stimulating an individual to take action that will lead to the fulfillment of a need or the accomplishment of a desired goal.

There have been many theories of motivation throughout the years. The traditional theory of motivation, which evolved from the Scientific Management movement at the turn of the century, is based on the assumption that money is the primary motivator. If the financial reward is great enough, workers will produce more. Therefore, financial rewards should be related directly to performance.

Figure 13–1. The process of motivation.

To begin, we would like to have you complete the exercise below, called "Factors Which Motivate Me." Check the six items on the list which you believe are most important in motivating you to do your best work. This should take you approximately five minutes.

A basic understanding of motivation theories can be useful to managers as they attempt to motivate people in their organizations. Consequently, we will present at length several theories which have relevance and application on the job for the manager and summarize some of the more popular ones of recent years.

YOU SHOULD REMEMBER

Motivation is the process of stimulating an individual to take action that will accomplish a desired goal. There have been many theories of motivation. One of the earlier ones is the traditional theory based on the assumption that money is the primary motivator.

"Factors Which Motivate Me"

Please indicate by placing an "X" next to the six items from the list below which you believe are most important in motivating you to do your best work.

1. _____ Steady employment
2. _____ Respect for me as a person
3. _____ Adequate rest periods or coffee breaks
4. _____ Good pay
5. _____ Good physical working conditions
6. _____ Chance to turn out quality work
7. _____ Getting along well with others on the job
8. _____ Having a local employee paper
9. _____ Chance for promotion
10. _____ Opportunity to do interesting work
11. _____ Pensions and other security benefits
12. _____ Not having to work too hard
13. _____ Knowing what is going on in the organization
14. _____ Feeling my job is important
15. _____ Having an employee council
16. _____ Having a written job description
17. _____ Being told by my boss when I do a good job
18. _____ Getting a performance rating
19. _____ Attending staff meetings
20. _____ Agreement with organization's objectives
21. _____ Opportunity for self-development and improvement
22. _____ Fair vacation arrangements
23. _____ Knowing I will be disciplined if I do a bad job
24. _____ Working under close supervision
25. _____ Large amount of freedom on the job (Chance to work not under direct or close supervision)

MASLOW'S HIERARCHY OF NEEDS THEORY

Probably the most widely publicized model of motivation comes to us from the work of the late **Abraham H. Maslow.** According to Maslow, only unsatisfied needs are prime sources of motivation. This means that only if you're hungry will you buy, grow, or—depending on the extent and duration of your hunger—even steal food to satisfy the primitive physiological need to survive. Likewise, only if you have an intense craving to succeed will you study and learn as much as you can in order to fulfill this ambition.

Maslow suggested that there are five needs systems that account for most of our behavior. These he placed in a hierarchy ranging from the most primitive and immature—in terms of the behavior they promote—to the most civilized and mature. Right now, if you'll look at Figure 13-2A you'll see that it features Maslow's hierarchy of five needs system: *survival; safety or security; a sense of belonging; ego-status;* and finally *self-actualization.*

According to Maslow, there is a natural trend in which individuals become aware of and therefore are motivated by each of these needs in ascending order. Progress up the Maslow hierarchy may be thought of as roughly equivalent to climbing a ladder one rung at a time; awareness of the next-higher rung presupposes successful negotiation of the lower one. The very lowest, consisting of physiological needs, reflects the individual's concern for survival. Next we move up to the safety rung, reflecting concern for safety and the avoidance of harm. The third rung represents the belonging needs, the normal human desire to be accepted and appreciated by others. The fourth is the level of ego-status needs, which motivates a person to contribute his or her best to the efforts of the group in return for the numerous forms of reward that recognition can assume. The highest rung on the ladder stands for the self-actualization needs, which are realized when the individual can experience a sense of personal growth and achievement, of satisfaction and self-fulfillment through doing.

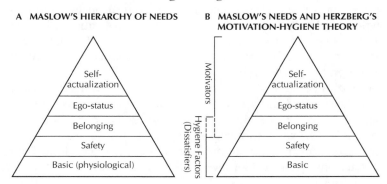

Figure 13–2. Needs and motives. *A* shows Maslow's Hierarchy of Needs Theory. *B* shows the relationship of Maslow's theory and that of Herzberg, who focused on motives as they relate to the workplace. As you can see, Herzberg thought that the upper level needs identified by Maslow served to motivate work performance; that lower level, or basic, needs acted as maintenance factors, possibly dissatisfiers; and that the need to belong could function as either a motivating or dissatisfying factor.

Maslow didn't mean to imply that any need ever receives *complete* satisfaction. Rather, he believed that some minimal degree of satisfaction is required before a need ceases to preoccupy the individual to the exclusion of higher needs. Once that point is reached, the person will be free to feel the tensions associated with the next level in the hierarchy and to experiment with a new set of behaviors designed to satisfy the new need.

YOU SHOULD REMEMBER

Maslow's Hierarchy of Needs Theory suggests that there are five needs systems that account for most of our behavior. He placed these in a hierarchy ranging from the most primitive and innovative in terms of the behavior they promote to the most mature. These needs systems range from the **physiological** or more primitive **factors,** to **safety, belonging, ego-status,** and **self-actualization** needs in that order.

TWO-FACTOR, OR MOTIVATION-HYGIENE, THEORY

Frederick I. Herzberg took a somewhat different approach to motivation. Maslow was concerned with the sources of motivation in a life-in-general sense, whereas Herzberg focused on sources of motivation which seemed pertinent to work and work accomplishment. Even so, Herzberg's investigations led him to conclude that needs very similar to those suggested by Maslow were operating in the job context.

Herzberg found essentially that only those needs systems that correspond to Maslow's *ego-status* and *self-actualization* levels serve as direct sources of motivation to work effectively. Belongingness concerns, he found, are somewhat linked to work motivation, especially in the area of supervisor-subordinate relationships, and to nonwork issues having to do with interpersonal satisfactions. These upper level needs in Maslow's hierarchy Herzberg called *motivators.*

The lower level needs systems, particularly those concerned with basic physiological needs and with safety, Herzberg termed potential *dissatisfiers* rather than sources of work motivation. The belongingness factors, he thought, overlapped both groups. See Figure 13-2B on page 239.

The upper level motivators, Herzberg felt, lead to behaviors that are directly relevant to the work to be accomplished, while the lower level dissatisfiers promote behaviors that focus on issues peripheral to the work itself.

Moreover, Herzberg concluded that even when the lower level needs are satisfied—and so, according to Maslow, are no longer sources of goal-directed behavior—there is still no reason to expect that individuals will perform any more effectively in their work. Why? Because the lower level needs—dissatisfiers—serve primarily as *maintenance factors*, those needs that people assume for the most part will be adequately met. A good boss and good working conditions are examples of such needs. Few managerial or professional people would cite these as the job factors that motivate them most. Yet the minute either boss or working conditions become a principal concern, factors like interesting job content and opportunity for advancement lose their power to motivate and the employer is in trouble. In short, effective job performance depends on the adequacy of both motivator and hygiene needs.

YOU SHOULD REMEMBER

Herzberg's **two-factor,** or **motivation-hygiene, theory** stated that basic needs corresponding to Maslow's needs of survival and security functioned as **dissatisfiers,** or **maintenance** factors, in the workplace, while higher level needs of ego-status and self-actualization were **motivator** factors.

MOTIVATING AND DEMOTIVATING FACTORS IN THE WORK SITUATION (ACCORDING TO HERZBERG)

MOTIVATORS (SATISFIERS):
  Work itself
  Responsibility
  Achievement
  Recognition
  Advancement
  Growth
MAINTENANCE FACTORS (DISSATISFIERS):
  Organization policy and administration
  Supervision
  Working conditions
  Interpersonal relations (with superiors, subordinates, and peers)
  Salary
  Status
  Job security
  Personal life

MOTIVATING FACTORS: THE SAME AND DIFFERENT

Why have we gone to such lengths in explaining theory? Because it's going to be important to you as you think about how you checked the exercise entitled: "Factors Which Motivate Me." What factors *do* motivate you? You have to remember that different factors may have different weights at various stages of your life. For example, say you're young, married, and have two small children. Good pay will absolutely be a primary consideration, but opportunity for advancement may be even more vital if you're thinking of the long haul. On the other hand, suppose your company's been merged with another company, and you, a top executive 56 years old, are out. You have to make a new connection. Sure you have to support yourself and your family, but looking at things realistically you realize you probably can't equal your old status and salary. So it's possible that as an alternative, interesting work and freedom on the job will become principal motivators for you.

Besides, whether we're talking about the achievement of personal goals or career goals, motivation is helped or hindered by existing conditions, by the environment in which we function. Doesn't it make sense, then, to seek out conditions, create an environment, in which the factors that motivate us to achieve will be dominant rather than those maintenance factors we've mentioned?

You may be interested in comparing the way you ranked the factors in that exercise with the rankings of others. How do you stack up against the norm, so to speak? We know there is no such person as an average man or an average woman, but sometimes comparisons are fun—and enlightening.

Gordon Lippitt, who has done a great deal of work in this field, had 6000 managers complete the same exercise you have in front of you. And what were their results? They ranked the following six items from the list on page 238 as most important in motivating them to do their best work:

2. Respect for me as a person.

4. Good pay.

6. Chance to turn out quality work.

14. Feeling my job is important.

21. Opportunity for self-development and improvement.

25. Large amount of freedom on the job.

Here is another set of results. We asked 500 senior-level executives from different companies and government agencies, all of whom were attending a university executive development program over a period of time, to do this exercise. These were their rankings:

2. Respect for me as a person.

4. Good pay.

10. Opportunity to do interesting work.

14. Feeling my job is important.

21. Opportunity for self-development and improvement.

25. Large amount of freedom on the job.

Remarkable, isn't it, how these two groups parallel each another. Yes, we can hear you saying, but isn't the distribution always pretty much the same on anything like this? No, *not* always.

The third group (50 recent college graduates—1999) ranked the motivational factors as follows:

1. Steady employment.

2. Respect for me as a person.

4. Good pay.

9. Chance for promotion.

21. Opportunity for self-development.

25. Large amount of freedom on the job.

These young men and women, Generation Xer's, were career oriented. Unlike the managers and executives, they weren't concerned immediately with promotability and steady progress toward high levels of responsibility and better-paying jobs. Yet, the factors they checked bear a marked resemblance to those chosen by the previous groups.

By way of contrast, let us tell you about how 150 current college students from a 1999 survey ranked these motivators. They ranked them by type the same way that the recent graduates did. Yet, these current college students represent Generation Y, and the motivators are markedly different from earlier generations. In fact, the Urban Institute's recent study "Long Term Trends in Workers Beliefs About Their Own Job Security" found that "anxiety about job loss has risen among workers as a whole. It lends credence to a view that growing fears about job insecurity have changed the employment relationship."* Employers should then create an environment in which the factors that motivate employees to achieve will outweigh the maintenance factors, the potential *dissatisfiers.*

We've said that motivation is affected by age and personal circumstances, by the phase of your life and career that you're going through at the moment. However, that's not all. Motivation is affected by the external environment as well. For instance, at times of economic slump, Item 1—steady employment—is checked very often, along with good pay. When the economy is flourishing, people often take both pay and job for granted.

---

* "Long Run Trend in Workers Belief About Their Own Job Security," *USA Today*, March 2, 1999, Section B, p. 1.

YOU SHOULD REMEMBER

The factors that motivate people may change at different stages of life (for example, when first married, when nearing retirement), but many studies have found surprising similarities in how people rank the factors most important to them. "Respect for me as a person" is a factor often cited. Also, in general, steady employment as a motivating factor is more important in times of economic slump.

What does the future hold? What changes in worker motivation are there likely to be? Look for a minute, if you will, at Figure 13-3: Major Needs—Value Shifts. This reflects data compiled by the Stanford Research Institute, using the Maslow Hierarchy of Needs we've been talking about.

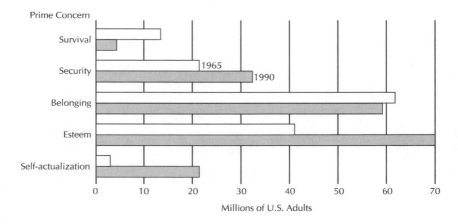

Figure 13-3. Major needs—values shifts.

In terms of 1965, the chart pictures a rather secure society—although, of course, that wasn't true of many underdeveloped countries in 1965 and isn't true now. But now let's take a look at the forecast for 1990. Notice that security by no means becomes less of a motivator; in other words, the people who provided the responses did not feel that they would be any more secure in 1990 than they are today. Belonging needs will still be important in 1990, but not to quite such a degree. Social needs for esteem—how we see the value of our job, our contribution to the world we live in, our overall importance in the scheme of things—will be much more important. Our needs for self-actualization are viewed as being four times more important by 1990, possibly because we expect to have more leisure time at our disposal.

In short, we have here a changing structure of values, changing ideas of what life should be. What are the implications of this picture? Well, if we consider the growing importance placed on satisfying the needs for esteem and self-actualization, it seems that the future will call for constant retraining to take advantage of changing career needs and opportunities plus constant attention to enriching our lives.

At this point please review what you said were the six factors that motivate you to do your best work. Now compare them with the factors checked by the groups we've reported on. We'd be willing to bet that you'll find your thinking closely in line with the general consensus, as well as with Maslow's and Herzberg's conclusions and the Stanford Research Institute findings. See Figure 13-4.

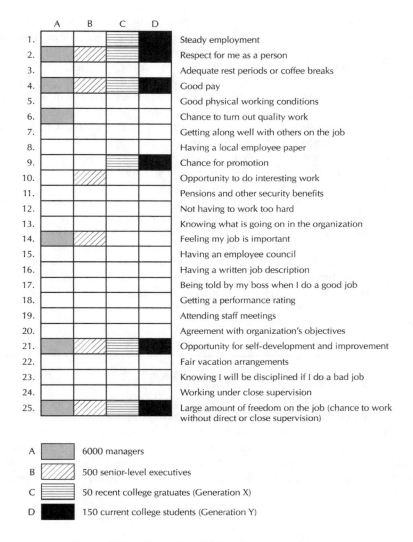

	A	B	C	D	
1.					Steady employment
2.					Respect for me as a person
3.					Adequate rest periods or coffee breaks
4.					Good pay
5.					Good physical working conditions
6.					Chance to turn out quality work
7.					Getting along well with others on the job
8.					Having a local employee paper
9.					Chance for promotion
10.					Opportunity to do interesting work
11.					Pensions and other security benefits
12.					Not having to work too hard
13.					Knowing what is going on in the organization
14.					Feeling my job is important
15.					Having an employee council
16.					Having a written job description
17.					Being told by my boss when I do a good job
18.					Getting a performance rating
19.					Attending staff meetings
20.					Agreement with organization's objectives
21.					Opportunity for self-development and improvement
22.					Fair vacation arrangements
23.					Knowing I will be disciplined if I do a bad job
24.					Working under close supervision
25.					Large amount of freedom on the job (chance to work without direct or close supervision)

A — 6000 managers

B — 500 senior-level executives

C — 50 recent college gratuates (Generation X)

D — 150 current college students (Generation Y)

Figure 13–4. Summary: Factors that motivate me.

OTHER THEORIES OF MOTIVATION
McCLELLAND'S THEORY OF HUMAN MOTIVES

The research of **David McClelland** stresses that there are certain needs that are learned and socially acquired through interaction with the environment. His theory concerns three motives—the need for *achievement*, the need for *power*, and the need for *affiliation*—and how these needs affect the individual's behavior in the work environment. Each person possesses these motives to varying degrees; however, one of the needs will tend to be more characteristic of the individual than the other two.

According to McClelland, individuals who exhibit a strong need for achievement are particularly responsive to work environments in which they can attain success through their own efforts rather than by chance. Entrepreneurs, for example, seek out such environments. In fact, *achievement motivation theory* is largely a theory of entrepreneurship.

The role of *power motivation* in managerial success is supported by studies by AT&T that track promotion rates of managers with different motive patterns. Research on the motivation to manage (i.e., managers with high levels of motivation to manage have been found to perform consistently better in the job and to progress more rapidly and further up the management hierarchy) also is consistent with McClelland's ideas. On the other hand, McClelland views *affiliation motivation* as a negative factor in managerial performance because it tends to make a manager too concerned subjectively with individuals and thus interferes with objectivity and rationality.

People with strong achievement and power needs should be placed in an appropriate entrepreneurial or managerial work context. Their intrinsic needs will motivate them sufficiently.

YOU SHOULD REMEMBER

McClelland's Theory of Human Motives concerns how motives of achievement, power, and affiliation affect behavior in the work environment. In general, McClelland believed that motives of achievement and power are positive factors leading to high performance, while affiliation motivation is a negative factor, interfering with objectivity.

REINFORCEMENT THEORY

This theory is based primarily on the work of **B. F. Skinner** and states that reinforced behavior will be repeated, and behavior that is not reinforced is less likely to be repeated. For example, if an individual is promoted for increasing sales substantially, then the individual is likely to continue to increase sales substantially if he or she wishes another promotion. Reinforcement theory assumes that the consequences of a person's behavior determine the level of motivation.

Skinner's work merged into the field of management through behavior and organizational behavior modification theory, which views behavior as occurring randomly in the beginning. Reinforcers are then applied selectively to those behaviors. Behaviors are learned as consequences accrue in the form of rewards and punishments. These reinforcers are applied contingent upon whether or not desired behaviors result. The focus of the operant learning approach is in the ways supervisors can orchestrate contingencies of performance—positive, negative, extinction, punishment—to obtain desired performances. Schedules or contingencies of reinforcements appear below.

Contingencies of reinforcements are:*

1. *Positive reinforcement*
   An existing set of circumstances→a particular behavior→the contingent positive consequence→increase in the frequency of the behavior.

2. *Negative (avoidance) reinforcement*
   An existing set of circumstances→a particular behavior→contingent termination or withdrawal of an unpleasant consequence→increase in the frequency of the behavior.

3. *Extinction*
   An existing set of circumstances→a particular behavior→the contingent positive consequence is withheld→decrease in the frequency of the behavior.

4. *Punishment*
   An existing set of circumstances→a particular behavior→the contingent negative consequences→decrease in the frequency of behavior.

According to reinforcement theory the manager can really make a difference, but for that to happen the manager must have substantial control over the work environment.

YOU SHOULD REMEMBER

The **reinforcement theory,** based on the ideas of B. F. Skinner, holds that the consequences of a person's behavior determine the level of motivation. Behavior that is reinforced—by a reward—will be repeated.

---

* Based on W. Clay Hamner, "Reinforcement Theory and Contingency Management in Organizational Settings," in *Organizational Behavior and Management: A Contingency Approach*, eds. Henry L. Tosi and W. Clay Hamner (Chicago: St. Clair, 1974), pp. 86–112.

EXPECTANCY THEORY OF MOTIVATION

Another important theory of motivation is the **expectancy theory of motivation** developed by **Victor Vroom.** The needs approach to motivation as developed by Maslow and Herzberg does not adequately allow for differences in individuals; Vroom's approach attempts to explain behavior in terms of an individual's goals and his or her expectations of achieving these goals. The expectancy theory assumes that individuals can determine which outcomes they prefer and can make realistic estimates of the chances of obtaining them. Consequently, it is sometimes referred to as the *preference-expectancy theory.* This theory emphasizes the need for organizations to relate rewards directly to performance and to ensure that the rewards provided are those rewards deserved and wanted by the recipients.

Motivation =	(Expectancy that increased effort will lead to increased performance)	(Expectancy that increased performance will lead to rewards)	(Preference of the individual for the rewards)
	$E \rightarrow$	$P \rightarrow$	O

As an example, assume that Bill Jones, a vacuum cleaner salesman, knows that he can sell four vacuum cleaners for every 20 calls he makes. Thus he sees a direct effort between his effort (E) and performance (P) or $E \rightarrow O$.

Since he is on straight commission, he also perceives a direct relationship between performance and rewards. Hence Bill's expectation that increased effort will lead to increased rewards is relatively high. Assume further that Bill is in a very high tax bracket and gets to keep only 50 percent of his commissions. Therefore he may not look upon the additional money that he gets to keep (the reward) favorably. Thus, the end result is that Bill's preference for the reward is relatively low even when this is multiplied by his relatively high expectations of receiving the reward. Therefore his motivation to work more may be relatively low.

YOU SHOULD REMEMBER

The **expectancy theory of motivation** allows for differences in individuals and holds that individuals will be motivated by their personal expectation of rewards and their preference for these rewards.

EQUITY THEORY

One of the major concerns of managers is the issue of equity in relation to the distribution of pay and other rewards. Although a number of views regarding the motivating effects of inequity and unfairness have been proposed, the ideas of **Stacy Adams** at General Electric seem to be the most significant. In Adams's view the perception of unfairness is one of the most powerful forces in the business world.

The major motivating force in **equity theory** is a striving for equity, which emerges only after some inequity or unfairness is perceived. Equity involves an individual comparing his or her performance and the rewards received with the performance and rewards others receive for doing similar work. When an employee receives compensation from the organization, perceptions of equity are affected by two factors:

1. Comparison of the compensation received to such factors as one's input of job effort, education, experience, skill, seniority, and endurance of adverse working conditions.

2. Comparison of the perceived equity of pay and rewards received to those received by other people.

In general, the research indicates that equity theory is a valid and valuable way of looking at human work and motivation.

YOU SHOULD REMEMBER

The **equity theory** holds that the perception of *unfairness* is a powerful motivating force in the workplace. It depends on comparison of perceived equity of pay and rewards among employees and comparison of compensation as related to factors such as education, experience, and seniority.

McGREGOR'S THEORY X AND THEORY Y

Douglas McGregor in 1960 stressed the importance of understanding the relationships between **motivation** and **behavior.** He believed that managers motivate employees by one of two basic approaches, which he termed **Theory X** and **Theory Y.** The traditional view, Theory X, suggests that managers must coerce, control, or threaten employees in order to motivate them. The alternative philosophy of human nature is Theory Y, which believes people are capable of being responsible. They do not have to be coerced or controlled by the manager in order to perform well. Some authors consider McGregor's work as a basic theory of motivation, whereas others feel it is a philosophy of human nature and fits more logically into a discussion of leadership rather than basic motivation theories.

KNOW THE CONCEPTS
DO YOU KNOW THE BASICS?

1. Why is it important to understand some of the basic theories of motivation?
2. Explain what occurs in the motivation process.
3. What is the traditional theory of motivation?
4. Explain Maslow's Hierarchy of Needs Theory of motivation.
5. How does Maslow's theory differ from Herzberg's theory?
6. What affects motivation?
7. What does the future hold in terms of motivation?
8. What does McClelland's Theory of Human Motives stress?
9. What is reinforcement theory?
10. Explain briefly the expectancy theory of motivation.

TERMS FOR STUDY

dissatisfiers	motivators
expectancy theory	needs hierarchy
human motives theory	reinforcement theory
hygiene factors	satisfiers
Generation X	self-actualization
Generation Y	Theory X
job satisfaction	Theory Y
maintenance factors	traditional theory
motivation	

ANSWERS
KNOW THE BASICS

1. It is important because highly motivated individuals can bring about substantial increases in job satisfaction and substantial decreases in absenteeism, tardiness, grievances, and so forth. Moreover, it is important for managers as they attempt to motivate people in their organizations.

2. Unfulfilled needs create tension, which produces motives which lead to behavior or activity to satisfy the human need or reduce the tension.

3. The traditional theory of motivation, which evolved from the Scientific Management movement at the turn of the century, is based on the assumption that money is the primary motivator. If the financial reward is great enough, workers will produce more. Therefore, these rewards should be related directly to performance.

4. Maslow identified five different levels of individual need in his theory of motivation—namely, physiological, safety, social, esteem or ego-status, and self-actualization. These needs exist in a hierarchy from physiological needs at the bottom to self-actualization at the top.

5. Maslow was concerned with the sources of motivation in a general sense, whereas Herzberg focused on those which seemed pertinent to work and work accomplishment. Herzberg found that only those needs systems that correspond to Maslow's ego, or status, and self-actualization levels serve as direct sources of motivation to work effectively.

6. Motivation is affected by age and personal circumstances, the phase of your life and career that you're going through at the moment, and by the external environment as well.

7. It seems that the future will call for constant retraining of managers to take advantage of changing career needs for security in terms of steady employment and opportunity plus constant attention to enriching the lives of employees by satisfying their needs for esteem and self-actualization.

8. It stresses that there are certain needs that are learned and socially acquired through interaction with the environment. His theory concerns the need for achievement, power, and affiliation and how these needs affect the individual's behavior in the work environment.

9. This theory is based primarily on the work of B. F. Skinner and states that reinforced behavior will be repeated, and behavior that is not reinforced is less likely to be repeated.

10. This theory was developed by Victor Vroom and attempts to explain behavior in terms of an individual's goals and the expectations of achieving these goals. It assumes individuals can determine which outcomes they prefer and make realistic estimates of the chances of obtaining them. Sometimes it is referred to as the preference-expectancy theory.

14
LEADERSHIP: THEORY AND PRACTICE

KEY TERMS

formal leaders those who are officially assigned leadership responsibilities within the organization

informal leaders those who are not officially assigned leadership experiences within the organization—but who may actually exercise the leadership function

organizational power those forms of power within the organizational structure that are used by managers, including (1) legitimate power, (2) reward power, (3) coercive power, (4) expert power, (5) charisma power, (6) referent power, and (7) information power

theories of leadership the various approaches that have been taken to systematically investigate and understand leadership over the years: (1) a genetic derivation of leadership, (2) a trait theory of leadership, (3) a behavioral explanation of leadership, and (4) situational or contingency theories of leadership

dimensions of leadership derived from studies done at the University of Michigan that characterized leadership functioning into two dimensions, task-centered and people-centered

Managerial Grid a practical method developed by Drs. Blake and Mouton of making use of the University of Michigan dimensions of leadership to categorize the leadership styles of managers

---

Leadership is the process by which one individual influences others to accomplish desired goals. Within the business organization, the leadership process takes the form of a manager who influences subordinates to accomplish the goals defined by top management. There may be two different kinds of leadership in any organization—those who are the *defined* or formal leaders and those who *act* as leaders in an informal manner. The two are not the same, yet both may exercise leadership behavior in influencing others.

A formal leader is someone *officially* invested with organizational authority and power and generally given the title of manager, executive, or supervisor. The amount of power is theoretically determined by the position occupied within the organization. Organizational promotion policies are designed to ensure that people with the necessary technical and leadership skills occupy the positions of power.

An informal leader will not have the official leadership title but will exercise a leadership function. This individual, without *formal* authority, assignment of power, position, or even responsibility, may by virtue of a personal attribute or superior performance influence others and exercise leadership function.

The biblical book of 1 Samuel recounts how the first king of Israel was chosen. The young man Saul possessed the personal attribute of stature—he is described in 1 Samuel, Chapter 9, Verse 2, as "from his shoulders upward he was taller than any of the people." He is made the formal leader (king) because of a personal attribute (height) that made him the informal leader and allowed him to influence others presumably because of the physical strength that accompanied his size. It is interesting to note that this ancient expression of personal attribute that denoted leadership is still used in the military to denote superior leadership performance in that such an individual is described as a "head and shoulders performer." The biblical example is not unique; the oldest theory of leadership, the *genetic approach*, is found throughout the ancient and medieval worlds, and we shall shortly turn to the ways in which people have sought to understand leadership. First, however, it is necessary to understand the nature of power within an organization, for effective use of individual power is the basis of leadership.

VARIETIES OF INDIVIDUAL POWER WITHIN THE ORGANIZATIONAL SETTING

Power, the ability to influence subordinates and peers by controlling organizational resources, is a hallmark of the leadership position. The successful leader effectively uses power to influence others, and it is important for the leader to understand the sources and uses of power to enhance the leadership functioning. The kinds of *organizational power* are (1) legitimate power, (2) reward power, (3) coercive power, (4) expert power, (5) charisma power, (6) referent power, and (7) information power. (Expert power, referent power, and information power are discussed in the pioneering work *The Bases of Social Power*. This book by **B. Raven** and **J. R. P. French** contains much of the early classification of organizational power.)

LEGITIMATE POWER

Legitimate power is that power inherent within the organizational structure itself. This power is assigned to an individual who occupies a specific position within that organization. Should the individual leave the position, the power remains with the position and does not follow the individual. This power is made legitimate within the organization, and the individual is vested with the power. This assumption of power is generally signified by an official title, such as Manager, Vice President, Director, Supervisor, and the like.

Organizations sanction various levels of power. These levels of power correspond to the hierarchical executive levels within the organization itself. Thus a position that is higher in the organization will have more power vested in it than a lower position, and a manager occupying the higher level position will be able to exercise more power than someone occupying a lower level position. In Figure 14-1, the Executive Vice President in position A has more organizational power than the Vice President in position B. If the Vice President in position B wishes to gain more power within the organization, he or she will have to move up the organizational hierarchy.

REWARD POWER

Reward power is also inherent within the organizational structure in that managers are given administrative power over a range of rewards. Since subordinate employees desire the rewards, they will be influenced by the possibility of receiving them as the product of work performance. Organizational rewards may be the obvious—pay and promotions. They may also be more

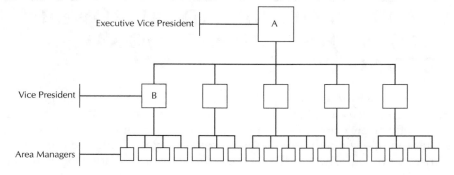

Figure 14–1. A corporate organizational chart (T/O, or table of organization) showing the hierarchical arrangement of power.

subtle—managerial praise, status, attention, greater access to information, an increased ability to design one's own job (autonomy), and others. Managers may employ a wide range of rewards to motivate work performance. A manager will possess reward power over an employee to the extent that there is managerial control over the reward potential and to the extent that the employee will value and seek the available rewards. If a manager cannot deliver a desired reward or if the available reward is not desired, the reward power of the manager will be greatly diminished.

The reward provided should be suitable to motivate the desired work performance. If management wishes to motivate an employee to sell $100,000 more of a product, giving a new wristwatch or a $100 U.S. Savings Bond will not be suitable since it will not be perceived as a suitable reward for the extra performance required. Management's task is to make effective use of scarce organizational resources to motivate genuine performance.

COERCIVE POWER

Coercive power is based upon the manager's ability to punish an employee. Punishment is performed across a range of options, from a mild warning to a suspension to actual termination. The major point to remember in conjunction with this kind of managerial power is that punishment or threat of punishment *does not* promote desired employee performance—it only discourages undesired worker actions. Even though punishment does not promote desired behavior, in serving to discourage undesired behavior, it is a powerful managerial tool. It may also have the greatest repercussions. A manager's ability to punish workers may be constrained by union contracts or the application of worker antidiscrimination laws. Additionally, as workers show an increased awareness of laws that protect them and a willingness to sue employers, it is vitally important to document all reasons for punishing an employee. This "paper trail" will be essential if an employer is to successfully defend punishment in a court of law.

A range of punishments is needed because the punishment applied should be suitable to the unacceptable action that gives rise to it. Management, in having a range of punishments from the mild to the severe, maintains a measure of flexibility. Several general principles govern the application of punishment—the use of coercive power—within the organizational setting:

- the punishment should be suitable to the action that led to the punishment.
- the punishment should follow as closely in time as possible the offense action; this links the action with the punishment.
- the punishment should have *educational* value; a person being punished should understand why.

- the punishment should not have a hidden reward. If a subordinate is being "chewed out" by a manager (who thinks that this is punishment) but secretly enjoys the attention, it isn't punishment, but reward.

- the manager doing the punishing shouldn't enjoy doing it.

EXPERT POWER

Expert power derives from the expertise possessed by the manager. This power is derived from the individual's special skills, knowledge, abilities, or previous experience. Any of these confer upon the individual power within the organization because the organization needs and values them. Expert power, derived from special knowledge or advanced education, can be relatively unrelated to age and job seniority since it often will depend upon educational achievement, not necessarily on time on the job (seniority). This form of power allows someone who is relatively young or new to the workforce to gain influence within the organization. It is important to remember that the value placed upon a specific expertise within the organization is transient; as times change so does what is needed and valued by the company.

CHARISMA POWER

Charisma power is the power of one individual to influence another by force of character, often called personal *charisma*. A manager may be admired because of a specific personal trait, and this admiration creates the opportunity for interpersonal influence. Advertisers have long recognized charisma power in making use of sports figures for product endorsements, for example. The charismatic appeal of the sports star supposedly leads to an acceptance of the endorsement, although the individual may have little real credibility outside the sports arena. A manager who is particularly handsome, talented, or just plain likable may be described by subordinates as inspiring and motivating. This person has charisma, and this will confer great power as a manager.

REFERENT POWER

The interesting thing about **referent power** is that it is gained by *association*. An individual's power may derive, not from his or her personality, but from that of the person with whom he or she is associated or has a relationship. The title of "assistant" or "deputy" is often used to denote those *associated* with individuals who possess great organizational power. Even though these assistants do not themselves have great power, they are often perceived as acting in place of those who do. An assistant empowered to sign correspondence in place of a superior, known as *by direction* authority, is perceived as having great power. Thus referent power, in addition to being charismatic, is also associative.

INFORMATION POWER

Information power is derived from possession of important information at a critical time when such information is necessary to organizational functioning. The possession of information may be totally unrelated to an individual's organizational position or given power. Someone who is "in the know" has genuine power. Thus, a manager's secretary may actually be in a powerful position if taken into the manager's confidence or given business knowledge. Conversely, if one's information is "old news," organizational power may decline.

YOU SHOULD REMEMBER

Managers acquire power within organizations in several ways. This power may be **legitimate, charisma, referent, coercive, expert, reward,** or **information power,** or a combination of these forms of power. With power, however, comes the obligation to use it in an ethical manner for the accomplishment of organizational goals. Managers accept responsibilities and the power necessary to fulfill these responsibilities and will be held accountable for the manner in which they make use of their power.

THEORIES OF LEADERSHIP

The various theoretical approaches to leadership represent attempts to understand its nature in a comprehensive manner. As we have already seen, there is a theory of leadership based on a personal attribute, enunciated in the biblical story of King Saul told in 1 Samuel. This approach to the understanding of leadership is called the *genetic theory* of leadership derivation and is the most ancient. Other approaches are the leadership trait theory, behavioral theory, and situational, or contingency, approaches. Each of these is discussed for they constitute the best understanding of leadership currently available.

GENETIC THEORY

The most ancient explanation of leadership is the **genetic approach,** the belief that leadership ability is transmitted genetically. The phrase "a leader is born, not made" sums up this approach. In the previously cited biblical story, the young man Saul is chosen to be king because of his height, a physical characteristic with which he was born. Kings have, from the earliest human history, believed that leadership ability was transmitted genetically from parent to child; generally, but not always, from father to son. This belief in the genetic transmission of leadership ability and right to a leadership position has been called the divine right of kings (or of royalty). This belief survived well into the 20th century until the carnage of World War I destroyed many of the royal houses of Europe. (The ancient Roman term for ruler, *Caesar*, could be found over 2000 years later in the German language as *Kaiser* and in the Russian language as *Czar*, both expressions denoting a military or political leader. Also, in the emerging 18th-century United States, there were those who believed in the divine right of kings and who urged the supreme colonial military leader, General George Washington, to become king. Much subsequent U.S. history stems from Washington's refusal to accept the offer of kingship because he apparently did not believe in the genetic approach to leadership.)

The strength of the genetic approach is that it readily explains the origins of leadership: if you are a leader, it is because you have inherited leadership genes from either your mother or father or both. As seen in the practices of royal families throughout history, those who subscribe to the genetic view of leadership tend to marry other royalty. This explains how the royal families of Europe came to be so intermarried, and why different kings bear a striking physical resemblance—they are descended from common ancestors. (Queen Victoria of England had nine children and married them into almost all the significant royal houses of Europe. Thus in World War I, English and Russian cousins were fighting their German cousin.) A great deal of intermarriage within a small group of families—in our example, among the royal houses of Europe—results in a "closed gene pool." New and different genes are rarely introduced into the pool, or, in other words, the same basic ingredients are mixed and remixed. Such a "closed gene pool" frequently results in a higher than normal incidence of birth defects. Even if the royal offspring did not show evidence of outright birth defects and therefore appeared normal in every respect, they often lacked the so-called leadership genes. This genetic phenomenon helps explain why this approach to leadership eventually proved inadequate.

Ultimately, the genetic theory of leadership failed because the world changed. Although the royal houses of Europe did see a decline in leadership abilities, this was a minor change compared with the rise of an industrial leadership in the 18th and 19th centuries, when men and women not of royal lines rose to positions of power and influence because of their personal abilities and creativity. The genetic theory could not adequately explain why these individuals achieved leadership positions.

TRAIT THEORY

The **trait theory of leadership,** which was seriously investigated after World War II, continues to be very popular today, and books by successful industrial leaders are routinely propelled to the top of the bestseller lists. The lives and management styles of well-known executives are subjected to close scrutiny by those seeking to determine the personal traits necessary for managerial success. Such traits as superior intelligence, imposing stature, self-confidence, effectiveness at communicating, ability to motivate others (being inspiring), and the need for achievement, decisiveness, and creativity have all been identified by various scientific researchers as traits characteristic of those who are successful in business. This is a *genetic approach* in that it is assumed that leaders are born rather than made. There is an explanation to a major difficulty raised in conjunction with the genetic approach: the offspring of a great leader may not have leadership abilities because the wrong traits were inherited. If common people achieved industrial leadership, it was because they did inherit a significant number of leadership traits. One need only look to employment advertisements that require "good qualities" to note that the trait theory still has relevance for many employers.

It would thus appear that the trait theory of leadership is a clear and concise view of the origins and nature of leadership, but such is not the case. Scientific investigation has produced extremely contradictory evidence. Traits denoting leadership in one scientific study are not found in others, and the situation is further complicated by the sheer number of supposed leadership traits. Management writers and scientists have claimed literally hundreds, if not thousands, of leadership traits. The final difficulty with this approach to the understanding of leadership is that, being a genetically based theory, it does not assume that traits are learned. That, however, appears to be the case; many leadership traits, such as communications skills, can be learned. They are not acquired by heredity, and such a method of trait acquisition is unacceptable with the trait theory.

Attention to those leadership traits that were learned, not inherited, caused managerial researchers to focus upon leadership behaviors. The focus effectively shifted from the leader and his or her traits to what the leader did. This attempt to understand leadership is called the Behavioral Approach to leadership.

YOU SHOULD REMEMBER

"Leaders are born, not made" is a concise way of stating the **genetic theory of leadership.** It is generally considered outmoded but was the authoritative view of leadership for centuries. Currently, management theorists believe that leadership can be taught. The **trait theory of leadership,** also a genetic theory of leadership, is not widely accepted today. It does, however, continue to be used in some employee performance appraisal systems.

THE BEHAVIORAL APPROACH

The change in focus from who the leader was to what the leader did was part of a larger movement in the study of management—the *human relations movement*—discussed in Chapter 2. The human relations movement focused on the individual as opposed to the task and sought to improve productivity by understanding the individual worker. This approach to the understanding of leadership also focused on the behavior of the individual. Making use of Frederick Taylor's earlier conceptualization of the "one right way," the **Behavioral Approach** to leadership sought to determine the "one best leadership style" that would work effectively in all situations. The focus of this approach to leadership behavior provides genuine insight into the origins and effectiveness of leadership, but its search for the one best leadership style is a weakness.

The Behavioral Approach is a research-based attempt to understand leadership. It was developed in several famous university studies of leadership in the business environment. Although the various studies used different terms to describe the dimensions of leadership, they are generally referred to as task orientation and employee orientation. *Task orientation* consists of actions taken by the leader to accomplish the job, such as assigning the task and organizing the work, supervising, and evaluating worker performance. *Employee orientation* consists of the actions that characterize the way in which a leader relates to and approaches subordinates; an example of this is the amount and kind of concern shown by a leader for employees. Figure 14-2 shows how these two dimensions of leadership are generally presented in a leadership-style matrix. In this example, three leadership styles have been placed within the matrix. Leader A shows a high concern for people and a low concern for getting the job done. Leader B shows an equal concern for both people and the task. Leader C demonstrates a high concern for getting the job done but not a high concern for workers. The classification and uses of these leadership styles will be discussed in depth later in this chapter in *The Managerial Grid*.

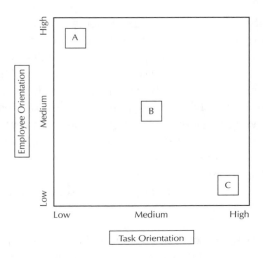

Figure 14–2. Two-dimensional leadership matrix.

The two research groups that are famous for their work along these lines were at Ohio State University and the University of Michigan. Their studies are known as the University of Michigan studies and the Ohio State studies. The **Ohio State studies** revealed two dimensions of leadership, which were called *initiating structure* and *consideration*. These leadership dimensions corresponded to the previously presented task orientation and employee orientation. The Ohio State researchers began their scientific investigation into leadership styles with the conviction that the successful leader would show both a high level of task orientation and a high level of employee orientation. This did not prove to be the case. In several studies making use of the leadership-style matrix, no one style emerged as always effective. Various combinations of task orientation and employee orientation were seen to characterize effective leadership. No one right style of leadership always proved effective. There were, however, assertions that the best leaders were high in both orientations.

The **University of Michigan** studies made use of the terms *job-centered* and *employee-oriented* to denote the dimensions of leadership corresponding to task orientation and employee orientation shown in Figure 14-2. The University of Michigan researchers compared two units within a large corporation and found that the units were different in leadership style even though both units were high producers. One unit had a leadership style high in employee orientation and evidenced high employee job satisfaction, low turnover, and low absenteeism. The other unit had a high task orientation leadership style and showed lower employee job satisfaction, higher turnover, and greater levels of absenteeism. Both units were highly productive, but worker feelings and behaviors were completely different.

The University of Michigan researchers concluded that the effectiveness of a leadership style could not be evaluated only on the basis of levels of achieved productivity. In this instance, in which both units were productive, one leadership style produced employee satisfaction and the other produced great employee discontent. The Michigan researchers concluded that evaluation of a leadership style requires an inclusive examination of such measures as employee satisfaction, absenteeism, and turnover rates. While concluding that *employee orientation* was most effective, the *University of Michigan studies demonstrated that even a leadership style judged less effective could lead to increased productivity.*

The researchers in both these studies and later scientists reached the following conclusions:

1. Leadership has at least two dimensions and is more complex than advocated by either a genetic or a leadership trait approach.

2. Leadership styles are *flexible;* managers can change the mix of task orientation and employee orientation as the situation requires.

3. Leadership styles are not innate; they can be *learned*.

4. There is no one right style of leadership.

Even though the Behavioral Approach to leadership failed to find the one right style of leadership, one of its original goals, it has contributed much to an understanding of leadership. It shifted the earlier focus from that which was given (genes and traits) to that which is learned (behavior) and advanced a more complex view of leadership. This more complex view led subsequent researchers to examine the relationship between leadership styles, abilities, and skills and the needs of the situation. These ways of explaining effective leadership are collectively known as *situational approaches* and are accepted as the state-of-the-art understanding of leadership. Even though the situational approaches have largely replaced the earlier behavioral methodology in the realm of research, the Behavioral Approach remains a powerful tool in the corporate world. This has largely been made possible by the work of **Drs. Robert R. Blake** and **Jane Srygley Mouton,** embodied in the Managerial Grid.

We shall complete the examination of leadership theories with a discussion of the situational approaches and then turn briefly to the Managerial Grid since, given its popularity, most managers will encounter it during their careers.

YOU SHOULD REMEMBER

The **Behavioral Approach** to leadership, part of the human relations movement in management theory, **focused on the individual,** not the task. Two basic dimensions of leadership—**task orientation** (initiating structures) and **employee orientation** (consideration)—were studied, particularly by two research groups, known as the University of Michigan studies and the Ohio State studies. The Behavioral Approach also stressed that leadership *can be learned* and should be *flexible* and that there is no one right style of leadership.

SITUATIONAL APPROACHES

As stated previously, the **Situational Approach** is a complex view of leadership that examines leadership styles, abilities, and skills and the needs of the situation.

The Situational Approaches are also known as **Contingency Approaches** since a leader's effectiveness in influencing others will be dependent (or contingent) upon the needs of the situation itself. An effective leader, in a Contingency Approach, must understand the dynamics of the situation and adapt his or her abilities to those dynamics. A situation must be understood from four different dimensions, each of which will influence leadership effectiveness. These are summarized in Figure 14-3.

The *personal characteristics of the manager* are the most obvious influence upon leadership effectiveness. These managerial abilities consist of the individual's needs, interpersonal and technical skills, personal motivation to achieve, past experience, and the value placed upon rewards offered by the organization. Some of these characteristics may be related to one's heritage or personality traits, but most are learned.

The second factor influencing leadership effectiveness is the *nature of the job itself*. If the job performance specifications are not stated clearly, effective leadership will be very difficult for it will lack direction and focus. Work that is highly challenging may evoke better performance than routine, boring jobs. The level of teamwork required to complete the job will also influence the nature and effectiveness of a leadership style. It is easy to see that a leadership style that is high in employee orientation will be more effective with a task requiring a high degree of teamwork.

Organizations are not neutral—*the nature of the organization* also influences leadership effectiveness. The organization's policies and rules may limit a manager's range of leadership styles. For example, if a company is unionized, the collective bargaining agreement (contract with the union)

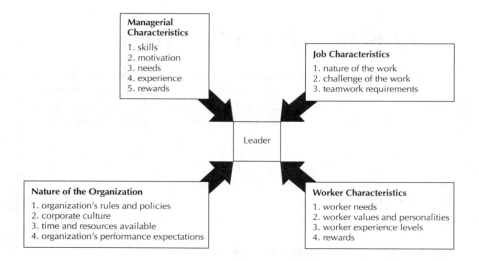

Figure 14–3. Contingency (situational) influences on leadership effectiveness.

may specify the types of rewards and punishment that can be used; this greatly limits the range of options available to the manager and will directly influence the effectiveness of a leadership type. If the business organization or individual department consists primarily of professionals, a different kind of leadership is required than that effective in an assembly-line situation.

Finally, *worker characteristics*—the personalities and values, needs, and past experience levels of the workers—will influence the choice and ultimate effectiveness of the manager's leadership style. Since the Contingency Approach to leadership stresses adaptability to the situation, managers can take individual differences in employees into account. One of the tasks of management is to understand the needs of the workers and provide organizational rewards that are meaningful and therefore motivational.

Each of these factors has the power to influence leadership behavior and the effectiveness of a leadership style. Taking these factors into account, several major management writers have created specific Contingency or Situational approaches to the understanding of effective leadership. Two of these deserve further attention. They are Fiedler's Contingency Model and the Path-Goal Theory.

• *FIEDLER'S CONTINGENCY MODEL*

The **Contingency Model** of **Fred E. Fiedler** was one of the earliest situational models. It is a contingency model in that a leader's effectiveness is contingent upon the leader's behavior and how it interacts with aspects of the situation. Fiedler began by assessing the manager's leadership style. He did this by making use of a variable that was called the *least preferred co-worker (LPC)*. He would ask a manager (actually many managers in different studies) to describe the worker (1) with whom the manager recently interacted on a job and (2) with whom he or she worked *least* effectively. Fiedler believed that a low LPC score indicated that the worker would not be accepted by a manager, and therefore, a low score indicated that the individual manager was high on *task orientation* (since he was rejecting the worker). The LPC test is used to determine the basic orientation of the leadership style; a low LPC score = high task orientation. A high LPC score indicates that the manager will accept even the worst worker on a project and is equated with a high *employee orientation*. Thus Fiedler is able to use his LPC test to determine leadership style.

The other variables in Fiedler's model are task structure, leader/member relations, and leader position power. The first of these situational variables, *task structure*, is the nature of the task itself. Fiedler classifies a task as being either *structured*, which is another way of describing a simple and routine task, or *unstructured*, which is a complex and nonroutine task.

The second situational variable, *leader/member relations*, is a measure of the relationship that exists between the leader and the workers. It is described as the amount of confidence and trust each has in the other, as well as the amount of shared respect. Fiedler's contention was that a higher measure of trust, confidence, and respect indicated better leader/member relations, and this improved leadership effectiveness. It will be easier for a manager to be an effective leader if employees trust and respect him or her. This measurement scale goes from good to poor, and when leader/member relations are evaluated as poor, a manager may have to take special steps to produce leadership effectiveness.

Fiedler's final situational variable is the *leader position power*, a measure of the actual power of the leader (within the organization). This power, measured on a scale from strong to weak, may consist of the forms of power or a combination of forms previously discussed. (These are (1) legitimate power, (2) reward power, (3) coercive power, (4) expert power, (5) referent power, (6) charisma power, and (7) information power.)

A major outcome of Fiedler's approach is that, given measures of the situational variables, an effective leadership style is recommended. Figure 14-4 illustrates how Fiedler would choose an effective leadership style based on measuring the situational variables. In a factory situation, for example, if leader/member relations are good and the task highly structured (a routine manufacturing assembly), and if the leader has strong power (assuming no union), Fiedler's leadership matrix would suggest a *task orientation* as the most effective leadership style. However, consider the case of a man who repairs potholes on the backroads of a rural county and is relatively unsupervised during the workday, an unstructured task. The leader/member relations are good, but given the unsupervised nature of the task, the leader lacks power. Fiedler's matrix would suggest that the most effective leadership style will be *employee orientation*. This makes sense if the manager will not be able to inspect the employee's work but will have to depend upon daily reports; the manager-employee relationship will be very important and should characterize the leadership style selected.

Fiedler's model has been used in much scientific research and has resulted in many new insights concerning effective leadership style. Its major contribution to management is the development of measures of *situational variables* and the integration of these measures into a total assessment mechanism of leadership effectiveness. Although some management scientists have disputed the use and content of the LPC measure, all Fiedler's measurement frameworks and scales have served to focus the attention of scientists and managers alike upon a true contingency view of leadership effectiveness.

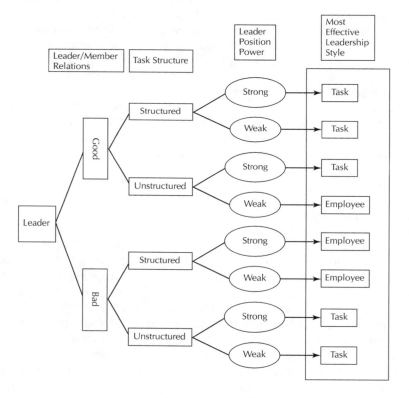

Figure 14–4. Fiedler's leadership contingency matrix.

• *PATH-GOAL THEORY OF LEADERSHIP EFFECTIVENESS*

A second major effort at developing a contingency theory of leadership effectiveness is that of **Martin G. Evans** and **Robert J. House.** Their theory, called the **Path-Goal Theory,** maintains that a worker will be motivated to perform on the job if:

1. he or she believes that the job can be accomplished (*expectancy*).

2. the rewards offered are suitable for the desired task accomplishment (*instrumentality*).

3. the rewards are meaningful to the individual (*valence*).

These reflect some of the previously presented situational variables found in the areas of worker characteristics and job characteristics. Evans and House maintain that there will be motivation to achieve the desired results when expectancy, instrumentality, and valence are all high. This approach to leadership effectiveness sees the task of the leader as facilitating each of these components, with the end result high motivation and good performance.

Evans and House recognize that there are situational variables that influence expectancy, instrumentality, and valence. These situational influences include worker characteristics, and the nature of the job (see Figure 14-3). The behaviors of the leader will also influence worker motivation and these scientists classify leader behaviors into four different classes:

1. *Instrumental behaviors* are the managerial functions of planning, task assignment, and controlling of worker behavior.

2. *Supportive behaviors* include behaviors that show interest in, concern for, and support of workers, for example having a birthday party for a worker.

3. *Participative behaviors* allow and facilitate worker participation by such activities as sharing of information and seeking worker suggestions and ideas.

4. *Achievement-oriented behaviors* include setting challenges for workers as a way of motivating peak performance.

Each of these kinds of managerial behaviors can have a profound effect upon leadership effectiveness. By showing the correct behavior, a manager can enhance leadership effectiveness by creating a high expectancy, instrumentality, and valence. When a leader helps create a clear path to a desired reward, the leadership shown is said to be effective. This may be accomplished by a combination of leadership behaviors.

The main contribution of the Path-Goal Theory of leadership effectiveness is to create a more complex view of a leader's interaction with both the situation and the subordinate. Although this approach is relatively new and is just starting to give rise to research to provide insight into effective leadership, it has proved to be a useful, systematic approach to the study of leadership. It has also pointed to the need for the prospective manager or leader to understand (or diagnose) the work situation. It is necessary to understand how all the elements that influence motivation and ultimate task accomplishment interrelate. This theory also recognizes that workers are influenced by a great many variables that impact upon the effectiveness of the leader.

The Path-Goal Theory of leadership is one of the most complex ways of approaching effectiveness. Because of its recent introduction and relative lack of exposure to scientific experimentation and verification, it has not yet found wide acceptance or application in the practical world of business.

YOU SHOULD REMEMBER

Situational, or Contingency, Approaches are complex, viewing leadership styles, abilities, and skills and the needs of the situation. Situational variables—the personal characteristics of the manager, the nature of the job, the nature of the organization, and worker characteristics—influence the effectiveness of a leadership style. Two specific models incorporating Contingency Approaches have become established. **Fiedler's Contingency Model** considers four variables—least preferred coworker, task structure, leader/member relations, and leader position power—in developing leadership recommendations. The **Path-Goal Theory** considers worker motivating factors—expectancy, instrumentality, and valence—plus situational variables in its situational model.

THE MANAGERIAL GRID

The most widely known and used approach to leadership does not reflect the complexity of a true contingency model but makes use of the Behavioral Approach to leadership effectiveness. This popular adaptation of the Behavioral Approach is called the **Managerial Grid.** It is presented here in a separate section because of its popularity and wide use in modern business.

Doctors Robert R. Blake and **Jane Srygley Mouton** adapted the behavioral data of the University of Michigan Studies and the Ohio State studies. These managerial scientists described the behavioral dimensions derived from the university studies in managerial attitudes that were expressed in what they called the two dimensions of leadership concern for people and concern for production, yet a different set of terms for the now-familiar task orientation and employee orientation. They produced a matrix—the Managerial Grid—concentrating on five major styles. Figure 14-5 is an example of the Blake-Mouton Managerial Grid.

The following leadership styles (highlighted in shaded numbered squares within the Managerial Grid shown in Figure 14-5) have received much attention by practicing managers:

Location 1,1. This location on the Managerial Grid shows equally minimal concern for both people and production. Because of this minimal concern, this is an *impoverished* or *laissez-faire management style*.

Location 1,9. This management style is characterized by a high concern for people but a minimal concern for production. A manager who shows such great concern for employees while paying minimal attention to getting the job done will be very popular and create a friendly and comfortable work environment. Work, however, may not get done. This is called a *country club management style*.

Location 9,1. This management style stresses a high priority for accomplishing the desired production while devoting little concern or attention to the needs of employees. This is termed a *task* or *authoritarian management style*. Managers who consistently practice this style may get the job done but will not be popular leaders.

Location 9,9. This style shows equal concern for both task and people and represents the ideal management style. It is rarely obtained by any practicing manager. Since concern for employees is equal to that for task, this is termed *team* or *democratic management*.

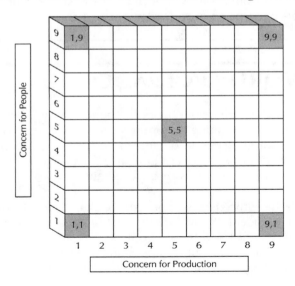

Figure 14–5. The Blake-Mouton Managerial Grid.

Location 5,5. This management style is in the middle of the Managerial Grid and is termed a *middle-of-the-road management style*. Blake and Mouton believed that this often characterized the realistic manager and therefore called it the *organization man management*. This expresses an adequate concern for and balance between task orientation and people orientation.

The Managerial Grid, although a behavioral theory of management, has been presented in a separate section in this chapter because it is so widely used by practicing managers. It has proved a useful and popular tool for advancing a more complex view of leadership in that it uses two different dimensions. The Managerial Grid has been criticized by management scientists in the same manner that all behavioral theories of leadership have been challenged—namely, that leadership is not just two-dimensional. The Contingency Approach to leadership, in particular, has stressed the influence of situational variables upon leadership effectiveness. This has led to the assertion that the Managerial Grid is too simplistic a view of leadership. Nonetheless, it remains a widely used tool.

YOU SHOULD REMEMBER

The **Managerial Grid** is the most widely used approach to leadership. An adaptation of the **Behavioral Approach,** it is a matrix concentrating on five major styles of leadership differing in the concern for people and concern for production.

AFTERWORD ON LEADERSHIP

Leadership theory has progressed from the genetic belief that "leaders are born, not made" to maintaining the opposite. "Leaders are made, not born" is an expression indicating that leadership can be learned. The following suggestions and observations represent guidance for everyone who aspires to a leadership position in business or government.

1. As the 18th-century English poet **Alexander Pope (1688–1744)** put it in a famous poem, "Know then thyself," know your strengths and weaknesses, and try to know those of others. Know the limits of your skills, abilities, and interests, but do not be intimidated by them. Seek to expand yourself by constant challenge. Seek to grow.

2. Learn from past experiences—both the successes and the failures. Analyze why you succeeded or failed. Try to learn from the past experience

of others. Read widely in the popular business press concerning the past and current success and failure of business leaders. Try to understand why they succeed or fail. Use the past—your own and that of others; it is a valuable tool for any manager.

3. Find a mentor. This will usually be a senior colleague who is willing to share past experiences and provide current guidance. Use this person as a sounding board to try out new leadership ideas. Welcome his or her criticism—even if he or she thinks your ideas are crazy, it's better to hear this from a mentor or friend than from your boss!

4. Maximize your managerial skills. If you don't have a needed skill, acquire it. Take advantage of formal and informal educational opportunities. Learning and the growth it stimulates are lifelong events.

5. As the Talmud, the ancient Jewish book of wisdom, law, and lore relates, "Who is wise? The person who learns from all others." Be open to learning from all you meet. Do not assume that your subordinates have nothing to teach you about effective leadership. Good and effective leadership is found at all levels within an organization, and if you find someone at whatever level who is such a leader, learn from him or her!

KNOW THE CONCEPTS
DO YOU KNOW THE BASICS?

1. Name the seven forms of organization power.
2. How does the organizational structure reflect the allocation of power?
3. How is punishment used within the organization?
4. Why was the genetic theory of leadership rejected?
5. What is the main difficulty with the trait theory of leadership?
6. Define the two dimensions of leadership found in the Behavioral Approach to leadership.
7. Define the terms of Fiedler's Contingency Model.
8. What are the main components of the Path-Goal Theory?
9. According to the Managerial Grid, what is the "country club" style of management?

TERMS FOR STUDY

authoritarian management
charisma power
coercive power
consideration structure
Contingency Approaches
country club management
democratic management
dimensions of leadership
employee orientation
expert power
Fiedler's Contingency Theory
formal leaders
impoverished (laissez-faire)
  management

informal leaders
information power
initiating structure
legitimate power
Managerial Grid
one best leadership style
organizational hierarchy
organization man management
Path-Goal Theory
referent power
reward power
situational variables
task orientation
theories of leadership

ANSWERS
KNOW THE BASICS

1. The forms of organizational power are legitimate power, reward power, referent power, coercive power, expert power, charisma power, and information power.

2. The T/O, or table of organization, a representation of the formal structure of an organization, reflects a power hierarchy. Positions that are higher on the organizational ladder have more power than those that are lower.

3. Punishment is used to eliminate undesirable actions; it does not promote desired behavior.

4. The genetic theory of leadership was rejected because leaders did not always have offspring who were leaders, and during the Industrial Revolution leaders arose by virtue of their own creativity, not genetic heritage. The genetic theory could not explain why these early industrialists emerged as leaders.

5. Management theorists could not agree on what was or was not a leadership trait.

6. The two dimensions of leadership found in the Behavioral Approach to leadership were concern for the employee (employee orientation) and concern for the job (task orientation).

7. The terms of Fiedler's Contingency Model are as follows. The LPC test is used to determine the basic orientation of the leadership style. The other variables in Fiedler's model are task structure, leader/member relations, and leader position power. The first of these situational variables, task structure, is the nature of the task itself. Fiedler classifies a task as either structured, which is another way of describing a simple and routine task, or unstructured, which is a complex and nonroutine task. The second situational variable, leader/member relations, is a measure of the relationship that exists between the leader and the workers. It is described as the amount of confidence and trust each has in the other, as well as the amount of shared respect. Fiedler's contention was that a higher measure of trust, confidence, and respect indicated better leader/member relations, and this improved leadership effectiveness. It will be easier for a manager to be an effective leader if employees trust and respect him or her. This measurement scale goes from good to poor, and when leader/member relations are evaluated as poor, a manager may have to take special steps to improve leadership effectiveness.

Fiedler's final situational variable is the leader position power. This is a measure of actual power of the leader within the organization. This power, measured on a scale from strong to weak, may consist of one of the forms of power or a combination of forms previously discussed. (These are legitimate power, reward power, coercive power, expert power, charisma power, referent power, and information power.)

8. The components of the Path-Goal Theory are that the worker believes that the job can be accomplished (expectancy); the rewards offered are suitable for the desired task accomplishment (instrumentality); and the rewards are meaningful to the individual (valence).

9. Under a Managerial Grid approach, the country club style of management reflects a manager who rates 1,9. This management style is characterized by a high concern for people but a minimal concern for production. A manager who shows such great concern for employees while paying minimal attention to getting the job done will be very popular and create a friendly and comfortable work environment. Work, however, may not get done.

15
MANAGEMENT: THE CONTROL FUNCTION

KEY TERMS

control process sequential actions taken by management to establish performance standards, measure and evaluate performance, and take corrective action where indicated

input controls corrective actions taken during the input phase of the organization's activities; also referred to as **steering controls**

process controls control actions that impact the organization's internal activities and serve to regulate and evaluate transformational activities

output controls actions taken by management to regulate an organization's output of goods or services or both

feedback information about job or organizational performance derived from the work itself that is used in a corrective manner

financial controls the formally stated financial objectives of an organization, setting forth, for a defined period of time, the financial parameters within which it will operate, the conditions assumed to exist during that time, and performance standards against which financial performance can be judged

behavioral controls actions taken by management that seek to specify, evaluate, and correct human performance within the organization, including performance appraisal techniques and production and operations planning

As we have seen in Chapters 6 through 8, *planning* is a major function of business management. The accompanying process by which management implements its plans and evaluates organizational accomplishment to gauge success or failure is that of control. Control consists of sequential actions taken by management to establish performance standards, measure and evaluate performance, and take corrective action where indicated. It is absolutely essential for effective planning. Management must know how it is performing in order to make the most effective use of scarce organizational resources. It must evaluate the manner in which resources are used, take corrective actions where needed, and effectively plan for more efficient resource use in the future. There are three major points concerning the importance of control:

1. Control is necessary to measure and evaluate organizational performance.

2. Control is a dynamic and ongoing process.

3. Control involves all facets of the organization.

THE CONTROL PROCESS

The **control process** is practiced by all areas and levels of an organization's management, although there is much variation in the application of control in different organizational areas. However, the basic process remains the same: (1) setting performance standards, (2) measuring the performance, (3) evaluating the performance, and (4) making effective use of feedback and taking corrective actions when necessary, when there has been a failure to meet the performance standards.

SETTING PERFORMANCE STANDARDS

As we have seen in the earlier chapters on managerial planning, goals are set for an organization at all levels. **Performance standards** are organizational goals and unit subgoals stated in *concrete and measurable performance terms*. By measuring the goal accomplishment of an organization, management can accomplish several important tasks:

• Management can determine relative degrees of success or failure by comparing actual performance with desired performance standards.

• Management can compare this year's performance results with those of past years, thus gaining perspective on how the company is doing over time.

• Management can compare the company's performance with that of other companies in the same industry, thus gaining a perspective on how the company is doing on a comparative basis.

For example, top management may state a business goal in strategic terms, such as, "to increase sales during this financial year," but this lacks a performance standard. To create a performance standard, midlevel management would restate this strategic goal in measurable terms, such as, "to increase sales by 20 percent over last year." This then creates a performance standard against which results can be measured and success gauged. There are several major issues that must be dealt with in creating effective performance standards: (1) What does management measure? (2) How is it measured? (3) When should it be measured? (4) What is a fair performance standard?

• *WHAT DOES MANAGEMENT MEASURE?*

That which is measured should be determined by an organization's goal. If the goal is to increase sales, as in the example cited earlier, then measuring the amount of sales is appropriate, but even here there may be questions. Does the measure include sales that are "booked" but not actually delivered and paid for? How does management consider sales that are made in one financial year but extend into the next? These questions may appear to be trivial, but such details must be considered in establishing an effective performance standards system. *That which is measured should reflect the actual business activity that fulfills management's business goals.*

The example just used may be misleading in its simplicity, for even with the problems cited, sales are relatively easy to measure. The reality confronting management as it creates performance standards is often more complex. Suppose one of top management's goals is to increase employee morale, believing that employees who are happier (higher morale) will be more productive. Is morale really related to employee productivity? This is not clear. How do you measure morale? These are questions management must answer before performance standards can be created. The former question regarding the relationship between morale and productivity raises the issue we began with: What do you measure? The latter question of how to define the abstract concept "morale" raises a different issue: How do you measure it?

• *HOW IS IT MEASURED?*

Once management has decided on what to measure, it must then decide how to do the actual measurement of performance. In the case of the abstract concept "morale," academic consultants and industrial psychologists might suggest that management measure such observable behaviors as employee absenteeism, tardiness, and turnover and create an index of morale. Such an index might be the number of employee days absent plus the number of employee minutes tardy plus the number of employees who quit during the year. Such a process would produce a number that is derived from behavior and would allow a company to compare departments in any given year as well as compare overall performance from year to year. Management would then have created a measure of morale and could evaluate performance in the area of morale improvement.

There are necessary financial considerations inherent in the decision of how to measure performance. Performance measurement of any form takes time and costs money, and there are compromises made in the name of financial soundness. For example, a company assembling passenger jet planes may find it cost effective, indeed mandatory, to inspect and test the quality of every part, even the smallest screw, before it is installed because of the dire financial and tragic human consequences which would derive from a bad part. A toothbrush manufacturer, however, would find it a tremendous and needless financial burden, and obvious managerial inefficiency, to inspect every toothbrush that comes off the assembly line. In this case, as evidenced by the routine use of product sampling methodologies and the application of statistical theory and probability measurement in Japan—advocated and taught by the pioneering American quality control expert **W. Edwards Deming**—inspecting one out of each 1,000, or perhaps one in 10,000, might be sufficient to ensure adequate quality control. Since quality control costs money, a task continually facing management is to achieve a system of such control that is both *efficient* and *effective*. Thus, how to measure performance will be determined by the *nature of what is to be measured* and the *cost effectiveness of measurement*, which is another way of saying the cost to the company (and risk) of not measuring quality.

• *WHEN IS IT TO BE MEASURED?*

Since measurement of performance takes time and costs money, companies will consider when to gather performance data. In general, performance is measured after it has taken place, but such a measure may employ data gathered before the performance. Parts used in the assembly of a computer may be tested to determine rates of failure *before* the actual assembly. The same company may test the circuit boards as they are assembled, performance data derived *during* the actual assembly. Or it may test product quality *after* assembly but before sale to the customer. These types of performance measures are *input* controls, *process* controls, and *output* controls and are discussed in much greater detail later in this chapter. They are summarized in Figure 15-1.

The nature of the product will influence when the measurement of performance should be made. It may be that the production process is slow enough to allow for product testing, but the reverse may also be true. The production process may be so rapid that it is impossible to test the components while assembly is taking place; the only practical testing methodology is to examine the completed product. Or it may be that the flaws and defects in the product will not show until much later, sometimes years after manufacture. In this case the manufacturer may decide not to do a final inspection but offer a long-term guarantee to deal with product defects that appear much later. Increasingly, the Internet has opened up significant new ways of gathering post-production performance data from computers and the electronic components that interface with them. The manufacturer is able

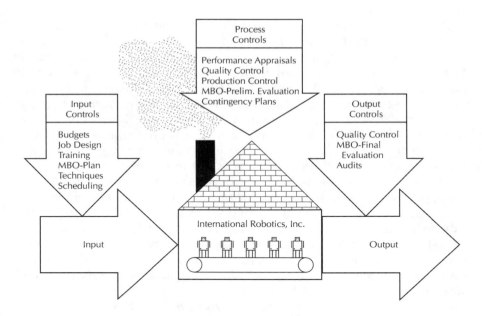

Figure 15–1. Open systems control model.

to gather diagnostic (performance) information from computers via the Internet while the purchaser is using the computer. (Alternatively, some computer programs are configured to go on the Internet to software company web sites and automatically download the latest versions of programming.)

The previous discussion of what, how, and when to measure has presupposed that management can create performance standards that are fair and equitable. If the standards created are not fair, then the other issues of measure will not matter; the standards will not function as useful and effective managerial tools. Each of the steps in the creation of performance standards ultimately revolves around the fairness of the standards created. It is therefore fitting that the discussion of standards end with some managerial consideration of the fairness of performance standards.

YOU SHOULD REMEMBER

Performance standards are powerful managerial tools for the control of a business. They serve as levels of desired performance against which actual performance can be measured and evaluated. Management must decide **what** performance to measure, **when** to measure, and **how** to measure. The measurement of performance is costly, so there is always a balance between the number of measurements and cost effectiveness. The guiding principle in deciding the frequency of measurement is what is required by the nature of the business activity. A business that exists in a rapidly changing environment may require more measures of performance than one in a stable situation.

• *WHAT IS A FAIR PERFORMANCE STANDARD?*

Performance standards are designed to provide management with a useful tool to measure and evaluate organizational actions. If the standards are unrealistically high, the organization will not obtain the desired results and will be judged a failure. If the performance standards are set too low, an organization may easily exceed the desired standards and be considered a success when a much more productive use of its resources was actually possible. The task confronting management is to create fair and equitable standards. This can be done by examining past performance as well as the performance of other companies in the industry.

Past performance data will give some indication of what is possible and therefore a realistic managerial expectation. Such data should not limit managerial expectation, however: they are an *indication* of what was previously accomplished, not a limitation of what can be accomplished. The current condition of the organization must also be taken into account, for it may be capable of higher levels of performance than in the past. Conversely, there may have been business reverses, the death of a key employee, or expiration of a vital patent, for example, creating a situation in which it will not be realistic to expect the achievement of past performance levels. In either event, the past as well as the present will provide a framework within which performance standards can be created. It should be noted that in a rapidly changing industry, characterized most notably by a changing technology, past performance data may seriously lag behind current performance capabilities. In this case, use of past performance data will probably not be an effective and challenging baseline from which to project future performance standards.

It will be helpful for management to examine what is being accomplished by other companies in the same industrial or service area. What other companies are doing also serves as an indication of what can realistically be expected. If a different company is achieving higher performance levels, management should seek to understand what factors make this possible. Does the other company have more effective applications of technology? Does it have better leadership? Are there geographic or economic factors that enable it to have better success? What are the lessons to be learned, and how can they be applied here in this company?

YOU SHOULD REMEMBER

Performance standards that can be achieved by workers are fair and reasonable. Performance levels that are not realistic will not serve to motivate worker achievement or provide management with a useful tool. The best data in the setting of realistic performance standards are past worker performance and the performance levels achieved by other workers in the industry. Management should be influenced by past worker performance but not constrained by that performance. Good management techniques and the innovative use of motivational theory and incentive design will often produce higher levels of worker performance and allow the setting of higher performance standards.

MEASURING PERFORMANCE

Some of the issues involved in **measuring performance** have already been discussed in terms of setting performance standards. It is of further use, however, to consider the different kinds of measurement data employed and the different time frames inherent in measuring performance.

The measurements stressed previously—for example, sales figures—are *quantitative* in nature. The numbers derived from such measures can be used to make comparisons and to keep records and in overall performance evaluation. There are those measures of performance, however, that defy quantification. For example, an airline that wanted to have some sense of customer satisfaction might attempt to quantify satisfaction by creating a satisfaction scale on a questionnaire, or it might define satisfaction in terms of the number of customer complaints about baggage and actually count the complaints. Both these techniques would quantify customer satisfaction. This same airline might invite some frequent flyers to a meeting and ask them to talk about their satisfactions and gripes regarding service. This discussion group (sometimes called in research a *focus group*) would not generally give numerical data, but there would be a sense of the quality of customer satisfaction. These nonnumerical data are called *qualitative* or *anecdotal data* and can also be useful in measuring performance.

Consider for a moment this example. **Sir Anthony Van Dyke (1599–1641)**, a Flemish painter of great renown who resided in England, created a painting entitled *Virgin and Child*. How much is this painting worth? An attempt to *quantify* its worth might add the value of the paint and canvas to the value of the artist's time to equal the value of the painting. This would produce a valuation of perhaps several hundred dollars. Or you could let the marketplace determine the value of this painting. Since there is a small supply of paintings by this artist and the demand is quite brisk, we would expect a high price to be paid for it. In fact, this particular painting sold for $365,000 in 1976, and art critics complained that the price was too low. Each of these attempts at valuation results in a quantification of the worth of this painting. But there are art lovers who claim that such art masterpieces are priceless, beyond monetary valuation. The claim that this painting is priceless is an attempt to place a *qualitative* value on its worth.

Evaluating organizational performance can encompass both qualitative and quantitative measures, just as a fine painting can be valued both quantitatively ($365,000) and qualitatively (priceless).

The timing of a performance evaluation is crucial. The nature of the product will influence when the measurement of performance should be made. It should also be noted that the time frame of the goal itself will influence the timing of the performance evaluation. Short-term goals should be evaluated on a short-term basis. Long-term goals require a much longer time frame. If the time frame of the goal is mismatched with the time frame of the evaluation, great confusion can result. A long-term goal evaluated too soon may appear a failure, and a short-term goal evaluated on a long-term basis, long after it has or has not been accomplished, may be irrelevant. Performance data should, therefore, be available in a timely manner to be truly useful as a managerial tool for planning and evaluating the efficacy of use of scarce organizational resources. Performance data that are either incomplete or untimely lack a utility value and, at best, will seem irrelevant; at worst, misleading. The issues of timing and format of performance data should be considered by managers prior to the gathering of such data or implementing a management information system.

YOU SHOULD REMEMBER

Performance may be measured in **quantitative** or **qualitative** ways. The nature of the goals (standards) set determines whether measurements should be made on a short- or long-term basis.

EVALUATING PERFORMANCE

Once the performance standard has been defined and the measures taken, the next step in the control process is to **evaluate the performance.** This is the process in which the measured performance is compared with the performance standard. Figure 15-2 shows the sequence of events in the control process. At this point—evaluate performance stage—in the control process one of two states will exist—the performance will meet the standards or it will not. In either case the information derived from the performance evaluation will be used by the organization in a constructive manner. This is called *feedback* and is information about job performance derived from the job itself that is used in a corrective manner.

As shown across the top of Figure 15-2, if the performance standards have been met, this information is fed back to the "measure actual performance" step in the control process and the process then begins anew from that step. There is no indication that the performance standards themselves have to be revised. If the performance standards have not been met, however, corrective actions are taken. This is shown across the bottom of Figure 15-2. After corrective actions are taken, this information is fed back into the control process to the "create performance standards" and "measure actual performance" steps. Perhaps the performance standards were not met because they were too demanding—the reexamination in the first feedback step will evaluate the standards created. If they are too demanding, they can be adjusted and the control process continues anew. The corrective actions are also fed back to the "measure actual performance" step since they will influence the manner in which the performance is measured.

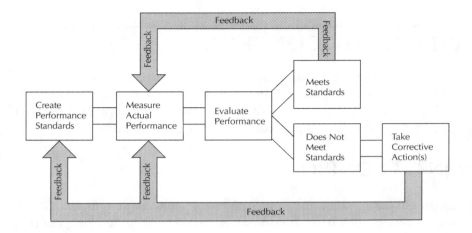

Figure 15–2. The control process.

YOU SHOULD REMEMBER

In performance evaluation the measured performance is compared with the performance standards set. The result produces useful information that is fed back into the organization and indicates where corrective action is needed. Effective use of **feedback** is a powerful management tool for the control of work performance.

USING FEEDBACK

As already indicated, if the actual performance does not meet the performance standard, management will take corrective action. This presupposes that the standards are fair and can be met. However, management may confront a different situation if the actual performance has exceeded the performance standard. This *may* indicate that the performance standards have been set too low—or that the individual under evaluation is a top performer.

Corrective action has as its purpose the promotion of desired performance and the meeting of the performance standards. Performance feedback data are analyzed to determine the most effective form of corrective action.

PHASES OF CONTROL

The control process operates at all levels of an organization. Managers find it useful to divide controls into three phases related to the open systems model. This was portrayed in Figure 15-1, in which organizational controls were broken down into input, process, and output controls.

INPUT CONTROLS

As stated earlier, when the control process operates *before* the actual business activity, it is called **input control.** It is also known as **steering control** since the organization will use such control to "steer" the activities of the business. One of the major advantages of this type of control is that it allows the organization to correct defective performance *before* making the final commitment of resources. Examples of input controls are *budgets, job design, training programs with skills evaluation* (discussed in Chapter 12), *MBO* (Management by Objectives, which is discussed in Chapter 9), *production and operations techniques* (discussed in Chapter 20), and *scheduling of work activities* (covered in Chapters 10 and 11 and in the operations framework in Chapter 20). Although this book deals with management, not finance, budgets are discussed later in this chapter. This does not represent an attempt to make managers into accountants but does emphasize budgets as a vital managerial tool.

PROCESS CONTROLS

If the control activity is done as the work is performed, it is **process control.** This function assures management that the actual performance meets the desired performance standards. If the standards are not met, the organization activity can be stopped and corrective action taken. Indeed, at some manufacturing plants, most notably automobile assembly factories, individual workers have the power to actually stop the assembly line until defective production activity has been corrected. The business activity will be resumed only when the standards are met. The following activities represent this kind of control: *quality controls*, which operate as the manufacturing process is underway; *MBO—Management by Objectives* (preliminary evaluations); and *contingency plans*, which allow management to adjust the production process to changing circumstance.

OUTPUT CONTROLS

The control process may operate after the activity but before delivery to the end user. This is an **output control.** Since this form of control operates only after the work is completed, it is the only form of control that can evaluate the entire work effort. This form of control may include *quality control of the final product* output, the final *MBO* (Management by Objective) evaluation, and *ex post facto* (after the fact) *audits.* Increasingly, as previously discussed, high-tech industries are making use of the Internet to gather *ex post facto* performance data. These are selective reviews of various aspects of the entire manufacturing process, seeking to better understand the compliance to and achievement of desired performance standards. By conducting an audit that evaluates the *entire* project, management can then shift its emphasis on planning to the appropriate aspects of organizational functioning. An overall evaluation may reveal the necessity to have more input or process controls, and management can then implement the needed forms of control.

Among the three kinds or phases of control—input, process, and output—each makes use of basic control processes. There are two broad divisions of control: *financial* controls and *behavioral* controls. The remainder of this chapter will focus on these two widely used forms of organizational control.

YOU SHOULD REMEMBER

Control can operate at all phases of the business activity. **Input** or **steering control** operates before the activity; it may include budgets, job design, and scheduling of work activities. **Process control** operates as the work is being done and may include quality control checks. **Output control** operates after the business activity but before delivery to the end user; it may include *ex post facto* audits and quality control.

FINANCIAL CONTROLS: BUDGETS AND AUDITS

DEFINITION AND PURPOSE OF BUDGETS

Budgets are formalized statements of the goals of an organization stated in financial terms. Budgets accomplish several important functions for managers. They state future projections of revenues, expenses, and expected profits. Since they embody organizational goals and expected future events, *budgets can be used as financial performance standards*. They are also extremely useful as managerial tools for planning. The creation of a budget forces managers to conceptualize future goals in specific (financial) terms and to immediately consider how to achieve these goals. No organization has unlimited resources, and budgets reflect this organizational limitation. Since budgets are created for organizations with limited resources, they furnish the financial framework and define the boundaries within which the allocation of those funds must take place. As performance standards, budgets help managers evaluate the financial performance of the business organization.

Budgets therefore aid management in the performance of the basic managerial functions of planning, organizing, and control. There is, however, an even more generalized and subtle function served by budgets and the financial evaluations of a business: budgets and audits, constructed and performed according to generally accepted financial and accounting standards, provide a universal evaluative framework. All businesses, no matter of what size or nature, can be compared based upon their level of achieved financial results.

THE BUDGETING PROCESS

Budgets can be prepared by top management and then imposed upon all other organizational levels, or they can be prepared by lower level managers and submitted to top management for approval. The first approach is the top-down budgeting method and the second is often called a *bottom-up* approach.

Top-down budgeting—budgeting prepared by top management—was a traditional approach in the past, and the top-level manager responsible for the budgeting process was given the title of Controller or CFO (Chief Financial Officer), Treasurer, or Vice President (or Senior VP, Executive VP and so on) of Finance. This process is shown in Figure 15-3.

The main advantage of this approach to the budgeting process is that it creates accountability, making a specific person responsible for budgeting. This individual, who is part of top management, has the "big picture," the overall financial condition of the organization. Although lower level managers may be able to comment on budgets, their major function is to carry out the budgets.

The major disadvantage of this managerial approach to budgeting is that budgets are not created by those who have to carry them out. Budgets that make sense on the top corporate level may prove wildly impractical on the lower organizational levels where they have to be carried out.

The bottom-up budgeting process—the process in which lower level managers prepare the budget and submit it to top management for approval—

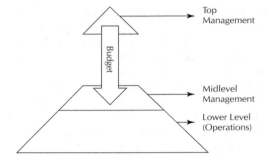

Figure 15-3. Top-down budgeting process.

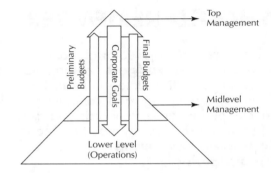

Figure 15-4. Bottom-up budgeting process.

begins with the creation by top management of the organization's goals. Lower level management then submits proposed budgets. The task of higher level management in a bottom-up budgeting system is to:

1. formulate and disseminate the goals of the business.

2. evaluate each individual departmental budget to ensure that it accomplishes or contributes to the accomplishment of the organization's goals.

3. integrate the various budgets submitted by subunits into a *total* organization budget.

An advantage of the bottom-up budget process is that it flows from those managers who have to carry out the actual budget. These managers bring a realistic appreciation for the use of resources within the organization. However, since all managers will be in competition for those organizational resources, such a budgeting approach may lead to maneuvering and manipulative behaviors by managers in an attempt to secure the needed financial resources. It may also routinely lead to the inflation of managers' budget requests so that when reductions are made by top managers in the final budget approval process, enough funds will be left to cover actual expenses.

The budgeting process should be flexible and subject to periodic review. Based upon the degree of goal accomplishment during this period, the budgets for the next planning period can be adjusted to help management meet organizational goals. If the goals themselves change, budget allocations may also be changed. As will be seen with "flexible budgets" later in this chapter, budgets may change not only at the end of a business year, but actually during the year if either goals are changed by management or economic conditions intervene to create new opportunities or thrust previously unanticipated hazards upon the corporate planners.

YOU SHOULD REMEMBER

Financial control, a major form of management control, involves budgets and audits. **Budgets** are formalized statements of the goals of an organization stated in financial terms. Important tools for planning, organizing, and controlling, budgets can be used as financial performance standards and as a framework for comparing businesses. Budgeting may be prepared by top management (**top-down budgeting**) or by lower level managers (**bottom-up budgeting**).

TYPES OF BUDGETS

There are several types of budgets: operating, financial, and flexible.

• *OPERATING BUDGETS*

Budgets, as managerial tools, are derived from specific organizational functions. **Operating budgets** reflect the operations of an organization and provide guidelines for managers. The specific content of operating budgets will vary between organizations, reflecting their different operational formats. Organizations that are primarily engaged in marketing have budgets that reflect this function, but a business that is mainly a manufacturing concern would feature a raw materials purchasing budget and may completely ignore marketing. In general, however, operating budgets reflect three basic approaches: the cost center, revenue center, and profit center approaches to budgeting.

COST CENTER BUDGET APPROACH

A **cost center approach** to budgeting constructs a budget that projects all the anticipated costs for a business (or a subunit) over a designated time period. It is considered an *operating budget* since it deals with projecting operating costs. This approach views each business unit as a cost or expense center and sets levels of spending for each area. If expenses exceed budget projections, management will be made aware that additional attention should be directed toward this area. This increased expenditure may be because of factors in the external environment of business, factors generally beyond the control of management. Another possibility exists, however, one that management will want to thoroughly explore: the increased expenditures may be due to managerial inefficiency. A cost center approach is often used in business departments where measuring output is difficult, for example professional staff areas, such as legal, research and development, personnel, and public relations. A cost center approach allows management to approximate a measure of departmental efficiency, however imprecisely. Although the cost center approach reflects a managerial concern with the costs of delivering goods or services, the revenue center approach focuses upon income projections.

REVENUE CENTER APPROACH

A **revenue center approach** deals with the profits produced by the business unit. It projects future profit goals for each separate business line, and these goals then serve as performance standards. A strict revenue center approach does not take costs into account but concentrates solely on projected profits. This leads to two major difficulties:

1. By not taking costs into account, it is difficult for management to know if the company (or subunit) is *actually* making a profit.

2. It is often difficult to accurately project profits since they are influenced by external economic and market forces that can be neither anticipated nor controlled by management. Management often combines the revenue center and cost center approaches into a profit center approach.

PROFIT CENTER APPROACH

The budget produced by the **profit center approach** combines both statements of revenues and costs to produce a statement of profits. It is used by management at the appropriate organizational level where there can be effective control over both revenues and costs. If management does not have control over both costs and revenues, this budgeting system will not be effective. When it is, it creates performance standards for management that involve meeting profitability targets. The profit center approach involves the most planning and organizational commitment.

YOU SHOULD REMEMBER

Operating budgets reflect the operations of an organization. A **cost center approach** to an operating budget holds management to account for all the funds spent in the course of doing business; it is a budgeting approach that lends itself to business departments where it is difficult to measure output—such as research and development departments. A **revenue center approach** holds management to account for the level of revenues achieved. The **profit center approach** combines both these approaches and holds management to account for profits achieved, which are revenues minus costs.

• *FINANCIAL BUDGETS*

Financial budgets are projections of how a business intends to spend its money during a given period of time. They are specific to an area and serve as performance standards against which actual expenditures can be evaluated. These budgets are cash and capital expenditure budgets, labor and material budgets, and a balance sheet budget.

CASH AND CAPITAL EXPENDITURE BUDGETS

Cash budgets are future projections over a given period of time of the anticipated cash flow through a business organization. Since cash flow is not constant, nor is the need for cash constant, management can readily project when excess cash will be available to be put to other uses. Management will also be able to project when there will be a need for cash beyond that which is provided by the cash flow. Short-term borrowing can be anticipated by means of cash flow analysis and arranged for in the most efficient and economical manner.

A **capital expenditures budget** details projected capital investment in new organizational physical resources such as plants, land, and machinery. Since many of these assets are of a long-term nature, they require a long-term organizational commitment of funds. These budgets may be very complex and express a multi-year commitment of organizational resources in yearly increments.

MATERIAL BUDGETS

Every organization makes use of raw materials. These constitute the input factors that we have seen before. These materials must be acquired; they include not only physical materials but also such things as labor. Materials and labor which go directly into a final product are called *direct cost factors* (or direct material and labor). Those organizational resources that do not go directly into a product, such as the cost of maintaining a company cafeteria, are called *indirect cost factors.* A **material budget** concerns the direct cost factors and details how and in what amounts an organization will acquire its future material needs.

BALANCE SHEET BUDGET

A **balance sheet budget** combines all the aforementioned budgets into one organizational master budget. It shows the relationship between an organization's assets (what it has), its liabilities (what it owes), and its owners' equity (whatever is left). If performance standards are not being met within one or more individual budgets, management can anticipate the probable effects upon the entire organization and take appropriate corrective action. Since the balance sheet projects the condition of an organization at a specific point in time, management cannot be sure that its projected results will become an actuality. A balance sheet budget is also called a *pro forma* balance sheet.

YOU SHOULD REMEMBER

Financial budgets project the ways in which a business intends to spend its money during a given period of time. There are several types of financial budgets: a **cash budget** projects anticipated cash flow; a **capital expenditures budget** details projected capital investment in new resources (such as machinery); a **materials budget** details direct cost factors—materials and labor; a **balance sheet budget,** combining all these approaches, shows the organization's assets, liabilities, and equity at a specific point in time.

Operating and financial budgets are called *fixed budgets.* Management has often found that it cannot make such rigid projections in rapidly changing environments that will influence the actual results. Under such conditions, several budgets will be constructed, each reflecting different environmental conditions. These budgets will be *flexible.*

• *FLEXIBLE BUDGETS*

Under conditions in which the projected financial results may vary greatly as the organization is influenced by rapidly changing environmental conditions, management may find it impossible to construct a valid fixed budget. The solution will be to construct several budgets, each one taking the potential environmental changes into account and their impact upon the organization's achievements. Since each of these budgets has a certain probability of occurring, this budgeting process is also called *probabilistic budgeting*. An example of this is a large photographic product company that uses huge quantities of silver in its manufacture of camera film. Budgets would be constructed assuming a $5, $6, and $7 price of silver per ounce. Every time the price of silver changes at least a dollar an ounce, a new budget takes effect. It is obvious that to ensure flexibility in the budgeting process, vis-à-vis such probabilistic forecasting, it is necessary to know a great deal about the changing environment and the parameters and determinants of the factors to the setting of budgets. It is for this reason businesses often consult industry experts and specialized consultants such as economists, to gain insight into future potentials as applied to relevant environmental factors. Money thus expended, if in a timely and thoughtful manner, can be an extremely good investment for the business manager.

YOU SHOULD REMEMBER

Flexible, or **probabilistic, budgets** take into account potential environmental changes and their probable impact on an organization's achievements.

AUDITS

Audits are formal evaluations of an organization's financial situation. Since budgets set forth financial performance standards, an audit seeks to answer:

1. Are the financial statements correct, do they accurately reflect the financial condition of the company, and have they been performed according to accepted accounting and auditing standards?

2. Does the actual financial performance of an organization meet the performance standards contained in the budget projections?

Audits are also presented to the general community as certifications of financial health. As such they are often performed by external accounting professionals—*certified public accountants (CPA)*— who certify the validity of the audits.

Audits are often performed on an internal basis to provide management with relevant and timely information so that more effective decisions can be made. These audits are done by internal auditors. The purpose of these internal audits is similar to that of the CPA audits, to ensure that the information thus derived is valid and that management can rely upon it in the decision-making process. Employees of the company generally have a greater familiarity with its operations than external auditors so they are able to go into greater depth in examining the organization's operations. *Internal audits* are useful tools for management and should be understood by all employees as such. If employees view the internal auditors as management's "secret police force," they will not be likely to cooperate, but if the internal audit is perceived as a tool, cooperation will be facilitated.

One form of audit—a **management audit**—consists of a periodic examination of managerial effectiveness. It examines the current content and condition of management's goals and the plans created to achieve these goals. Such an audit might examine the current state of all organizational resources and management's policies regarding the acquisition, inventory, and use of resources.

Management audits can be conducted by internal personnel or external professional consultants or a combination of both. There are advantages to both: internal personnel know the firm best, as already mentioned, but may have personal stakes in the outcome of the evaluation. An external professional consultant may be more objective in evaluation but not know the firm well and be quite costly. A hidden benefit of using a consultant, however, is that if bad feelings are created by what prove to be realistic but unpopular recommendations, such feelings will attach to the consultant, an outsider, and will be somewhat mitigated by the fact that this individual leaves the company after the assignment is completed.

Financial controls furnish management with extremely useful tools to control the organization, but there is also a different major classification of controls that are valuable for management—*behavioral controls.* Although financial controls involve dollars, behavioral controls center upon the human side of the enterprise. Control of worker behavior is inherent in the reward and motivational systems' use of coercive power and discipline of workers, and performance appraisal systems leading to corrective action as the direct result of managerial evaluation.

YOU SHOULD REMEMBER

Audits are formal evaluations of an organization's financial situation. Performed by external accounting professionals or by internal auditors, an audit evaluates the accuracy of financial statements and performance compared to budget projections. A **management audit** examines managerial effectiveness.

KNOW THE CONCEPTS

DO YOU KNOW THE BASICS?

1. Why should performance standards be realistic?
2. Where can management get data to set the realistic standards referred to in Question 1?
3. What is feedback, and what is it used for?
4. If performance standards are not met, what might management conclude?
5. What are the general forms of control used by management?
6. How does top-down budgeting differ from bottom-up?
7. What is an operating budget?
8. How do the cost center, the revenue center, and the profit center approaches differ?
9. What are financial budgets?

TERMS FOR STUDY

balance sheet budget	input
behavioral controls	management audit
control process	operating budgets
cost center approach	performance standards
CPA	probabilistic budget
direct cost factors	process controls
feedback	profit center approach
financial controls	pro forma balance sheet
fixed budget	qualitative measures
flexible budgets	quantitative measures
focus group	revenue center approach
indirect cost factors	steering controls

ANSWERS

KNOW THE BASICS

1. If performance standards are realistic, they will serve to motivate workers and provide management with useful data on worker performance as the workers either achieve the goals or fail to do so. If the standards

are realistic and the workers do not achieve them, then management will know that there is organizational inefficiency.

2. The best data on worker performance will be derived from past worker performance achievements. Management will also wish to examine the worker achievements of other employees within the same or similar industries. This will indicate what has been possible in the past. However, if management has introduced some technical or managerial improvement, it may wish to raise the work performance standard.

3. Feedback is information about job performance derived from the job itself that is used to indicate to management where and in what form corrective action is needed.

4. If performance standards are not met, management may conclude one of two possibilities: (1) the standards are set too high and therefore the responsibility lies within the standards themselves or (2) the standards are realistic and the workers are responsible for not meeting them.

5. The control process operates on all levels of an organization and, derived from the open systems model, can be divided into three phases—input, process, and output controls.

6. In top-down budgeting, the budget is essentially created by top management and handed down to the lower managerial levels to be implemented. Middle and lower level management have little input and no control over the finalized budget. In bottom-up budgeting, management transmits the organization's goals to the lower levels of management. These lower levels then formulate budget proposals that go back to top management for final integration into an overall organizational budget and final approval.

7. Operating budgets reflect the operations of an organization and provide guidelines for managers. These budgets are derived from different operational business formats. A marketing company will have an operating budget that will project marketing expenses; a service company will not have the same expenses in its operating budget as the marketing company.

8. A revenue center approach holds management to account for the level of revenues achieved. A cost center approach sets expenditure levels as performance goals. A profit center approach combines both in that managers are held to account for profit, which is revenues minus costs.

9. Financial budgets are cash and capital expenditure budgets, labor and material budgets, and a balance sheet budget. They set organizational performance levels in financial terms.

16
WORK GROUP DYNAMICS AND CREATIVITY

The basic definition of an organization given earlier in this book was a group of people united by common goals and objectives. This is a *macroscopic* organizational view since the entire organization can be seen as a large single group. A more *microscopic* view sees organizations as a collection of interrelated groups and recognizes that all employee behavior takes place within and between these many worker subgroups. These two approaches to an organization are shown in Figure 16-1. Because groups are so important to the modern business organization and to the management function, we shall now examine their many facets as confronted by the contemporary manager.

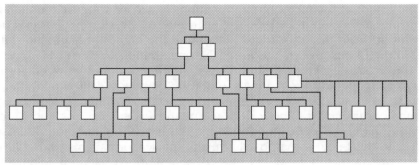

Macroview: the organization as one group

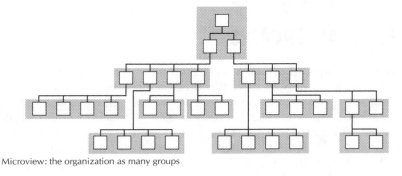

Microview: the organization as many groups

Figure 16–1. Micro and macro organizational views.

GROUPS: BASIC CHARACTERISTICS

In general, the organization confronts two kinds of groups: *formal* and *informal* groups. Before discussing the specific nature and behaviors of groups, it is useful to distinguish between these two general types.

FORMAL GROUPS

A **formal group** has the sanction of the organization within which it exists, possesses legitimate power within the organization, and generally is formed to accomplish a designated task or function. A finance department and a regional division of a company are examples of formal organizationally defined groups. Since it is formed by the organization to accomplish a task or to fulfill an ongoing function, the goal of the formal group is efficient and effective task accomplishment. Its relative position and power allocation within the larger organization are geared to its goals; it is, or should be, given enough power and resources to fulfill its assigned task.

The leader of the formal group functions in accord with the hierarchical principle of organizational design encountered previously; power flows downward from the organizational top, and the highest ranking individual within the formal group in terms of the organizational design will normally be the group leader. Not surprisingly, *communication* between formal group members follows channels established by the organizational design, flowing from superior to subordinate in a formal manner. Discipline and group cohesiveness will be maintained by the leader's use of the organization's rewards and punishment system. The formal organization discussed earlier in this book is composed of many smaller formal groups. However, just as we saw that there was an informal organization existing simultaneously with the formal organization, there are also informal groups existing simultaneously with formal groups.

INFORMAL GROUPS

Informal groups arise within an organization as a function of the proximity, personality, and needs of individuals. Employees choose to affiliate with each other because they work together in the same location (proximity), because they share similar interests outside work (hobbies, civic activities, religious memberships, children in the same school, and others), or because they have the need or desire to work with friends. These groups are neither planned nor sanctioned by the company—they emerge in a spontaneous manner. Their purpose is to provide satisfaction and identity for the group members.

The leader is not designated but emerges by virtue of a personal characteristic that is related to the nature of the group itself. For example, if the group is a computer users' group, the leader may be the most knowledgeable participant. It matters little if there is a senior vice president in the same interest group as the mailroom messenger; if the messenger is the more experienced or skilled computer user, he or she will probably be recognized as the group leader. Power and position within the informal group may be completely independent of formal organizational position.

Communication between informal group members is likely to travel via the informal means of a *grapevine*. Because there is no investiture of formal organizational power in these informal groups, there can be no application of the formal organizational reward and punishment system as a means of group control. Discipline and group cohesiveness are maintained by group sanction and peer pressure. These social forces are often as real and as potent as any formal reward and punishment system. Figure 16-2 shows an organizational chart with the informal groups indicated. As shown in this figure, the indicated informal group cuts across organizational lines and involves three different organizational levels.

Within the two general groups, formal and informal, there may be many specific forms. It is often helpful for managers to know exactly which type

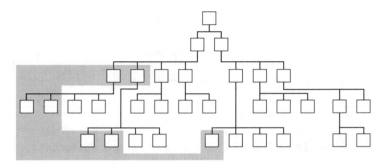

Figure 16–2. The informal group within the organization.

of group is operating or which type of group should be operating within the larger organization. Employees (and managers, too) usually belong to several different groups at work. These specific group forms are discussed later in this chapter, but first we must turn to some of the technical factors that influence group size. A useful way of establishing group size is by the concept called span of control.

YOU SHOULD REMEMBER

The **microview** of an organization sees it as a combination of interrelated groups. These groups can be classified according to orientation: formal and informal groups. **Formal groups** are those designated and sanctioned by the organization. These groups adhere to the scalar principle of organizational power, receive their legitimacy from the organization itself, and feature communication that flows according to organizational design. An **informal group** is one created by the employees themselves, not sanctioned by the organization. These groups may be created around a workplace issue (interest group) or an activity outside the workplace (friendship group).

SPAN OF CONTROL

Span of control refers to the number of subordinates supervised by one manager; generally expressed as a ratio of manager to employees (thus a span of control of 1:4 means that a manager is supervising four employees), it is also known as *span of management*. Several spans of control are shown in Figure 16-3.

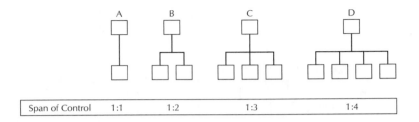

Figure 16–3. The 1:1, 1:2, 1:3, and 1:4 spans of control.

The formal structure of a business can be described by listing the spans of control at each organizational level. Let us create an organization structure that has the following spans of control by organizational level: level 1, one employee; level 2, one employee; level 3, three employees; level 4, three employees (two in one department and one in a different department); and on level 5, four employees in one department and zero employees in the other two departments. This organization has five levels, and they are shown in Figure 16-4.

Much management research has been directed at determining the best span of control to facilitate effective management control. This research has shown that there is no single best and most effective span of control for organizations. Scientists have, however, reached the following conclusions:

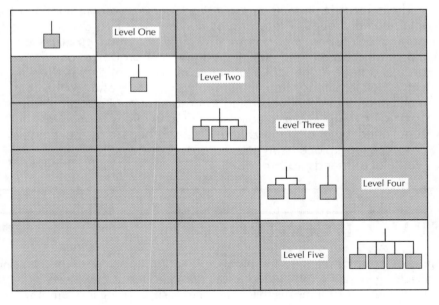

Figure 16–4. Organizational chart with five levels.

- The greater the degree of routinization in the jobs to be supervised, the greater is the number of employees that one individual can effectively manage.

- The more skilled are the manager and the employees, the greater the number of employees supervised.

- A manager can supervise more employees if they physically work closer together than if they are widely dispersed.

- The smaller the variety of job types to be supervised, the greater is the number of employees that can be supervised.

- The less a manager has to perform nonmanagerial tasks, the greater is the number of employees that can be supervised.

- The greater the use of technology, the greater is the number of employees that can be supervised.

It is evident that the span of control depends upon:

1. the skills of the manager

2. the kinds of employees

3. the nature of the jobs

4. specific application of technology, for in some jobs the use of computer monitoring has allowed a manager to supervise a greater number of workers, a trend that continues to increase with greater and more innovative utilization of the Internet.

A business that has small spans of control is called a *tall organization*, and a business that has large spans of control is called a *flat organization*.

YOU SHOULD REMEMBER

Span of control is a useful way of describing the formal organization. At every organizational level there exists a span of control relationship between manager and subordinates. The span of control will be influenced by the skills of the manager, the nature of the jobs to be supervised, the levels of technology involved, and the kinds of employees to be supervised. In organizing work and designing jobs, management must consider the effectiveness of the span of control relationship.

GROUPS: BASIC FORMS

The size and structure of the various formal groups within an organization will be influenced by the span of control. And while informal groups are not represented on the formal T/O (Table of Organization), the same influences operate to determine group size. The forms of individual groups within an organization are functional groups, task groups, interest groups, peer groups, and formal committees. Where we formerly classified groups according to *orientation* (formal or informal), these classifications are by *purpose*.

FUNCTIONAL GROUPS

Functional groups are defined by the business organization and, understandably, adhere to the organizational hierarchical structure of authority relationships. Groups form part of the organizational chart, known as the T/O, and will be distinguished by a designated leader and subordinate members. The size of the group will directly reflect, therefore, a defined span of control. A skilled group leader will be able to manage a larger group—in this case the increased span of control will flow directly from the managerial abilities of the group leader. As these groups always have a leader or someone designated in command, they are also referred to as *command groups*.

TASK GROUPS

Task groups are created by an organization to do as their names imply—complete an assigned task. A *project team* is an example of a task group. Since they are created for a specific task accomplishment, they tend to have a limited life span: the duration of the project. Individuals brought together by management in a task group are linked together by the common task and will have something, in general or specifically, to contribute to its accomplishment. Given that the organization creates them, they are considered formal groups. Although these groups may follow a normal hierarchical organizational relationship with a designated leader supervising subordinates, the task group may also have a leader who is not senior according to the T/O. Such an individual will be an appointed or chosen leader because he or she is the most effective leader for the immediate project. Special task forces, project teams, matrix organizations, and committees are examples of task groups. Since committees are so prevalent and significant in their impact upon modern business, they will be discussed separately.

INTEREST GROUPS

Interest groups are informal groups, created not by the organization but by individuals who are affiliated because of a common interest in the workplace. The interest group may be of real significance to the company in that it will present a united front before management on an issue important to its members. Some of the employees in different departments of a factory may create a workers' safety committee to seek better working conditions from management. This is considered an interest group in that it is not created by the organization. Rather, it is composed of employees united for the advancement of a common interest and is composed of individuals who are members of different functional and task groups. The interest group is similar to the task group, however, in that it is usually of limited duration; once the goal of interest has been achieved, the group typically disbands. This group usually has the shortest life span of any of the groups but will quickly be replaced by a different interest group. Some interest groups, however, such as a safety committee, may have a continuous existence.

PEER GROUPS

A **peer group,** also known as a *friendship* or *social group*, is similar to the interest group in that it is informal, not created by the organization, and may involve individuals from all parts and levels of the organization. However, unlike the interest group, which exists *within* the workplace, the peer group usually exists primarily *outside* the workplace. It consists of individuals who join together in a group based upon a common characteristic. This may be religious affiliation (church or synagogue), common interest (civic, service, or sports club or hobby, for example), political party membership, or just about anything that brings people together after working hours. Sharing this common interest, it is natural that these individuals have some form of relationship within the organizational context. During coffee breaks and at lunchtime they may group together and share their common interest, from a discussion of the latest model of personal computer to what's going on in the National Football League. Common interests bring people from all aspects of the organization together.

It is significant for business entities to understand that worker participation in peer groups is not within the organization's power to prohibit or even regulate other than in a superficial manner even though such groups operate during work hours and in the workplace. The best that management can hope for is to limit access time for socializing during the workday by careful work layout and scheduling social times (e.g., coffee breaks or lunch hours), although such actions cannot stop the creation of such social or peer groups. Many businesses have found a positive value in actually sponsoring such peer groups centered around a common interest where socializing is combined with an activity such as a company-sponsored bowling team, a baseball team, a club, or a charitable group. Meeting under company auspices offers social benefits for the employees and presents the company to both worker and community as a good corporate citizen.

YOU SHOULD REMEMBER

Groups, classified according to their purpose, can be **functional** (command) **groups; task groups** created to complete a specific task; **interest groups** formed within the workplace by a common interest; **peer groups** joined by friendship outside the workplace; and formal committees.

COMMITTEES

Committees are formal groups in that they are organizationally created. They exist for a purpose, but it is usually not as specific as that of the task group. Committees are routinely used for:

- resolving conflict within the organization (the well-known "conference" committee, which meets to resolve differences between the House of Representatives and Senate in Washington, D.C., is an example of this function)

- recommending decisions to senior management (a worker safety committee charged with making recommendations regarding safety in the workplace is an example of this kind of group; so is a "quality circle," which will be discussed at the end of this chapter)

- generating ideas and innovative solutions to problems confronting the business (a brainstorming group is an example)

- making decisions (groups or individuals placed in a committee to solve a specific problem)

Committees have come under a great deal of ridicule over the years. Who has not heard the joke that "a camel is a horse designed by a committee" or "a committee of ten people has twenty legs and twenty hands and no brains." This is an indication that many committees do not, in fact, function in an effective and efficient manner, but it is also an unjust indictment of all committees. The persistence and pervasiveness of committees in the contemporary business organization points to their worth and contribution. Committees can be a tremendous waste of time and energy, but they can also be a valuable resource and method by which management can harness workers' creative power.

Studies have shown that committees can make better decisions than the average individual members. This is because a committee has a greater database in the form of the knowledge and experience of its members than any individual. Do not assume, however, that all members of a committee have equally accurate information or equally valuable previous experience. Some committee members have excellent data for the group, and other committee members have poor information to contribute to the database. Committees function to filter out information that is at the extreme—either extremely good or extremely bad. The resulting information and subsequent decision by the group is better than the average that may be arrived at by the individual. Additionally, note that the information that is extremely good or extremely bad—shown at the far right and left of the data distribution curve—is filtered out by the group.

Committee effectiveness depends upon several factors: the skills of the chairperson, the composition of the group, and the nature of the assigned task. Many companies have found that committees are so important to the accomplishment of needed actions that they have offered workers formal training in committee leadership and participation skills.

• *COMMITTEE CHAIRPERSON*

The first effectiveness factor, the skills of the **committee chairperson,** is the most important to ensure group success. It is necessary for the chairperson to be skilled in group processes since the group will take direction from his or her leadership. The task of the leader is to allow enough freedom to encourage interpersonal debate and differences of opinion while accomplishing the desired goal and nurturing group creativity. Groups may, under the leadership of an unskilled leader, waste time in endless discussion and squander valuable energy in interpersonal conflicts and personality clashes. The skilled chairperson, however, can effectively channel the group's energy into creative and effective problem-solving. Conflicts between group members often mask expressions of creative energy, and a skilled committee leader guides those in conflict into a synthesis that will be more than a compromise.

A manager seeking to be an effective committee chairperson should:

- establish a committee agenda before the actual meeting

- encourage all group members to participate

- recognize his or her personal bias and keep it out of the group

- not judge the opinions expressed and ideas generated; the judgmental function is for the group

- keep the group focused on the organizational goals, within the timetable established

- act quickly to extinguish personality conflicts; keep focused on the organizational goals, not on personalities

- insist that ideas be evaluated only on their professional merits

- provide for the keeping of a record of committee accomplishments

- provide for individual and group rewards for task accomplishments

The leader is influenced by the kind of group members and the task assigned. There is no single universally successful leadership style for all groups. All the group variables will act to determine the leadership styles that will be effective in the specific group situation. The task assigned to some groups may be of such an urgent nature to the organization that the chairperson will justifiably assume the authoritative role of dictator. Such a leadership style is grossly inappropriate, however, in a different circumstance with other group members and different assigned tasks.

• *COMMITTEE MEMBERS*
Committee participation should be perceived as a valued function by management and employees alike. If either group thinks that committee participation is a waste of time or, even worse, punishment, it will be difficult to attract willing and skilled managers and employees to serve on the committee. The committee is not likely to achieve its goals if it cannot attract willing and skilled members. Committee members should be chosen because:

- they are willing to cooperate with others, rather than compete

- they are, or can become, skilled in communication

- they volunteer and are willing to serve

- they possess technical skills or knowledge necessary for the group task

- they are task oriented

• *NATURE OF THE COMMITTEE TASK*
The final variable that influences committee success is the nature of the assigned goal or task. Having read the previous chapters on goal formation, it is not surprising that the goals given to committees should be stated in definitive terms with behavioral performance standards. This will prove motivational for the group because it then has an identifiable target toward which its efforts can be directed. When committees are delegated tasks, they should also be given the organizational resources necessary for task accomplishment. These resources may be something as concrete as clerical support or as intangible as organizational power. A committee lacking the necessary resources for task accomplishment is doomed to failure.

It should be noted that certain issues are not suitable for committee assignment. An example of this kind of issue is a labor-management dispute in which there is a collective bargaining agreement (CBA) in force. This CBA specifies a mechanism for resolving disputes, and the union has dispute resolution means ranging from mediation to arbitration to strikes. These labor-management issues normally should not be sent to a committee. Since the committee has no authority to resolve the issue, it is an inappropriate use of the committee within the organization. Also, issues that do not readily lend themselves to goal formulation or that do not have obtainable solutions are not proper topics for committees, since common goals serve to unite group members and to target group efforts.

Additionally, any issue that potentially could place the business in conflict with current law or regulation will generally not be suitable for committee action unless it possesses the necessary legal expertise, such as a group of lawyers.

We shall return, toward the end of this chapter, to a discussion of an emerging employee-management group that may have great promise for organizational productivity and effectiveness, the quality circle (QC). First, however, let us describe the formation and development of groups in greater detail.

YOU SHOULD REMEMBER

Committees, although much criticized for wasting organizational time and resources, can be creative and valuable if they are strong and have skilled leadership, willing and enthusiastic members, a focused and defined goal, support from higher management, and the necessary resources to achieve the goal. If any of these is missing, a committee may indeed become a gigantic waste of time, energy, and resources.

Management should examine carefully the issues sent to a committee: issues of labor-management relations, for example, are inappropriate for committees.

FORMATION AND DEVELOPMENT STAGES OF GROUPS

Most groups exhibit similar states of formation and development. It would be tempting to say that management merely has to define a problem or a goal, assign members, and a group is created. This is an erroneous and overly simplistic view of group formation. First, there are groups, such as interest and peer groups, that are informal, *not* the result of managerial action. Second, the development of a group identity and the evolution of member effectiveness are more complex than the mere action of members coalescing around a common goal. Groups *evolve,* and it is important that managers understand the course of this evolutionary process. In general, groups evolve through four stages.

FORMATION AND FIRST PHASE

After the assignment of individual members has taken place, a group may flounder for an identity. Although it would seem that a group's identity would immediately revolve around the assigned task, the assimilation of that task takes some time. The initial group process is to define itself in terms of its members and assigned task, and it takes time for group members to begin to know one another and understand the skills, education, and experience that each member brings to the group process. This first phase of a group after formation is often called a *mutual acceptance stage* because it is during this initial period that members meet and get to know each other. This process of mutual acceptance takes time, and management should under no circumstances expect several individuals to immediately become a fully functioning group. Sufficient time must elapse for the group members to (1) get to know one another, (2) deal with their mutual mistrust, (3) learn about one another's capacities, skills, talents, knowledge, and so on, and (4) begin to develop confidence in one another and start to rely upon one another.

This first phase of group formation is sometimes very painful because the designated group participants are initially unsure of the adequacy of their skills and abilities. They may not completely understand the assigned task, they may be unsure of the adequacy of the resources available, and they may not yet know if they can accomplish the task assigned. Groups must evolve their own style of leadership and participatory process—a *group identity*. This will be the product of the individuals as they relate to the task assigned. By the end of the first phase, individuals have begun to constitute a group defined by a distinct identity. The members have ideally begun to trust each other and can approach the assigned task with a growing confidence. The group processes are still in development, however, and some significant events must take place before the group can approach the task.

During group activities, strong personal and professional differences emerge. One of the major tasks of the group leader is to help reconcile such differences of professional opinion and limit the impact of the ever-present personality clash. The group must devise a mechanism by which decisions are made and a consensus created. This may be by dictatorial decree when there is an autocratic group leader; or it may be by majority vote if the group atmosphere is democratic. If the latter is the decision-making methodology used by the group, it is important to have an odd number of group members so that tie votes are impossible. In the second phase of a group, problem-solving and decision-making are actively undertaken.

GROUP DECISION-MAKING

After a group has created a distinctive identity, learned to trust and rely upon one another, and understand the assigned task, it enters the second phase. In this stage of group functioning, problem-solving and decision-making are begun. The members of the group have become a team, relying upon one another and specific individual contributions to accomplish the task. The group defines the problem in operational terms and begins to determine the alternative solutions. Information will be needed and subsequently gathered for evaluation. While this is taking place, the group tests the limits of the assigned resources. If the resources prove inadequate, the group may be forced either to disband or to seek additional resources from top management.

As the workers labor together, they come to know one another better and to know better the limitations of the group's human resources of skills, education, and previous experience. The group members are growing closer together, the group identity is becoming stronger, and the internal environment of the group is characterized by increasing trust and confidence. The group will, as a result of shared experience, develop methods and procedures for problem-solving. As a result of this shared experience, the group will achieve a greater efficiency in problem-solving. At this stage there may be some residual competition between group members. When this competition has been replaced by cooperation, the group will have moved to the next stage of development.

GROUP MATURITY

The replacement of individual competition by cooperation marks the achievement of group maturity. The group identity has solidified, and the members are working with maximal efficiency and effectiveness. They know one another well by this point, and personality differences assume a minor role, if any. The group identity is reinforced by shared experiences and the creation of "in-group war stories" and may be expressed in such seemingly frivolous manifestations as mottoes, slogans, and logos on tee shirts. Group members feel a sense of purpose as they share a common directionality of effort. There is an increasing responsibility toward the group and a general willingness to put in the extra time, give the additional effort, "go the extra mile."

CONTROL PHASE

The final phase of group development has been called a **control phase**. The group has assumed its final form; all who did not fit in have left, and those remaining feel a deep sense of identification with the group. This stage is similar to the previous group maturity stage, but it differs in that now group sanctions are operating. The group has solidified to the point at which norms embody expected behaviors. *Group norms* are forms of behavior, ideals, or opinions that are expected within the group as accepted and desirable. The group is prepared to exercise sanctions when these norms are not met. These sanctions can be mild disapproval of group members but may extend to extreme peer pressure. The members of the group have learned to trust and rely upon one another.

It is important for management to know the group's stage of development. A group in the mature and control phases of development can be given a more complex task than a group in one of the earlier developmental stages. It can be relied upon to function in a more autonomous, efficient, and effective manner. This is not to suggest that groups in earlier developmental stages are not able to make different contributions, and management can foster growth and maturity in a group by carefully and sequentially assigning tasks of increasing complexity and responsibility.

YOU SHOULD REMEMBER

As groups evolve through the four stages of **mutual acceptance, decision-making, group maturity,** and **control,** their ability to deal with different and increasingly complex problems also evolves. Management should be aware of the progress of a group and assign problems accordingly. As a group matures and grows, it evolves standards of expected behaviors and attitudes. These are the **group norms** that are very important in the reinforcement of group loyalty and identity.

SPECIFIC CHARACTERISTICS OF GROUPS

This chapter began with a discussion of the general characteristics of groups. It is helpful for management to understand some specific characteristics. Three of these are group behavior, group size, and group status.

GROUP BEHAVIOR NORMS

Behavior within a group conforms to the expectations of its members. This expected behavior takes place within a range defined by upper and lower performance standards. The group accepts a minimal level of performance—and if an individual performs below this lower acceptable level, he or she is ostracized and is made to feel potentially severe peer pressure for performance improvement. Management can readily understand this; any individual not performing at an acceptable level detracts from overall group accomplishment. Perhaps even more significant is that the other group members may feel that they can no longer rely upon the employee whose performance is deficient. This erosion of reliance threatens the very foundations of the group identity.

It is easy to understand that a poorly performing group member is pressured to improve, but it may be difficult to understand that a group member who has an excellent performance record may also feel group pressure. In this case the excellent performer is pressured by the other group members not to do so well. This is the upper limit of acceptable group performance. Any employee performing above this upper level is viewed as a *rate buster* whose performance makes everyone else look bad. The behavior within the group takes place within this lower and upper range, and this range constitutes the **group behavioral norm.** If management wishes to improve group performance, it will not be sufficient to raise the lower group performance norm—this will not function to raise the overall group performance. It will be equally inappropriate to attempt to improve group performance by raising the upper level of acceptable performance. This will also not function to raise the overall group performance. The most effective way to improve group performance is to raise the range of group performance—raise both the lower and upper limits.

YOU SHOULD REMEMBER

Group behavior takes place within a range of acceptability. Management (or the workers themselves) defines the minimum acceptable performance standards, but the workers also define the acceptable upper performance level. If management wishes to increase worker productivity within the group, it must change both the lower and upper performance standards.

GROUP SIZE

No universally accepted group size ensures maximal efficiency, but management can follow some guidelines in assigning group members:

- A group should not be too small; it should have enough human resources to accomplish the assigned tasks.
- A group should not be too large; too many people make effective communication and leadership difficult.
- The ideal group size allows its members to know and rely upon each other; if there are too many members, some will be strangers.
- Members should feel a sense of obligation to the group; if the group becomes too large, this sense of obligation suffers.

GROUP STATUS

Different groups have different levels of status within the organization. This status is related to five major factors:

1. the importance of the assigned task
2. the level of group accomplishment
3. the status of the individuals within the group
4. the nature of an organization's rewards to group members
5. the perceived external status of the group

Groups that are given important tasks are perceived as important groups. Others see that the organization has entrusted the group with matters of great significance, perhaps even related to organizational survival. Seeing that top management trusts the group to accomplish important tasks, others invest the group with great status. In this sense, the group's status is derived from the importance or status of the assigned job.

Groups that succeed in accomplishing the assigned task are more highly valued by top management than groups that fail. Success confers status upon a group; failure lessens group status. Top management knows that it cannot rely upon the particular group, and others know that the group has failed. Failure results in a diminished group reputation and loss of status within the organization.

Certain individuals have more status than others within the organization. This may be because of individual past accomplishment or educational achievement or possession of specific abilities and skills. For whatever reason or combination of reasons, these individuals are given greater status than others. If a high-status individual is included within a group, the group may itself achieve greater status than if the person were not included. Some of the individual's status will "rub off" on the group, as the group is perceived as being worthy of the particular individual. This suggests that management, desiring acceptance of a group by the rest of the organization, assign a high-status individual as a group participant. However, this high-status individual should be a willing participant within the group. If the individual is assigned to the group merely as "window dressing," the group itself will suffer in that it is burdened with a member who does not fully participate. Others outside the group will become aware that the high-status individual does not really confer a similar status level upon the group. Management can also influence the perceived status of a group by rewarding group participation after genuine achievements.

YOU SHOULD REMEMBER

The **status** of a group is dependent upon four major factors: the importance of the task assigned, the success of the group, the status of the individual workers, and the nature of the rewards to the group's members by the organization. An organization should enhance the status of a group if it wishes willing and enthusiastic participation by the workers. If the reverse is true—namely, that there is no status attached to group participation—workers do not willingly participate in the group.

GROUPS: MANAGERIAL IMPLICATIONS

This chapter began with the observation that an organization was a group of individuals united to achieve a common goal. The microview of an organization pictured it as a collection of groups. If we take part of this earlier organizational view and actually divide it into three groups with spans of control of 1:2, 1:3, and 1:4, it looks like Figure 16-5. This shows three different smaller groups with the manager at the top of the triangle.

This is the *linkpin view* of an organization, a conceptualization of **Rensis Likert (1903–1981)** in which a large organization is seen as a series of interrelated groups. The three different groups have been recombined into a single group in Figure 16-6. The linkpin function of the manager can be seen. Each organizational level is linked through the leader of a group to another group. If the group leader fails to link the group with the group

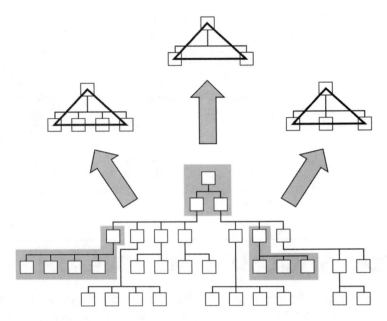

Figure 16–5. Linkpin view of an organization. Top: three small groups, each with a different span of control. Bottom: the three small groups as part of a single group—the organization.

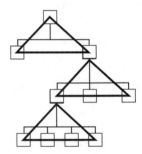

Figure 16–6. Simplified view that shows how the manager of each group links the group to other groups in the organization.

on the higher level, all in the group suffer. Employees, although they may be leaders of one group, are probably also members of another group. Thus the organization truly is a series of interrelated groups bound into an organizational whole by common goals. How management structures the relationship of these interrelated groups can have a dramatic impact upon business success or failure.

A recent example of this is the way in which the Ford Motor Company restructured the relationships between the design teams for the Taurus and Sable automobiles.

The Taurus and Sable automobiles are sleek, aerodynamic models that cost over $3 billion to design and produce. Before these models were developed, Ford, a pioneer automobile manufacturer and one of the largest companies in the world, designed and produced new models with separate groups of engineers and stylists working on the different parts. Each group worked independently and in sequence. The stylists produced the body design, then the engineers designed the engine and mechanical components, and then the mechanical engineers specializing in manufacturing systems designed the machines that would actually manufacture the automobile. The final step was for the service specialists to determine how to repair the completed model. The system was cumbersome, inefficient, and sometimes produced inadequate results. It was entirely possible to have an automobile that looked good but was underpowered because the interior styling and space requirements did not allow sufficient room for an adequate engine. The buyer would have to spend several hundred dollars in labor costs to replace a part costing less than a dollar because of the way in which parts had been arranged under the hood. A European model was infamous for having a $5 oil filter placed in such a manner that one had to remove the entire engine to change the oil. Since this process cost several hundred dollars, oil filters were rarely changed. The engines rapidly wore out, and this particular model earned a just reputation for being a disaster on wheels.

Ford decided to take a new approach to the way in which the engineering and styling groups related to each other. A management team was created with representatives from all the functional departments: engineering, styling, marketing, manufacturing, and service. This team or management group provided a forum within which the various groups' efforts could be coordinated. It quickly progressed through the group developmental stages discussed earlier and assumed a strong identity. The group came to be called Team Taurus. Because group coordination was set up at the beginning of this project, no group worked in isolation from the others. The styling, design, engineering, marketing, and servicing of these two automobiles were a unified effort. The top management of Ford also decreed that any member of the coordination group—Team Taurus—had the right to delay the project completion date to correct design or production defects. This resulted in an increased project cost and time factor, but the resulting design was judged remarkably free from defects.

Taurus and Sable are consistently best-selling automobiles and the Ford Motor Company has benefitted greatly from changing the way in which the various work groups related to each other. There is no doubt that these automobiles will eventually be replaced by others with newer styling and features, but the lessons learned about group relationships may well have an impact upon the way U.S. cars are created for years to come. This sort of intergroup cooperative effort is new to the U.S. automobile industry but is common in Japan. U.S. managers have increasingly turned to other industrialized countries to learn new ways of increasing worker productivity and product quality. Many contemporary managers have attempted to learn from Japan since its post-World War II productivity rate increase has been four times greater than that of the United States and over twice that of the leading industrial nations in Europe. U.S. companies are experimenting with the joint management-labor quality control group technique invented by two U.S. management consultants but adopted and developed most effectively in Japan. This group is known as the quality circle, and the total approach is called TQM (Total Quality Management) or TQL (Total Quality Leadership).

YOU SHOULD REMEMBER

In the **linkpin view** an organization is seen as a series of interrelated groups with each level linked through the leader of a group to another group. Management must understand how groups relate to one another if they are to achieve success.

QUALITY CIRCLES

A **quality circle (QC)** consists of workers and managers assigned the task of improving manufacturing efficiency and product quality. This group is trained in the methodologies of quality control and problem solving. The concept of the quality circle makes use of the statistical methodology developed by **W.E. Deming,** an expert on quality control and production. Approximately 100,000 quality circles operate in Japan and the Deming award for quality control is awarded with much public acclaim.

The quality circle consists of between eight and ten workers and managers. Since this group is designated and sanctioned by management, it is a *formal group*. They meet at least once a week *on company time* and are trained by personnel and industrial relations specialists in the basic skills of problem identification, information gathering and analysis, basic statistics, and solution generation. The specialist may continue to serve as a consultant to the circle but will not be a regular group member or have a vote.

Once trained in the basic problem-solving skills, the quality circle meets on a regular basis during working hours to identify and solve problems in the specific area in which the QC participants work. A problem is identified, alternative solutions are proposed, consequences are evaluated, and recommendations are made to senior management. Not surprisingly, this is the same problem-solving methodology identified in Chapter 5 as used by management. The difference here is that the problems are solved by those closest to the job and, presumably, with the most immediate and intimate knowledge of the day-to-day problems inherent in the office or on the factory floor.

The stimulus to participate in the QC comes from one of two sources. In some companies, the workers who participate in the QC receive a monetary reward, generally a percentage of the money saved as a result of those recommendations by the group that are successfully adopted. Even if there is no financial reward, workers desire to participate in the QC if such participation contributes to receiving promotions. Many companies that have instituted a QC program have realized great savings derived from worker-generated suggestions, and its successes have been widely heralded by QC consultants.

Many companies have not been very successful, however, and have abandoned the program. A successful QC program requires the support of both unions and management, and when this is lacking, the program finds the going rough and success elusive. Management is often not willing to grant to the QC any real power to identify problems or recommend solutions. In this case, the QC members will quickly realize that they are not being taken seriously and participate half-heartedly, if at all. Management is often not willing to allow the QC to meet during working hours; this costs the company money in terms of lost productivity and management may not want to bear the costs. Additionally, for the QC to succeed, it is necessary for workers and management participants to be trained in problem-solving, performance standards formation, communications, and statistical skills. Without these skills the workers will not be able to participate effectively in the QC.

Unions also may view quality circles with great suspicion—as a management attempt to increase worker productivity. Some unions have been in favor of the QC approach only when there has been a management commitment to provide workers with security and a commitment to refrain from raising worker performance standards without union consent. For the QC approach to work, there must be an understanding by both union and labor that no issue or problem is raised in the QC that rightfully belongs at the bargaining table or is already covered by the union contract. Unions are often assured of management's integrity when both a union member and a manager are appointed cochairpersons of the group.

The QC, as well as TQM, is emerging as one of the most potentially productive work group approaches in the labor arena. The U.S. Navy, an organization of almost a million servicepeople and civilians, has adopted TQM as its main managerial model. As shown in Figure 16-5, the group has access to a larger database than the individual and has the potential of making better decisions. Other forms of worker groups also provide a creative resource for the organization. This chapter ends with a discussion of three of these, one of which we have encountered before, in Chapter 5.

YOU SHOULD REMEMBER

The **quality circle,** pioneered in Japan, is a formal group of eight to ten workers and managers trained in quality control and problem-solving methodologies that meet about once a week on company time to identify problems and recommend solutions to ensure improved efficiency, quality, and productivity.

GROUPS AND CREATIVITY

Groups can be used in several ways to develop new ideas. Among techniques to increase creative input are brainstorming, the nominal group technique, and the Delphi technique.

BRAINSTORMING

As was described in Chapter 5, **brainstorming** is a technique that is often used with a small group of employees (6–12 participants) to generate a large number of alternatives in a short period of time. In brainstorming, the group is confronted with a business problem defined by management, not the employees, and then arrives at potential solutions. This is the *alternatives generation phase*. No criticism is voiced during this process because this would interrupt the generation of potential solutions. The quality of the solutions proposed is enhanced by the group's being composed of employees who possess expertise in the area and are familiar with the problem to be solved. The potential soutions to the problem are recorded on a chart or chalkboard. Each potential solution is evaluated in detail by the group only when the participants have exhausted their imaginations. The *evaluation phase*, since it comes after alternatives generation, does not intrude with criticism on the generation of proposed solutions. This technique encourages group participants to be imaginative and innovative without fear of ridicule from other employees.

NOMINAL GROUP TECHNIQUE

This technique, used in conjunction with the planning activities of management, has proved valuable in creating managerial contingencies and future projections. It is known for the high quality of idea generation and levels of innovation achieved. It is similar to brainstorming in that a managerially defined problem is presented to a small group of between six and twelve participants. Each member individually generates as many potential solutions to the problem presented as possible, *in writing*. There is no communication between group members. After a given period of time, usually no longer than half an hour, the group members present their ideas. The group members can ask the presenter to clarify the ideas, but no criticism is voiced during these presentations. The ideas of each presenter are recorded. After all group members have completed their presentations, the recorded ideas are discussed and criticized.

After the group discussion of the recorded ideas, each participant is asked to rank the ideas. This ranking is usually done in writing and in an anonymous manner. The final group ranking of the proposed solutions is then presented to management for consideration. Those who favor this technique point to the strength of the solution generation efforts: the lack of criticism prevents the inhibition of individual creativity. When criticism is voiced, it is directed toward the solution, not the personality of the individual making the suggestion.

The group is called nominal because the grouping of individuals is only temporary and ceases after the session is over. This prevents individuals from dominating the group and using it to fulfill personal ambitions. If management accepts the final group recommendation, the participants will have a developed loyalty toward the solution since they created it. On the other hand, if management rejects the proposed group solution, the participants may be resentful and may not be willing to participate again in a nominal group.

DELPHI TECHNIQUE

Feeling that any personal interaction will influence the quality of the information generated, a manager may decide to make use of the **Delphi technique.** This technique is used to identify future trends. In this method, management presents a series of questions centering on an identified problem to a panel of experts. Although these experts constitute a group, they never physically meet. The questions are sent by the Delphi group coordinator, in writing, to the individual group members. Each member is asked to answer the questions anonymously. These answers are sent back to the coordinator to be tabulated and summarized. The summaries are then returned to the group members, who are asked to examine the criticisms and modify their original answers if necessary. Note two important points: the coordinator sends the summaries back to each participant *without the names of the critical group members*, and the group members are instructed to react *in an anonymous manner*. At no point does any group member know who proposed a specific idea or who criticized it. The focus is exclusively on the merits of the ideas, never on individual personality.

The summaries are again returned to the group members, and they are asked to examine their ideas, make adjustments if necessary, and justify their ideas if they differ from those proposed by the majority of group members. Again, the focus is exclusively on ideas, not on personality.

A final summary of the responses is prepared, and the group members are asked to respond a third time, with the only difference being that every idea must be justified. Each time the individual participants respond to a summary is called a wave, and after the third wave a summary is prepared and a forecast made by the coordinator. This is particularly useful in situations in which the future is unclear and the opinions of the experts will be valuable for management. The Delphi technique places a premium on the expert's knowledge and ability to justify opinions while isolating the process from the destructive intrusion of participant personality. The benefit of gathering expert opinion regarding future events must, however, be balanced against its being a time-consuming and somewhat expensive process. It is a method by which a group, however anonymously, contributes in a creative manner to the success of contemporary business ventures.

KNOW THE CONCEPTS
DO YOU KNOW THE BASICS?

1. Distinguish between the micro and macro views of organizations.
2. What are the differences between formal and informal groups?
3. What are the factors that determine the span of control?
4. What kinds of groups are found within the organization?
5. How should management regulate a "friendship group?"
6. What issues are inappropriate for a committee?
7. How can management improve group performance?
8. What determines the status of a group?
9. What is the linkpin view of an organization?
10. What is a QC?

TERMS FOR STUDY

formal group
formal organization
group norms
informal group
informal organization
linkpin organizational view

mutual acceptance phase
QC (quality circle)
rate buster
span of control
span of management

ANSWERS
KNOW THE BASICS

1. In the macro view, the overall organization is seen as one large group. In the micro view, the overall organization is seen as a collection of interrelated groups.

2. Formal groups are created and sanctioned by the organization. Given legitimate authority within the organizational structure, these groups follow a hierarchical scalar pattern and communications are according to the organizational structure. Informal groups are created by the workers, either to pursue a work-related issue (an *interest group*, e.g., worker safety committee) or a nonwork-related issue (a hobby group or bowling team, for example). These groups do not necessarily follow the hierarchical scalar pattern, and communications cross the regular organizational structure in an informal, "grapevine" arrangement. These groups are not sanctioned by management.

3. The span of control (or span of management) is influenced by the skills of the manager, the kinds of employees, and the nature of the jobs.

4. The forms of individual groups within an organization are functional groups, task groups, interest groups, peer groups, and formal committees.

5. Management cannot nor should it attempt to regulate friendship groups. Managers can, however, *influence* these groups by limiting access time for socializing during the workday by careful work layout and the scheduling of social times (such as coffee breaks). Such managerial actions influence the creation of peer groups but do not stop such groups.

6. Certain issues are not suitable for committee assignment. An example of this kind of issue is a labor-management dispute in which a collective bargaining agreement (CBA) is in force. Labor-management issues normally should not be sent to a committee. Also, issues that do not readily lend themselves to goal formulation or that do not have obtainable solu-

tions are not proper topics for committees since common goals serve to unite group members and target group efforts.

7. Since behavior within the group takes place within a lower and an upper range, this range constitutes the "group behavioral norm." If management wishes to improve group performance, it will not be sufficient to raise the lower group performance norm—this will not function to raise the overall group performance. It will be equally inappropriate to attempt to improve group performance by raising the upper level of acceptable performance. This will also not function to raise the overall group performance. The only way to achieve improved group performance is to raise the *range* of group performance—raise both the lower and upper limits.

8. The status of a work group is determined by the status of the assigned task, the level of group accomplishment, the status of the individuals within the group, and the nature of organization's rewards given to group members.

9. The linkpin view of an organization sees the organization as a series of interrelated groups. A manager is head of one group and member of a group of managers. As such, the manager links the two groups.

10. A QC, or quality circle, is a formal group of workers and managers charged with the task of improving manufacturing efficiency and product quality. This group is trained in the methodologies of quality control and problem-solving and consists of between eight and ten workers and managers.

17

COMMUNICATION SKILLS AND MANAGEMENT EFFECTIVENESS

KEY TERMS

sender the originator of a **stimulus** (known as a **message**)

encoding the act that begins the communication process

decoding the process of understanding a message

filtering the altering of a message as it passes through the personalities of either the sender or the receiver; **filters** are part of either the sender or receiver

receiver one who receives the stimulus, or message

noise anything that changes or interferes with the message but is not part of either the sender or receiver

denotative meaning the explicit definition of a term

connotative meaning meaning by association

common vocabulary words that have formally defined meanings accepted by a specific group and that facilitate communication by eliminating or greatly limiting the connotative meanings of words

This book began with the observation that an organization is a group of individuals united to achieve a common goal. Many of the previous chapters have centered upon the functions of managers as they plan, organize, direct, motivate, and control subordinates in the achievement of the organization's goals. Effective communication is absolutely essential for managerial and organizational success. If a manager cannot communicate with subordinates, there will be little success in any of the managerial functions. Communication is the bridge between goal and the creation of performance standards and worker accomplishment. Workers who do not understand what is expected within the workplace have little if any chance of accomplishing the desired results. It is for this reason that this chapter deals with the communication process.

Communications assume two different dimensions within the contemporary business structure: the *organizational perspective*, which looks at how the organizational structure itself promotes or hinders effective communication, and the *interpersonal perspective*, which examines communication effectiveness as a function of the basic communication process involving two individuals. Both perspectives are necessary, for a business is structured to promote effective communication, but if the individuals in that business have poor communication skills, effective communication will be difficult. The reverse is also true; individuals can be highly effective communicators and yet fail to be effective if the organizational structure itself hinders communication.

This chapter begins with a discussion of the basic communication process and the influences upon that process that promote effective communication between individuals. This topic is discussed first because it forms the basis for communication success at every organizational level. The chapter concludes with a discussion of how the structure of the organization influences communication effectiveness.

COMMUNICATION PROCESS MODEL: AN INTERPERSONAL PERSPECTIVE

The basic **communication process model** consists of the following phenomena: encoding, filtering, sending, noise (interference), receiving, filtering, decoding, and feedback. A stylized version of this process is shown in Figure 17-1.

Communication begins with the action of encoding the message, here shown as a computer. The act of encoding a message is a complex procedure involving not only a selection of what to communicate but also the selection of the channel of communication (the *medium*). The message then passes through the individual's personal filters and is sent. The sending here is shown as a mechanical process of a radio wave that is then influenced by atmospheric factors, called *noise*. This atmospheric noise can distort the message before it is received. The message is received, passes through the personal filters of the receiver, and then is decoded. As can be seen, even the basic communication process is complex; little wonder that people often misunderstand each other. Misunderstood communication is even more possible as the workforce more accurately reflects the multicultural and ethnically diverse general population. When the sender and receiver are from different cultural traditions, poor communication may result, which in turn

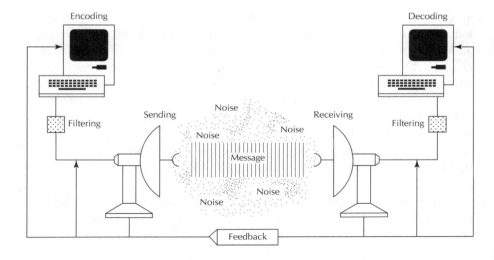

Figure 17–1. Basic communication process model.

may lead to reduced morale, ineffective teamwork, and negative impacts on organizational productivity.

YOU SHOULD REMEMBER

Communication begins with the sender **encoding** a **message** and ends with the receiver **decoding** it. Between these end points the message passes through the **filters** of both sender and receiver and through external **noise,** all of which can interfere with effective communication.

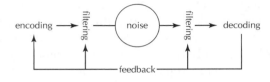

THE MESSAGE

In its basic form, the **message** is any *stimulus* that can evoke a response. Most communication commonly takes place in one of three ways: written, oral, and visual. The first two are used routinely by managers; they either speak or write to subordinates. The third takes place every time we look at something and receive a message. In most cultures the color red, conveying a sense of danger, is used in traffic signs and signals to tell the pedestrian and driver to stop. Conversely, green functions to give permission to proceed. Each of these colors transmits a message visually without any accompanying spoken or written words.

Images also convey messages. Everyone has seen the stylized figure of a man or a woman on a restroom door in a restaurant or hotel, immediately recognizing where the appropriate facilities are located. Using symbols that are universally accepted and recognized becomes an important communication device for sponsors of international sporting events, such as the Olympics.

That messages can be conveyed visually and orally creates a problem for communication effectiveness; a person may intend to convey one message with spoken words and a different message visually by means of what has been called body language. An example is a manager who speaks to an employee with words of praise and encouragement while staring down at the floor and showing a lack of sincerity. The words convey one message, but the body posture conveys a different one. The task left to the receiver is to decide which message is correct—to reconcile the differences in the received messages. This unique issue of message reconciliation is discussed under the topic of decoding.

There are three other human sense dimensions capable of receiving stimuli and responding: tactile (touch), taste, and olfactory (smell). These senses may also be used in communication. For example, the tactile sense is used by the blind to communicate. The Braille system of raised dots on a page allows the blind to "read" by touching.

The olfactory sense can also communicate a message. This is less common with humans even though it is widely employed in the animal kingdom. Some animals have an extremely well-developed sense of smell, but this appears to be the least developed sense in human beings. It does operate, however, and is occasionally used to communicate messages, however unconventional. Industrial essences have been developed that mimic the "new car smell" of polished leather. This essence, contained in aerosol cans, is used by car dealers to spray in used cars to convey the message that these cars are almost new. The same company has canned a "baking bread smell" for supermarkets that don't have a bakery on the premises but want to stimulate shoppers to buy bread.

YOU SHOULD REMEMBER

Any **stimulus** can be used to send a **message.** The senses of hearing and sight are usually the major avenues of communication within the work setting. Smell, taste, and touch can also be used to convey messages and under certain specialized conditions may be the most appropriate method to communicate a message. A manager should remember that several messages may be communicated simultaneously: an oral message and an accompanying body posture message may be sent at the same time by the message sender, which will force the receiver to reconcile the different messages. Managers who desire effective communications should minimize conflicting simultaneous messages.

ENCODING AND SENDING

Encoding a message involves the formulation of contents and the selection of an effective medium for its transmission. A message, then, has these two different components—*contents* and *medium*—and they must complement each other. If either is inappropriate, effective communication will be difficult, if not impossible.

Managers have to choose *what* they want to communicate and must decide *how* to communicate. This is an important decision. If the way chosen to communicate is inappropriate for the message, there will be a destructive interference between the channel of communication and the contents of the message. Consider the following example. A manager yells at a subordinate to do an ordinary task immediately. The channel of communication is oral and the contents of the communication, the task. The problem arises because the manager yelled at the subordinate, implying urgency. The task, however, was ordinary and the sense of urgency created was inappropriate. The subordinate may wonder why the urgency is necessary when the task is clearly ordinary and routine. If such a case occurs often with this manager, subordinates will quickly learn to disregard the implied urgency, and when the manager has a truly urgent command, the employees may disregard the manager. For effective communication, managers must be sure the contents and medium of the message are appropriate. Only in this manner can a manager both gain and maintain credibility with subordinates.

Managers are faced with the question of how to communicate in an appropriate and therefore effective manner. Do I speak to the employee? Do I send a memo? A formal letter? Do I yell and scream, or remain calm, cool, and collected? Such questions are answered as part of a larger consideration: What will most effectively convey the message? A major problem confronting the manager is what words to use, in either a letter or a conversation, to effectively get the message across. The issue of an effective vocabulary is considered later in this chapter when we discuss communication effectiveness.

The means selected for transmission should also be suitable in all respects. If a manager wishes to convey a sense of importance and seriousness, a formal letter is appropriate. If there is a desire to convey a sense of informality, however, a memo will do. The means selected, the *medium*, will directly influence communication effectiveness. If the intent is to convey a warning, a siren is sounded, not a symphony. A telegram will convey kinds of intent that are different from those conveyed by a postcard. And increasingly, e-mail (electronic mail) and instantaneous communication via the Internet are becoming the usual mechanism for communication with employees on a daily basis. As such, use of stylistic elements such as **bold,** *italics,* or underlining, distinguished by their visual impact, are increasingly important for communicating emphasis. The selection of the most appropriate medium is one of the most important decisions made by a manager in effectively marketing a new product. If one wants to influence the purchase behavior of consumers to buy a Steinway grand piano, it will be more effective to advertise on a radio station that features concert music and opera than on a station featuring heavy metal or rap music.

A separate issue that will be considered when we discuss decoding the message is the conflict of simultaneous messages. Individuals are capable of sending several messages at the same time, some intentional and others unintentional, and these messages interfere with each other.

FILTERING

This is a process that takes place within both the sender and the receiver of a message. It is both a physiological and a psychological process and is a common experience. Consider the conversation conducted between two people at a loud party. They are able to converse even though there is much background noise by speaking more loudly than normal and by filtering out the background noise. They become aware of the filtering process if someone elsewhere in the room mentions one of their names—no one filters out their own name. They will immediately become aware of the background noise and that they are filtering it out. This is a physiological process in that the background sounds are impacting upon the human auditory system but not being acknowledged by the recognition centers of the brain.

The process of filtering is also of a psychological nature; a personal prejudice or bias will cause distorted communication. A manager who is biased against women in the workplace may communicate with his female subordinates in a demeaning manner and not be aware that his bias is influencing the nature of his communication. It is important to recognize that the filtering process operates in both sender and receiver. For example, the biased manager tells a female subordinate, "That's a great job" [the message he wants to send] "for a woman" [the message is distorted because of his bias against women in the workplace]. The female subordinate hears the message, "That's a great job" [I did a great job!] "for a woman" [So I didn't do such a good job—a man would do a better job]. Her filtering causes her to discount the compliment. If the female subordinate replies, "Are you saying that I am not doing a good job?" the manager may well be astounded. He may reply in genuine surprise and indignation, "What's the matter? I said you're doing a *great* job." The manager is unaware of the filter operating in the sending and receiving that distorts the message. Filters are part of both the sender and the receiver and have the power to distort the message. Noise also has the power to distort the message but differs from filtering in that it is not part of either the sender or receiver.

YOU SHOULD REMEMBER

The parts of a **message**—the **content** and the **medium**—must complement each other. Effective managers must be sure of the appropriateness of the entire message they send. They must also realize that both the sender and the receiver filter messages and that the message they thought they sent may not be the message that was received.

NOISE

Noise, in the communication process, is situated between the sending and receiving and can distort the message. In Figure 17-1, it is represented by atmospheric disturbance that changes the message. Consider the example of our biased manager who is speaking to the female subordinate. In the background is a construction worker operating a very loud jackhammer. The female subordinate cannot hear each word clearly because of the jackhammer. The jackhammer sound is *noise*, and it distorts the message (which in this case is for the best because, as we have seen, the female subordinate will not like what the manager is saying). Noise, then, is anything not part of either the sender or the receiver that has the power of distorting the message. It is an obligation of the sender to minimize noise to ensure communication effectiveness.

DECODING

Decoding is the understanding of the message by the receiver. It is important to recognize that the message may have been changed three times before being decoded: (1) changed by the filtering of the sender, (2) changed by noise, and (3) changed by the filtering of the receiver. Decoding the message is not merely the process of accepting and understanding the filtered message, however. As previously noted, a message can be any stimulus that elicits a response, and since more than one sense can be stimulated at the same time, the receiver can receive more than one message simultaneously. It is during decoding that contradictory messages are reconciled.

Let us return to the previous example of the manager who conveyed one message with spoken words and a different message visually by means of body language. The manager speaks to an employee with words of praise and encouragement while staring down at the floor or off into space with general disinterest. The words convey one message, the body posture a different message. The receiver must decide which message is correct—must reconcile the differences in the received messages in the decoding phase of the communication process. The context of the communication will influence the selection of the correct message by the receiver. In this case, if the relationship between the manager and the subordinate is good, the employee will be likely to believe and accept the words while ignoring the visual message of the body language. If the relationship is one characterized by much past criticism and animosity on the part of the manager, however, the subordinate is more likely to accept the "I really am not interested in your terrible performance" message conveyed by the body language. The task of a manager desiring to effect successful communication is to minimize contradictory messages and, when there are simultaneously transmitted messages, to help the receiver in the decoding function. This can occur during feedback.

FEEDBACK

There is a channel of **feedback** placed in the communication process, in Figure 17-1 shown as a *feedback loop* that connects receiver to sender. This has been done because even as an individual is sending a message, feedback information is received that has the power to modify the message sent. For example, if a manager disciplines a subordinate by speaking harshly and sees that the employee is becoming angry, the manager may soften the message and so lessen the employee's anger.

Feedback is crucial to the message sender. By examining and evaluating the feedback, the sender can gain valuable insight into the way in which the message is being received. If a manager sends a favorable message to an employee but discovers during feedback that the employee has received a negative message, the manager can conclude that the original intent of the message has become distorted. Many managers build a formal feedback request into a message by asking for confirmation. By this mechanism the manager can ascertain if the intended message was the message that was received and decoded. Managers may also attempt to gain immediate feedback by asking the subordinate to repeat the message.

YOU SHOULD REMEMBER

Noise is anything not part of the sender or receiver that can distort a message. A manager must try to minimize noise to ensure effective communication. He or she must also be aware of all of the factors that influence the decoding of a message and pay particular attention to **feedback.** An important tool for managers, feedback provides valuable information about *what* is being communicated and *how well* it is being communicated. The processing of feedback by the sender takes time, but it is time well spent for the manager desiring effective communication.

BARRIERS TO SUCCESSFUL COMMUNICATION

There are several barriers to successful communication. Among the most common are message overload or complexity; personal distortion mechanisms, such as inattention and lack of common vocabulary; and psychological distortion mechanisms, such as rationalization and denial.

MESSAGE OVERLOAD

Advertisers are aware that the placement of too many ads on the printed page is very ineffective because the ads end up competing with one another for the reader's attention. Each ad's message is a visual stimulus, and too many messages presented simultaneously result in what is called **message** or **stimulus overload.** In message overload too many competing messages arrive simultaneously, and the result is either that none are decoded or that those that are decoded are distorted in the midst of the message competition.

Managers should limit the number of messages transmitted at any one time. Too many messages will create an overloaded condition and severely interfere with effective communication. Messages must be *prioritized*, with the most important for the immediate situation transmitted first. After there has been time to decode these messages, then others can be sent according to their priority. Consider the situation of the manager who wishes to notify the members of the department, by placing information in the weekly pay envelope, of a new procedure for taking vacation, information regarding a change in the health plan, and news of a pay raise. If all three pieces of information are placed on the same insert, they may create an information overload. A better way of presenting this information is either to stagger the information over three pay envelopes or to place three separate inserts into the same envelope. The messages, read separately, will be more sequential than simultaneous and reduce the competition for the attention of the receiver.

And, as employers make increasing use of e-mail, particular care must be given to the initial description of the subject matter of each e-mail message sent. When employees receive many messages daily, there is a great tendency to view the subject descriptions in the e-mail inbox, and either to immediately delete those that appear unimportant or to merely skim the opening paragraph. In either case, the result is the same—ineffective communication. With electronic messages, it is vitally important to "grab" the reader quickly so that he or she is motivated to read the whole message.

MESSAGE COMPLEXITY

There is greater difficulty in decoding a complex message than a simple message. With a complex message the receiver must try to understand not only the many components of the message but also the interrelationships of these components. The task of the manager is to reduce message complexity, if possible. This often can be accomplished by *message incrementalizing*, which is the process of breaking a complex message into several smaller and simpler messages.

Incrementalizing is not merely inserting periods into a message that contained commas—the making of a complex sentence into many simple sentences. It is an organized sequential breakdown of the message. If, for example, the message being simplified contains instructions for sequential actions, the sequence of instructions must be preserved in the order of the simplified messages. To indicate the sequence in which the messages should be read, they may be placed in numbered order or may even contain an *overlap section*. This is a summary paragraph, or even the final section from the previous section. By reference, it reminds the reader of what came immediately before.

YOU SHOULD REMEMBER

Effective communication can be impeded by too many messages or by messages that are too complex. A **message** or **stimulus overload** occurs when too many messages arrive at the same time making the distortion in decoding likely. A **complex message** should be broken down into parts and the relationship of the parts carefully explained.

PERSONAL DISTORTION MECHANISMS

People may also have personal mechanisms that interfere with successful communication. These **personal distortion mechanisms** include inattention, early evaluation, and lack of a common vocabulary.

• *INATTENTION*
Inattention can be produced by the difference in the speed at which a person speaks and the listener hears. The brain of the listener can process information at a much faster rate than the message can be delivered by the speaker. The process of rapid understanding is further accelerated by the psychological process known as *closure*. The mind of the receiver completes a message even if it is incomplete and assembles the parts into a whole. In communication this process operates to fill in the gaps of a partial message so that it can be understood. This means that messages are understood even before the speaker finishes sending them. Consider the following message: "United States of America." Most listeners would know what the message was by the time the speaker had said "United States," and some might even complete it upon hearing "United."

When the message has been decoded, even if the sender isn't finished speaking, the receiver's attention may momentarily wander. The listener may then appear to be "tuning out," making further communication effectiveness difficult. The difference in speed between sending and receiving also leads to a different difficulty—that of early evaluation.

• *EARLY (PREMATURE) EVALUATION*
Because the receiver completes the message even before receiving it, the receiver may prematurely evaluate the contents of the message. This may lead the receiver to draw false conclusions and assume the message to be something that it is not. "Leaping to conclusions" can obviously be very destructive to effective communication as what will be assumed to have been said may be at great variance with what was actually communicated. And, since messages are discerned incorrectly from only partial communication,

the few words used, if carelessly chosen by the sender, may exacerbate further the difficulties, particularly so if the sender and receiver misunderstand the words used. This circumstance is characterized as a "lack of a common vocabulary," and is a common and serious communication problem.

• *LACK OF A COMMON VOCABULARY*

A word can have several different meanings. It has one *denotative meaning*, the explicit definition of a term, but may have many *connotative meanings*, or meanings by association. The meaning intended by the sender is often determined by the specific context within which it is found. Consider the following example of using the word *crash:*

- The disk crashed (computer programming)
- The plane crashed (air traffic control)
- The project was crashed (project management)

In this example, the word has three distinctly different meanings that depend on the specific context. In computer programming, when a disk drive fails it is said to crash. When an airplane crashes, it is a tragic event. When a project is crashed, it means that the shortest possible time for completion has been reduced by the application of additional organizational resources. The same word has three different meanings, and the receiver must make use of the context in which the word is used to decipher the correct meaning.

Sometimes the different interpretations of what was said come from an intrinsic ambiguity in the words used. For example, a manager tells a subordinate that he wants the report completed by "next week." On Monday the manager asks the employee for the completed report, and the employee replies that it will be ready, on time, later in the week. The manager is angry because the report isn't completed; the employee is confused by the anger and disappointment of the manager. The source of the difficulties in this case is to be found in the differing interpretations of the phrase "next week." The manager meant "by Monday," but the subordinate understood the same phrase as meaning "by Friday." The manager coded and sent one message; the employee received and decoded a decidedly different one.

A *common vocabulary* consists of words that have formally defined meanings that are accepted by a specific group and that facilitate communication by eliminating or greatly limiting the connotative meanings of words. Professional groups, such as engineers and physicians, develop a specific vocabulary, words that have denotative meanings acknowledged by all within the profession. The medical profession, for example, needs a vocabulary that is relatively immune from change and often uses Latin words for derivatives to name body parts and drugs.

Some words acquire unique meanings when used within a profession. Some of this profession-specific vocabulary may seem arcane to the general public, but some may pass from the specific profession into the general vocabulary as "jargon." A nonengineer, overhearing a highly technical conversation between two engineers, would probably not understand much of the conversation. The important point is that the two engineers would understand each other exactly, and this is the function of a common vocabulary.

A manager may have to use a different vocabulary when speaking with senior managers than when speaking to the union rank and file. This is not linguistic snobbery but the recognition that effective communication depends upon understanding, and a manager desiring to be understood must use words that are understandable. When the first Sears and Roebuck catalogue was published, it featured farm tools under the heading of "Agricultural Implements." The farmers who received this catalogue responded with a new American expression: "Call a spade a spade!" The farmers were reacting to the use of the term "agricultural implements"—they wanted the words they commonly used. Managers who use words not understood by employees will have extreme difficulty in communicating accurately with them.

YOU SHOULD REMEMBER

Communication difficulties arise, in part, because of personal distortion mechanisms. Some of these are **inattention, early (premature) evaluation,** and **lack of a common vocabulary.** Managers desiring to facilitate effective communication should attempt to pay attention to the message being transmitted, avoid early (premature) evaluation of messages, and make use of a vocabulary common to the individual to whom the communication is being directed.

PSYCHOLOGICAL DISTORTION MECHANISMS

Many psychological phenomena can interfere with effective communication. Psychologists have identified defensive reactions that operate in everyone without the individual being conscious of their operation. Any communication from either a senior or a subordinate that is considered threatening can evoke a defensive reaction. These defensive reactions create difficulties for good communication in both senders and receivers. Senders of threatening messages cause the defensive reactions to come into play and interfere with communication. Receivers, reacting to threatening messages, will react in a defensive manner and pass bad information via the feedback loop to the sender.

• *RATIONALIZATION*

Rationalization is a psychological process by which an individual justifies behavior and thought that is unconsciously evaluated as unjustified. We have all had the experience of doing something that was dumb and yet justifying it to friends because we didn't want to appear dumb to others. This also creates distortion within the communication process and must be considered by managers desiring an effective communication style.

Within the communication process, managers rationalize their behavior before peers and subordinates. This rationalization forms the basis for the message that is encoded, but if the same rationalization is *absent* at the decoding end, the receiver will have great trouble understanding the nature of the communication and will probably respond with feedback that points out that the sender is rationalizing. Managers need to become aware of when they are rationalizing and realize that this may be the source of difficulty in communication.

• *DENIAL*

Denial is the process by which an individual refuses to acknowledge feelings or opinions when challenged. A subordinate, having voiced an opinion (communication) to a manager, may deny such an opinion if challenged. This will impact the communication process when it creates confusion; the manager will have trouble understanding the subordinate's denial. What seems obvious to the manager will not be obvious to the subordinate engaged in the denial reaction.

YOU SHOULD REMEMBER

Psychological distortion mechanisms are psychological processes that operate to distort interpersonal communications. Either the receiver or the sender can be affected by these processes. Two of the best known are **rationalization** and **denial.** Rationalization is the self-justification of a specific message interpretation; denial is the lack of recognition of a message's meaning.

IMPROVING INTERPERSONAL COMMUNICATION

As is evident from the previous discussion of the barriers to effective communication, a difficult task confronts managers. The following points represent guidance derived from scientific research and the experiences of practicing managers that will help in overcoming these barriers.

- The communication process should begin with the formulation of a message that is *clear* and *concise*. By knowing exactly what you wish to communicate, it will be easier to do so. If you are confused about your message, the person to whom you are sending the message will probably also be confused. By making the message as concise as possible, you will avoid the confusion caused by message complexity.

- Use words that are part of the common vocabulary of the individual with whom you wish to communicate and recognize that *different groups have different common vocabularies*. You should be prepared to change vocabularies as needed. The same message may be communicated in different terms to different groups to facilitate effective communication.

- After sending a message and allowing sufficient time for its transmission and decoding, perform an accuracy check: ask the individual to whom you are communicating to repeat the message. Be hesitant to conclude that communication has been successful if the message is repeated with the same language as originally transmitted. This may be simply rote recitation without real understanding. Seek confirmation of understanding in words other than those originally used to transmit the message.

- Try not to communicate in great haste. Spend as much time as necessary to communicate effectively. Transmit the message in several different forms if you think that you have not been successful in one format. Remember, the goal is to communicate effectively, not quickly.

- Listen to your employees. Be attentive to simultaneously transmitted nonverbal messages, in both sending and receiving. If there appears to be a conflict in simultaneous messages, seek clarification and reconcile the messages if necessary. Listening is such an important communication skill that many companies formally offer training in this area. If you feel you could be listening more effectively, investigate such training as an investment in your business career.

- For communication that is of long-term significance, such as the messages containing performance standards, keep a written record so that later disputes regarding meaning can be resolved by consulting the original message.

The chapter has, to this point, dealt with communication effectiveness as a function of the basic communication process model. This was, as noted, an *interpersonal perspective*. Communication effectiveness is also influenced by the organization itself. It is for that reason that this chapter concludes with a discussion of the *organizational perspective*.

COMMUNICATION PROCESS MODEL: AN ORGANIZATIONAL PERSPECTIVE

It is useful here to refer to the formal organizational structure in Chapter 16. This organizational structure is shown in Figure 17-2, which also indicates three different kinds of communication within the organization: upward, downward, and across (lateral and diagonal). Each of these is discussed here.

DOWNWARD COMMUNICATION

Management routinely communicates information regarding the directing and controlling of performance downward to subordinates in the organization. Since business policies that impact the entire organization are formulated at the highest organizational level, it is not surprising that communication from top management also sets forth organizational rules and policies. The top managers of a company usually assume that if they send out a memorandum or make a speech, everyone in the organization will "get the word"—receive the message. This is often not the case, and personnel who are lower in the organization regularly complain that information is being withheld from them by top managers. This suggests that one of the hazards of downward communication is the organizational filtering that takes place with both superiors and subordinates.

It may be that the top manager does not correctly estimate the amount of information needed by the subordinate and transmits a less than adequate amount. This results in incomplete communication and distrust of top

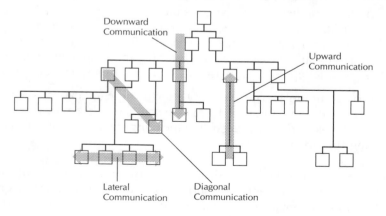

Figure 17-2. Forms of organizational communication.

management by the subordinate. This distrust will make subsequent communication difficult. This transmission of less than adequate information is not intentional, however. It is a different but equally destructive condition when the failure to transmit adequate information downward is a *deliberate* act.

A second reason that top managers may not transmit enough information is to foster dependence. By deliberately controlling the necessary information, the manager will make the subordinate dependent on him or her for needed data. Although this fostered dependence may meet the needs of the insecure manager, it also ultimately creates resentment on the part of the subordinate and increases the possibility that the subordinate does not have the information required at the appropriate time to accomplish the assigned task. Such a lack of needed information increases the chance of failure on the part of the subordinate with a negative impact upon organizational goal achievement. Because of the potential for negative impact upon the organization's eventual success, the withholding of data should be discouraged as a managerial style.

The third reason that managers may withhold data from subordinates is that they are not fully trusted. If there is a reason for believing that an employee cannot be fully trusted with important corporate information, the withholding of needed information is a temporary solution that will not be in the best long-term interests of the business. There is no assurance that the distrusted employee will not eventually acquire the information from a peer (a lateral communication, discussed later). Furthermore, if the information is genuinely needed to do the job, the lack of adequate data precludes successful task accomplishment. Clearly this is the wrong person to have in this position, and the company should seriously consider termination or reassignment.

If the individual is not trustworthy because of a transient condition—temporary extreme financial difficulty, severe emotional stress (brought about by such conditions as a death or divorce in the family or difficulty with children), or personal illness, a transfer to a position that does not require the information may be in order. This allows the business to retain an employee in a position where the possibility of task accomplishment is more likely. Even if the employee becomes frustrated by being placed in a less trusted position with perhaps less responsibility and organizational power, management can make it clear that the transfer is related to the transient condition. When the condition passes, the individual employee can receive renewed consideration for placement in the former position.

If the individual is mistrusted because of a character flaw as evidenced by past behavior that is not acceptable to the business, termination may be in order. Examples of such actions that call an employee's trust into question are long-term drug addiction, stealing, revealing corporate information to competitors, and conviction of a serious crime. Even if this person is retained within the company, there will always be doubt on the part of subordinates, peers, and managers as to his or her trustworthiness. It may be better for the individual and the company to terminate employment—better for the individual to begin anew somewhere else where trust can be built up without the immediate stigma of past deeds, and better for the company, which can now acquire an employee for the position who can be trusted with the information needed to accomplish the assigned tasks.

None of these reasons applies, however, if the manager's lack of trust in a specific employee is unjust. If a manager has no basis for distrusting an employee but persists in doing so, this is a reflection of a poor manager. By refraining from providing needed information because of an unjust distrust, the manager is ensuring that the subordinate will likely fail at the assigned task. If the subordinates of a manager consistently fail to accomplish their assigned tasks, this may be a sign of poor managerial practice, not subordinate failure.

YOU SHOULD REMEMBER

Management routinely transmits information downward to lower organizational levels. For this communication to be successful, managers must ensure that all necessary information is included in the transmission in a form that is acceptable to the subordinate. This means that the communication must be in a common vocabulary that is easily understood. Downward communication may therefore force the manager to make use of a decidedly different vocabulary than is normally used when communicating with senior managers. Given the importance of a **common vocabulary** to facilitate effective communication, that a manager uses a different vocabulary to speak to subordinates than that used with peers or superiors should not be mistaken for snobbery.

UPWARD COMMUNICATION

Just as filtering operates in the downward transmission of information, it also operates in the upward transmission. Since the information that is transmitted upward is used for planning and decision making, it routinely concerns performance achievement and problem identification. The subordinate who informs top management of the achievement of success may do so willingly, but there is often great reluctance when the news to be transmitted is not favorable. No one wishes to be the bearer of bad news, fearing with some justification that bad news may become associated with the messenger. Information regarding poor performance or an unfavorable situation may be transmitted upward in a censored form or may even be withheld from top management. Top management will be denied the information regarding poor performance, which is filtered out by subordinates.

Managerial decisions that depend upon information can only be as good as the information upon which they are based. If the information has been censored, the subsequent decision-making suffers. Top management may find itself making decisions based upon poor or incorrect information because subordinates have withheld poor performance data. There are other reasons that poor information is transmitted upward. As we saw in Chapter 16, behavior within organizations takes place within an acceptable range defined by upper and lower limits. Subordinates desiring organizational rewards (pay and promotions) tend to transmit information that falls within this acceptable range. Such information is "safe" and does not cause the sender to be regarded with closer than normal scrutiny. Such employees may be regarded by their peers as "yes men" who tell the boss whatever he or she wants to hear. Ultimately this is not good for either the individual or the company. The individual does not display originality or take any risk by always playing it safe, and the company loses a subordinate's creativity and the new ideas that would come from it.

Additionally, just as a manager may distrust subordinates, subordinates may come to distrust the manager. This distrust may be based on past experience. A manager who is not loyal to subordinates and betrays their confidence will not have a good reputation and will not be trusted. Such a reputation becomes part of the informal organization—new employees may be informally told by other workers not to trust a specific manager—and the distrust is passed from organizational generation to generation. If a manager acquires a reputation for distrust, it will be hard to achieve success since subordinates will regard all attempts to motivate, direct, and evaluate worker performance with a degree of suspicion. Managers should make it a priority to earn and maintain the trust and confidence of their subordinates.

Sometimes it is the manager, not the organization, who is responsible for the filtering by subordinates. Managers may let it be known that they don't want to know about something, and subordinates will oblige. A manager who says that "padding an expense account is OK as long as I don't know about it," or "make the sale, but don't tell me how you did it," is telling the subordinate, "lie to me, don't give me this information!" Managerial expectations may lead to subordinate filtering of specific information, and although this may be acceptable to the manager who has communicated these expectations, it is not beneficial to organizational decision-making, which depends upon valid information.

YOU SHOULD REMEMBER

Managers should remember that the key to successful upward communication is the trust of the subordinate who is doing the communicating. If there is no trust, the subordinate will be tempted to play it safe and only transmit desired information. A manager should never presume the trust of subordinates—it cannot be ordered or demanded but must be earned. Managers have to work at earning and keeping an employee's trust.

LATERAL AND DIAGONAL COMMUNICATION

There are two additional forms of organizational communication, but they do not follow the traditional hierarchical T/O (table of organization) as do upward and downward communication. They are the lateral and diagonal forms of communication, and they differ from each other in terms of the organizational levels involved. **Lateral communication** is, as shown in Figure 17-2, between different individuals or departments on the *same organizational level*. **Diagonal communication** involves communication between *two different organizational levels*. Research has shown that managers spend a large portion of each day involved in lateral and diagonal communication; the greater the interdependence of various departments within the larger organization, the greater the necessity for such diagonal and lateral communication and message transfer. To a very real extent, then, the growing complexity of the modern business structure has necessitated the creation and growth of lateral and diagonal forms of communication. Even though these forms of communication do not follow the traditional organizational structure, they are vital to the workings of the complex contemporary business.

Since lateral and diagonal forms of communication violate the traditional top-down, bottom-up forms of organizational communication, they often disrupt the normal format of work. Subordinates participating in these non-traditional communication forms often become aware of new events *before* their managers. The advantages of these forms of communication are that they (1) spread information more quickly than the traditional formats, (2) serve to link groups that otherwise would either have to communicate through the much slower upward-downward organizational communication channels or not communicate at all, and (3) enable individuals with diverse knowledge in different parts of the organization to contribute to problem solution, enhancing the effectiveness of resource use within the organization.

The major disadvantages of these forms of communication are that they interfere with the normal organizational routine and they cannot be effectively controlled by the organization. Nevertheless they are here to stay, and most managers and employees alike use them to function more effectively and efficiently within the organization. These informal communication networks are often referred to as the "grapevine" or the "water-cooler network." They exist in all organizations and are used by almost all successful managers to monitor employee communications and "put out the word" when the goal is to reach employees quickly without the often cumbersome official organizational communication channels.

YOU SHOULD REMEMBER

Lateral communication occurs between different individuals or departments on the same organizational level. **Diagonal communication** occurs between two different organizational levels. Both are vital to the workings of a complex contemporary business, to allow individuals with diverse knowledge to contribute to problem solution in different parts of an organization and serving to link groups and spread information.

AFTERWORD

Organizational communication has but one function: to facilitate and co-ordinate the efforts of individuals and groups and, ultimately, to contribute to the achievement of the organization's goals. Success at both interpersonal and organizational communication greatly determines overall success. Some well-known corporations have spent large sums of money from the human resources development budget to train employees in communication skills; it would appear to be money well spent.

KNOW THE CONCEPTS
DO YOU KNOW THE BASICS?

1. What is the difference between the *organizational* and *interpersonal* communication perspectives?
2. Why are both perspectives discussed in Question 1 important?
3. What are the origins of conflicting messages?
4. Define message reconciliation.

5. What is message overload?

6. How would you advise a manager to deal with message overload?

7. What causes inattention in the message receiver?

8. What are the different meanings of a word, and how do they cause communication problems?

TERMS FOR STUDY

connotative meaning

decoding

denotative meaning

diagonal communication

downward communication

early (premature) evaluation

encoding

feedback

filters

grapevine

inattention

interpersonal communication perspective

lack of common vocabulary

lateral communication

medium

message overload

noise

organizational communication perspective

overlap section

rationalization

receiver

sender

stimulus

upward communication

water-cooler network

ANSWERS
KNOW THE BASICS

1. The interpersonal perspective views communication effectiveness as a function of the basic communication process. The organizational perspective views communication effectiveness as a function of the organizational structure.

2. Both perspectives are necessary, for if a business is structured to promote effective communication but the individuals in that business have poor communication skills, effective communication will be difficult. The reverse is also true; individuals can be highly effective communicators and yet fail to be effective if the organizational structure itself hinders communication.

3. That messages can be conveyed visually and orally creates a problem for communication effectiveness: a manager may convey one message with spoken words and a different message visually by means of what has been called body language. Conflicting messages originate when two or more messages are sent at the same time.

4. Message reconciliation becomes necessary in the decoding process when contradictory messages are received simultaneously. The receiver generally makes use of the message context to determine which message is intended.

5. Message overload occurs when too many messages arrive at the same time. It differs from message reconciliation in that here the messages are recognized and must be reconciled. In message overload, however, too many messages are arriving and they in effect cancel each other out and are not decoded or are decoded incorrectly.

6. A manager deals with message overload by staggering the sending of messages so that they arrive at different times and so can each be decoded.

7. Inattention is produced by the difference in speed at which a person speaks and the listener hears. The brain of the listener can process information at a much faster rate than the message can be delivered by the speaker. The process of rapid understanding is further speeded up by the psychological process known as "closure."

8. A word can have several different meanings. It has one denotative meaning, the explicit definition of a term, but may have many connotative meanings, or meanings by association. These may interfere with effective communication since the message sender intends one meaning but the receiver assumes a different meaning. Unless the sender uses feedback to learn of the misunderstanding, he or she may not know that faulty communication has taken place.

18
MANAGING ORGANIZATIONAL CHANGE

KEY TERMS

change the process of transforming the manner in which an individual or organization acts from one set of behaviors to another; may be systematic or planned, or may be implemented in a random manner

organizational development the concept of changing the behavior of an organization, either in its entirety or in parts, by changing the way employees work, the structure of the organization, or the technology used

resistance to change a force active in individuals and in groups that minimizes or limits the amount of change that will occur

organizational climate the overall economic and social environment of an organizational entity, taking into account such notions as power structure, external forces, and perceived needs

change processes the ways in which changes are accomplished; may be imposed from above or participative, depending on the organizational philosophy and nature of the change

CHANGE: AN INTRODUCTION

Plus ça change, plus c'est la même chose. Loosely translated from the French this means "the more things change, the more they stay the same." In the words of **Machiavelli,** "There's nothing more difficult to take in hand, more perilous to conduct, or more uncertain in its success, than to take the lead in introducing a new order of things." These quotations point out two basic and somewhat opposite concepts about change:

No change is final. This really means that a static mode in management is almost impossible. The organization that chooses, by either design or default, not to adapt to changing opportunities and environments may be doomed to go out of business. Each change creates a set of other changes. (See Chapters 7 and 8 on Planning for a fuller discussion of these concepts.)

Change is difficult. Most people and most organizational entities become comfortable with the way business is done. BAU (business as usual) is often the easier route to getting one's job done. Managing change implies changing people's habits, behavior patterns, and sometimes attitudes about how jobs are performed.

The concept of change encompasses the future—that is, the unknown. Change brings uncertainty, and each action of change produces a reaction. A memorandum from senior management indicating a new set of work hours, a new system for sales orders, or a new claims processing method is sure to evoke discussion among those responsible for implementing the change. This chapter focuses on change in organizations, how its need is assessed, how alternatives for change are evaluated and decisions made, and how implementation efforts may be approached.

YOU SHOULD REMEMBER

Change occurs daily in organizations, by design, spontaneously, or by default. Change is oriented to the future, and each individual change may provoke a reaction that in turn provokes another future reaction. Hence, change often triggers a chain effect of future events.

ORGANIZATIONAL CLIMATE FOR CHANGE

Why do some organizations adapt to new markets, see opportunities for their product or service, centralize and/or decentralize their management structures, develop innovative programs for training their employees, and other organizations glide along in the same basic mode for many years? Recognition and acceptance of forces for change—*external* or *internal*—is a key element in foreseeing change.

EXTERNAL FORCES

Key among **external forces** for change is recognizing the need for more, less, or different goods and/or services. Consumer needs and wants change; other similar businesses change their promotion or pricing structures; and shifts occur in the spending ability of various groups of consumers. The manager and the firm that avoid recognizing these changes may well be outpaced by others who have seen the trend and have adapted their operation to take advantage of an opportunity in the marketplace.

Changes in laws or regulations can also be potent external forces for change. Here there is usually less choice about compliance. The change, however, can impact the amount of resource outlay for a firm, the amount and type of records that must be kept, and the way a supervisor performs. For example, consider a new safety regulation requiring safety glasses in a machine shop department. The organization is obliged to ensure that workers have the glasses (perhaps even at the employer's expense) and that the workers wear the glasses. Unless introduced carefully and with some consideration of the workers' views, the need to meet or comply with an external force could be viewed very negatively ("Why do I have to wear those ugly glasses?" "What happens if I don't wear them?")

A third external force can be termed "technology." Examples abound: sensing devices that read codes at supermarket checkout counters; light pens reading department store tags for inventory and price; automated warehouses; robots that perform in steel mills and automobile assembly lines; containerized cargo processing; and others. These technological advances continue to appear at an extremely high rate. Managers who ignore these advances run the risk of slower processing, longer term obsolescence, or, in some cases, high cost-benefit ratios.

INTERNAL FORCES

One of the most important **internal forces** for change is the power structure or organizational arrangement of the firm. Such areas as control systems, formal authority structure, information channels, and reward systems tend to influence managers' incentives to develop ideas for change and even to implement those ideas. Consider the firm with very stringent control systems, a hierarchical power and decision structure, and a minimal merit raise compensation system. These organizational attributes, separately or in combination, may represent considerable hurdles to developing and/or implementing change. Many times a crisis situation (e.g., stockholder uprising or a bankruptcy threat) is needed to "unfreeze" the organization.

A second internal force that exerts pressure for or against change is the force of people. People—human resources—are generally necessary to produce the firm's goods or services. Many people prefer the business-as-usual approach and resist change. Others, anxious for new ideas, are always looking for new and better ways. Imagine that the "new and better ways" person is supervising a group of "business-as-usual" subordinates. The possibility of conflict and the need for some intervention to resolve the conflict are apparent.

YOU SHOULD REMEMBER

Forces for change can be **external,** such as the market itself, laws or regulations, and technology, or **internal,** focusing on the power structure of the organization and its human resources.

CHANGE: A CONTINUUM AND A PROCESS

One of the basic laws of nature is that each action produces a reaction. So, too, in the management of an organization, each change, whether the introduction of a computer system, a change in an assembly line, or a change in the pay raise system, produces a different pattern of behavior on the part of those affected. If the desired pattern of behavior is not achieved, chances are that another change intervention will be developed to try to achieve the desired goal. This tends to produce a **continuum of change** or, stated alternatively, an absence of sameness.

Most organizations prefer to implement change in a systematic, orderly manner. In general, some stimuli (external or internal) to change trigger an idea or recognition of a problem. Alternatives are then developed and analyzed and a decision made and implemented. Results are then evaluated and data used to provide feedback for further changes.

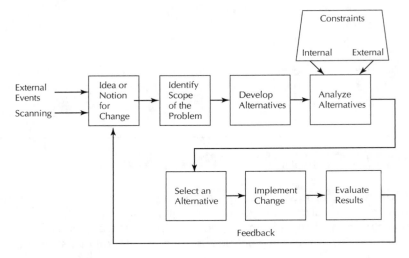

Figure 18–1. A systematic approach to managing change.

STIMULI TO CHANGE

As discussed previously, events external or internal to the organization may stimulate a need for a change. (Also, please refer to Chapter 7, which discusses environmental scanning from a planning perspective.)

The idea or notion for a change is sometimes referred to as *perceived* need, that is, the necessity for the form or entity to make a change or to alter its behavior. It is the sense that "something's wrong"—that "business as usual" needs to be altered or that an improvement can be made to make the firm an entity that is more efficient or effective. Note the difference between these two terms: *efficient* means doing things correctly, *effective* means doing the correct thing.

Examples abound of ideas for change in the work environment:

- A new safety regulation requires workers to shower as they enter or leave an area producing lead batteries.

- Data from an internal survey show employee absenteeism and lateness to be increasing (or decreasing) in one department.

- An automobile assembly plant finds its quality control measurements lowest of all of comparable plants in the United States. (In fact, this plant closed, laying off thousands of automobile workers in a rural area of the United States.)

- The firm reviews its financial statements and decides that it is undercapitalized for its anticipated level of production.

- A revision of the federal tax code may influence the firm's investment strategy or capital expenditures or the manner in which it acquires or divests assets.

These represent some externally generated and some internally generated forces for change. Returning to Figure 18-1, these are inputs to the idea or notion for change.

YOU SHOULD REMEMBER

Ideas for change can be generated by external forces or by reviewing internal control systems through regular or one-time evaluation studies. Change in this systematic process can focus on management of people, production, finance, or any other aspect of the business.

DETERMINE THE SCOPE OF THE PROBLEM

One of the most difficult and critical aspects of the change process is identifying the scope of the problem. Sometimes referred to as *problem diagnosis*, this function delineates the problem itself, separates the symptoms from the problem, and addresses the question of desired outcomes and also the measures by which to evaluate outcomes.

In an organization, it is sometimes difficult and complicated for a manager to succinctly determine a particular problem. Let us return to one of the examples noted in the ideas for change discussion—a new safety regulation requiring workers to shower as they enter or leave an area producing lead batteries. Which of the following is the problem?

- The regulation is unacceptable and should be rescinded.

- There are no showers, not enough showers, or only one shower in the men's locker room and none in the women's locker room. To comply, more showers are needed.

- The workers have refused to shower and threaten a walkout. To implement this change, some human resources intervention may be necessary.

The balance of the change process depends heavily on how the problem is perceived and how it is focused. The alternatives, constraints, and paths for implementation differ considerably depending on which way the problem or need for change is perceived.

YOU SHOULD REMEMBER

The actual step of determining the scope of a problem from an idea or notion for change is a critical part of the change process. If done correctly, the management of the change can more easily produce the desired outcome. Note that, in the examples, some statement of anticipated action is made.

DEVELOP ALTERNATIVES

For every complex problem, there is usually a simple solution—and it is usually wrong. Managing change in today's business environment is complex and may involve the analysis of many alternatives, each of which may require different levels of resources and have varying probabilities of success.

After the need for a change and the scope of the problem are identified the next step is to develop possible approaches to the problem in terms of who, what, where, how, and when. Without any constraints, which will be discussed later in this chapter, alternatives can easily be developed depending on which way the scope of the problem is determined.

If, for example, the problem is that the regulation is unacceptable, a manager can think of several alternatives:

- Lobby with an industry group for repeal.

- Call one's government representative for possible action.

- Disregard the regulation and risk a possible penalty; get others in the industry to do the same.

In developing potential alternatives to managing change, managers may use a "brainstorming" technique in which several people gather to focus on ways to manage a solution to a particular problem. Initially, suggestions of any alternatives are encouraged, regardless of how impossible the alternative may appear on the surface. After myriad alternatives have been suggested, the evaluation process begins.

YOU SHOULD REMEMBER

Alternative change techniques are developed based on the scope of the problem. One way to develop these alternatives is **brainstorming.**

ANALYZE ALTERNATIVES IN THE CONTEXT OF THEIR CONSTRAINTS

The key to analyzing alternatives is recognition of internal and external constraints. These may relate to:

- *People:* the norms and values the workforce brings to the job

- *Structure:* the lines of communication and power, both formal and informal

- *Environment:* the technologically driven forces that inhibit or propel change

- *Costs and benefits:* the financial resources required or anticipated to make the change

Each of these four areas must be addressed in evaluating alternatives to change. Returning to the example of rescinding the regulation regarding showers, the "people factor" may (or may not) provide letters or telegrams supporting the organization's position to rescind the legislation. On the other hand, let us suppose your immediate superior had been on a commission that drafted the substance of the legislation; it is unlikely that this alternative would even be considered. This illustrates the informal structure constraint. Costs and benefits are fairly straightforward; both may be tangible or intangible. For example, consider the situation in which workers in the department had been asking for showers for years. If management chooses the alternative of installing the showers, thereby implementing the proposed new legislation, an intangible benefit may result: worker morale may increase, and thereby production may increase.

YOU SHOULD REMEMBER

Alternatives for making any change must be analyzed in the context of their constraints. Each alternative will become more or less attractive given the constraints and probability of success.

SELECT AN ALTERNATIVE

After analyzing various alternatives, management makes a choice of which approach to use in managing the change. The decision process may be formal—for example, a review of the proposal by the vice president's group, by a department head group, by a committee of the board of directors, or by the board of directors itself—or it may be informal—for example, an agreement among workers and the supervisor of a section of a department to change the sequence of workers who assemble a particular part. In general, the bigger the problem is or the more costly the proposed solution, whether in dollars, sensitivity, or magnitude of change, the more formal the selection process—usually.

> # YOU SHOULD REMEMBER
>
> Decisions may be made **formally** through the organizational hierarchy, or **informally** by groups of people with similar interests. A lack of a decision is, in effect, a decision to continue with business as usual.

IMPLEMENT THE CHANGE

Implementation of a planned change is a key component of any managerial job and involves translating upper management's decision into activities that will produce the desired outcomes.

In implementing change, it is important to note varying styles of leadership (see Chapter 14, which describes in detail a variety of management styles). In a continuum, one may describe these styles as ranging from autocratic to participative. In the *autocratic style*, change is assumed to be implemented by an edict from top management. This may be in the form of a memorandum or a special videotape or cassette or letter. The initial intervention is a written or verbal communication instructing workers to change their behavior pattern. It is a one-way form of communication that assumes that lower level managers and workers will change their behaviors to achieve the desired outcome. Such an autocratic approach does not take into account several factors, chief of which are:

- the natural resistance to change

- the need to unfreeze current behavior patterns

- the tendency to continue doing business as usual

Another approach to managing change is to involve subordinates in developing and implementing the change. This participative approach shares the responsibility and authority for change by bringing the subordinates on board very early in the process. This principle is, in fact, one of the basic concepts of the quality circle approach, developed in the United States in the mid-1940s and adopted and popularized by Japanese industry in the late 1970s and early 1980s. For this highly participative approach to work, several conditions must exist:

> Subordinates must wish to be involved. A managerial leadership climate that encourages employees to take part in solutions to the problems of the organization must exist. They must believe that their par-

ticipation is not simply a rubber stamp to support a solution predetermined by management.

Managers must be confident in their roles. Normally a manager considers it his or her responsibility to solve problems. The concept of involving subordinates who may come up with a better solution takes a high degree of confidence and an understanding of the broader role of the manager.

Employees must be willing to voice new ideas, and managers must be willing to listen to new ideas. These two conditions complement each other. If one is absent, the other will be defeated. As a manager, you may be faced with a situation in which you would like employees to participate, but your predecessor practiced the autocratic management style and employees were unaccustomed to any participation. Given the first opportunity of participation, it is highly likely that employees will initially offer few, if any, suggestions to solve problems. Consistent involvement, over time, is needed to build this relationship.

Once subordinates and managers develop confidence in the participative approach, problems may be presented and solutions discussed. Implementation becomes easier because of the earlier involvement and because subordinates have "bought in" to the problem, the process, and the solution.

YOU SHOULD REMEMBER

Implementation of new ideas is an important part of each manager's job. Management styles can vary from autocratic to participative. Implementation may be easier or smoother if subordinates have participated throughout the process.

EVALUATE THE RESULTS

Evaluation asks the basic questions, "Did we manage to attain the objectives?" and "What could we have done differently or better?" Returning to our earlier example, the following might be evaluation questions:

- Was the regulation rescinded?
- When? Was the change accomplished within the appropriate or planned time frame?

- Was another, more onerous regulation passed?

- Were costs and benefits realized?

In a day-to-day operational environment, evaluation techniques often include reports, such as sales data, budget analyses, production run data, absenteeism analyses, and quality control measure data. These techniques tell the manager whether the change intervention was successful in terms of the desired outcomes and also provide measures of the degree of success.

Evaluation also serves another role: it provides feedback in terms of future ideas for change. If the initial change intervention was not successful, evaluation studies or reports would point this out. In turn, these data help to identify a potential need for changes in the future. The change process may be reinitiated to develop and analyze future change interventions.

YOU SHOULD REMEMBER

Evaluation can provide valuable data in terms of the degree to which the planned outcomes were achieved. It can also provide feedback through which future changes can be developed and analyzed.

In order to test your knowledge of some of the principles of change described earlier, as well as some of the other management areas covered thus far in the text, the following case is presented. As you read through this case, make a list of the problems as you see them and their probable causes.

INTERNATIONAL TELEPHONE AND TELECOMMUNICATIONS SUPPLY CORPORATION*

The International Telephone and Telecommunications Supply Corporation had started out as the Brussels Telephone Supply Company in 1919. Through the years, the company had expanded with small manufacturing plants and marketing offices in several European countries until, in 1992, they had plants and country headquarters locations in seven nations. In 1984, they had changed their name in order to better fit their product line and to avoid being identified with one country as they attempted to broaden

---

* This case material has been developed as a basis for discussion of organizational situations. All names have been disguised. Darrell T. Piersol, 1993 (revised 1994).

their market. They specialized in a number of products used by the giant national telephone organizations and could generally count on a far better cost structure to help their marketing strategy.

In 1990, they were facing increased competition on all sides, and the European economy was sinking. President Emile Montan knew that he had to increase efficiency, since sales were not increasing, to maintain profitability in a shrinking market. For some time, he had felt that the purchasing function could be more effective if it had central control and guidance. He knew that this idea would not be easily accepted by his Country Executive Directors, as they had their own suppliers in their countries and after many years had built up strong relationships. Also, with the growing cutbacks in people, they hated to do anything that might harm their individual nation's employment situation.

After discussing the matter with other top executives and his board of directors, it was decided to hire Mr. Pierre La Fond, Assistant to the Managing Director of one of the largest European national telephone organizations, to improve their purchasing organization. In one of his earlier assignments, Mr. La Fond had been Director of the Centralized Purchasing Division for his national telephone exchange. To help Mr. La Fond become acquainted with the International Telephone and Telecommunications Supply Corporation, President Montan assigned Mr. Charles Briemont, a former Executive Managing Director of one of the country organizations, to serve on La Fond's staff. Mr. Briemont had been invited to headquarters in Brussels after a mild heart attack to remove him from the stress of daily operational decisions.

After Mr. La Fond spent several days meeting with executives at the headquarters, Charles Briemont suggested that they might visit the various Executive Managing Directors to discuss the role that Mr. La Fond intended for his new position in the corporation. The only communication with the country organizations had been a notice that Mr. La Fond had joined the corporate staff, but no mention of his job responsibility had been given except for his new title. Mr. La Fond said that he really did not have time for a visit as he wanted to take action as quickly as possible. He preferred his instructions to be in writing so that no mistakes would be made in understanding his directives. He sent the following letter to the seven purchasing directors in the headquarters of the various country organizations. (See Figure 18-2.)

> Dear _____,
>
> I am very pleased to have joined the International Telephone and Telecommunications Supply Corporation in this time of tremendous change and explosive growth in the industry. This highly competitive arena demands that we operate as effectively as possible. My experience in the _____ National Phone Company has increased my awareness of the absolute necessity of cost control in every part of our business.
>
> Please fill out the attached questionnaire regarding your current purchasing practices and give me a detailed up-to-date report on your purchases this year. In this way, I can better comprehend the

problems faced by our organization and can develop a plan to make the structural changes needed to improve our competitive position. Until my plans are finalized, please send for my review any purchase of $10,000 or more.

Since this will take some detail work on your part, I expect your report in three weeks from the date of this letter. I look forward to meeting you in the future and working with you in this vital endeavor.

Sincerely,

Pierre La Fond
Corporate Vice President
Purchasing

Mr. La Fond received several letters of congratulations on his new assignment from other corporate staff executives and two letters of welcome from purchasing executives in the country organizations. However, after the three weeks had passed, he had received no information from the country purchasing executives and no purchase orders over $10,000 had been sent to headquarters for his review. This lack of response to his directive had never occurred in his previous executive position where his orders had been obeyed promptly. He was irritated and decided he had waited long enough. He now began to plan his strategy to compel compliance with his directive.

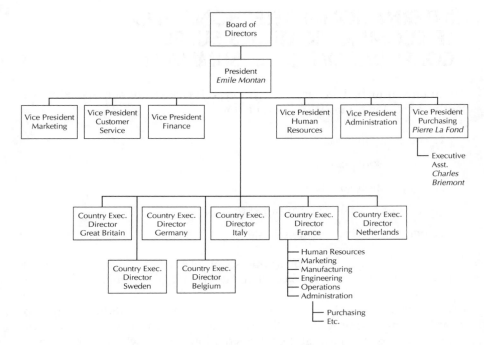

Figure 18-2. Partial organizational chart for International Telephone and Telecommunications Supply Corporation.

PROBLEMS AND CAUSES

INTERNATIONAL TELEPHONE AND TELECOMMUNICATIONS SUPPLY CORPORATION CASE: SUMMARY

You have now had a chance to explore this case. Generally speaking, we can break it down into five different points:

1. organizational communication

2. interpersonal behavior

3. organization structure

4. short-term vs. long-term pressures

5. personnel recruitment

La Fond's predicament, apparently so simple at first, encapsulates many important problems that we face each day as managers or members of organizations.

Whether or not we have ever sent or received a memorandum on the approval of purchase orders, we all know what it is like to have someone new imposed on us. We have all been in situations either where our assumed power to communicate and direct was not matched by the responses we received, or where we acted to ignore messages or directives that seemed to us inappropriate.

Managers who have discussed this case over the years have drawn many interpretations and lessons from it. Some have defended La Fond and argued that the top officers of International should have done more to endorse and back his directives. Others have treated the problem as one growing out of La Fond's failure to understand the kind of purchasing practices required in the company and have suggested that it was a mistake to hire him for the job.

But most often the discussion has centered around a theme that we now want to develop in a more general way: while structure, size, tradition, available communication levels, and sometimes even employee expectations favor one-way transmission of information, guidelines, and instructions, effective management requires two-way communication.

Interactive dialogue among members of organizations often is hard to arrange, especially beyond the confines of small work teams, and, as this case shows, it is often rejected as a strategy because it is expensive in time and energy for those who get involved.

Discussion of this case hints at many ways in which a better dialogue among the parties involved would have helped to ensure that La Fond was the best person for the job, provide for his early integration into the organization, and speed constructive changes in purchasing practice.

The form of two-way communication used in this exercise illustrates one of a number of ways in which the techniques of "structural communication" can be employed to further two-way interaction in company communication, training, and personnel assessment.

KNOW THE CONCEPTS
DO YOU KNOW THE BASICS?

1. A carefully planned change will be easy to implement: true or false?
2. Name the major external forces that cause change.
3. Internal forces are important in managing change. What are these forces?
4. Why is determining the scope of the problem important to managing change?
5. Name four factors to consider in evaluating alternatives in the context of their constraints.
6. Decisions in a change strategy of an organization are always made formally: true or false?
7. Describe the continuum of management styles in implementing change.
8. Name the conditions that must exist for successful participative management.

TERMS FOR STUDY

alternative solutions
decisions: formal, informal, and
   default
evaluation methodologies
external constraints

external events
implementation styles
internal constraints
scope of a problem

ANSWERS
KNOW THE BASICS

1. A planned change may be easy or difficult to implement depending on the magnitude of the change, the organizational climate, and the involvement of those who will make the change occur.
2. The major external forces causing or promoting change are (1) the marketplace, (2) laws and regulations, and (3) technology.

3. Internal forces that contribute to the accomplishment (or non-accomplishment) of change are (1) the power structure of the organization and (2) resistance to (or acceptance of) the change on the part of the workforce.

4. Determining the scope of the problem is the key to managing any change. This activity involves stating the specific problem, not its symptoms, and describing expected outcomes. If the scope of the problem is incorrectly determined, alternatives and analysis of those alternatives will focus on an incorrect problem.

5. The four factors that are generally considered in evaluating alternatives are people, the structure of the organization, the technological or future environment, and the costs and benefits of the particular alternative.

6. False. Decisions involving major changes or major reallocations of resources are usually made formally, but decisions may be made quite informally as well. Additionally, the failure to make a decision results in a decision by default.

7. Management styles range from autocratic to participative. The autocratic manager tends to implement change by formal written or oral communication, specifying each person's role in implementing that change. The participative manager involves his or her subordinates early in the process and asks for subordinates' assistance in determining the scope of the problem, development and analysis of alternatives, implementation, and evaluation.

8. There are three major conditions for successful participative management: (1) subordinates must wish to be involved, (2) managers must be confident in their roles, and (3) employees must be willing to voice new ideas, and managers must be willing to listen to new ideas.

19

CONFLICT: ORGANIZATIONAL AND PERSONAL DIMENSIONS

KEY TERMS

conflict disagreement within the organizational setting between two or more parties, or between two or more positions, as how to best achieve the organization's goals

avoidance a management strategy for dealing with organizational conflicts, which includes nonattention or creating a total separation of the combatants or a partial separation that allows a limited interaction

smoothing a conflict management technique that stresses the achievement of harmony between the disputants; treating a problem superficially, denying its importance to the organization, or complete denial that a problem exists are examples of smoothing

dominance or **power intervention** another conflict management technique, the imposition of a solution by higher management (other than the level at which the conflict exists)

compromise a conflict management strategy that seeks a problem resolution that satisfies at least part of each party's position

confrontation a conflict management strategy that features a thorough and frank discussion of the sources and types of conflict and the achievement of a resolution that is in the best interests of the group but that may be at the expense of one or all of the conflicting parties; the strategy most oriented toward genuine and effective problem-solving

---

Prehistory, that time before people began to keep a written record of events, was likely characterized by many disputes between various groups of people. The roots of conflict, as revealed by ancient languages, seem to be found in the competition for food supplies. No matter what the origins of conflict between groups, however, it is apparently as old as humanity. It is not surprising, therefore, that conflict continues into modern times and into the world of business. In fact, the cover of a book on ways to achieve business success, entitled *Corporate Conflict*, showed a business executive dressed in a suit wearing a tie featuring a camouflage design. The point of the book was that the modern manager could ensure success in the world of business conflict by applying principles of military conflict. Indeed, recent compilations of management practice seek to invoke the implication of success by reference to historical military leaders such as Attila the Hun, Generals George Patton and Ulysses S. Grant, and the Mongol leader Ghengis Khan.

Conflict within the organizational setting is defined as the disagreement between two or more parties or between two or more positions as to how to best achieve the organization's goals. This definition has two major facets.

TYPES OF CONFLICT

A conflict can obviously be between two or more parties, whether those parties are individuals, groups, departments, divisions, companies, political parties, or even entire nations. Two-party conflicts can be divided into several different formats: between individuals, between individuals and groups, between groups, and between total organizations. Each of these two-party conflicts is discussed, but first we must present the seemingly unique case of a single-party conflict.

SINGLE-PARTY CONFLICTS

This **single-party conflict** would be two opposing opinions within a single individual. We have spoken previously of the individual manager's value system. That value system may be in conflict with the organization's values; for example, an individual manager may believe in "fair play" but the company asserts that "anything goes" and "all's fair in love, war, and business."

Individuals involved in situations in which the individual's sense of values conflicts with what the organization expects or when the individual's ethical sense is radically different from the values embedded within the corporate culture may experience internal conflicts that can assume life-threatening dimensions. Ulcers, sleeplessness, elevated blood pressure, inattention, higher accident rates, and marital stress have all been related to personal conflicts in the workplace. The organization may not be very sympathetic to the individual in conflict, believing that the worker should "get with the program"—either go along with what the organization desires, or get out.

Single-party conflict may also arise when there are two methods of accomplishing an organizational goal and the individual cannot decide which method to select. The two methodologies may be in conflict within the same manager, and a third party, such as an organizational superior, might be needed to resolve the conflict.

Yet another single-party conflict may involve an individual presented with two choices of action, both equally bad. An example is a manager confronted with the choice of (1) continuing to operate a money-losing business or (2) entering into a Chapter 11 business bankruptcy. Since both courses of action are bad, the owner of the failing business may have trouble resolving the conflict and choosing one course of action over the other. This example of a single-party conflict might conceivably take the actions of a disgruntled creditor to force the company into involuntary bankruptcy to resolve the conflict.

There is a great temptation to regard conflict, especially the single-party form, as destructive. Conflict wastes limited managerial time and energy. It has the power to interrupt the flow and effectiveness of organizational communication. Ultimately, the desire to avoid conflict may produce uncontroversial decisions designed to "fit" within the acceptable range of organizational behavior.

However, it must also be recognized that conflict can stimulate innovation in problem solving and thereby be beneficial for the organization. Individuals caught in a single-party conflict may become truly creative in finding a satisfactory solution that effectively reconciles both opposing opinions or courses of action. A sharp disagreement of opinion often leads to criticism and testing of the opinions, which will produce a better solution. The necessity of finding a solution that reconciles the conflict can spur the individuals involved in multiparty disputes into risking new solutions that previously would have gone unconsidered by either party. The emotional turmoil in the lives of managers occasioned by conflict can be offset by the creation of better solutions and managerial action.

YOU SHOULD REMEMBER

Conflict—disagreement between two or more parties or between two or more positions—is not necessarily bad for an organization, even though it may waste valuable managerial effort and organizational resources. Conflict can release creative problem-solving energies and lead to genuine innovation within the organization. Management should regard conflict as a constant force within the modern organization and seek to manage it in a beneficial manner.

CONFLICT BETWEEN INDIVIDUALS

An organization is, at the most basic level, a collection of individuals. It is therefore not surprising that the most basic form of conflict within the organization is between individuals. Conflicts between individuals within the organization have traditionally been viewed as the result of personality differences. There is some basis for accepting this view, and the only remedy for such a personality clash has traditionally been the termination or transfer of the lower ranked or less valued employee. A more contemporary view of interpersonal conflict within the organization, however, sees such conflict as the product of the organizational roles assigned to each individual, not the personalities involved. Individuals, while fulfilling their corporate roles, are brought into conflict as they compete for scarce organizational resources. Thus a marketing manager and a vice president of research and development may have excellent personal relations but clash vehemently as each argues for resource allocation for their individual departments. However valid and rational this insight, it should be noted that it has been estimated fully one half of all terminations occur, not because of poor employee performance, but because of personality clashes.

CONFLICTS BETWEEN INDIVIDUALS AND GROUPS

Two previously noted factors of organizational life contribute to the origin of the conflicts between individuals and groups. Group behavior takes place within an acceptable range, and organizations evolve a distinctive corporate culture. The individual who does not agree with the group behavioral norms or with the values found within the corporate culture will be in conflict with the work group or with the entire organization. An initial task of the new employee is to determine if there is a fit between his or her individual values and behavioral patterns and what is expected by the corporate group. If such a fit does not exist, there is certain conflict.

The organization, as part of its recruitment and screening procedures, attempts to make a similar determination as to the quality of fit. However, since initial screening and interviewing takes place in a limited time period when the employee and the company are attempting to show each other the very best picture, neither the individual nor the organization may have enough information to assess accurately the nature and quality of fit.

The result may be that the individual chosen for the job will not really fit in. The manager's values and work expectations may have changed over time, and now are no longer congruent with those of the organization. In either event, the stage is set for conflict between the individual and the group.

CONFLICT BETWEEN GROUPS

The microview of organizations discussed in Chapter 16 stressed that an organization was composed of many different groups. Conflict between these groups is inevitable given two basic factors of organizational life: (1) the competition for scarce resources and (2) the different managerial styles necessary for the effective operation of different departments. The inherent time frames of various departments may necessitate radically different points of view and planning frames. Take the previous example from this chapter—the marketing manager and the vice president of research and development. The marketing manager strives to achieve maximum flexibility and the ability to adjust product marketing activities in a rapidly changing consumer environment. The planning and decision-making frame is decidedly short term. The vice president of research and development is forced to assume a much longer view and planning framework. This is because the activities of the research and development department are of a long-term nature, involving capital expenditures to purchase expensive equipment. This equipment will be used in both basic research and specific inquiry that will take a long time, if ever, to become marketable. It is inevitable that these departments come into conflict as they compete for organizational funding since each has a fundamentally different view of resource utilization.

Different organizational groups may require different managerial styles because of the nature of their functions. An accounting department is run differently from a marketing sales force. The differences in managerial policies and practices may occasion a conflict between each department as employees compare and contrast their jobs and how the organization regulates and rewards them.

CONFLICT BETWEEN TOTAL ORGANIZATIONS

The U.S. free enterprise economic system is characterized by vigorous competition. Each business seeks the consumer's dollar in the marketplace, and this brings total business organizations into conflict. Such conflict is often regulated by state and local governments, which have enacted laws designed to promote competition and prohibit anticompetitive business behaviors. The outlawing of a monopoly is an example of government regulation to prohibit anticompetitive business behavior. The marketplace rewards companies that are triumphant with economic rewards and continued survival. Organizations that do not compete efficiently and effectively suffer financially and may even pay the ultimate financial price. Companies go out of business or lose their corporate identity as they are acquired by other, more successful business organizations. Survival is by no means assured in the highly competitive world of contemporary business, and there are scores of famous-name companies from yesteryear that are no more because they failed to remain competitive. Some organizations, indeed even countries like Japan, view business as a kind of conflict, and the only important reward is victory. And it is vital to recognize that with the advent of the incredible growth of the Internet, business has increasingly been globalized—almost every business now faces, and must respond to worldwide competition.

YOU SHOULD REMEMBER

Conflict between individuals, groups, or entire organizations is an inherent part of the modern business environment. People and groups compete for resources within a company; companies compete with one another for the marketplace.

SOURCES OF CONFLICT

As the basic forms of conflict within the organization have been described, several potential **sources of conflict** have emerged, and this section examines these and other sources in detail. Organizational conflict arises from the following sources: (1) differences in goals, (2) resource competition, (3) communication failure and misinterpretation of information, (4) disagreement over performance standards, and (5) organizational structure incongruities.

DIFFERENCES IN GOALS

As seen in Chapters 7 and 8, which dealt with the planning process, there should *ideally* never be any goal conflict between different groups (departments or units) within the total organization. Top management determines the business policy goals and frames these goals in general terms. Midlevel management chooses strategic and tactical goals, and supervisory or lower level managers supervise the day-to-day operations as the goals are then implemented. There is no goal incompatibility between any organizational level. This *ideal* situation rarely, if ever, exists, however; in fact, goal incompatibility is cited as the most common cause of organizational conflict. This is due to two main reasons:

1. Individual managers are not neutral in this process—they have goals of their own that often clash with or at least influence the timing and ultimate achievement of the organization's goals.

2. There are inherent differences in subunit goals within the organization—all divisions do not have the same goals, time frames for accomplishment, or performance standards. What is deemed success in a newly started division might well be considered outright failure in an established one. Subunit differences are the source for interunit conflict.

Let us consider a conflict between two divisions of an automobile company. The design department wants to install a $50 battery in a new automobile because it is smaller and provides more space for the engine in the front compartment. The department responsible for car maintenance systems desires a $90 battery that is maintenance free and will last longer. This latter battery, however, is a third larger than the former and will require a different engine design. Each of these two divisions has a valid point of view and performance goal, with the end result that the unit goals themselves are in conflict.

This problem of automobile design was discussed earlier in the case of the Ford Taurus. By creating groups that interfaced with each other, Ford provided the opportunity for such diverse engineering groups to arrive at a unified solution, but not to meet in design conflict destined to produce an unworkable compromise, such as the military jet with a radio installed under the pilot's seat. Every time a technician wanted to service the radio, which was often, an explosives expert had to disarm the pilot's ejection seat mechanism.

Consider another example. The president of a large department store wants to increase sales in the month of July, traditionally a quiet merchandising interlude between the beginning of summer and the back-to-school buying rush in late August. The president decides to hold a sale in the shoe department because it is in the back of the second floor of the department store. He reasons that by luring customers to the back of the second floor, they will make more purchases on the way out of the store. Since the shoe department is the most remote department in the store, only a dramatic sale will entice customers to the second floor, and the president decides to offer a two-for-one sale. The shoe department manager, however, has a unit goal of selling as many shoes as possible because the compensation of all the shoe salespeople depends upon total dollar sales volume. When the president announces that the shoe department will hold a two-for-one sale, the manager is stunned and then gets very angry. This anger comes from the differences between the manager's goal and the president's goal.

RESOURCE COMPETITION

Another source of conflict within the organization is found in the competition for limited available resources. One of the tasks facing top management is to allocate the available resources among the departments and organizational subunits. This is not always an easy task, since each department believes that it has a valid claim upon the organization for support of individual projects and departmental activities. Increasingly, as businesses create service departments that offer a common but limited resource to many departments, there is competition for that resource. An example of this kind of interdepartmental competition is the competing claims upon the data-processing facility. Conflicts commonly arise over such organizational resources as:

- project funding
- office space
- consultant time
- use of facilities, tools, equipment, and so on
- project opportunities
- data-processing facilities

Even as top management allocates the available resources among the various competing organizational claimants, there may be those who believe that they have been slighted and not received their "fair share." Although the individuals (or groups) that believe they have not received a fair share will probably not act in an openly aggressive manner, they may act in a *passively aggressive manner*. They will retaliate by noncooperation, withholding needed data, and performing organizational tasks on a minimal level. A group that believes it has not received its deserved allocation of organizational resources has the power to disrupt the orderly and effective conduct of business activities.

COMMUNICATION FAILURE AND MISPERCEPTION OF INFORMATION

It is not likely that all departments and individuals in an organization will simultaneously possess the same information. The very nature of departmental specialization leads to different groups possessing different information. Much of the interaction between groups in the organization consists of the trading of information. Information is used in decision-making, and since one department's information may not be known by a different department, the decisions made by the former will often not be understood by the latter. Both lack of information and lack of understanding decisions that flow from that information can lead to serious misunderstanding between departments.

Additionally, even if departments do possess the same information, they may have significantly different points of view. A marketing department may be delighted at an increase in sales, but the production department views the same increase in sales with genuine dismay since the machinery in the factory will not be able to efficiently produce the required inventory. Different information and points of view lead to interdepartmental misunderstanding and conflict.

Akira Kurosawa, the legendary Japanese film director, made his famous film *Rashomon* in 1951 and introduced a renaissance in Japanese cinema. The film, considered one of the greatest of all time and still being shown years later, centers upon an alleged act of violence viewed by four different witnesses. As the story is told from the different viewpoints, the viewer is presented with four radically different versions of what happened. Each witness has such a different story that by the end of the movie the viewer is not really sure what has happened. That different points of view produce significantly different understandings is Kurosawa's point so brilliantly made.

DISAGREEMENT OVER PERFORMANCE STANDARDS

Departments within a large contemporary organization may be highly interrelated as each individual subunit both gives and receives information. Since the performance of one division can impact upon another's, it is important that the performance standards of each be compatible. If a performance standard incompatibility exists, there may be an adverse impact upon the task achievement of one or both departments. For example, the planning department in a large corporation needs information from the marketing department. The planning department is charged with the task of submitting plans on a quarterly basis—by the first of January, April, July, and October. However, the marketing department expects that the marketing estimates will be submitted on a twice-yearly basis—by January 10 and July 10. Each of these departments has a different performance standard—in this case different delivery dates. They are out of sync, and the performance of the marketing department will directly impact upon the eventual success of the planning department. In this case, the differences between performance standards will probably lead to direct conflict between the two departments.

Disagreement over performance standards may also manifest itself on the level of the individual, something learned by many U.S. business executives working in Japan. In the United States, a manager is praised if he or she works efficiently and finishes all the needed work by the end of the day. The Japanese executive is often expected to return from dinner and work until the evening hours. U.S. executives often learn to leave some work for the evening hours to meet Japanese work standards. A U.S. manager who fails to understand the difference in performance standards while working in Japan may be regarded as a poor employee.

ORGANIZATIONAL STRUCTURE INCONGRUITIES

The organizational structure itself may also be a source of conflict. We have discussed the differences in power between the line and the staff employees within the organization. It is not surprising that this difference in organizational power leads to conflict. Staff employees derive their power from the value the organization places upon their unique skills and expertise. Line employees are assigned their power by the organization, symbolized by the hierarchical T/O (table of organization), and are delegated both authority and responsibility. Staff employees, making use of their expertise, advise the line decision makers. Often, however, staff believes that it should be making decisions, not merely influencing the decisions. This dynamic often leads to conflict when the advice of staff is ignored.

The line-staff conflict assumes some predictable forms. The line complains that the staff does not understand or take responsibility for daily operations. The staff complains that the line employees do not listen to their advice or know how to use the staff experts correctly. Each of these departments, despite their fundamentally different orientations, has much to contribute to the other and to the ultimate success of the organization. This eventual success, however, necessitates cooperation, not conflict.

YOU SHOULD REMEMBER

The sources of organizational conflict are (1) differences in goals, (2) resource competition, (3) communication failure and misperception of information, (4) disagreement over performance standards, and (5) organizational structural incongruities. Management can make use of conflict resolution techniques that seek to resolve the conflict but do not deal with the causes—like a doctor treating the symptom, not the disease. However, the conflict may break out in a different form if the causes are not treated.

STRATEGIES FOR MANAGING GROUP CONFLICTS

Since conflict seems a universal part of organizational life, executives must learn techniques for the management of these conflicts. By mastering various methods, an individual can increase managerial effectiveness. Some of the most used and effective methods are avoidance, smoothing, dominance or power intervention, compromise, and confrontation. Table 19-1 on page 377 compares conflict resolution strategies.

AVOIDANCE

Management may practice **avoidance** as a strategy for dealing with organizational conflicts. For this technique to work, two factors must be true: (1) management must be willing to ignore the causes of the conflict and (2) the conflict itself or its resolution must not be vital to the organization. If management is not willing to ignore the causes of the conflict, or if one of the consequences of avoiding dealing with the conflict is significant harm to the company, avoidance is not an appropriate conflict management technique. Since these two conditions are rarely both true, there is a gradation of avoidance responses. The avoidance response can range from nonattention to partial separation that allows for only limited interaction between conflicting parties to finally creating a total separation of the combatants.

• *NONATTENTION*

In this form of avoidance response, management totally ignores the conflict and never deals with its causes. Some managers believe that if the problem is totally ignored, as if it did not exist, it will eventually go away. To a certain extent this may appear to be true—given the passage of time, some conflicts are either resolved or, more likely, *appear* to be resolved. Even under the best of circumstances, when the problem actually gets resolved with an avoidance response of nonattention, management never deals with the causes of the conflict. In medicine, a fever is often a symptom of the disease. Likewise, a conflict itself is often a symptom, and with a nonattention avoidance response, the basic cause may later result in the emergence of a different symptom. (In medicine, if the disease is not treated, another symptom may appear.)

The nonattention methodology often results in the conflict getting worse. This leads management, committed to avoidance techniques, to employ other methods such as a limited separation of the combatants or, ultimately, a total separation. Each of these, to a certain extent, recognizes that a conflict exists, but still does not deal with the cause of the conflict directly.

• *LIMITED SEPARATION*

When management cannot ignore that a conflict exists between two departments (or individuals) but still does not want to deal with the causal factors, it can avoid dealing with the problem by enforcing a **limited separation** of the combatants. This seeks to minimize the impact and expression of the conflict by severely limiting contact between the combatant parties. This technique is also called *limited interaction* because the conflicting parties are allowed to interact on a limited and sometimes supervised basis. This interaction is usually only that needed for organizational functioning, and there will be great emphasis on formality of relations. Often the meetings between the two parties will be characterized by a strict agenda, and no deviations from this agenda will be permitted. Such an agenda serves to control the limited interaction and prevent the conflict from starting anew. The agenda is like a cork placed on top of an active volcano; it prevents an eruption, at least temporarily, but it really does not stop the underlying fire.

This approach is similar to the inattention method in that it does not deal with the causes of the problem, only its symptoms. The problem can readily break out anew and be expressed in different symptoms. There are two major difficulties with the technique of limited separation as a managerial response to organizational conflict:

1. Keeping the parties apart and "policing" the limited interaction can consume valuable managerial time, effort, and organizational resources.

2. There will be constant tension between the two parties that can influence the rest of the organization in a negative manner and adversely influence daily operations.

A final limitation of this approach is that it may be unworkable with conflicting groups that must have a great deal of interaction. The close supervision required to prevent open conflict may consume too much of management's attention and the organization's resources.

Table 19–1. Styles of Conflict Resolution Within Organizations

Strategy	Rationale	Strength	Weakness
Avoidance	Because managers wish to avoid having to deal with the problem, sometimes in the belief that a problem avoided will simply "go away"	Enables managers to avoid spending a lot of time on problems that may solve themselves	Does not deal with underlying causes; allows managers to ignore issues vital to the organization
Smoothing	Because managers wish to stress harmony in the organization	Harmony of relations; surface peace between workers	Does not deal with underlying causes; often only creates the illusion of solving the problem
Dominance or Power Intervention	Because managers wish to resolve the conflict quickly and maintain the existing power structure	Conflict is resolved in the quickest manner	Does not deal with underlying causes; conflict may not be resolved; bad feelings between boss and employees may develop
Compromise	Because managers wish to satisfy at least part of each party's position	Each party receives something—"wins" partly	Does not deal with underlying causes; does not provide either party with satisfaction
Confrontation	Because managers wish to get the "roots" or causes of the conflict	Management deals with the causes of conflict and arrives at a workable solution that forces all involved to reconcile their demands with the realities	If not properly managed, will create bad feelings; also a danger that managers will be caught up in dealing with the roots of the problem and never solve it

• *TOTAL SEPARATION*

Total separation is the final avoidance technique open to management. This conflict management technique features a total physical separation of the disputing parties. It is only feasible when no actual interaction is needed for organizational functioning. If the warring departments or groups are dependent upon each other in even the slightest degree, contact will be necessary and total separation impossible. The theory behind this approach is that the conflict will be totally avoided if the parties are kept totally apart.

The major disadvantages to this approach to conflict management are similar to those of the limited separation; tension persists and may even be reinforced by the total separation as the groups are divided between "us" and "them." Stories will circulate about the other group that recount, magnify, and perhaps even create a mythology of past wrongs and misdeeds. Because the causes of the conflict are never dealt with, there is no real resolution and the conflict will continue to cast its shadow over the organization. The enforced separation will require the continued attention of management, consuming executive time, energy, and organizational resources.

YOU SHOULD REMEMBER

The **avoidance** method of dealing with organizational conflict ranges from a partial separation of the combatants (limited interaction) to a total separation. This range recognizes that a problem exists but seeks only to control the conflicting parties. Management may totally ignore the problem by making use of inattention; the hope is that the problem will go away or get better, and sometimes this appears to be the case. Usually, however, conflicts are not resolved unless management takes a more active approach, addressing the causes, not the symptoms, of the conflict.

SMOOTHING

Unlike the techniques just discussed, which seek to avoid the conflict, **smoothing** begins with a recognition that a problem exists. The emphasis, however, is on harmony and peace within the organization—the conflict is "smoothed over" as management emphasizes the similarities and common features shared by the two contentious groups rather than their differences. Management seeks to create a consensus between the two groups so that they realize that what they share is greater than what is different.

The major advantage in smoothing is that it preserves surface harmony and peace, but this is also its major weakness. This surface harmony often serves only to conceal the conflict. It is always just beneath the organizational surface. There is the possibility, perhaps inevitability, that the smoothed-over conflict will rise to the surface. The newly risen problem may have festered and grown and become even more serious than the original conflict. Smoothing, if it works at all, is effective only in the short term. Over the long term, it will probably be an ineffective conflict management technique as the causes of the conflict are never identified nor is the conflict really resolved.

YOU SHOULD REMEMBER

Smoothing as a conflict management technique stresses harmony within the organization. Although recognizing that a conflict does exist, smoothing does not deal with the underlying causes of the conflict. Since it does not deal with the causes of conflict, it has limited use, but it may be the most appropriate technique if organizational harmony is the most important managerial goal.

DOMINANCE OR POWER INTERVENTION

The simplest form of conflict resolution within the organization is for a higher level manager to impose a resolution on the two parties—**power intervention.** Also known as **dominance** because the senior manager can dominate both parties, this form of conflict resolution has two major advantages:

1. It is the fastest method of resolving a conflict.

2. It conforms to and confirms the existing power structure of the organization.

Power intervention also has two major disadvantages, which must be considered by managers considering its use:

1. Even though it resolves conflicts quickly, it may not deal with the causes of the conflict—the conflict can recur at a later date in a more serious form.

2. Either one or both the combatants may resent the intervention of senior management in what they perceive as "their problem." The disputing parties may believe that top management is "butting in," and long after the conflict has been resolved, the resentment at top management's intrusion will persist.

Under the best of circumstances, when one party believes that the imposed conflict resolution has vindicated its specific position, the other party may well believe that it has been slighted, even humiliated. For every winner there will be a loser, and if the imposed conflict resolution slights both parties, both sides will believe that they lost. It is this feeling of being a loser when senior management intervenes in the organizational dispute that has led many managers to avoid power intervention and to try compromise.

YOU SHOULD REMEMBER

Power intervention is the conflict management technique that features the imposition of a solution by senior management. This is a quick way of resolving a conflict, but will likely leave a residue of employee resentment. Although the senior manager will have greater knowledge of the overall organizational goals, he or she will often not have a detailed knowledge of the individual conflict.

COMPROMISE

Compromise is a conflict management strategy that seeks a problem resolution that satisfies at least part of each party's position. This technique gives something to each party, and if no one disputant can believe he or she has been a complete winner, neither is he or she a complete loser. The emphasis is on finding a solution that resolves the conflict in a satisfactory manner; hence this procedure may create a solution that conforms to the lowest common factor of both groups in the attempt to compromise the opposing viewpoints. Neither of the competing groups will be completely satisfied with the solution, and this lack of satisfaction is a negative feature of this form of conflict resolution.

There are several weaknesses to this approach. First, it usually fails to deal with the underlying causes of the conflict by focusing solely on the solution. Second, by its very nature the compromise fails to satisfy either party to the conflict. Finally, in reaching a compromise, there is the chance that the real problem will not even be solved as the decision-making criterion is that of compromise—thus, if the most effective solution to whatever problem presented is to favor one group over the other, this solution will not be reached in the compromise mode. Because the reasons for the problem are not reached, no one is completely satisfied. Also, because the problem may not actually be solved, there may be residual dissatisfaction and sometimes actual grudges. In addition, there is a false assumption that compromise assumes the contending groups are relatively equal in organizational power, communication ability, negotiation, and interpersonal skills, all of which may be untrue. If either group is significantly more skilled than the other, compromise will be improbable because the more powerful group will simply impose its will upon the less powerful group.

YOU SHOULD REMEMBER

Compromise strategy tries to satisfy at least part of each party's position. However, it leaves neither party completely satisfied and, like all the methods so far discussed, does not deal with the *causes* of the conflict.

CONFRONTATION

In **confrontation,** unlike the previous conflict resolution techniques discussed, the causes of the conflict will be considered. This process emphasizes the understanding and attainment of the organization's goals rather than the individual goals of the disputing parties. There is the desire on the part of the participants to understand the other group's positions, and to that end groups may exchange personnel for a limited period of time. This is to facilitate understanding and is referred to as *mutual personnel exchange*. It does not solve any problems, but it does aid in creating a climate of mutual understanding between the groups.

Another useful confrontation technique is to emphasize the organization's goals that are more important or superordinate to individual group goals. This emphasis on the *superordinate goals* requires two managerial actions:

1. Employees must have an understanding of the organization's goals.

2. Management must convince the parties in the conflict that neither can achieve the desired organizational goal alone—they need to cooperate.

Confrontation is useful when both parties are willing to enter into the process. Confrontation cannot be forced since this defaults into a power intervention or dominance situation. Each party must be willing to enter into a frank exchange of views and make a genuine attempt to understand the other side. The benefits of a confrontation can be outweighed by the impact of the emotions let loose. Confrontation consumes a great deal of managerial attention and energy, and if there is no organizational ability and willingness to devote the necessary resources (time and attention), confrontation should be avoided.

YOU SHOULD REMEMBER

Confrontation as a conflict managing strategy considers the *cause* of the conflict and emphasizes *superordinate*—overall organization—*goals*, not individual or group goals. Conflict can be resolved but often at the expense of emotional outbursts and a great deal of managerial energy.

ORGANIZATIONAL CHANGE AS A SOURCE OF CONFLICT

Change within the organization often leads to conflict. As we have previously discussed, change often produces resistance and management may seek to overcome some of that resistance by *incrementalizing* the change as it is introduced. People resist change because, however well intended, it threatens the status quo, the known. Individuals often exhibit self-interest as they act to resist change and preserve that which they know and are comfortable with. This is sometimes called *parochialism*. Change is also often resisted because of a lack of information—its content and intent are not known. One of the ways in which management can deal with the lack of information is to educate the workers.

Because the world of the contemporary manager is continually changing and businesses wish to remain competitive, change is continual. Many business organizations have approached the necessity to change in a systematic and deliberate manner, called organizational development.

ORGANIZATIONAL DEVELOPMENT

Organizational development stresses an active approach to conflict management. It brings individuals and groups together to build teams and discuss the causes of organizational conflicts. This is a carefully controlled forum in which perceptions and opinions can be voiced and critically examined. Since this can be an emotionally trying process, the organizational development (OD) process is facilitated by a professional specialist. This individual may be part of the human resources or personnel department but also may be someone from outside the organization. Although hiring an outside consultant can be an expensive proposition, it has the advantage of utilizing a facilitator with no vested interest in the outcome of the dispute.

OD specialists make use of the latest findings in industrial and personal psychology to effectively facilitate change. Such an approach may make extensive use of survey research techniques to gather information about the current state of the organization's and employees' attitudes. It should be noted that OD is an eclectic approach making use of a variety of change-agentry techniques. It is not an inclusive theory and is not founded on a comprehensive body of research. If the theory behind organizational development is problematic, it persists as a managerial tool because of its pragmatic success.

The OD approach has traditionally made extensive use of organizational histories to teach managers how particular past business problems have been confronted and resolved. These histories are called *case studies*, and the *case study methodology* produces several identifiable benefits for the manager student: (1) managers learn how to analyze a business problem or conflict and identify possible alternative solutions and (2) managers learn how specific problems have been solved in the past—in this, managers can benefit from the experience of others. The case study methodology is also used in most college-level business school studies.

YOU SHOULD REMEMBER

Conflict often arises at times of change within an organization. To decrease conflict many organizations use an eclectic approach known as **organizational development (OD)** (often based on *case studies*) to manage conflict at times of change.

ALTERNATIVE DISPUTE RESOLUTION

Modern business organizations are developing more effective methodologies for dispute resolution, and this area, **alternative dispute resolution (ADR),** is rapidly growing. The benefits of ADR are speed and often modest costs, especially when compared with the expenses and time associated with litigation in courts of law, or the human and organizational costs associated with interpersonal conflicts. Additionally, ADR resolves disputes in a manner that may be more confidential and appropriate to the individuals. In other words, ADR can be truly customized to the specific conflict. The parties to a dispute may ask a third party to help them arrive at a mutually acceptable resolution (mediation); may actually ask the third party to propose a solution (arbitration); or agree in *advance* to the third party's proposed solution (binding arbitration). Parties to a dispute may even agree to a private trial with a qualified judge (usually a retired court judge) and a suitable jury.

AFTERWORD ON ORGANIZATIONAL CONFLICT

No organization is free from conflict, and virtually every company both suffers and benefits from these conflicts. Conflict can consume managerial energy and organizational resources, but it can also release creative energy and innovative potential. It is often the skills of the individual manager and the commitment of the organization to the conflict management process and methodologies that will determine how conflict will impact upon a business.

KNOW THE CONCEPTS
DO YOU KNOW THE BASICS?

1. Is a conflict always bad for an organization?
2. Why do organizations and individuals conflict?
3. What are the basic types of organizational conflict?
4. What is the range of avoidance responses available for the management of organizational conflict?
5. How does smoothing differ from the avoidance response?
6. What are the pros and cons of power intervention?
7. What is mutual personnel exchange, and how does it contribute to organizational conflict management?
8. What are the benefits of the case study method?

TERMS FOR STUDY

alternative dispute resolution (ADR)
avoidance
communication failure
compromise
conflict
confrontation
differences in goals
disagreement over performance standards
dominance
incremental innovation
misperception of information

mutual personnel exchange
nonattention
organizational structure incongruity
parochialism
partial separation
passive aggression
power intervention
resource competition
smoothing
superordinate goals
total separation

ANSWERS
KNOW THE BASICS

1. No, a conflict is not always bad for an organization. Although it is true that a conflict can consume managerial effort and organizational resources, it can also lead to creative problem-solving and innovative program development.

2. Group behavior takes place within an acceptable range, and organizations evolve a distinctive corporate culture. The individual who does not agree with the group behavioral norms or with the values found within the corporate culture will be in conflict with the work group or with the entire organization.

3. Organizational conflict arises from the following sources: differences in goals, resource competition, communication failure and misperception of information, disagreement over performance standards, and organizational structure incongruities.

4. The avoidance response can range from nonattention, to a partial separation that allows for a limited interaction, to finally creating a total separation of the combatants.

5. Unlike the avoidance techniques of managing organizational conflict, which do not recognize that a problem exists, smoothing begins with the recognition that a problem exists. The emphasis is on harmony and peace within the organization—the conflict is smoothed over as management emphasizes the similarities and common features shared by the two contentious groups rather than their differences.

6. Power intervention, the imposition of a solution to an organizational conflict by senior management, is a quick way to stop a conflict. Its speed and conformance with the hierarchical power structure are its major advantages. The major disadvantages are that the senior managers who impose the solution to the problem may not be acquainted with its minute details, and after the solution has been imposed the conflicting parties may come to resent senior management interference.

7. In confrontation, the causes of the conflict will be considered. This process emphasizes the understanding and attainment of the organization's goals rather than the individual goals of the disputing parties. There is the desire on the part of the participants to understand the other group's positions, and to that end groups may exchange personnel for a limited period of time. This is to facilitate understanding and

is referred to as mutual personnel exchange. It does not solve any problems but does aid in creating a climate of mutual understanding between the groups.

8. The case study method provides managers with a methodology by which a business problem can be systematically analyzed. Further, by analyzing past business problems and examining how other managers have solved their problems, executives can gain valuable problem-solving experience without actual involvement.

20

PRODUCTION AND OPERATIONS MANAGEMENT (POM)

KEY TERMS

break-even analysis a managerial planning technique used to determine the *minimum* units of sales necessary to pay the total costs involved with producing and selling a product; this minimum number is called the "break-even quantity" or **BEQ;** computation of the BEQ makes use of fixed costs, variable costs, and the price of a product

payoff matrix or **decision table** a technique used to project profitability from various managerial decisions; employs a formal arrangement (table or matrix) showing the relationship between managerial choices, external conditions (states of demand), and the potential payoff or profit from the various courses of managerial action; a powerful planning tool to aid management widely used in most businesses

economic order quantity (EOQ) model relates carrying costs of inventory, ordering costs, and usage to determine the most economical size of an inventory order that minimizes inventory costs

project evaluation review technique (PERT) a managerial technique that (1) breaks down a project into its component tasks, (2) arranges the tasks in a logical sequence, (3) determines if the component tasks are sequential or simultaneous, (4) diagrams the component tasks in a **PERT chart,** and (5) determines the shortest time that the project can be completed (called the **critical path**)

MRP (materials requirements planning) a technique for determining the amount and timing of the components used in manufacturing process; often used with **CRP** (capacity requirements planning), which takes the materials required derived from MRP and converts them into "standard work hours," which are related to the labor and equipment capacities of the business work centers, to effectively schedule the required production

linear programming a production and operations technique that determines the optimal allocation of resources (either most profitable or least costly) to alternative product choices

Before the advent of industrialism, productivity was severely limited by the abilities and capacities of the individual craftsman. The mechanization of work, begun slowly in England and France, heralded the beginning of the end of the craftsman as a major feature of the workplace, and the modern manufacturing world began to emerge. The invention of the steam engine by **James Watt** in the late 1700s further accelerated the industrial process by allowing manufacturers to site factories away from the waterwheels that had previously served as the power source for the early power looms, the source of English supremacy in the 18th-century fabric industry. With a portable power source, the 1800s saw the growth of the factory system and the development of prototypic transportation networks based upon the same portable power source, the steamboat and steam locomotive.

The work of **Frederick W. Taylor** in the late 19th and early part of the 20th century, previously discussed in Chapter 2, dealt with the relationship between the worker and work in the emerging industrial world. Not only did Taylor's work make the human resources component of the assembly line possible, it focused on what was rapidly becoming the major issue of the industrial age, increased productivity. As Taylor, and later **Elton Mayo** and his human relations colleagues and the later management theorists and practitioners developed new techniques for increasing human resources productivity, other specialists and practicing managers were developing forecasting tools for better planning, scheduling techniques, and controlling methodologies. These techniques collectively are known as **production and operations management (POM).**

Although the theoretical basis for many of these production and operations techniques and methodologies are beyond the scope of this book on management, several are presented and their uses in the contemporary business organization discussed. Many of these techniques involve mathematical procedures, a quantitative side of management that may seem foreign to the managerial endeavor as previously presented in this text. But POM, with its quantitative emphasis, is emerging as a powerful managerial tool, and modern executives will have to be well versed not only in human resources methodologies but also in production and operations management.

BREAK-EVEN ANALYSIS

Break-even analysis is a managerial planning technique using a production model featuring fixed costs, variable costs, and the price of a product to determine the minimum units of sales necessary to break even, or to pay the total costs involved. The necessary sales are called the BEQ, or *break-even quantity*. This technique is also useful to make *go/no-go decisions* regarding the purchase of new equipment. Each of these uses is illustrated, but first it may be helpful to describe the various costs associated with production.

COSTS ASSOCIATED WITH PRODUCTION

There are several types of costs associated with production:

- *Variable costs (VC)*—the costs of production that vary *directly* with the quantity (Q) produced; these costs generally include direct materials and direct labor costs.

- *Semivariable costs*—the costs of production that vary with the quantity (Q) produced, but not directly.

- *Fixed costs (FC)*—the costs of production that do not vary with the quantity (Q) produced.

For the purposes of discussion here, it is useful to consider only the first and last of these, the variable costs (VC) and fixed costs (FC). There are accepted cost-accounting practices that allocate the semivariable costs to the other two categories, so considering all costs as either fixed or variable is reasonable.

Fixed costs do not vary with the quantity produced. Figure 20-1 illustrates fixed costs of $10,000 and a production run of 5 units. The costs are constant across the production range—$10,000 whether the production is 0, 1, 2, 3, 4, or 5 units. Examples of fixed costs are insurance and the mortgage expenses that have to be paid even if there is no production.

Figure 20–1. Fixed costs of $10,000 for a production quantity = 5.

Variable costs, on the other hand, vary directly with production and are shown in Figure 20-2 for the same production run of 5 units. The variable costs are $5 per unit and are shown on the vertical axis, and the production run is shown on the horizontal axis. The total variable costs increase directly by $5 for each unit of production. It costs $15 to produce 3 units, $25 to produce 5 units. An example of variable costs is the amount of raw materials needed for 1 unit of production.

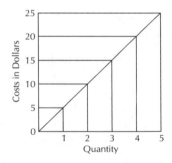

Figure 20–2. Variable costs $5.00/unit.

The fixed and variable costs have been combined in Figure 20-3 for the 5 units of production. The zig-zag in the vertical axis shows the discontinuity in the two scales. The $10,000 in fixed costs is shown on the bottom, and the $5/unit variable costs are higher. The shaded portion represents the combination of the fixed and variable costs, which, when added together, are the total costs associated with a production run of 5 units. The total costs (*TC*) for a production run are equal to the fixed costs (*FC*) + (the variable cost (*VC*) × the number of units produced (*Q*)). These are shown in Figure 20-3. The total costs are the costs that must be met in order to break even.

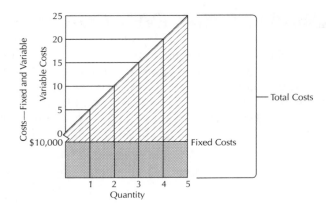

Figure 20–3. Fixed costs + variable costs = total costs.

Figure 20-4 illustrates the break-even point. The fixed and total costs are shown on the graph as is the total revenue line *(TR)*, which represents the number of units, or quantity *(Q)* sold times the price *(P)* of each unit. Where the total revenue line crosses the total costs line is the point at which the manufacturer breaks even. In other words, when revenue equals expenditure (costs), the manufacturer breaks even. Or, the point at which one breaks even is the sales level at which the total revenues received are exactly equal to the costs. The break-even point shown in Figure 20-4 also represents the number of units, shown on the horizontal axis, that need to be sold if total revenue is to equal total costs. This quantity is called the *BEQ*, or *break-even quantity*. Note that if more than the *BEQ* is sold, the manufacturer begins to make a profit as total revenues are greater than total costs.

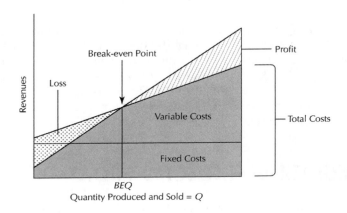

Figure 20–4. *BEQ.*

DETERMINING BREAK-EVEN QUANTITY

Remember, total revenues are equal to the price times quantity sold; and total costs are equal to the fixed costs plus the variable costs/unit times units sold. When these elements of production are set equal, the point of breaking even, the result is that the *BEQ* can be determined by a simple equation in which the total fixed costs (*FC*) are divided by the price minus the variable cost/unit (*P* = *VC*).

$$BEQ = \frac{FC}{P - VC}$$

The price minus the variable cost/unit is called the *contribution margin*. It represents the amount left after the sale of each unit and the paying of the variable costs in that unit that "contributes" to the paying of the fixed costs.

The following is an example of how this formula might be used to determine the *BEQ*. We shall use the data found in the previous examples. The fixed costs are $10,000. The variable costs are $5/unit. The selling price is $10/unit. The *BEQ* is determined in the following manner:

$$
\begin{aligned}
BEQ &= \frac{FC}{P - VC} \\
&= \frac{\$10,000}{\$10 - \$5} \\
&= \frac{\$10,000}{\$5} \\
&= 2000 \text{ units}
\end{aligned}
$$

Note that the *BEQ* is stated in terms of units since the dollars cancel out from both the top and the bottom of the equation. If the company fails to sell the *BEQ*, the 2000 units, it loses money. If it sells *exactly* the 2000 units, it breaks even. If it sells more than the 2000 units, it makes a profit.

If you wish to know how much in dollar sales is needed to break even, this can be determined by multiplying the *BEQ* by the selling price. In this instance, 2000 units times the $10 selling price yields $20,000 in total revenue needed to break even.

CALCULATING PROJECTED PROFIT

It is possible to calculate **projected profit** by making use of the same elements in the *BEQ* formula. Profit is the total revenues minus the total costs.

$$
\begin{aligned}
\text{Profit} &= TR - TC \\
&= (P \times Q) - [(VC \times Q) + FC] \\
&= PQ - VCQ - FC \\
&= Q(P - VC) - FC
\end{aligned}
$$

This formula, by projecting profit, is useful to make go/no-go decisions with regard to buying new machinery. Consider the following example. Under the present conditions, the following data apply:

$$
\begin{array}{ll}
FC = \$10,000 & P = \$10/\text{unit} \\
VC = \$5/\text{unit} & Q = 3000 \text{ units sold}
\end{array}
$$

Using the projected profit formula, given the sales volume of 3000 units, the projected profit is:

$$
\begin{aligned}
\text{Profit} &= Q(P - VC) - FC \\
&= 3000\ (\$10 - \$5) - \$10,000 \\
&= \$5000
\end{aligned}
$$

The problem confronting management is whether to purchase a new machine for the factory. The machine will add $5000 to the fixed costs but will have two beneficial effects. It will allow management to increase production by 10 percent and reduce costs/unit by $1. (Production will go from 3000 to 3300; VC will be $4 instead of $5/unit; and the fixed costs will rise to $15,000.) Should management authorize the purchase of the new machine, or stick with the old arrangement? This question, a go/no-go decision, to purchase or not to purchase the new machine, can be made by computing the potential profitability of the purchase. This potential profitability can then be compared with the data derived previously. The potential profit given the purchase of the new machine is:

$$
\begin{aligned}
&= Q\ (P - VC) - FC \\
&= 3300\ (\$10 - \$4) - \$15,000 \\
&= \$4800
\end{aligned}
$$

Since the present arrangement yields $5000 profit, but the projected profit from the machine purchase is $4800, the purchase of the machine is not recommended. This technique is useful in making a decision that has only two possibilities, hence the name go/no-go. If there are more than two possibilities, however, management may make use of a payoff matrix or decision table approach.

YOU SHOULD REMEMBER

Break-even analysis is a planning technique that uses fixed costs, variable costs, and the price of a product to determine minimum sales necessary—the **break-even quantity (BEQ)**—if revenues are to equal costs. Further analysis can yield data for go/no-go decisions and allow managers to project profit.

PAYOFF MATRIX OR DECISION TABLE

A **payoff matrix,** or **decision table,** is a formal arrangement showing the relationship between managerial choices, external conditions (states of demand), the probability of occurrence of these external conditions, and the probable payoff or profit from the various courses of managerial action. It is a widely used planning tool to aid management in choosing a specific strategy or course of action; it evaluates potential returns in cases in which there are more than two possible managerial courses of action.

Let us consider a few examples of how management may use this technique as an aid to decision-making. This is the basic situation. The XYZ Soda Store has to make a decision about how many soda cases to order. The managerial choices are 2 cases, 4 cases, 6 cases, or 8 cases each day. The demand for cases of soda varies from day to day. Some days customers want a total of only 2 cases, but other days the demand can be as much as 4, 6, or 8 cases. The cost to the soda store for each case is $5; each case is resold for $10. The profit, therefore, from each case is $5. However, if a case remains unsold, it is returned to the dealer for a $1 return charge. A careful analysis of all these elements allows management to make the best decision about how many cases of soda to order.

It is important to recognize all the elements involved in the situation. Management can make choices: these are *courses of action* within managerial control. The *states of demand,* or *states of nature,* for the cases of soda are not within the control of management. The construction of a payoff table, or decision table, is based on the following:

- List the states of nature on the horizontal axis.

- List the managerial choices down the left vertical side axis.

- Given a specific state of nature and managerial choice, compute the probability of occurrence.

- For each managerial choice, determine the possible payoff.
- Choose a course of action based upon the decision-making criterion employed (this is amplified later in the chapter).

Table 20–1   Payoff Matrix/Decision Table

States of Nature

	Demand will be for 2 cases	Demand will be for 4 cases	Demand will be for 6 cases	Demand will be for 8 cases
Order 2 Cases	A $10.00	B $10.00	C $10.00	D $10.00
Order 4 Cases	E $8.00	F $20.00	G $20.00	H $20.00
Order 6 Cases	I $6.00	J $18.00	K $30.00	L $30.00
Order 8 Cases	M $4.00	N $16.00	O $28.00	P $40.00

Managerial Courses of Action

This is usually done in the form of a table or matrix. See Table 20-1. In the table, the states of nature are listed across the top—demand for 2, 4, 6, or 8 cases of soda. Listed down the left side are the managerial decision possibilities, the order possibilities open to management. Each box in the matrix has been given a letter identification, and the computation for the profitability of each box is shown in Table 20-2.

Once the payoff matrix or decision table has been constructed, management can then determine the most desirable course of action. To show how management goes about making a decision, it is necessary to add three columns to the matrix. We shall add columns to the right of the matrix showing, for each course of action, the maximum row payoff, the minimum row payoff, and the average row payoff. These are shown in Table 20-3 (see page 397).

The course of action chosen by management depends upon the decision-making criterion employed, and this directly reflects the philosophical attitude of the managers. If management assumes an optimistic view, it chooses the course of action with the best single result. This decision-making criterion is called the *maximax solution*. It is accomplished by choosing the course of action with the highest row value, shown on the right as the maximum row value. Since ordering 8 cases produces the highest maximum

Table 20–2   Payoff Matrix/Decision Table Computation

Square Number	You Ordered	Demand Was	You Sold	You Made	Return Penalty	Final Profit
A	2 Cases	2 Cases	2	$10	0	$10.00
B	2 Cases	4 Cases	2	$10	0	$10.00
C	2 Cases	6 Cases	2	$10	0	$10.00
D	2 Cases	8 Cases	2	$10	0	$10.00
E	4 Cases	2 Cases	2	$10	−$2.00	$8.00
F	4 Cases	4 Cases	4	$20	0	$20.00
G	4 Cases	6 Cases	4	$20	0	$20.00
H	4 Cases	8 Cases	4	$20	0	$20.00
I	6 Cases	2 Cases	2	$10	−$4.00	$6.00
J	6 Cases	4 Cases	4	$20	−$2.00	$18.00
K	6 Cases	6 Cases	6	$30	0	$30.00
L	6 Cases	8 Cases	6	$30	0	$30.00
M	8 Cases	2 Cases	2	$10	−$6.00	$4.00
N	8 Cases	4 Cases	4	$20	−$4.00	$16.00
O	8 Cases	6 Cases	6	$30	−$2.00	$28.00
P	8 Cases	8 Cases	8	$40	0	$40.00

value ($40), it is the managerial course of action given a maximax solution. This is referred to as an optimistic view since it *only* considers the best possible results of each managerial alternative course of action and ignores the worst possible results. It is the maximum (best result) of the maximum (best results). That is why it is called the *maximax solution.*

Management may, however, instead of being optimistic, take a decidedly pessimistic view and assume that the lowest row value is the most likely, in effect assuming a "worst-case scenario." This decision-making criterion is called the *maximin solution.* Management first determines the worst result in each row, here shown as the minimum row value, and then chooses the course of action that yields the best result. Because this solution chooses the maximum (best result) of the worst row results (minimum), it is called the maximin solution. In our example, ordering 2 cases would produce the best of the worst results, $10. Under the maximin decision-making criterion, management would order 2 cases.

Table 20–3   Payoff Matrix/Decision Table

States of Nature

		Demand will be for 2 cases	Demand will be for 4 cases	Demand will be for 6 cases	Demand will be for 8 cases	Maximum Row Value	Minimum Row Value	Average Row Value
	Order 2 Cases	A $10.00	B $10.00	C $10.00	D $10.00	$10	$10	$10
	Order 4 Cases	E $8.00	F $20.00	G $20.00	H $20.00	$20	$8	$17
	Order 6 Cases	I $6.00	J $18.00	K $30.00	L $30.00	$30	$6	$21
	Order 8 Cases	M $4.00	N $16.00	O $28.00	P $40.00	$40	$4	$22

Managerial Courses of Action (left vertical label)

If management were neither optimistic nor pessimistic, but took a realistic view, it might assume that neither the best nor worst possible result would occur. Rather, management might assume that the most likely result would be an average of all possible results. Therefore, management would consult an average of all row values, here shown as the average row value. Given this orientation, in our example management would order 8 cases since this yields the highest average return of $22. This is referred to as the *equally likely solution*.

Finally, the personality of the decision maker may be such as to avoid, as much as possible, regret. *Regret* is defined as the difference between the best possible outcome (maximax solution) and worst possible outcome (maximin solution) for each managerial choice. It is computed by subtracting the maximax from maximin solution for each choice; the resulting sum is defined as the amount of regret occasioned by that choice. The manager seeking to avoid regret will select that course of action that produces the smallest amount of regret. In this example, ordering 2 cases yields zero regret while ordering 8 cases could result in $36 of regret (maximax – maximin).

The profit matrix or decision table methodology is a powerful managerial tool and is used often. The example presented here is simplistic, in keeping with the introductory nature of this chapter, but it should be noted that far more complex models of potential profitability are possible. In this example we have assumed that each state of nature or demand state has an equal probability of occurring. In reality, higher or lower demand states may be likely. In the summer, for example, there may be a 70 percent chance of an 8 case demand for soda, but in the winter the most likely demand for soda may be only 2 cases. Using a more complex format, but basically the same payoff matrix technique, it is possible to introduce differing probabilities of occurrence for the various states of nature.

YOU SHOULD REMEMBER

A **profit matrix** or **decision table** is a decision-making tool that shows the relationship between managerial choices, external conditions (demands) and their probability of occurrence, and the probable payoff or profit from each managerial choice.

ECONOMIC ORDER QUANTITY (SIMPLE)

U.S. managers have sought to understand the reasons behind the Japanese economic miracle. Although there are many reasons for the emergence of the strong Japanese economy, one often cited is the *just in time* (JIT) inventory policy, which ensures that the raw materials inventory arrives exactly when it is needed. Even though many U.S. companies are attempting to make use of this technique, managers have noted that this may be effective only in a Japanese-like environment where most raw materials suppliers are located within 50 miles of the factory. U.S. managers more often employ a useful technique for calculating the **Economic Order Quantity (EOQ)** to determine:

- when to place an order for raw materials inventory

- how much to order to be most cost efficient

Inventory costs money, primarily *carrying costs* and *ordering costs*. Although there are often more complex costs involved, we shall consider only these two costs associated with inventory. Further, we shall assume that the inventory yearly demand and order times are known quantities. The costs factors are defined as follows:

- *Carrying costs* are the costs incurred by the holding of raw materials inventory. Examples of these kinds of costs include the cost of storage, insurance, theft allowance, spoilage allowance, and opportunity costs.

- *Ordering costs* include all costs associated with the ordering of inventory, including clerical labor, forms, and labor to process an order.

Inventory can be ordered in single-unit lots. In this case there are no carrying costs but maximal ordering costs. A company could order one large order. In this case there would be minimal order costs but maximal carrying costs. Carrying costs and ordering costs are indirectly related—as one goes up, the other goes down. The total inventory costs = the carrying costs + the ordering costs. This is shown in Figure 20-5. The inverse relationship between ordering and carrying costs is shown here; the *total cost curve* is the sum of both ordering and carrying costs. The point at which the total inventory costs are lowest is where the carrying costs and ordering costs are equal. The order quantity for which costs are lowest is called the *economic order quantity.* Because the *EOQ* is determined when the ordering and carrying costs are equal, it is possible to derive a formula to calculate this amount. First, however, it is helpful to examine how inventory is used.

Let us consider the case of a company that uses 5 units of inventory each week. Since the use is constant, 1 unit is used each day. The week's inventory use is shown in Figure 20-6. In this case, several factors are evident: (1) inventory usage is constant, (2) the maximal amount of inventory is on the first day, and (3) the lowest amount of inventory is on the last day. In this example we assumed a weekly inventory usage of 5 units (1 unit/day), which would be a total annual inventory demand of 5 units/week × 52 weeks = 260 units. This would mean that there would be 52 orders/year and that each order would be for 5 units.

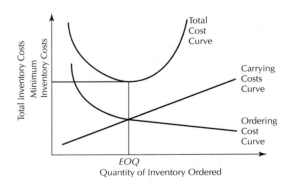

Figure 20–5. Inventory costs.

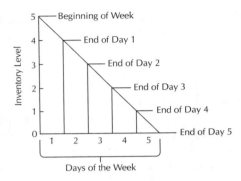

Figure 20–6. Inventory usage pattern.

However, we did not determine if the 5 units were the most economical order quantity, that amount of inventory that minimizes the total costs of inventory. We can determine that quantity since it is at the point where the carrying costs are equal to the ordering costs, as shown in Figure 20-5. The following are the elements in determining the *EOQ*, which is also called *Q**.

$$Q = \text{number of units ordered (when the ordering and carrying costs are set equal, this will become } Q^*\text{)}$$

$$Q^* = \text{optimal amount of each inventory order}$$

$$D = \text{annual demand for inventory units}$$

$$O_c = \text{cost per each inventory order}$$

$$C_c = \text{cost of carrying each unit of inventory for a year}$$

The derivation of the *EOQ* or *Q** formula is shown in the following. Determine ordering costs:

$$\text{Ordering costs} = \text{number of orders/year} \times \text{cost/order}$$

$$= \frac{\text{annual demand of units}}{\text{number of units per order}} \times \text{cost/order}$$

$$= \frac{D}{Q} O_c$$

$$\text{Ordering costs} = \frac{D}{Q} O_c$$

Determine average inventory level:

$$\text{Average inventory level} = \left(\frac{\text{order quantity}}{2}\right) \text{carrying cost/unit/year}$$

$$\text{Carrying costs} = \frac{Q}{2} C_C$$

To determine Q^*, make ordering costs equal to carrying costs:

$$\frac{D}{Q} O_c = \frac{Q}{2} C_c$$

Solving for Q, we cross-multiply and get:

$$2DO_c = Q^2 C_c$$

Reversing the terms gives us:

$$Q^2 C_c = 2DO_c$$

Solving for Q^2, we arrive at:

$$Q^2 = \frac{2DO_c}{C_c}$$

Finally, solving for Q, the following emerges:

$$Q = \sqrt{\frac{2DO_C}{C_c}}$$

But since we originally set ordering costs equal to carrying costs, we have derived the *EOQ*, or:

$$Q^* = \sqrt{\frac{2DO_C}{C_C}}$$

Here is an example of how management would apply this formula. The Conduit Pipe Company has an annual demand for 25,000 couplings used in its pipe manufacturing enterprise. The cost of each coupling order is $10, and it costs the company $2/coupling each year in carrying costs, which includes allowance for theft, spoilage, and insurance. How many should the company order to minimize its inventory costs? The calculations of the *EOQ* or Q^* are as follows:

$$Q^* = \sqrt{\frac{2DO_C}{C_C}}$$

$$= \sqrt{\frac{(2)\,(25{,}000)\,(\$10)}{\$2}}$$

$$= \sqrt{250{,}000}$$

$$BEQ = 500 \text{ units}$$

This means that the most economic inventory order is 500 units. Since the annual demand is for 25,000 units, this means that there will be 50 inventory orders per year.

To carry this simple inventory model a step further, let us look at the inventory pattern in the Conduit Pipe Company. The *EOQ* is 500 units, so the inventory usage pattern looks like Figure 20-7. The highest level of inventory is achieved when the shipment of 500 couplings arrives. That inventory is used up at a constant rate until none is left. A new shipment of inventory then arrives, and the cycle starts over. Suppose the company wanted to keep an amount of inventory on hand as a form of insurance just in case the regular inventory order was delayed. This insurance amount is called *safety stock* and is shown in Figure 20-8.

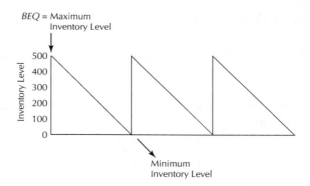

Figure 20-7. Inventory usage pattern where *EOQ* = 500.

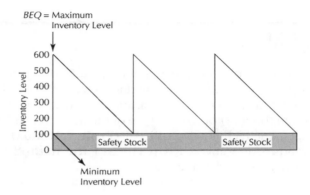

Figure 20–8. Inventory usage pattern where *EOQ* = 500 and safety stock = 100.

Therefore, the maximum inventory will be:

$$500 \ (EOQ) + \text{safety stock} = 600$$

Note that this now changes both the maximum and minimum inventory levels. The maximum now becomes 600 (*EOQ* + safety stock) and the minimum now becomes the safety stock level. If the annual demand, the annual carrying costs/unit, or the cost/order changes, the *EOQ* must be recalculated as it too will change.

This is a simple inventory model, but the business world is rarely this simple. It introduces the basic concepts of inventory modeling and demonstrates how management can make use of this concept to more efficiently accomplish the organization's profitability goals.

YOU SHOULD REMEMBER

The technique known as **Economic Order Quantity (EOQ)** helps managers determine when to place an order for raw materials inventory and how much to order to be most cost effective. The EOQ formula takes into account units ordered, optimal amounts of each inventory order, annual demand for inventory units, ordering costs, and inventory carrying costs to determine the most economic inventory order.

PERT/CPM

The beginnings of complex engineering and manufacturing projects, such as the construction of the nuclear submarine, created the need to develop techniques to schedule, monitor, control, and coordinate an often bewildering variety of component subprojects. One of the most well known of these project management techniques is **PERT (Project Evaluation Review Technique)** and its derivative **CPM (Critical Path Method).**

PERT is a managerial technique that:

1. breaks down a project into its component tasks.

2. arranges the tasks in a logical sequence.

3. determines if the component tasks are sequential or simultaneous.

4. diagrams the component tasks in a PERT chart.

5. determines the shortest time in which the project can be completed (called the *critical path*). The *critical path events* indicate to management areas for effective application of additional resources to complete the project more quickly.

A brief introduction to PERT/CPM will demonstrate the power of this managerial tool. The first step in applying the PERT methodology is to organize the project into its component events and tasks, or activities. *Tasks* or *activities* are self-explanatory—they are behaviors performed by employees. *Events* are points in time, and each activity, or task, has two events, a starting point in time and an ending point. These two components of the PERT methodology are shown graphically in Figure 20-9. These two graphic components can be used to represent all the activities that comprise the many subtasks that combine to form the total project. Using these graphic components, we have represented activity A by two events, a starting and ending time, and the activity itself. This is shown in Figure 20-10. Activity A begins at event 1 and ends at event 2 (note that it is customary to give the events numbers). Activity A can then be called activity 1-2, and this is a particularly useful notation since it pinpoints not only the activity but its timing.

Figure 20–9. PERT components.

The next step in PERT is to place all the events in *sequential order*. The following PERT table shows five activities placed in sequential order.

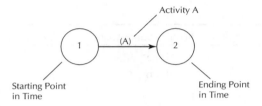

Figure 20–10. PERT chart representation of activity A, which begins at event 1 and ends at event 2. Activity A then can be called Activity 1-2.

Activity	Immediate Predecessors
A	None
B	None
C	A
D	B
E	C, D

Before showing the PERT chart for this five-activity project, two points must be noted: (1) *immediate predecessors* tells you which specific event or events must be completed before going to the next activity, and (2) since we are representing an activity by its starting and ending points, the ending point of one event becomes the starting point for the next activity. The events can be represented as starting and ending points. The five events listed in sequential order in the PERT chart are represented in Figure 20-11.

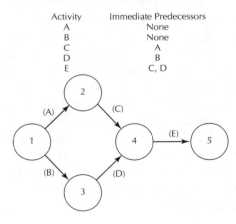

Figure 20–11. PERT chart (network).

The events listed previously can now be represented in the revised PERT table as follows:

Activities	Immediate Predecessors	Event Description
A	None	1-2
B	None	1-3
C	A	2-4
D	B	3-4
E	C, D	4-5

We show activities A and B starting at the same time since neither has a predecessor; these activities are *simultaneous* since both can be going on at the same time. Activity A must be completed before activity C can begin, and this is shown by having C begin at event 2, the completion for A. For the same reason, activity D begins at event 3 after B has been completed. Since activities C and D must be completed before E can begin, we show C and D both ending by event 4 and only then can E begin. This then is the PERT chart or network for these five events.

Since the event notation (1-2, 2-3, and so on) is sufficient to represent the network, let us take out the alphabetical description of the events and substitute the amount each event will take. The new PERT chart showing the time alloted for each event is shown in Figure 20-12. These times allow computation of the *critical path*, which is defined as the longest path through the PERT network, which is the shortest time for total project completion. This appears to be a contradiction, but examination of the PERT chart in Figure 20-12 illustrates this seeming contradiction. It will take three days to complete activities 1-3 and 3-4, but it will take four days to complete activities 1-2 and 2-4. Activity 4-5 cannot begin until both activities 2-4 and 3-4 are completed. This time sequence is shown plotted against a time line in Figure 20-13. As has been previously noted and now shown here, activities 1-2 and 2-4 take a total of four days, but activities 1-3 and 3-4 take only three days. This means that activity 3-4 contains an extra day, here shown in the white as slack time. **Slack time** is defined as waiting time while another activity is completed. Activities 1-2 and 2-4 occur simultaneously with activities 1-3 and 3-4, but the requisite time to reach event 4 is four days. Activities 1-2 and 2-4 are the longest time to reach event 4 and are called the *critical path*. The critical path for project completion, here shown in darker lines, are activities 1-2, 2-4, and 4-5.

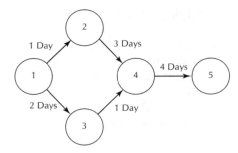

Figure 20–12. PERT chart (network) showing duration of activities.

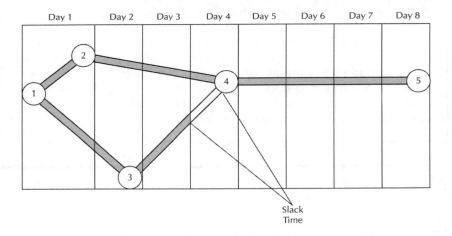

Figure 20 –13. PERT chart with absolute time line showing "slack time."

The critical path is important because it is the shortest time a project can be completed. If management wishes to finish a project more quickly, it must shorten the critical path. When organizational resources are applied to accomplish a critical path activity more quickly, this is referred to as **crashing the project.**

The critical path helps guide management in allocating organizational re-sources. Let us suppose that cost figures can be derived for each activity in the previously discussed project. Activity 1-2 costs \$100/day; activity 1-3 costs \$50/day; activity 2-4 costs \$75/day; and activity 4-5 costs \$50/day. If management wanted to shorten the project by one day, it must shorten a critical path activity. These are 1-2, 2-4, and 4-5. Note that to shorten activity 1-3 or 3-4 would not shorten the total project completion time as these activities are not on the critical path. Of those activities on the critical path, the cheapest on a per day cost basis is activity 4-5. A one day cost savings can be accomplished by spending an extra $50, whereas to shorten activity 2-4 would cost $75.

The previous discussion has presented the basic concepts of PERT/CPM. It should be noted that we have assumed a knowledge of the exact time necessary to accomplish the various component tasks of the project. This is often not the case, and advanced applications of PERT/CPM have methodologies for developing estimated completion times. PERT/CPM are powerful management tools for project management, and it is not surprising that many computer applications have been developed to make use of these techniques.

YOU SHOULD REMEMBER

PERT and **CPM** are management techniques used to schedule, monitor, and coordinate complex manufacturing and engineering projects made up of many component subprojects. The component tasks of a project are arranged in sequential order and diagrammed or charted to show the **critical path,** or shortest time in which the project can be completed.

MRP-CRP

As manufacturing has become more complicated, management has created a variety of tools for its planning and control. Widespread application of computer technology has enabled the development of information-based POM methodologies. These computer systems are discussed in Chapter 23, but here it should be noted that this technology has been used in POM to create a new control approach, called **Materials Requirements Planning (MRP).**

The purposes of MRP, a computer-based scheduling program, are to:

- establish an economic inventory policy (EOQ) to maintain the correct (most economic, efficient, and timely) inventory levels

- correct priorities for inventory quantities

MRP is a systematic approach to determining the quantity and timing of inventory so that an optimal level of production can be maintained. The MRP derives its data from documents associated with the production process; each projected unit of production has a corresponding *bill of material* or *product structure* stored in the master MRP computer program. When the desired number of units to be produced is designated, the computer program then details the necessary raw material inventories and formulates a time schedule for inventories acquisition. Management designates a specific production number, and the MRP computer program *explodes* this, or breaks down the unit number into all the inventory and raw materials components necessary to produce the unit production target. All this is designed to ensure that, for a specific amount of planned production, the company will have the necessary raw materials in a time-efficient manner.

Once the MRP system has determined the needed inventory levels, **Capacities Requirements Planning (CRP)** is then used to schedule the actual production. This computer program converts the planned production into *standard hours of load* to be applied to the human and machinery resources of the business. The goal of converting the production goals into standard hours of load is to make sure that there is sufficient time to accomplish the production. Since the load capacities of both the firm's labor and its machines are known, it is easy to compare the available load with the desired load. If the former is smaller than the latter, schedule adjustments are necessary since the required production is not possible under the original schedule. It becomes necessary to lengthen the production schedule so that the production facilities are not overloaded.

The MRP and CRP are combined into a *Master Production Schedule (MPS)*. The computer integrates all the individual time and materials requirements, compares them against the inventory and production resources of the company, and formulates the MPS, a total approach to production. This approach is a versatile and flexible planning and scheduling tool that is made possible because of the increasing availability of computer technology to even small businesses.

YOU SHOULD REMEMBER

A **Master Production Schedule (MPS)** is a computer-based scheduling program that combines and integrates individual time and materials requirements (MRP) and compares them against the inventory and production resources of the company (CRP) to develop a total approach to production.

SIMULATION MODELING

A managerial decision-making tool growing in acceptance and application involves the creation of a *model*, a *simulation* of a real-world situation or environment. The model can then be manipulated to predict outcomes given a specific set of conditions. In a physical sense, this is what the major car manufacturers accomplish when they construct a clay model of a proposed auto design and place it in a wind tunnel. The model in the wind tunnel is used to predict how an actual full-sized car will behave on the road.

In the business world, this technique is used to create models of operation and predict potential profitability. A simple example shows how simulation modeling is used. Management wishes to determine if a particular mini-parking lot design will be profitable. Here are the specifications:

- The parking lot will hold *only* ten cars.

- The cars park for the entire day.

- Even though each car space is the same size, the prices charged for different-sized cars vary.

- Limousines are charged $20/day.

- Regular cars are charged $15/day.

- Compact cars are charged $10/day.

Construction of the model consists of defining the variables (done earlier) and determining the maximal performance parameters. In this instance, the maximum profit is stated by the following. Let the number of limousines parked any one day = L. Since each limousine is charged $20/day, the total profit derived from limousine parking in any given day will be $20L. Let the number of regular cars = R, and the total daily profit from regular cars = $15R. Compact cars will be designated C, and the total profit from this kind of car = $10C. The total profit for this 10-spot parking lot = $20L + $15R + $10C.

The key issue is how many of each vehicle type will be parked in the lot each day. Here is where the simulation techniques are employed. Research determines that 10 percent of all vehicles that park downtown where this parking lot is located are limousines, 30 percent are compact cars, and the remaining 60 percent are regular cars. The model then defines the following values. Given numbers 00–99, 0–9 will represent limousines, 10–39 will represent compact cars, and 40–99 will represent regular cars. We use only two-digit numbers (00–99) to be able to make use of the two-digit random number table. Note, however, that 00–99 equals 100 numbers, which represents 100 percent.

We now make use of a table of random numbers derived from a *random number table* or created by a *random number generator* computer program. These numbers are totally random and are neither related to each other nor dependent upon any other factor. Having consulted such a table, we arrive at the following numbers: 1, 22, 78, 65, 32, 12, 7, 99, 56, and 45. We choose only ten numbers because there are only ten parking spots to be filled in a day (assuming that a car once parked will remain all day), and these ten numbers become the simulated parking for a day. There are two limousines, numbers 1 and 7. There are three compact cars, numbers 22, 32, and 12. The remaining five cars are regular sized, numbers 78, 65, 99, 56, and 45. Therefore, the total projected profitability for this proposed parking lot is $2 \times \$20 + 5 \times \$15 + 3 \times \$10 = \$145$/day. Assume that the parking lot is open for paid customers 5 days/week × 52 weeks = 260 days. The total yearly projected profit is 260 × $145, or $37,700. This figure can be used to make business decisions.

The complex contemporary computer model, characterized by the tracking of millions of variables, and defining the interrelationships between such variables, is exactly that—a model, however cunningly arrayed. If the model is good, the predicted and obtained results will be close. If the model is not good, then there will be great divergence between the two. Thus, models always need refinement and are continually being improved, or even completely changed.

YOU SHOULD REMEMBER

Simulation modeling is yet another decision-making tool available to managers. A model, or simulation, of a real-world situation is created and manipulated to predict outcomes given specific conditions.

AFTERWORD

Production operations management is a constantly changing world in which new techniques are introduced, refined, and eventually discarded in favor of even newer developments. This chapter has only touched upon some of the more popular techniques and methodologies; there are many others widely used that will be introduced when the student studies POM.

One such advanced technique is *linear programming*. Linear programming is a production and operations technique that determines the optimal allocation of resources (either most profitable or least costly) to alternative production choices. Computer technology has greatly enhanced this technique since a greater number of production variables can be considered. Another technique not dealt with in this book but widely used is that of *decision trees*. These are visual representations of the decision-making process showing the states of nature, managerial choices under each state, and the probability of occurrence of each state of nature. Both these are considered in a more advanced POM text.

KNOW THE CONCEPTS

DO YOU KNOW THE BASICS?

1. Define fixed and variable costs.
2. Given the following data, determine the *BEQ*. The XYZ Company has fixed costs = $20,000. It charges $25/product unit. The variable costs for each product = $15.
3. The XYZ Company of the previous question is selling 1000 units above the *BEQ*. It can purchase a new machine that will add $5000 to its fixed costs but reduce the costs/unit of production to $12.50. Should the company purchase the new machine?
4. Given the following payoff table, determine the maximax solution.

States of Nature

		Demand will be for 2 cases	Demand will be for 4 cases	Demand will be for 6 cases	Demand will be for 8 cases
Managerial Courses of Action	Order 2 Cases	$16.00	$16.00	$16.00	$16.00
	Order 4 Cases	$14.00	$21.00	$21.00	$21.00
	Order 6 Cases	$13.00	$16.00	$26.00	$26.00
	Order 8 Cases	$12.00	$15.00	$24.00	$28.00

5. Using the same payoff table in Question 4, determine the maximum solution.
6. A company uses 10,000 gaskets/year. Every time it places an order it costs $25, and each gasket costs $0.50 to carry per year. Determine the *EOQ*.
7. In Question 6, if the company wants to maintain a safety stock = 100 units, what will the maximum inventory level be?
8. Construct the PERT chart for the following activities: 1-2, 2-3, 3-4, 3-5, 4-6, 5-6, and 6-7.

9. Given the following times for the following events, determine the critical path: 1-2 = 2 days, 2-3 = 3 days, 3-4 = 1 day, 3-5 = 2 days, 4-6 = 4 days, 5-6 = 2 days, 6-7 = 2 days.

TERMS FOR STUDY

activities	model
average row payoff	MPS
BEQ	MRP
bill of material	optimistic view
break-even analysis	ordering costs
carrying costs	payoff matrix
contribution margin	PERT/CPM
courses of action	pessimistic view
critical path	POM
CRP	$Q*$
decision table	random number tables
EOQ	regret
equally likely solution	safety stock
events	semivariable costs
fixed costs	sequential order
go/no-go decision	simultaneous activities
linear programming	slack time
maximax solution	standard hours of load
maximin solution	states of demand
maximum row payoff	states of nature
minimum row payoff	variable costs

ANSWERS
KNOW THE BASICS

1. Variable costs (VC) are the costs of production that vary directly with the quantity (Q) produced, generally direct materials and direct labor costs. Fixed costs (FC) are the costs of production that do not vary with the quantity produced.

2.

$$FC = \$20,000$$
$$VC = \$15/\text{unit}$$
$$\text{Price} = \$25/\text{unit}$$
$$BEQ = \frac{FC}{P - VC}$$
$$BEQ = \frac{\$20,000}{\$25 - \$15}$$
$$BEQ = 2000 \text{ units sold}$$

3. In the current case, the company is selling 1000 units beyond the *BEQ*. Since all *FC* by selling the *BEQ* (= 2000 units) are covered, only the *VC* need to be covered in the next 1000. The rest is profit. For each of the 1000 units a $10 profit is made: *P − VC*. Therefore, selling 1000 units beyond the *BEQ* yields a profit of $10,000. Under the proposed machine purchase, the total profit realized will be:

$$\begin{aligned} \text{Profit} &= Q(P - VC) - FC \\ &= 3000\ (\$25 - \$12.50) - \$25,000 \\ &= \$12,500 \end{aligned}$$

Therefore, since the old machine yields a $10,000 profit but the new machine yields a $12,500 profit, the company should purchase the machine.

4 & 5.

States of Nature

		Demand will be for 2 cases	Demand will be for 4 cases	Demand will be for 6 cases	Demand will be for 8 cases	Maximum Row Value	Minimum Row Value	
Managerial Courses of Action	Order 2 cases	$16.00	$16.00	$16.00	$16.00	$16	$16	**Maximin Solution**
	Order 4 cases	$14.00	$21.00	$21.00	$21.00	$21	$14	
	Order 6 cases	$13.00	$16.00	$26.00	$26.00	$26	$13	
	Order 8 cases	$12.00	$15.00	$24.00	$28.00	$28	$12	

Maximax Solution

6.

$$EOQ = \sqrt{\frac{2DO_c}{C_c}}$$

$$= \sqrt{\frac{(2)\,(10{,}000)\,(\$25)}{\$0.50}}$$

$$= \sqrt{1{,}000{,}000}$$

$$EOQ = 1000 \text{ units}$$

7. 1000 units (*BEQ*) + 100 units safety stock = 1100 units (maximum inventory).

8 & 9.

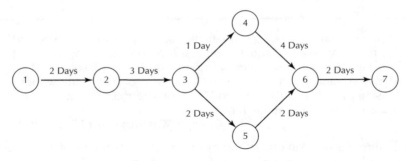

21
TIME
MANAGEMENT

> Take two managers and give them the same number of laborers, and let these laborers be equal in all respects. Let both managers rise equally early, go equally late to rest, be equally active, sober and industrious, and yet, in the course of the year, one of them, without pushing the hands that are under him more than the other, shall have performed infinitely more work.
>
> **George Washington (1732–1799)**

This chapter focuses on one of the most precious resources of a manager—**time**—and how we can manage it for greater results and productivity. In discussions of planning, the lack of time comes out rather clearly. We all have the same problem, but we can do something about it.

The purpose of this chapter is to get you to do something differently when you go back home or to the office—or even right now—something that will help you buy back some time.

What is there that is unique about time? Basically, there are five unique features about time:

1. The supply is totally *inelastic;* no matter how great the demand, the supply never increases.
2. It is totally *irreplaceable;* yesterday's moment is gone forever.
3. It is totally *perishable;* it cannot be stored; there is no price for it.
4. You *cannot rent or buy it.*
5. It is always in *short supply.*

The standard advice to people who want to improve their use of time is to plan their work. This sounds reasonable but seldom works. The plan always remains on paper.

Effective managers of time do not start with the tasks, they start with the time; they do not start with planning the time, they start by finding out where the time goes.

YOU SHOULD REMEMBER

Time is unique because the supply is totally inelastic, irreplaceable, perishable, and always in short supply and cannot be bought or rented. Effective managers of time, if they expect to manage time, begin by finding out where the time goes.

We would like you to think for a few minutes about where your time goes. Try to think in terms of the kinds of activities on which you spend your time, and record this information in the time column of Table 21-1. Estimate the percentage of time you spend on each type of activity in a typical week. One purpose for this exercise is to provide a basis for comparison between what you *think* you spend time on and what you *actually* spend time on. This will become apparent to you upon completion of another assignment, so you will have to refer to Table 21-1 again.

Table 21–1 Time Spent on Various Managerial Activities

Type of Activity	Time (%)
1. Phone: seeking information	_____
2. Phone: giving information	_____
3. Attending meetings	_____
4. Vocational work	_____
5. Training others	_____
6. Administrative work	_____
7. Discretionary time	_____
8. Other	_____

YOU NEED MORE TIME: WHAT KIND?

You need more *discretionary time*, for this is time to do what you wish. It is time that is regulated by one's own choice.

To help sort out your thinking relative to where your time goes, refer to Figure 21-1, which will help you understand the various categories of time we use when we perform certain managerial tasks.

The lowest level in Figure 21-1 shows that our time is taken up by three basic types of tasks: *boss-imposed, organization-imposed,* and *self-imposed.* Note that there are penalties for boss-imposed tasks that are not performed. It is clear that, if these tasks are not performed, you may find yourself out of a job.

If we work for an organization, the organization also imposes tasks upon us. Penalties can also be attached to not accomplishing these types of tasks. In other words, if you do not play ball with the organizational system, it will not play ball with you. The penalties are not as swift or direct as those for uncompleted boss-imposed tasks; nevertheless they exist and cannot be treated lightly.

The third type of task is self-imposed. These tasks are exempt from penalties. Only you know you have them. They are in your mind. The more self-imposed tasks you generate, the faster your career success will be.

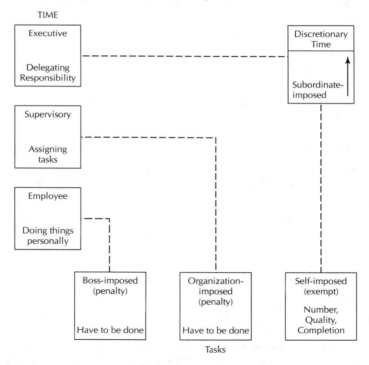

Figure 21–1. Categories of managerial time and managerial tasks. Arrow represents the pressure exerted by subordinates on a manager's discretionary time. (Based on the work of William Oncken, Jr.)

The problem of time management must also be viewed from the perspective of how we spend our time. Note that on the left side of the figure there are three time categories: *employee, supervisory,* and *executive.* When you spend time doing things personally, regardless of your level of management, you are working in the employee category. When the things you do yourself are too much for you to handle alone and you spend time assigning tasks to others so that you can get more done than by yourself, this is working in the supervisory time category. When you reach the point or level of management in which you spend time delegating authority and responsibilities to others for getting things done, you are working in the executive time category. This is the time for which you are paid in management. Remember our definition of management in Chapter 1: *Management is working with and through other people to accomplish the objectives of the organization and its members.* The only way you can achieve results through others is to become proficient in the art of delegation.

One of the greatest reasons managers do not have much discretionary time, as you will also note in examining Figure 21-1, is that they allow their subordinates to take time from them. The box in the upper right-hand corner of Figure 21-1 demonstrates this "monkey-on-the-back" analogy. If we allow it, our subordinates will rob us of our discretionary time. As managers we will then spend our time performing work that rightfully belongs to subordinates.

As technology aides us in the vocations, so should it aid us in management. However, if technology is misapplied in management, it can destroy our discretionary time, and limit our judgment and influence, leading to deterioration in our relationships. According to William Oncken, in a recent article*, the solution is to accept that you must ignore some requests and recognize that you must have two priority systems: *political* and *objective.* Some 80 to 90 percent of the support you need to get your job done comes from 10 to 15 percent of all the people you know, so you need to prioritize what comes to you via e-mail first based on political considerations. List those people who can "make or break you" in key areas of your job. Since you cannot get anything done without their support, you must influence people to say "yes" who do not have to say "yes"; hence, you are at times a politician. You might call this your *constituent list.* Remember that what you know will not get off the ground without the active support of whom you know. This list gets first call on your time, regardless of the merits of the issues they send you, because you need their active support to get your job done. On the objective part of the solution, if the priorities represented by your core constituencies are not yours and are not in the best interest of the organization, you can lay out cogent arguments customizing your recommendations in such a way that your target audience will see that it is in their own best interest to adopt the objective priorities you suggested. If

---

* "Technology Misapplied," *Executive Excellence*, September 1998, vol. 15, no. 9, p. 14.

you succeed, now your priorities are their priorities and you have their backing.

We are paid to develop an active political constituency. To do that, we need discretionary time. Technology can help us in our quest to exercise our judgment and influence.

YOU SHOULD REMEMBER

There are three types of tasks: **boss-imposed, organization-imposed,** and **self-imposed.** There are three time categories: **personal, supervisory,** and **executive.** Your objective in management should be to spend as much time as possible in the executive time category so you can generate more self-imposed tasks. This will not happen if you allow your subordinates to take away your **discretionary time.**

APPORTIONING MANAGERIAL TIME

Figure 21-2 is a model or guideline for **apportioning managerial time** (see page 421). At the first or supervisory level of management, approximately 70 percent of your time should be spent in operating by doing (personally assigning tasks to others) and 30 percent of your time should be spent managing through delegation. At the middle management level the proportion should be 50:50, and at the top management level (i.e., vice president) 70 percent of your time should be spent in managing through delegating and only 30 percent in operating by doing. At the chief executive level, 90 percent of your time should be spent in managing through delegation and only 10 percent in operating through doing.

Knowing that we have to live within the system and must handle the boss-imposed and organization-imposed tasks, how do we gain more discretionary time—executive time—to carry out our self-imposed tasks? Undoubtedly you have some ideas, but by the end of this chapter you will have many more.

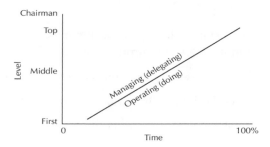

Figure 21–2. Model for apportioning managerial time, with the level of management plotted against the percentage of time spent in assigning tasks (doing) and in managing through delegation.

YOU SHOULD REMEMBER

As you move up the managerial hierarchy, more of your time should be spent in managing through delegating and less in operating through doing.

USING TIME BETTER

We are poorly equipped to manage our time. We lack a reliable time sense. The principle involved here is our inability to judge time, especially after the fact. What then is the answer to this dilemma? There are two steps to better time utilization:

1. Record time.

2. Consolidate and manage time.

RECORD YOUR TIME

Let us first discuss **recording time.** The only way to manage your time is to first find out where it is going—how you spend it. That means taking inventory of your time. Table 21-2 is a time sheet arranged in the form of a diary. It represents the other assignment we mentioned earlier in this chapter. Reproduce this sheet in your office or elsewhere and start keeping a time record for two weeks. With this information you can analyze where your time goes. Even if you keep a record for a few days it will prove very helpful.

You will undoubtedly be surprised.

Note the time you start a discussion with someone and the time you finish. The amount of "people time" is high.

Your time is fragmented—bits and pieces versus chunks.

Unproductive time is the greatest piece of the total.

Less than one-quarter of your time is discretionary.

Table 21–2 Managing Time: The Time Log

Day of the week: _____		Date: _____	
Time	Name	Subject or Activity	Code
8:15 AM			
8:30			
8:45			
9:00			
9:15			
9:30			
9:45			
10:00			
10:15			
10:30			
10:45			
11:00			
11:15			
11:30			
11:45			
12:00 PM			
12:15			
12:30			
12:45			
1:00			
1:15			

1:30	
1:45	
2:00	
2:15	
2:30	
2:45	
3:00	
3:15	
3:30	
3:45	
4:00	
4:15	
4:30	
4:45	
5:00	
5:15	
5:30	
5:45	
6:00	

Code: (A) I wasted time. (B) Can consolidate time with _____. (C) Somebody else can do this. (D) Too much time (10:90 concept).

Table 21-3 contains the instructions for using the Time Log; review this table before you take inventory.

Table 21–3 Instructions for Using the Time Log

List date and goals for day in terms of *results*, not *activities*. (Complete agenda within time allocated for sales meetings: do *not* hold the sales meeting.)

Record all significant sets in terms of results during each fifteen-minute period. Do *not* wait until noon or the end of the day, when any major benefit is lost.

Answer the following questions, *immediately after completing the log:*

1. Did setting daily goals and times for completion improve my effectiveness? Why or why not?

2. What was the longest period of time without interruption?

3. In order of importance, which interruptions were most costly?

4. What can be done to eliminate or control them?
   a. Which telephone calls were unnecessary?
   b. Which telephone calls could have been shorter or more effective?
   c. Which visits were unnecessary?
   d. Which visits could have been shorter or more effective?

5. How much time was spent in meetings?
   a. How much was necessary?
   b. How could more have been accomplished in less time?

6. Did you tend to record "activities" or "results"?

7. How many of your daily goals contributed directly to your long-range goals and objectives?

8. Did a "self-correcting" tendency appear as you recorded your actions?

9. What two or three steps could you now take to improve your effectiveness?

From R. Alec Mackenzie, *The Time Trap*, New York: Amacom, 1972.

The next step is to pinpoint wasted time from your inventory. Here are some test questions to ask of all activities:

What would happen if this were not done at all?

Which of these activities could be done just as well, if not better, by somebody else?

Is the pattern of continuous time spent on one activity dribs and drabs or chunks?

Most of us must accept that a large part of our time must be wasted on things that apparently must be done but that contribute little or nothing. Anything we can do to convert even some of this nonproductive time pays off. This is known as the *10:90 concept*, and it is shown in Figure 21-3. What it points out is that a very small number of events, perhaps as few as 10 percent, account for most (maybe 90 percent) of the results. However, our efforts tend to allocate themselves to the 90 percent of events that produce little or no results unless controlled.

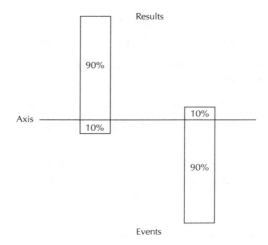

Figure 21–3. The 10:90 concept.

CONSOLIDATE AND MANAGE YOUR TIME

Let us expand the idea of **consolidating time.** We will call this the *chunk concept.* Most important tasks require, for minimum effectiveness, a fairly large period of time. To spend less than this minimum in one stretch is a sheer waste. Nothing is accomplished; you simply start all over again. Therefore you must ask yourself, what are the really important activities for which you need chunks of time, and how large should these chunks be?

One key to time management and performance success is to determine which "to do's" are priorities, and then address them in that order. You should always attend to the things that are most urgent and important. Stephen Covey reminds us that "you should spend as much time as possible doing important things that aren't urgent." That is, do not forget to invest your time wisely by always working on important (those things that have the highest payoff in terms of results) rather than unimportant things.*

In the last analysis, you really do not have much discretionary time. Thus, you must learn to consolidate what you have. Here are some tips on **managing time:**

---

* Stephen Covey and Roger Merrill, "New Ways to Get Organized at Work," *USA Weekend*, February 6–8, 1998, p. 8.

1. Make a plan for the day (see Figure 21-4).

2. Set deadlines; if these are not met you know your time is slipping away.

3. Set aside some time each day, if possible, for thinking and creating. The morning is usually best.

4. Concentrate on doing one thing at a time (chunks).

5. Start first with the task that is preying on your mind, then strike a balance between important jobs and necessary jobs.

6. Take a five- or ten-minute break every two hours. Relax your muscles and mind, and then take up some other activity.

Figure 21–4. Managing time: the day plan.

Now, let us go back to a frequent comment made during discussions of managerial planning. We very often hear, "I don't have time to plan—I'm too busy." On the surface, this may be a legitimate comment, but we ask the question, "Can you afford not to find the time to plan?" Let us explore this area a bit more. What are your barriers to time? Why can you find so little time to plan? List some of your time wasters:

_____

_____

_____

_____

After you have completed a list of your time wasters, make a list of the ways in which a manager can find time to plan. List these factors:

_____

_____

_____

_____

For a more comprehensive list of time wasters, see Figure 21-5, which shows thirty-five time wasters allocated by the functions of management.

We are sure that by this time you have concluded that the management process and time management are very closely related and interrelated. You have or will have responsibilities in management, none more important than to get things done through other people. You are responsible for converting ideas into plans and for translating plans into action and results. This definition of your responsibilities gives you the approach you want when you search for ways to make better use of your time.

How can you use your time more advantageously? In summarizing this chapter, let us get more specific. There are three approaches: (1) production, (2) administration, and (3) delegation.

• *PRODUCTION*

Separate the essential from the nonessential. The ability to know the essentials and to stick to them is a mark of maturity. Children start a great many projects and finish few; their attention is easily distracted. If you are

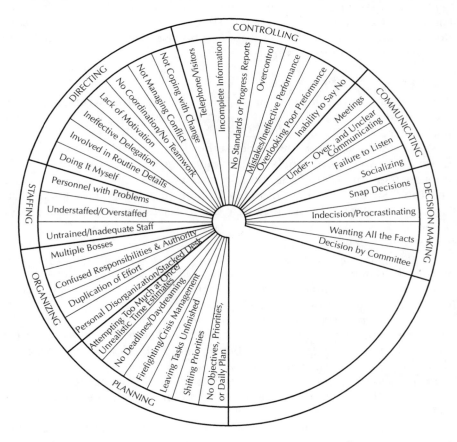

Figure 21–5. Managerial time wasters.

From *The Time Trap* by R. Alec Mackenzie. (New York: Amacom, 1972)

not getting as much done as other people are, it may be that you are wasting your time on nonessentials.

Be persistent. The way to make better use of time is to develop better work habits. Keep alive your ability to exert effort by forcing yourself to do things, if necessary, until the habit of work is stronger than the human inclination to loaf.

Learn to work anywhere. Keep a pencil and a pad of paper in several places in your home: within reach from your favorite chair where you sit to watch television or on your bedside table, for example. Do not take the chance of forgetting a good idea once it is hatched.

Put your spare moments to work. The doctor does by reading medical journals between office appointments, the farmer on rainy days by fixing fences when field work cannot be done. Professional singers and musicians are always using spare minutes for practicing.

Decide trifles quickly. A lot of people do not accomplish more things because they waste time deciding trifles. Trifles are important. However, many decisions are so minor that they can often be made by tossing a coin rather than by wasting time worrying over them.

• *ADMINISTRATION*

The second important area of responsibility is **administration.** This is the implementation of the job, the machinery setup with which to accomplish the responsibilities assigned.

Stop marking time; schedule time. At the close of each business day, write down on a slip of paper the six most important tasks for tomorrow. Next, number them in order of their importance. Put this paper in your pocket, and the first thing the next morning look at item 1 and start working on it until it is finished. Then tackle item 2 in the same way, then item 3, and so on.

Do not be concerned if you have only finished one or two tasks. You will be working on the most important ones, and the others can wait. If you cannot finish them all by this method, you could not with any other method either, and without some system, you would probably not even have decided which was the most important.

Do this every working day. Have your employees do the same thing. Organize the little things. If you can organize the little things well, you can save time and thought for tackling the bigger ones: the telephone, correspondence, reports, and training staff.

Practice for perfection. It is a human weakness to practice the easy things and neglect the more difficult, but progress comes from practicing what is difficult.

Do the job correctly the first time. Why is it we never have enough time to do the job right, but we always have enough time to do it over? Let us not be like the recruit who chose the infantry instead of joining the paratroopers where the pay was higher. When asked by a friend about the reason for his choice, he offered the logical explanation, "I don't want to do any-thing if the first time you do it, you have to do it right."

Develop good work habits. Put habit on your side. People who get things done are the same people who waste no time in the organization of their administrative duties.

• *DELEGATION*

This brings us to the third very important key to the better use of time, **delegation.**

Get help from others. Learn to get the help of others, whether it is your fellow students, your children, your fellow workers, or your neighbors. Know which task you can safely delegate to others; figure out who can help you most effectively.

People show unexpected initiative and develop responsibility if given an opportunity. "The best executive," Theodore Roosevelt observed, "is the one who has sense enough to pick good people to do what he wants done and self-restraint enough to keep from meddling with them while they do it."

Keep these thoughts in mind:

Success is the progressive realization of successive goals and worthy ideals.

Every day is a building block with which a person builds the tower of life.

To advance to the desired position, keep your eye on the goal and out-grow your present size as a person in competence and ability.

Promotions, as a rule, are not given to people; people promote them-selves by becoming too big for their present jobs, and by identifying the bigger and better jobs they are shooting for.

YOU SHOULD REMEMBER

There are two steps to better time utilization. First, record your time—the time you actually spend doing various things. Second, pinpoint wasted time and make an effort to consolidate and man-age time. Make a plan for each day and use approaches involving production, administration, and delegation to use time effectively.

The subject of time management can be wrapped up by quoting some-thing that was originally written in Sanskrit over 4500 years ago, entitled Sal-utation to the Dawn.

"Yesterday is only a dream and tomorrow is but a vision. Yet, each today, well lived, makes every yesterday a dream of happiness and each tomorrow a vision of hope. Look well, therefore, to this one day, for it and it alone is life."

KNOW THE CONCEPTS
DO YOU KNOW THE BASICS?

1. Why is time unique?
2. With what do effective managers of time begin?
3. What single area of time do most managers want more of?
4. What are the three types of tasks we perform?
5. What are the three time categories in which we perform these tasks?
6. Why should managers strive to work in the executive time category?
7. What is the major reason that managers do not have much discretionary time?
8. What does the model for apportioning managerial time reveal?
9. What are the three steps to better time utilization?
10. What are some ways to manage time?

TERMS FOR STUDY

boss-imposed tasks
consolidate time
discretionary time
executive time category
organization-imposed tasks
reverse delegation

self-imposed tasks
subordinate-imposed time
supervisory time category
time inventory
time wasters

ANSWERS
KNOW THE BASICS

1. There are five unique features about time: The supply is totally inelastic, no matter how great the demand the supply never increases. Time is totally irreplaceable; that is, yesterday's moment is gone forever. It is totally perishable, for it cannot be stored. You cannot rent or buy it, and it is always in short supply.

2. They start with their time, and they do not start with planning their time. They start by finding out where their time goes.

3. Managers most want discretionary time, the time to do what they wish.

4. These tasks are boss-imposed, organization-imposed, and self-imposed.

5. The time categories are personal, supervisory, and executive.

6. Managers work in the executive time category because getting results effectively through others is what they are paid for. This can only be done through assigning responsibilities and delegating the commensurate authority to go with these responsibilities.

7. Managers allow subordinates to take discretionary time from them.

8. As you rise in the manager hierarchy, more of your time should be spent in managing through delegating and less in operating through doing tasks personally.

9. Three steps to better time utilization are record time, analyze it so you can manage it, and consolidate time.

10. Make a plan for the day; set deadlines; concentrate on doing one thing at a time; balance between important jobs and necessary jobs; and every so often take a break.

22
PLANNING THE
MANAGERIAL
CAREER

Career life planning is a relatively new process in the United States. The process is best illustrated by the questions, Where am I heading? What do I want? Can I get it? How do I get it? Most students and even many practitioners in the field of management do not know the answers to these questions. In planning your managerial career, it is most important to know yourself.

Each of us has a lifelong challenge to realize our full potential. This requires a continuing process of self-appraisal, which is too important to be left to chance. It calls for the assessment of personal values, personal interests, and personal goals, followed by the conscious structuring of a life plan and a strategy for carrying it out.

We hope that the series of exercises for life planning provided in Appendix 2 starting on page 518 will help you get started on the process of assessing yourself—your strengths and weaknesses, your likes and dislikes—and developing a career life plan for your future. Put away your inhibitions and start taking inventory of yourself. The results may be very surprising.

Once you know yourself and where you are heading, or would like to go, and have explored the possibilities out there (see Careers in Management in Appendix 3 on page 525), the career management process will usually call for the development of a resume, cover letter, and preparation for an effective interview. This chapter focuses in depth on these key areas of career management. A list of firms and directories offering services relating to employment is provided in Appendices 4 and 5 on pages 531–532.

THE RESUME
GENERAL RULES FOR RESUME WRITING

The purpose of the **resume** is to stimulate the interest of the reader in order to gain an interview. It is a misconception that a good resume will guarantee a job for you. A resume is a selling tool used to market your abilities. It is an advertisement of your skills and accomplishments.

Remember the following general guidelines in writing your resume:

Approach. Your resume must be completely honest. Giving false information can be cause for dismissal.

Length. Keep your resume short, organized, and easy to understand (one to two pages). Be brief and to the point, highlighting your skills and accomplishments.

Focus. An effective resume is designed with a specific job in mind and a clearly articulated objective, substantiated by the reasons you are qualified for that particular type of work. If you are seeking employment for several different positions, develop a separate resume for each job objective. Emphasize the aspects of your background that relate to each job objective.

RESUME FORMAT

There are several **resume formats.** Those formats used most often are *chronological, functional,* and *the combination.* Examples are on the following pages.

• *CHRONOLOGICAL FORMAT*

The **chronological format** is the most widely used format and is most familiar to employers (see Figure 22-1). Jobs are listed chronologically, beginning with the most recent. List dates of employment first, then job title and name of employer. Begin a new paragraph for each position held and describe your accomplishments.

Use this format when there are few or no gaps in your employment history.

• *FUNCTIONAL FORMAT*

The **functional format** categorizes your experience into three- to five-job functions that you wish to emphasize for a specific job target (Figure 22-2). It emphasizes impressive job capabilities and de-emphasizes dates, names, and places. It shows your knowledge of critical job areas. Organization, leadership, planning, and communication are examples of job functions.

Use this format if there are gaps in your employment history or if you have changed jobs several times in a given period.

• *COMBINATION FORMAT*

The **combination format** utilizes the functional format and indicates title held, company name, and dates employed (see Figure 22-3). It emphasizes valued skills and abilities. However, it tends to be longer than the other two forms.

Use this format if your experience has been largely with one company.

YOU SHOULD REMEMBER

The purpose of the resume is to stimulate the interest of the reader to gain an interview. It should be accurate, brief, and designed with a specific job in mind. The three resume formats are **chronological, functional,** and a **combination of the two.**

RESUME DON'TS

The following guidelines will help prevent your resume from being tossed into the wastebasket:

Do not include personal data (age, height, weight, and marital status, for example, are unnecessary).

Do not include references. State a willingness to submit them on request. Always obtain the permission of prospective references before using their names. Avoid using the names of relatives.

Do not use highly technical language unless it is appropriate for the particular job for which you are making application.

Do not place the resume in a fancy binder or cover. This does not add anything, and it seems like a gimmick.

Resumes sure to be tossed are:

those that lack a logical order, have spelling errors, or are too wordy or flowery (life history type).

those that are vague and badly organized.

those three or more pages long.

those poorly typed and duplicated.

those that look as though they have been mass-produced.

those on colored paper other than white, light gray, or beige (sand and buff, for example).

(Continued on page 439.)

ROBERT MELTON
674 Washtenaw Street
Milwaukee, Wisconsin 53201
(414) 980–7683

OBJECTIVE

A position as a <u>Sales/Marketing Representative</u> in a growing, dynamic organization where there is a need to expand markets and develop new marketing concepts and services.

EDUCATION

MBA Degree, University of Texas, San Antonio, 1984–86
Major: Finance and Marketing
GPA: 4.0/4.0 Overall

B.A. Degree, University of Texas, Austin, 1979–82
Major: Finance
GPA: 3.7/4.0 in major
Special study area in marketing and sales. One semester internship in securities division of local bank.

EXPERIENCE

1986   – <u>Sales Representative</u>, Jagger Associates
Present   – Successfully sold photographic equipment through most levels of distribution.
             – Increased volume products 25 percent with premium users as well as catalog and plant firms in first year. Import/Export experience.
             – Direct mail know-how.
             – Cognizant of distribution patterns in electronics and photographic industries.

1982   – <u>Sales Coordinator</u>, Arco, Inc.
1985   – Determined product desirability in the marketplace.
             – Involved at most levels of product design.
             – Knowledge of patent and trademark regulations.

COMMUNITY ACTIVITIES

             – Member of Public Relations Society of America
             – Toastmasters International, Sigma Delta Chi
             – International Council of Sales Representatives

Figure 22–1. Chronological resume format.

GENE HARRIS
7895 Clinton Street
Bridgeport, CT 06606
(203) 785-3982

OBJECTIVE

A position as an Administrative Specialist providing effective coordination of administrative functions for increased efficiency in the area of troubleshooting, higher personnel production, and lower operating costs.

EXPERIENCE

ORGANIZATIONAL: – Improved job performance among eleven units of Naval Reserve in Bel Air area. Acted as troubleshooter to analyze causes of poor productivity.

LEADERSHIP: – Established a new system for recruiting highly qualified technical personnel.
– Motivated personnel to performance through clearer guidelines and closer coordination of operations.

COMMUNICATIONS: – Provided technical and administrative direction to five engineering divisions.
– Raised production by motivating personnel in badly demoralized department.

EMPLOYMENT HISTORY

Employment Representative, HUGHES AIRCRAFT CO., 1980–99.

EDUCATION

Graduate of Armistad High School, Greensboro, North Carolina.

Numerous professional and technical courses in plant engineering.

COMMUNITY ACTIVITIES

Active in Civic Affairs: NAACP, United Givers Fund, Naval Affairs Committee.

REFERENCES and further data upon request.

Figure 22–2. A functional resume format.

PAT W. FORRESTER
4022 West Palm Lane
Pendleton, Oregon 97801
(503) 596-8734

OBJECTIVE

A position as a Systems Software Programmer/Analyst for an organization with strong emphasis on improved data communication and individual creativity.

EXPERIENCE

Instructor Programmer, UNIVAC, 1992 –
– Specialized in assembly and machine language programming and software analysis.
– Utilized Teletype 35 and Friden 7511 communication terminals.

Equipment Programmer, BURROUGHS, 1990–92
– Designed and wrote production programs and software for Burroughs systems.
– Experienced in multiprocessing on the B3500 and real-time processing.

EDUCATION

B.A., Florida State College, 1990

20 weeks of specialized USAF data processing training from basic to advanced during college years through Air University. Stayed in top 5 percent of class with a 3.4 average.

HONORS/AWARDS:

Honor Student, three years
President of Economics Club

OTHER FACTS:

Experienced public speaker and technical writer.
Ability to address large groups and communicate highly technical material.
Member: Data Processing Management Association, Institute of Electrical and
　　　　Electronic Engineers.

REFERENCES and further data upon request.

Figure 22–3. The combination resume format.

YOU SHOULD REMEMBER

Resumes should not include personal data, references, highly technical language, fancy binders, or spelling errors or be poorly organized.

THE COVER LETTER

A **cover letter** is written to a potential employer with your resume attached (Figure 22-4). The letter is usually no more than three paragraphs long and is written on a printed, personal letterhead, if possible.

If you are responding to an advertisement from a newspaper, use some of the language from the advertisement in your cover letter. We suggest that you tailor your cover letter to each particular job.

If you are sending twelve resumes to twelve companies, write a separate cover letter to each company.

A good cover letter includes the following information:

1. The name and title of the individual with whom you want the interview.

2. A particular skill you can bring to the company that meets the company's needs.

3. A suggested interview time at the close of the letter.

THE INTERVIEW
HOW TO HAVE A WINNING INTERVIEW

• *PERSONAL PREPARATION*

APPEARANCE
The most important nonverbal communication you make about yourself is your **appearance.** An interview demands attention and focus on appearance and grooming.

In the first few minutes, the interviewer will quickly "size you up" and form an impression that may affect other important judgments made during the course of the interview.

1642 North Drive
Denver, Colorado 80206
February 15, 2000

Ms. Joan Evans
Personnel Manager
Jones, Smith and Klein
6209 Girard Avenue
Denver, Colorado 80206

Dear Ms. Evans:

Entering the job market these days is not easy. The same thing applies to staying and growing with a firm. I am interested in working for your organization as a public relations worker and have good qualifications.

My educational background and personal flexibility, as shown in the attached resume, will allow me to adapt quickly to any situation. Because I am interested in growing and learning about the job, you will find me a sound addition to your company.

I would very much like to get together to talk about a position. I will call your secretary in a few days to set up a time that is convenient.

I look forward to meeting you soon.

Yours very truly,

(Name)

Enclosure

Figure 22–4. A cover letter.

Dressing for success means dressing neatly and appropriately for the environment for which you are interviewing. By wearing the quality and style of clothing you would wear if hired, you help the interviewer visualize you on the job. Your appearance should make the interviewer think, "This person will fit in well."

Buy a special job-hunting outfit. (Remember, this is tax deductible.) To add to your professional image, carry a briefcase or attaché case.

TIMING

This refers to the time of day you actually set for the interview. Know when you function best (your metabolic clock).

PERSONAL STORIES

Be ready to briefly describe specific personal accomplishments you want the interviewer to remember. These accomplishments are reinforcers of your successes and capabilities—that is, your ability to identify a problem and how you solved it.

PUNCTUALITY

Be on time. In fact, it is wise to be early.

If you are not sure of the location of the interview, take time before the appointment to learn how to get there.

Determine how long it takes you to arrive; check for parking, location of elevators, and so on. Check to see if parking tickets are validated. Bring extra money in case of an emergency.

• FACTUAL PREPARATION

One of the most positive ways to ensure a successful interview is to demonstrate a knowledge of the company—its size, product line, major problems (if any), programs, and needs.

Do your homework. Completing an interview data sheet like the one shown in Figure 22-5 is essential. Investigate the company before your interview. This will gain you credibility. For example, if you are seeking a position with a major cosmetics firm, discover how their product is sold locally. If asked, you will then be ready to offer a tactful appraisal of displays, sales approaches, and advertising, for example.

Some of the possible sources of information about companies are annual reports, trade journals, news magazines, other people in the field, and brokerage houses. Other sources are listed in Appendices 4 and 5.

• DURING THE INTERVIEW, REMEMBER:

1. While waiting for your interview, be aware of the image you are projecting. If possible, bring a serious popular magazine (such as *Time* or *Newsweek*) or a journal from the trade.

2. You should know the proper pronunciation of the name of the interviewer. If necessary, call and ask the secretary.

3. Greet the interviewer with a firm handshake, and establish eye contact.

4. Wait until the interviewer sits or offers a seat to you. Position yourself comfortably; avoid awkward movements and excessive mannerisms. Look alert, be interested, and smile naturally.

5. Do not smoke, even if offered a cigarette.

6. Do not be afraid to initiate the interview discussion by commenting on the office décor, building, and general environment.

7. Be a good listener. It is important to *listen* so that you will *hear* what the interviewer is saying about the kind of person they would like to hire.

8. Be enthusiastic, honest, and sincere. Convey a warm, positive attitude.

9. Learn something about your interviewer before leaving to use in your follow-up letter (i.e., company needs, interests, or hobbies).

10. Send a brief thank-you note within four days after the interview.

YOU SHOULD REMEMBER

To have a winning interview, dress appropriately, be on time, and prepare yourself with knowledge of the organization. Also, keep in mind the ten points to remember during the interview.

Interview Data Sheet
Complete this sheet before each interview

Company Name	
Address, Phone	
Major Products And Services	
Size Of Organization	
Financial Status	
Brief History And Growth Rate	
Reputation In Field	
Company's Programs And Problems	
Job Title And Description	
Name Of Interviewer	
Interviewer's Job Title, Department (Correct Spelling)	
Telephone And Address Of Interviewer	
Time And Location Of Interview	
List Questions You Might Ask (Reason Job Is Available, Training Programs, Company Growth Plans, Job Description, Duties, Etc.)	1 2 3

Figure 22–5. A sample interview data sheet.

STRUCTURE OF THE INTERVIEW

The interview is a structured conversation. It allows the interviewer to assess your potential and your future job performance. It allows you to evaluate whether this is the job for you.

The interview generally consists of four segments: *the greeting, typical questions asked, questions you ask,* and *the close.*

• *THE GREETING*

Establish rapport; make small talk to put you both at ease.

The interviewer may begin by giving the background of the company, describing the job, or asking a question. If the interviewer waits for you to begin, initiate the discussion with a well-prepared statement or question relating to your job target.

Remember to maintain good eye contact and to listen attentively. Appear relaxed and in control.

• *TYPICAL INTERVIEW QUESTIONS*

Much of what you say in job interviews is in reply to important questions. Your knowledge of these questions and your ability to respond to them intelligently and fluently ensures a better impression with the interviewer.

Throughout the interview, *watch for nonverbal feedback.* If the interviewer's eyes begin to wander or he or she gives some other indication of impatience, shorten your answer and switch to another subject. Omit superfluous details from your conversation. Stress the benefits you can bring to the job and the company.

Do not panic if you do not know the answer to a technical question. Admit that you do not. Remember, no one is expected to know everything.

If you do not agree with an opinion expressed, say so honestly and tactfully. Mention one or two of your strongest selling points toward the end of the interview. Remember to take your time, think about your answers before replying, and relax.

The questions and suggested replies listed in Table 22-1 cover three main areas: education and training, work experience, and personality factors.

Table 22–1 Typical Interview Questions and Suggested Replies

Question	Reply
1. Tell me about yourself.	Keeping your resume in mind, mention a few important facts about yourself and your experience and relate this to the company.
	Mention your major strengths, and relate them to the specific job for which you are applying. Also, mention

Table 22–1 Typical Interview Questions and Suggested Replies

Question	Reply
	something personal, such as values or interests. The interviewer has given you the initiative.
2. What are your major strengths?	This is the opportunity to sell yourself. Show that you are proud of your accomplishments. Discuss a key quality you possess that you believe would be in great demand on the job.
	Emphasize your initiative, knowledge of the industry, leadership ability, and specific skills needed for the job. Substantiate these qualities with evidence from past experiences on other jobs or in other areas.
3. What are your major weaknesses?	This is not the place to confess your insecurities or weaknesses. Give a self-confident reply, and point to unimportant, nonjob-related areas that need improvement.
	The best strategy is to present a strength as a weakness; for example, I find it difficult to keep my promise to myself to read a book once a week, or I get upset with myself if my timetables are not met.
4. Why are you interested in working for this company?	Emphasize your interest in the company and do your homework so that you are prepared with facts and figures, such as a description of the virtues of their product(s) or its success in the field of marketing.
5. Why have you chosen this field?	This is an opportunity for you to impress the interviewer with your interest and knowledge and to explain that your chosen career utilizes all your skills and abilities and, as a result, you have been very successful.
	This field may have good fringe benefits, vacations, or other benefits. However, this is not the time to discuss them. Your emphasis should be on the opportunities for you in this field.
6. Why should I hire you?	This is a direct invitation for you to sell yourself. Take a moment and think seriously about this question before replying, and relate your previous successes to this job and the company.
	Some suggested responses are: I learn quickly. I'm experienced in this field. I'm highly motivated for success in this job.

Table 22–1 Typical Interview Questions and Suggested Replies

Question	Reply
7. What are your long-range goals?	Your answer to this question will reveal much useful information about you—your foresight, realistic outlook, preparation in career planning, knowledge of self, and commitment to the company and your profession. In your reply, describe your career plan and discuss your commitment to the field and the company. From your prior research, you will have determined what position you could reasonably expect to have in five years and in ten years. Let the interviewer know you will work hard, as you are determined to reach your goals. If asked, What do you expect to be doing in ten years? you could reply, I want to be the best, or one of the best, at whatever I am doing at that time.
8. What is your current salary and what do you expect?	This should not be discussed until you have had an opportunity to sell yourself in person during the interview. Discuss salary only *after* the interviewer tells you a specific job is available and the company wants to hire you. Ask the interviewer to state the intended salary, which will then open negotiations. Keep in mind the minimum salary you are prepared to accept. You should talk to other individuals working in the same position, and read professional and trade magazines in the field to determine this amount. When you know the typical salary range for your job, always seek the top portion of the range. Do not hesitate to let the interviewer know you have a career plan and an interest in growing with the company.
9. How do you handle pressure?	Give examples of how you handled pressure situations in previous jobs.
10. What is important to you in a job?	Impress the interviewer by stressing your desire to do a good job. Do not discuss salary or benefits until you have been offered the job. A suggested reply might be, What is most important to me, and what really motivates me, is to know that I'm doing a good job in a company where my opinions really count and where I can contribute to meeting the goals of the company.

Table 22-1 Typical Interview Questions and Suggested Replies

Question	Reply
11. How is your previous experience applicable to the work we do here?	Slant your previous experience toward this present opportunity. If your previous experience does not exactly fit, emphasize your strengths, such as initiative, perseverance, punctuality, and organizational abilities, and how they apply to the job.
12. Why did you leave your former job?	One of the worst interviewing errors you can make is to respond to this question by ventilating your negative feelings from a previous job. Always remember that there are two sides to a conflict and that between you and a company, the company generally has more credibility.
13. What are your interests outside of work?	Stress that you use your time wisely, have varied interests, and get along well with others and that you are a participant, not a spectator. If you have a special talent, hobby, or skill, mention it briefly.
14. How do others describe you?	Paint a positive picture of your social relationships on the job by letting the interviewer know you get along well with coworkers and subordinates and are respected by your prior employers.
15. Tell me about your education.	Keep your reply positive. Your speaking well of your alma mater indirectly speaks well of you. If you worked to put yourself through school, be sure to mention it.

• QUESTIONS YOU ASK

When it is appropriate, ask questions throughout the interview. Convey the impression that you, too, have to be sold on the job and the company. This is an opportunity to demonstrate what you learned about the company before the interview. The following questions are suggestions; use them at your discretion.

1. May I see a copy of the job description?

2. With whom would I be working?

3. Where would I appear on the organization chart? (If position is appropriate to this question.)

4. What is the growth rate of the company?

5. What are the advancement opportunities two years from now? Five years from now?

6. What happened to the person who last held this job?

7. What are your major markets?

8. Who are your biggest competitors?

9. What is the most important qualification for this position?

10. Who is your biggest customer in this area?

11. When will you be making a decision about this position?

12. To whom would I be responsible?

13. What are the employee benefits? When does coverage begin?

14. How much travel would you consider normal for this position?

15. Would relocation be required at this time or in the future?

• *THE CLOSE*

By now, you should be able to determine if all information has been adequately communicated. If you feel comfortable that it has and the interviewer has not offered the next step, firmly ask, Does my experience fit the company's needs? or Is there anything else you need to know about me?

State that you think your experience would be valuable to the company.

If the interviewer is interested and wants you to come back, you may want to ask to spend some time with one of the employees or on location if you need more information.

Ask to have the hiring procedure defined so that you are fully informed and know what to expect.

What is the next step?

If there is no interest from either side, you may ask for contacts in similar companies, if you are comfortable with this question. Also, ask for an evaluation of your interview and resume.

Be courteous, offer a firm handshake, and a pleasant, Thank you for your time or We'll be in touch.

YOU SHOULD REMEMBER

The interview is a structured conversation and consists of **the greeting, typical questions asked, questions you ask,** and **the closing.**

AFTER THE INTERVIEW: THE THANK-YOU NOTE

The object of the **thank-you note** is to obtain a fast and positive response and to serve as a reminder of your capabilities in relation to the job (see Figure 22-6).

Try to highlight the areas of company needs mentioned in the interview, and suggest how you can fill them. Briefly review the points covered during the interview. Express your continuing interest. (The note should be written on your personal stationery.) If there is no response within a few days, telephone and offer to supply additional information or to have another personal meeting.

Remember to consult Appendices 2, 3, 4, and 5, starting on page 518, for further guidance on planning a career in management.

Finally, remember in planning your job hunt strategy to hunt everywhere for jobs, call everyone you know or can get to know about jobs, go fill out job applications, leave your resume, get interviewed.

Keep in mind the following points in finding your job openings: work out your finances, cut costs, line up your skills and assets, work out a marketing

---

(date)_____

Dear Mr. Marks,

This note is to reiterate my interest in the position we discussed during our recent interview. I am confident I can contribute to the company's growth.

Enclosed is an addendum to my resume, describing the techniques I used to increase circulation in the Western region.

Since I am considering several alternatives and must arrive at a decision shortly, I would like to talk with you in the early part of next week.

I look forward to meeting with you.

Sincerely,

(name)

Figure 22–6. A thank-you note.

presentation (you're the product), line up your networks, contact people, ask for their help, read want ads, follow up, and scan the news headlines for business changes.

Last, but not least, *dress the part.* Go to the interview dressed conservatively. You will never be faulted if you are dressed more formally than the person interviewing you. If you're a man, do not wear loud color shirts, ties, or sport coats. Keep your hair neat and well-groomed. Cut and clean your fingernails. Do not wear wrinkled or soiled clothing. Have your shoes shined. Do not wear white socks. The same guidelines apply to women. Do not wear overly bright colors or have excessively long nails. Nail polish should be a muted color. Heels should be of moderate height. Do not dress provocatively.

Finally, do not chew gum, bite your fingernails, smoke, or adopt mannerisms that make you appear nervous or ill at ease.

KNOW THE CONCEPTS
DO YOU KNOW THE BASICS?

1. What is the purpose of the resume?
2. What are the various formats for preparing the resume?
3. What are some ways to prevent your resume from being tossed into the wastebasket?
4. What should a good cover letter include?
5. What are some things to keep in mind to have a winning interview?
6. What are some things to remember during the interview?
7. What are the four segments of the interview?
8. What is the purpose of the job interview?
9. What is the object of the thank-you note?
10. What is the purpose of career life planning?

TERMS FOR STUDY

career exploration
career life planning
career management
chronological resume
combination resume
cover letter
executive search
functional resume
job interview

life inventory
long-range goals
peak experience
personal objectives
personal strengths
resume
self-exploration
values

ANSWERS
KNOW THE BASICS

1. The purpose of the resume is to stimulate the interest of the reader in order to gain an interview. It is a selling tool to market your abilities.

2. Resume formats are chronological, functional, and a combination.

3. Do not use highly technical language, fancy binders or covers, or illogical organization. Do not have spelling errors or use flowery language, poor typing, or poor duplication.

4. The cover letter should include the name and title of the individual with whom you want the interview, a particular skill you can bring to the organization, and a suggested interview time.

5. Dress appropriately, set the time for the interview when you function best, and be on time.

6. Know the proper pronunciation of the name of the interviewer. Greet the interviewer with a firm handshake, and establish eye contact. Do not smoke. Be a good listener and be enthusiastic, and send a brief thank-you note within four days after the interview.

7. The parts of the interview are the greeting, typical questions asked, questions you ask, and the close.

8. The interview allows the interviewer to assess your potential and your future job performance. It allows you to evaluate whether this is the job for you.

9. The thank-you note is a way of trying to obtain a fast and positive response. It allows you to review the points covered in the interview and remind the interviewer of your capabilities.

10. Career life planning enables a fast and positive response during the interview and serves as a reminder of your capabilities in relation to the job.

23

MANAGEMENT INFORMATION SYSTEMS

KEY TERMS

IFCA information for competitive advantage, coined by the Management Information Consulting Division of Arthur Andersen & Co., a dynamic view of information that stresses that information is valuable to management because it confers competitive advantages in the marketplace

MIS management information system, the integrated total of all corporate people, procedures, data, and equipment into a comprehensive system that produces the required information for all levels within the organization

MRS management reporting system, which makes use of computer-processed information to generate standard reports in predetermined formats that are employed by managers to make routine and recurring decisions

CPU central processing unit, the basic electronic unit of a computer, which performs the desired calculations to acquire, sort, calculate, manipulate, and store data

hardware includes not only the CPU but also all physical devices that input data, store data, and output data

LAN local area network, a methodology employing both hardware and software to link individual computers and hardware devices together to enable sharing of individual components and maximal efficiency of equipment use

WAN wide area network, serves to link LANs

software programs of instructions that control the actions of the hardware components; such functions as data acquisition, processing and manipulation, and storage are facilitated and controlled by software programs

The latter half of the 20th century may well be regarded by future historians as the age of information. The invention of the computer and the creation of new communication technologies have made it possible for managers to acquire, manipulate, and evaluate more information than ever before in human history. As with so many other mechanical discoveries, it was preceded by the emergence of a new philosophy of information. This philosophical change, evident in virtually every public library book catalog, is only now coming to be valued as an informational watershed and dividing point between the medieval and modern worlds. Although it began in revolutionary France of the 1790s, it was fully, if undramatically, stated in the preface of a scholarly but little-heralded book published in 1897.

Medieval libraries, generally located in monasteries, great church centers, or the castles of nobility were cataloged and recorded in a sequential list by subject in a bound volume. This format was maximally durable but minimally useful since these lists were not flexible and became immediately obsolete. The change from recording book lists or merchandising accounts in bound volumes to using card files (the beginning, no doubt, of paper shuffling) marks the change from the view of information as static and rigid to the view that information is dynamic and can be periodically rearranged to serve people's needs.

The first patent application for a flexible card file was submitted in 1849, and by the end of the century the Library of Congress had adopted the practice of distributing book reference cards to public libraries. The card catalog, previously found in every public library, with its thousands of *movable* cards, embodied that change from the medieval world to the modern, from information as static to information as flexible. In 1897, **Sidney** and **Beatrice Webb** extolled the virtue of index cards for the organization of scholarly information. Their comments on academic methodology, contained in the preface of their book *Industrial Democracy*, set the tone for the organization of information by scholars ever since.

Modern computer technology, with the unparalleled ability to generate, manipulate, and evaluate data, embodies this concept of *flexibility of information* just as the movable card catalog did a generation before. The abilities of computer technology to superbly embody the concept of information flexibility make it a powerful, useful, and essential tool for contemporary managers. Indeed, current managerial theory and practice stress the importance of up-to-the-minute market data to make effective decisions. The manager's day now routinely begins with an evaluation of the latest information that may impact on that day's business.

THE VALUE OF INFORMATION

As was previously stated in the discussion of decision-making, decisions based upon information are only as good as the information upon which they are based. Computers can produce a tremendous amount of information, but the impact of this technology is not in the quantity but in the quality of information produced. By improving the quality of information, computer technology can improve the quality of management decision-making. **Jean-Louis Gassee,** former director of research and development for Apple Computer, Inc., in an interview about personal computers, made the following statement, but his insightful comments refer to computers in general:

> Do we really think we can measure productivity in the information age as Frederick Taylor did with manufacturing in the industrial age, by the mile of text produced? Information should not be evaluated by volume alone. Do we evaluate a meal by the number of calories ingested? The point of personal computers is precisely to enhance content as well as production. In that way, personal computers become true intellectual power tools.

Management decision-making has become dependent upon information, and the computer and its allied technologies—that make the acquisitions of information routine—have vastly increased the amount of such information available. As Gassee suggests, although computers are the newest intellectual tools, the mere quantity of information will not promote better decision-making. Rather, the strength of information acquisition technologies lies in the ability to improve significantly the quality of information, and that has a direct impact upon managerial success.

Information is also a dynamic method for gaining advantage in the marketplace. This now well-accepted concept is **IFCA, information for competitive advantage**, a term coined by the Management Information Consulting Division of Arthur Andersen & Co. It is a dynamic view of information that stresses that its value to management is that it confers competitive advantages in the marketplace. Some have gone so far as to assert that information is a *weapon* to be used in corporate competition. Although this may be an overly dramatic view of information, it does point to the increasing value placed upon it by managers. This dynamic view of information within the modern business organization leads to an equally dynamic view of the acquisition, management, and security processes with regard to corporate information. This process is seen in Figure 23-1. It is clear from this dynamic process view of organizational information that the first step is the determination of the manager's or the organization's informational needs.

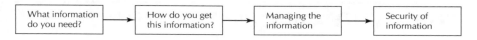

Figure 23-1. Dynamic systems view of information.

YOU SHOULD REMEMBER

Information is necessary to the modern business because it gives a significant competitive advantage. This concept of information is known as **IFCA (Information For Competitive Advantage).** Business organizations that do not take active measures to acquire and use information risk extinction. Information systems must be flexible to adapt to changing circumstance.

THE INFORMATION NEEDS OF MANAGERS

Different managers have different kinds of information needs, and a dynamic systems view of information allows these various informational requirements. The highest level of corporate management, which is responsible for the formulation of corporate business policy that will realize the organization's goals and determine its directions, has a need for information that is broadly based and strategic in nature. This level of information, however, is not appropriate for a first-line supervisor or operational manager. A supervisor requires detailed information on day-to-day operations and does not generally have a use for the same sort of broad strategic information provided to a company president. The general guideline is that the information provided should match the information required. This information is provided by the **management information system (MIS)**.

MIS, the management information system, is the integrated total of all corporate people, procedures, data, and equipment into a comprehensive system that produces the required information for all levels within the organization. This MIS focuses both internally and externally as it provides information derived from within the organization (for example, weekly production totals) or from without (changes in the Consumer Price Index). Indeed, the emerging field is more encompassing than MIS and is contained in and implied by the term **IT, information technology**. IT now reaches beyond the company vis-à-vis the Internet and access to the growing body of world information. Companies, and even individual managers, are now connected to countless others and incredible amounts of information—and the paralysis occasioned by information overload is a daily difficulty.

Before examining the hardware and software components of the management information system and the selection criteria that operate in its design, it is necessary to delineate the characteristics of the information itself.

INFORMATION REQUIREMENTS

Since information is a managerial tool used by all levels within an organization, it must meet certain requirements. As any tool, it must be *appropriate* for the task. Additionally, the information should be *complete* and *accurate* and must be delivered in a *timely manner* to be useful. If any of these requirements are not met, management may find a less than useful tool. Since the quality of information greatly influences the quality of managerial decision-making, the failure to meet even one of these informational requirements can lead to organizational disaster.

Consider the following example of complex decision-making:

> Management is going to make a decision by flipping a coin. The odds are 1 of 2, or 1/2, or 50 percent, that the decision will be correct. Suppose, however, that two decisions have to be made in a row, that is, *sequentially*. The odds of making the first decision correctly are 1/2, and the odds of making the second decision correctly are also 1/2, *but the odds of making two sequential decisions correctly are $1/2 \times 1/2 = 1/4$.* The odds of making a series of decisions correctly is $1/2^n$ where n = the number of decisions in the series.
>
> If a manager has to make five decisions in a row, the odds of all of them being correct are $1/2 \times 1/2 \times 1/2 \times 1/2 \times 1/2 = 1/2^5$, which equals $1/2 \times 2 \times 2 \times 2 \times 2 = 1/32$.

Thus, even though the flipping of a coin gives 50:50 odds of being correct, when management has to make a series of sequential decisions, the possibility of making all the decisions correctly rapidly decreases. Ensuring that information used by managers in the decision-making process meets all the necessary requirements increases the possibility of making correct decisions.

Information costs money, and as previously seen with inventory, acquiring and maintaining unneeded information will waste organizational resources. Managers must be cost conscious in designating their information needs; too little or poor quality information will not help decision-making, while too much information will certainly waste money and may cause good and useful data to become lost.

YOU SHOULD REMEMBER

A **Management Information System (MIS),** part of the corporate area called **Information Technology (IT),** is a comprehensive system that produces all the required information for all levels within the organization. To be a useful tool, information should be complete, accurate, appropriate for the task and the person to which it is delivered, and delivered in a timely manner. The information provided should match the information required for decision-making.

MIS SUBSYSTEMS AND THE USES OF INFORMATION

As discussed in Chapter 5, managers are called upon to make routine and nonroutine decisions. Each of these requires different forms of information, and different informational systems have been created to aid management in its decision-making. The *transaction processing system (TPS)* is the most basic part of the MIS, gathering and organizing basic business transactions; this component of the MIS does not involve decision-making. For routine decisions that recur within the business organization, a *management reporting system (MRS)* has been created. For nonroutine decisions, a *decision support system (DSS)* is utilized.

TRANSACTION PROCESSING SYSTEM

A transaction is any event that takes place either within the business organization or between that organization and the external environment. Such regular transactions include regular ordering of raw materials, customer billing, and bank deposits. This information is not directly involved in the decision-making process but is needed by management. It must be compiled and classified, perhaps calculations must be made, and finally it must be summarized in a form in which it will be maximally useful to management.

TPSs are needed at all levels of an organization, and although the exact nature of the system employed is different in each case, there are certain similarities in every case:

- There must be a large volume of transactions to justify the creation of a TPS.

- The transactions must be repetitive—that is, essentially the same each time, with no or few exceptions.

- The way in which the information is to be gathered, processed, and presented is well understood.

The transaction processing system is characterized by extreme routinization. Since the information-gathering and -processing steps are well known, they are often described as *standard operating procedures (SOP)*. The computer is ideally suited to the TPS in that it is capable of the needed degree of accuracy, can handle a high volume of transactions, and does not become bored by the repetitive task.

MANAGEMENT REPORTING SYSTEM

Most business decisions are of the routine nature. They are distinguished not only because they recur with regularity but also because the decision-making parameters are well understood. Because they are well understood, these kinds of decisions are often called *structured decisions*. Because the decisions are well understood, the information needed to make these decisions is also well understood. This information fits into a predetermined format that is used in the regular reporting process. The specific part of the corporate MIS that generates this information is called the **management reporting system.** This makes use of computer-processed information to generate the standard reports that are employed by managers to make routine and recurring decisions.

The design and execution of a successful MRS is a slow and deliberate developmental process that is focused on the derivation of information in a useful format to aid managers in decision-making, and is always subject to evaluation and improvement. Indeed, as information needs change in response to the challenges of managerial decision-making in often fast-changing business environments, the MRS must also change. Managers who fail to evaluate their information systems periodically risk obsolescence, not only of the system but also of their entire business. The rapid pace of contemporary business demands constant attention. To fall behind is to court failure, and making critical decisions based on bad data almost ensures poor performance in a marketplace that is totally unforgiving of such performance.

DECISION SUPPORT SYSTEM

The second type of decisions made by management are those cases that are nonrecurring and nonroutine. They may even be one-time decisions characterized by their uniqueness. As we saw in Chapter 5, these problems and their decisions are referred to as unstructured, and their informational requirements are not well understood. Since the kinds and amount of information needed to make a managerial decision in an unstructured situation are not readily apparent, it is difficult to design a system to provide the information, but it is not impossible. The key to designing a successful DSS is *flexibility*.

An example of an unstructured decision is the hiring of a new manager. To a large extent, each hiring decision is unique, and in each case different information is considered important. The interviewer or personnel department has the ability to request needed information in each case, and when additional information is deemed necessary to the hiring decision, it can also be requested. The exact kind and amount of information is not known before the event. Because of the lack of predetermination of the kind and amount of information needed in the managerial decision process, this DSS requires managers who are flexible and comfortable in an uncertain environment.

HOW INFORMATION TECHNOLOGY WORKS

Each IT subsystem is facilitated by the use of computer technology, the basis of which is hardware and software.

HARDWARE

Computer **hardware,** an extremely rapidly changing area, includes all physical equipment that comprises the management information system. Although a computer may be self-contained, it is more likely that it will consist of components designed to maximize the acquisition input, processing, storage, and output of data. A useful way of classifying hardware is shown in Figure 23-2. This diagram itself may be outdated even as you are reading it because new input devices, faster CPUs, and innovative output systems are constantly being introduced.

• *INPUT DEVICES*
Input is provided to the central processing unit (CPU) in a variety of ways. Since the input is converted to electronic signals that the CPU will recognize, any electronic signal generator may be capable of providing data input. In Figure 23-2, input is provided by a visual signal generator (video camera); a touch-sensitive monitor which converts touch upon a monitor screen into an electronic signal; the keyboard of a personal computer, via a telephone link and signal processor; and a digital signal source. This is not an exclusive listing of signal sources; scientific instruments, weather data sensors, burglar

alarms, magnetic tape readers, and audio outputs (microphones and tape recorders) can all be connected to central processing units.

• CENTRAL PROCESSING UNIT

The **central processing unit (CPU)** is the basic electronic unit of a computer. It performs the desired calculations to acquire, sort, calculate, manipulate, and store data. It has a memory that consists of thousands of small switches that can be positioned in either the on or off position. These switches are contained on the surface of a small silicon wafer. By either opening or closing these switches, meaningful patterns are established. Computer memory is described in terms of *bits* of data. A 64K memory actually can hold 65,536 characters of data (1K = 1024), and current computers can hold billions of characters. The switches in the CPU are of two kinds: (1) those that are *permanently* positioned in an on/off pattern and (2) those that can be turned on or off by input instruction. The former is *read only memory (ROM),* and the latter is *random access memory (RAM).* When a computer programmer formulates a series of instructions on how input is to be processed (known as a *program*), this is input into the RAM. This process is described in the discussion of software, but first we must turn to the methods by which the results of the computer processing emerges from the CPU. This is done by means of various output devices.

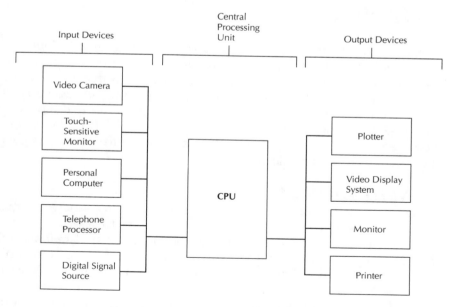

Figure 23–2. Hardware components of MIS.

• *OUTPUT DEVICES*

Traditionally, output from the CPU has been either to an appropriate printer [here shown as a *plotter* used by engineers, a video display system (e.g., projector), a letter-quality or laser printer used for higher quality output] or to a monitor. Output can be sent to any device capable of decoding electronic signals. This is having a major impact not only in the office but also on the concert stage: computers are used to generate audio output and simulate virtually any musical instrument or even the human voice.

SOFTWARE

Software consists of programs of instructions that control the actions of the hardware components. Such functions as data acquisition, processing and manipulation, and storage are facilitated and controlled by software programs. These programs place specific switch on/off patterns into the random access memory. These instructions are formulated according to a set of predetermined rules called the *computer language*. There are many different languages, some of which are better suited for specific programming applications. New languages are constantly developed and introduced into the marketplace. Computer programs, the application instructions, are the "drivers" that enable management to utilize the processing power of the CPU, and this leads to the correct method for purchasing the hardware for the MIS. Since this method is so often violated by managers impressed with the latest gadget, it deserves special attention.

The correct way to purchase hardware is to first choose the desired software. The software is what makes the computer a useful and effective tool. Management must:

- decide what the MIS should be able to do
- choose the appropriate software to do it
- *then select the hardware that will run the software*

Software is written by a *computer programmer* who is expert in one or several computer languages. Programs may be written for specific applications (a personnel database for a hospital) or for a general application (an accounts-receivable processing program) that can be customized by individual users. A program may be sold to an end user or merely leased. Programs are described by their version number. As these programs are improved, the newer versions receive different numbers and are referred to as *program updates*.

As the use of computers has increased, it has become apparent that greater productivity is possible by linking individual computers into a network that can share specific devices. Thus a costly plotter can be shared or "accessed" by several different user computers. Networking of computers in the office appears to be one of the keys to greater IT productivity. This is done often by means of a local area network (LAN) or wide area network (WAN).

LOCAL AREA NETWORK

LAN denotes **local area network,** a methodology employing both hardware and software to link individual computers and hardware devices together to enable sharing of individual components and maximal efficiency of equipment use. The complexity of the LAN varies with the size, dispersion, and complexity of the computer processing to be networked. Networks have often been developed by individual equipment manufacturers and are, not equipment specific.

A typical office network is shown in Figure 23-3. Such a network arrangement allows several different types of computer users to share plotters, printer buffers, printers, disk drives, and other peripheral devices. This facilitates maximal use of expensive equipment and efficiency. Computer scientists are learning how to more efficiently and effectively link hardware together, and greater integration of functions will be a hallmark of the office in the coming decade.

Note that the network is becoming the computer as increasing amounts of software are now stored, not in the individual computer, but on the network itself. When the individual user wishes to perform a computing task, the program is accessed on the network. The advantage to the business or-

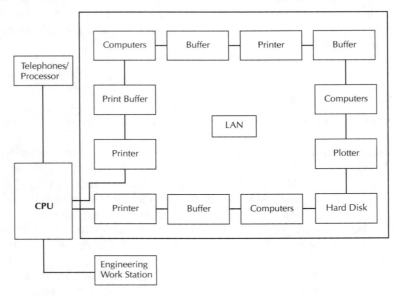

Figure 23–3. Local area network (LAN).

ganization that has such computing is that a network-based program can serve multiple users, may allow worker collaboration on tasks, and will allow more sophisticated computing to be performed on the individual manager's computer, which now can be a relatively inexpensive terminal.

YOU SHOULD REMEMBER

The effectiveness of an **information technology** system depends upon the interrelationship between (1) the task to be accomplished, (2) the selection of software to accomplish the desired task, (3) the efficiency of the hardware, and (4) the skills and facility of the human operators of the **IT.** The cornerstone of IT system design is the selection of the initial software to accomplish the desired task.

NEW TRENDS IN MANAGEMENT INFORMATION SYSTEMS
HEALTH CONCERNS

Unions have expressed concern about the health effects of cathode ray tubes. These tubes are thought to emit low-level radiation, and there is growing suspicion that this may have a negative impact upon workers whose primary job function is to work before the computer screen. Although there is little scientific evidence to substantiate this assertion, research studies are being funded and the unions of clerical employees who work before such screens are funding regional and national conferences in which the experts will present their research findings.

Since employees do spend so much time before the computer screen, there is a growing effort on the part of scientists to create the most efficient forms of furniture and computer design that maximize comfort and promote employee concentration and productivity. This effort to achieve design efficiency is *ergonomics*.

Additionally, various physical ailments, such as carpal tunnel syndrome, resulting from repetitive wrist movement (e.g., typing or using a computer mouse/trackball) and computer vision syndrome (known as CVS, with symptoms of eyestrain, blurred vision, and/or headaches, and related to extended computer use), have been well documented. The workplace is increasingly being challenged to design and employ technology that is more health-promoting and avoids repetitive stress injuries.

LINKED NETWORKS AND DATA PROCESSING SERVICE ORGANIZATIONS

The cost of computing power has fallen dramatically in a very short period of time. Contemporary analysts who follow the computer field have described this dramatic fall in computing prices by relating it to automobiles. If automobile prices had fallen as dramatically as computer prices, a Rolls Royce would today cost a mere $5 or less. It is anticipated that the price of computing power will continue to decline, although perhaps not as dramatically as in the past.

As various offices and departments of a company are linked by means of phone lines and satellite data transmission, an increasing number of companies will create subsystems of computing for more effective data management. These office subsystems (LANs) can be linked electronically to remote mainframe computers, and the use of each individual office of the remote CPU will be accomplished by means of distributed data processing.

Many companies elect not to purchase computers for an IT but to acquire computing power. This is done by contracting with a *data-processing service organization (DPSO)*. A company can thereby avoid the large capital expenditures necessary to acquire a mainframe computer and its accompanying LAN, avoid having to deal with equipment obsolescence, and avoid having to acquire and maintain the necessary skilled human resources to run the system. All these will be provided, for a fee, by the DPSO. Data can be sent via the phone or through the mail, the required data processing done, and the results communicated back to the contracting company.

USER-FRIENDLY PROGRAMS

Computer programs are now continually introduced that do not require a sophisticated programming background but prompt the user in easily understood language commands and allow interaction between the program and user to clarify the task commands. These programs are referred to as "user friendly" and have opened the world of IT to nonsophisticated users.

This trend toward *user-friendly programs* is an ongoing hallmark of the most widely accepted programs and has become almost a prerequisite for programming success. The focus is shifting from the ability to construct programs to the ability to use those programs. It should be anticipated that contemporary managers will have to be comfortable with IT concepts and programs to keep aware of the latest developments in the area.

SECURITY

With the proliferation of individual computers tied into the LAN and telephone connections to corporate mainframe computers, more employees than ever before have access to data. On well-publicized occasions this access has lead to abuse by those who were not authorized, called *hackers* in the popular lexicon. Much heralded security systems have merely served to challenge talented but misguided individuals to crack the computer system, whether a bank database or the grade records at the local college. From the local savings and loan to the Pentagon, all have fallen prey to the talented hacker. This has forced the realization that where there are data, there must also be attention to the **security** of those data.

This security comes in several forms. The *physical security* of data is related to the physical measures to protect the data. This includes the locks, combinations, cameras, watchpersons, and so on, that protect a data system. This protection, however, must consider not only the willful violator but also the real possibility of natural disaster (such as fire) that could rob a company of its data far more efficiently than any criminal. It is for this reason that companies routinely make copies of data, a process called "*backing up*" the data, and place the copies in secure circumstances. Copies of data may be stored in a bank vault, but enterprising business people have created an industry of storing data in such unlikely but suitable locations as salt mines in Utah or in abandoned and obsolete U.S. Air Force Titan missile silos.

Security also includes dealing not only with the possibility of physical violation of the computer system but also with intrusion into the programming or database. Think of the havoc caused by a violator's reading a competitor's database or, worse, altering that base to insert false information. There are documented instances in which an unhappy employee altered an existing program to slightly change the information entered so that the results of data analysis looked probable but actually were inaccurate. A program was changed to include subroutines that, at a certain point, erased the data bank. Programs that have been changed to include unpleasant outcomes, such as erasing data banks, are said to contain a virus, "bombs," or "worms" and are often called "Trojan horse programs."

Not only is it evident that the hardware must be protected, but the software must be protected as well. Access may be limited by requiring a series of passwords to gain entry to programs, and these passwords can be made necessary for several sequential program levels. By using sequential passwords, individuals can be given access to specific program functions while being closed out from other levels. Individual users may be assigned specific identification numbers or code names with which they will have to "log on" the computer, creating a record of who was using which program or program feature.

In line with the concept of information for competitive advantage, companies are taking extraordinary measures on the software level to protect data. This involves the use of a software program that codes the data in such a way that, without the programming code or password, it becomes impossible to understand the data. This process is *data encryption* and consists of scrambling the original data in such a way that it is unrecognizable until it is descrambled. Similar coding programs protect the secrets of most modern nations, but what is new is that the software encryption programs available for even the basic personal computer are so effective that many contain a warning that if the program password or "key" is lost, it will be virtually impossible to unscramble the data.

MANAGERIAL IMPLICATIONS OF IT TRENDS

A satellite placed in a 22,500-mile-high orbit rotates at the same speed as the earth, thus effectively remaining continually over one spot. This is called a geosynchronous orbit (synchronized with the earth) and makes possible data transmission to virtually anyplace on earth where there is a satellite dish receiving station. Information can be relayed through a series of geosynchronous orbit satellites almost instantaneously, and it is now possible to receive data as it is actually happening, *real-time data*. This makes it possible for management to make decisions based upon absolute and current data, more valid data than ever before. The IT must be able to process such data and fashion it so that it is useful to management. Managerial decision-making, which had in the past a buffer of time in which to evaluate information before using it, will not have such evaluative time in the future. Judgments will have to be made more quickly about the validity and usefulness of real-time information.

As management comes to rely on the IT to provide better and more immediate information from any site, however remote, the quality of the decisions produced will depend upon the quality of the information provided. Care will be taken to ensure that the flow and quality of data remain uninterrupted, necessitating both hardware and software security measures as they relate to satellite data transmission. Recently, a disgruntled executive gained control of a satellite transmitter (called an uplink) owned by the Home Box Office cable movie service. This individual interrupted data transmission (of a movie) to millions of households in the United States. This illustrates only one of the threats and opportunities to data transmissions that may dramatically impact upon the MIS.

KNOW THE CONCEPTS
DO YOU KNOW THE BASICS?

1. What is IFCA and why is it important?
2. All levels of organizational management require the same information. True or false?
3. What are the characteristics of information?
4. List the components of the IT.

5. Which should be selected first, hardware or software? Why?

6. How can management protect important data in the MIS?

TERMS FOR STUDY

CPU

CRT

DSS

distributed data processing

DPSO

encryption

ergonomics

hacker

hardware

IFCA

IT

LAN

MIS/IT

MRS

nonroutine decision

programmer

RAM

ROM

routine decision

software

SOP

synchonized work

TPS

user-friendly software

WAN

ANSWERS
KNOW THE BASICS

1. IFCA, information for competitive advantage, is the view that the possession and use of relevant information confers an advantage in the marketplace and enables a company to compete more effectively. It also suggests that information, either generated internally or acquired externally, must be secured in such a way that it remains available and useful to those requiring it but unavailable to those who should be denied access.

2. False. Different organizational levels require different amounts and kinds of information. Top management needs strategic information, but a first-line supervisor needs operational data derived from day-to-day production efforts.

3. The characteristics of information are that they must be appropriate to the task, complete and accurate, and delivered in a timely manner to be useful.

4. The components of the IT are the transaction processing system (TPS), the most basic part of the MIS, gathering and organizing basic business transactions. This component of the MIS does not involve decision-making. For routine decisions that recur within the business organization, a management reporting system (MRS) is used. For nonroutine decisions, each of which is unique, a decision support system (DSS) is utilized.

5. Software should be selected first. It may be a general program or a specific application but in either case is designed to accomplish the desired task. Once the software has been selected, the hardware component can then be purchased. It must be done in this order since, if the order is reversed, there is the real possibility that the selected hardware will be unable to run the necessary software. Select the software first.

6. Data can be protected by (1) physically protecting the IT hardware, and (2) duplicating data and storing the backup copy in a secure location. The software can be protected by the use of sequential passwords that grant access (or limit access) to its data-processing programs. Data can be encrypted or scrambled to keep it from unauthorized viewers.

24
INTERNATIONAL MANAGEMENT

KEY TERMS

MNC multinational company, company established in one country (parent country), doing business in a foreign country (host country); business may be the telemarketing or manufacturing of a product or service

absolute advantage concept that asserts that a country that can produce a product exclusively, or nonexclusively but more cheaply than others, possesses an absolute marketing advantage for that product

comparative advantage principle that asserts that countries should specialize in producing those products in which there is the greatest advantage or the least disadvantage *in relationship to other countries*

global marketing concept popularized by **Theodore Levitt,** marketing expert and editor of the *Harvard Business Review*, which stresses that what people value in product characteristics is converging or becoming alike. This convergence of preference becomes the basis for universal marketing of products with the same or similar marketing techniques no matter what the country.

GATT general agreement on tariffs and trade, international treaty among the leading industrial nations administered through a permanent organization called a secretariat; through this permanent organization, member nations act to jointly reduce tariff and trading barriers

GAAP generally accepted accounting principles, standards of accounting practice developed in an individual country; furnish a standard by which the worth of accounting statements in a country may be evaluated; highly individualistic to specific countries and vary greatly from country to country

Raise the hood of a late-model U.S. automobile, and the realities of contemporary business are immediately apparent. The fuel in the gas tank probably began as crude oil beneath the Arabian desert and may have been refined into gasoline in the Bahamas at an oil refinery owned by a European conglomerate and sold by a local service station. Parts of the engine bear foreign manufacturing labels, and at tune-up time, even the U.S.-made original parts may be replaced by those of foreign origin. Go to any large foreign city and the reverse is true. Films from the United States play in movie theaters, U.S. automobiles abound on the streets, and U.S. products are readily available. Blue jeans, the uniquely American product designed by Levi Straus in the gold fields of California in the 19th century, have become a status product worldwide. International business is a fact of life for everyone, and it is essential to understand its nature, for such business scope and activity present unique but increasingly common problems for management.

A **multinational company (MNC)** is a company established in one country (parent country), doing business in a foreign country (host country). This business may be the marketing or manufacturing of a product or service. This is the most visible form of international business but not the only way in which a company can enter the international arena. Before dealing with the problems of international management, it is necessary to understand why and how companies enter international business. It is certainly true that the rapid growth of the Internet as an international phenomenon has lead to increasing globalization of business. Any search on the "Net" is likely to produce hundreds or even thousands of *hits* or references to web sites located all over the world. If you are going to do business via the Internet, you will be engaged in international business!

INTERNATIONAL BUSINESS: WHY?
ABSOLUTE ADVANTAGE

In general, owing to their geographic location and natural resources, some countries possess what is described as an **absolute advantage.** This describes a condition in which the country can produce a product exclusively, or nonexclusively but more cheaply than others, and therefore possesses an absolute marketing advantage for that product. Although the former rarely exists, there are instances in which natural resources are so concentrated in one or a few countries that companies in those countries possess immense advantage in the marketplace. The production of diamonds in South Africa and tin in Bolivia are prime examples. The latter condition is more common, namely that there are cost advantages to foreign production that confer marketplace advantage. The lower labor costs of Japan in the manufacture of automobiles and lower costs per ton in steel production in Korea give the Japanese automobile companies and the Korean steel companies a strategic advantage in the marketplace. The amount of these products exceeds the ability of the local economy to absorb the units produced, and the excess production is exported to foreign markets. Thus even the little regional steel center in the U.S. heartland may find itself competing against a gigantic Korean steel mill.

COMPARATIVE ADVANTAGE

Since an absolute advantage is rare and—even if derived from price advantages or production efficiencies—difficult to maintain, a different general rationale for international business comes from the concept of comparative advantage. **Comparative advantage** is the principle that asserts that countries should specialize in producing those products in which they have the greatest advantage or the least disadvantage in relationship to other countries. This may be thought of as "job specialization on the international level," and the products created in one country where there is a comparative advantage find their way to areas of the world where local producers cannot match the quality or price. This principle implies that some nations excel in the production of specific goods but other nations do not but will be a ready market for that production.

This made perfect sense in mid-19th century England, which was becoming an economic power by doing what it did best—manufacturing. This manufacturing was fueled by what seemed to be unlimited coal supplies. England sought a colonial empire to achieve a steady stream of raw materials; it would manufacture, what it did best, and the colonies would do what they did best, provide raw materials. Since manufacturing is a value added process, England became a wealthy, powerful, and influential nation. The colonies, viewed merely as suppliers of raw materials, generally remained poor.

This result of the principle of comparative advantage would be merely a remnant of history except that it is present now in the world of contemporary business. The United States and the other major industrial nations possess comparative advantages of production efficiency and technological sophistication. Often the less-developed countries (LDC) that are just emerging into the industrial arena cannot compete with the major industrial nations—cannot match the comparative advantage of advanced technology. Ideally, these LDCs provide raw materials for the industrial nations. However, just as in the last century, given that the manufacturing of a product—not the selling of raw materials—is what produces the highest profit, the LDCs remain much poorer than the industrial nations. Not surprisingly, the LDCs often resent this and have erected barriers to international trade to protect local industry that, lacking the comparative advantage, cannot successfully compete. Any individual active in international business must take such local protectionism into account. The forms of such protective activity are discussed later in this chapter.

YOU SHOULD REMEMBER

Two reasons for companies entering international business are **absolute** and **comparative advantage.** In each of these the individual company, because of a unique circumstance in the geographic environment (cheaper labor, availability of natural resources, and others), achieves a competitive advantage in the marketplace. This advantage is either absolute or relative but rarely lasts for very long. Companies exploiting these advantages should be aware that "necessity is the mother of invention," and the use of absolute or comparative advantage often spurs competitors into new research efforts to overcome the competitor's advantage. (When the supply of natural rubber was cut off to the United States during World War II, scientists developed artificial rubber.)

SPECIFIC REASONS FOR ENTERING THE INTERNATIONAL ARENA
DESIRE TO EXPAND MARKETS

Other than the general philosophical reasons for international business (absolute and comparative advantage), there are several specific factors that might lead a company into the international arena. The first of these factors is the **desire to expand markets.** A company that has saturated a local market may choose to enter a foreign market to find new customers. Given the variation in local taste and custom, it is not surprising that what sells successfully in one country may fail dismally in a different country. Cadbury-Schweppes, the famous and highly successful English food company, once tried to introduce a soft drink called Rondo® into the United States. It had been created in England and successfully introduced into the Australian market. Cadbury's top management could not understand why the drink failed in America until a local marketing expert pointed out that consumers thought that the name Rondo® was a dog food! The need to take local taste into account will be expanded later in this chapter, but it is a general principle that in order to enter a foreign market successfully, it is first necessary to understand that market, its tastes, needs, wants, customs, and even its history.

SEARCH FOR NATURAL RESOURCES

Another reason for a company to enter a foreign country is **availability of natural resources.** A company may need natural resources that are perishable or which do not ship economically. The logical way of minimizing spoilage or transportation difficulties, then, is to locate the production facility in close proximity to the required resources. A fruit juice manufacturer, for example, may locate its processing facility in a country close to the fruit growing grounds and thereby realize great savings.

GLOBAL MARKETING

Yet another reason for the growth of international business is the acceptance of the concept of **global marketing.** This is a concept popularized by **Theodore Levitt,** marketing expert and former editor of the *Harvard Business Review*, which stresses that what people value in product characteristics is converging or becoming alike. This convergence of preference becomes the basis for universal marketing of products with the same or similar marketing techniques no matter what the country. It opens the possibility for a company to greatly expand its market by creating products that appeal to an international audience. The Apple Computer Company builds universality into its Macintosh® computer by printing symbols on the back of the computer case instead of English words so that the model can be sold in foreign countries. IBM now sells its PC® in Arabic-speaking countries with the appropriate keyboard. In both these cases, the product was designed from the beginning to be sold in an international market.

PROXIMITY TO CONSUMER

A fourth reason, similar to the second, that a company might enter the international arena is **proximity to the final consumer or end user.** This is the case when a parent company (located in one country) is producing a product to be sold exclusively in the host country. The economics of such production are that savings can be realized and profits increased by producing in the host country. Transportation costs are minimized, and production can be directly and effectively related to marketing success. This may not be the case if production is done in one country and marketing is accomplished in another. By the time that local marketing trends are recognized, it may be too late for management to react in the host country.

LABOR SAVINGS

A fifth reason for a company to enter into international business is to **realize labor savings.** Business historians have recognized that the genius of

Henry Ford was not that he adapted the assembly line (which existed previously) to automobile production, or even that he invented the automobile (he did not), but that he paid his workers $5/day. This was an extraordinary wage for its day, and not the product of Ford's generosity. He rather despised or disliked workers, and especially labor unions, but realized that such a wage would give workers enough extra money to afford to buy the automobile. In creating customers, Ford did much to create the U.S. middle class and the automobile market.

Ever since the time of Ford, U.S. labor costs have often been among the highest in the world, and many companies have gone overseas to manufacture their goods because such foreign labor costs are often substantially less. Even after factoring in the costs of transporting the manufactured goods back to the U.S. market, the reduced labor costs in the foreign country provide a crucial cost savings. Although the foreign country may believe that, because of its reduced standard of living and wage structure, U.S. manufacturers are exploiting its workers, such manufacturing activity is viewed as desirable. Foreign manufacturing brings in needed U.S. currency, and local workers often gain valuable job skills training in more advanced technologies.

YOU SHOULD REMEMBER

Practical reasons for entering into international business are desire for market expansion, need for natural resources, availability of cheaper local labor, global marketing, and proximity to the consumer or end user.

Almost all the reasons, both general and specific, stated for a company to enter the international arena assume that this is done by means of actually manufacturing a product or delivering a service in the host country. In actuality, international business can assume several different formats. It is now necessary to examine these formats to more fully understand the difficulties faced by managers of international businesses.

INTERNATIONAL BUSINESS: HOW?

International business assumes several different formats. The easiest is the exporting of a company's production to the foreign country, and the most complex form is actual manufacturing in the host country. Each of these is discussed briefly.

EXPORTING

This is when a company sends a product to a foreign country. Many companies have deliberately sought to export their goods to new markets, but still others may be *unintentional* or *passive exporters*. The latter condition exists when a subcontractor supplies parts to a main manufacturer, who then exports the end product assembly to a foreign market. The subcontractor may have no knowledge of the eventual export and only discover its existence when a request for spare subassembly parts is received. Exporting entails much planning, and managers involved with this activity frequently encounter major difficulties in both planning and execution.

Exporters require a license that is secured from the U.S. Department of Commerce. This government regulatory agency considers both the proposed goods and destination in its consideration. In most cases, a *general export license* is issued, and it is not necessary to receive individual permission each time a company wishes to export. However, if the products are of strategic value (valuable and rare) or of potential military use (for example, a powerful computer), it is necessary to secure a *validated export license*. Each case requiring this specific export license is considered on individual merit. Without this specific export permit, the products cannot legally be exported. Any person who subsequently exports such a product without the validated export license is guilty of a punishable crime. A validated export license is also required to export goods to a country that is declared unfriendly to the United States.

Security of technology is a major concern and requires priority attention by management. For example, in recent years such export of potential military technology was not possible to Spain. This was not because Spain was unfriendly to the United States but because it had not joined Cocom, the group of Western countries that had formally committed themselves to withhold technology with potential military applications from the Eastern bloc countries. Thus AT&T was not permitted to sell advanced phone-switching technology to Spain in 1984, even though Spanish officials were willing to meet AT&T's financial terms. Because the U.S. Department of Commerce feared that this technology could be adapted for military communications use, it refused to issue the needed export permit. Spain, seeing that it could not obtain the needed technology and products without assuring the U.S. Commerce Department of its security, formally joined Cocom in 1985, and a state-of-the-art computer chip manufacturing plant was under construction by AT&T in 1986 under the name of AT&T Microelectronics of Spain.

YOU SHOULD REMEMBER

Just because a company wishes to export is no guarantee that it can. It must first secure a **general export license.** If the country to which the exported good is destined is deemed unfriendly to the United States, or if the exported goods are considered of potential military or strategic use, a more restrictive **validated export license** is necessary. Each of these latter cases is considered individually on its specific merits.

International export also requires specific expertise in the area of international shipping, finance, and currency transactions. If a company does not have such resident expertise, it may acquire it by engaging a consultant. For example, some banks specialize in export banking and are equipped to handle the complex aspects of international bill collection and currency transaction. However, many foreign governments have set up offices in this country to facilitate the acquisition of U.S. products. These *resident buying offices* handle all details of export, often help in the obtaining of export licenses by providing documentation, and greatly facilitate exporting success. Because there are often many small companies selling to a single foreign country, a *foreign freight forwarder* is a specialized shipper that consolidates many small export loads into one large economical shipment. Such a specialized shipper constitutes a valuable source of expertise for the small exporter since the forwarder possesses the necessary expertise in dealing with foreign governments and with foreign currency systems.

Although exporting is the most common form of involvement in international business, there are other challenging formats. One of these is foreign licensing, and it presents the manager with both opportunities and difficulties.

FOREIGN LICENSING

Foreign licensing is more complex than merely exporting a product to a different country. In this arrangement, a company in the parent country (called the *licensor*) gives the right to a company in the host country (called the *licensee*) to make use of an exclusive patent, trademark, process, or technology. This license is granted in exchange for a sum of money, usually either a fixed annual fee or a percentage of the derived profits. This is potentially very profitable to the licensor, which (1) already has a proven process or technology, (2) assumes minimal risk, and (3) makes little or no investment other than the transfer of the desired license. However, this is not without risk.

The licensor will want to ensure that the technology transferred with the license is applied correctly. Quality standards may be different in the foreign country, and it can be difficult to ensure quality control from thousands of miles away. Furthermore, needed human and physical resources may not be available or may not be available in the numbers needed. Both the acquiring and selling companies will want to carefully consider the potential effectiveness of a licensing agreement. The interests of neither are served by the licensing if the technology or products are inappropriate.

FOREIGN ASSEMBLY

In this form of international business, a company exports parts from the parent country to the host country, where final product assembly takes place. This offers several benefits to the exporter. Any tax on imported goods imposed by the host country (called an *import duty* or *tariff*) is usually less on parts than on assembled goods. Many foreign countries now require foreign assembly as a way of providing local employment and job skills acquisition in the local workforce. Although providing such employment and job skills training, a company may realize significant labor cost savings because the foreign workers doing the final assembly are paid less than are U.S. workers.

FOREIGN PRODUCTION SUBSIDIARIES

In this form of international business, a company actually establishes a factory in the host country. This may be in conjunction with a local company, called a *joint venture*, or independent of local involvement. Many countries require a joint venture to ensure that local interests are adequately represented. In some instances the host country may even require that a local business own a majority interest in any joint venture before granting the necessary permits. Since this involves the company in the complex array of foreign influences upon the manufacturing venture, from foreign labor unions and local social customs to the very political stability of the host country, it requires utmost managerial attention and abilities. Many companies enter upon the establishment of foreign manufacturing subsidiaries lacking the necessary knowledge of the foreign influences or without having adequately assessed the political risk factors or done the necessary homework. Such situations usually end badly, and it should be remembered that the obvious benefits to be derived from having a manufacturing subsidiary in a foreign country (labor savings, proximity to the end market and to natural resources, and so on) may be outweighed by the risks.

An additional benefit to be derived from the establishment of a foreign manufacturing subsidiary can be seen from the actions of Honda and Volkswagen, which have both opened U.S. assembly plants. The automobiles produced at these plants do not count against any import quotas and allow these companies to increase their share of the U.S. market. Although the situation is not always identical to that of a U.S. manufacturing subsidiary located in a foreign country (in that its production will not be counted within import limits), a U.S. company can make a strong case that such foreign subsidiary production (1) brings needed capital into the foreign country by providing local employment, (2) trains local workers in modern manufacturing job skills, and (3) helps establish links with industrialized countries and may lead to further opportunities.

YOU SHOULD REMEMBER

Foreign business can assume the following forms: **exporting, foreign licensing,** or **foreign assembly of products.** This last form may be either a **joint venture** with a local partner (which may be required by foreign law) or a wholly owned **foreign manufacturing subsidiary.** Each of these forms offers advantages to the parent company, and they all illustrate the need to understand the foreign culture in which business will be done.

INTERNATIONAL BUSINESS: THE PROBLEMS

International business, ranging from exporting to a foreign manufacturing subsidiary, involves management in a wide variety of problems that are not present in a domestic operation. As more companies become involved in forms of international business, there is an increasing need for managers who have the abilities to deal with the associated problems.

COMMUNICATION

One of the first and most obvious problems encountered by managers in the international environment is that of language differences. Even when a company engages the services of an expert translator, the idiomatic or slang meanings of words often give rise to unintended communication. For example, consider the following:

- The General Motors Corporation once touted the quality of its automobile bodies, in the United States with the end phrase "body by Fisher." In Flemish, however, this became "corpse by Fisher."

- This same company tried to sell its well-received Chevrolet model, called the Nova, in Puerto Rico, only to discover that the name (which meant "Star") was being pronounced "no va," which means "no go" in Spanish. It was not surprising that sales were disappointing until the name was changed to Caribe.

- The Rolls Royce Motor Car Company, Ltd., of England, makers of the most expensive and prestigious automobiles in the world, thought that they had a winner in the Silver Mist model name. It was intended to convey a sense of luxury and softness, of absolute and uncompromising quality. In German, however, the translation of the word "mist" really meant "excrement." Understandably the name was changed for the German market.

Communication difficulties are not only to be found in product marketing; they also interfere with business negotiations.

- During business negotiations, a U.S. manager proposed that the issue under discussion be "tabled." The English negotiator subsequently brought the same issue up, much to the confusion of the Americans. To "table an issue" means to *not* bring it up to Americans, but to the British it means exactly the opposite, to bring it up.

- A different U.S. business negotiator created havoc when he proposed, quite innocently, that the French buyers of a foreign bank put their purchase payments temporarily into an "escrow account." The French buyers became incensed, shouted "never," and so rattled the sellers that the deal was canceled. It seems that an "escrow account" was translated into French as a "gyp account."

CULTURAL DIFFERENCES

Anyone wishing to do business in a foreign country can commit no greater error than to assume that what works at home will work elsewhere. In past decades, the tendency of Americans to insist that foreign businesses do it the U.S. way has been termed the "ugly American syndrome." It should not be surprising that many Americans were regarded with great derision. There is an increasing sophistication in the way in which U.S. managers approach the international arena. They seek to understand the cultural differences that dictate the form for effective operations in a foreign country. How might a company err in the foreign country? The following examples graphically illustrate the point.

- A company selling baby food in an African country pictured a smiling child on the outside of the jar. The local customers assumed, with a certain justification, that there were canned babies inside and avoided the product.

- A manager, negotiating a deal in Greece, lost a major contract when he failed to understand local customs as they involved attitudes toward time and negotiations. His Greek counterpart could not understand the American's insistence upon setting time limits for their business meetings. The American also insisted that the senior managers work out the general principles of the deal and leave the details to subordinates. The Greeks regarded this as devious since they had a different view of time—they were prepared to spend as much time as necessary working out all the details.

- Another hapless U.S. manager almost lost a large contract when he refused to accept a cup of coffee from an Arab executive. This ill-informed American did not realize that coffee was not only a social amenity, but also a formality of friendship and trust. When he turned down the cup of coffee, he insulted his host and called into question the validity of the negotiation. The deal did not fall through, but negotiations were much more difficult.

- It is well known that in the Islamic religion alcohol is forbidden to the faithful, and few if any Western business people would offer such a gift to their Arab counterparts. It is less well known that giving a cloak in the People's Republic of China can kill a deal because the Chinese word for cloak sounds like the word for funeral. This has extremely negative connotations for the future of any business deal. One should also not give knives or handkerchiefs in Latin America since they imply, in many countries and cultural settings, either the cutting off of a relationship or the eventuality of a tearful event.

It is necessary, then, to consider a foreign culture before doing business in that culture. Learning about a culture involves becoming familiar with its history, customs, and beliefs, including local conceptualizations of time, space, friendship, and obligation.

Since culture is such a complex enterprise extending over not only a geographic area but also duration of time (sometimes thousands of years), it is generally recognized that it is impossible for a foreigner to completely understand its depth and richness. A company can greatly enhance its chances of success in the foreign environment, however, by preparing managers in a formal and rigorous manner to do business in the foreign country with lectures and presentations detailing that culture *before* sending the manager to the country. Ability to speak the host language, although not absolutely necessary, should be considered *highly* desirable. Screen out executives who are in some way biased against the foreign culture; they may be fine managers in the United States but should not be sent overseas. Finally, hire local managers as employees or consultants to advise U.S. executives as to the proper manner in which to conduct business. Such an expense, although costly at the beginning, pays off in the long run in terms of establishing the company as serious about the foreign involvement and sensitive to local culture.

YOU SHOULD REMEMBER

It is absolutely necessary to understand a foreign culture in order to successfully do business within that culture. This understanding should be provided to employees before they are sent overseas. The company should also seek local counsel and advice as to business practice. To insist that all business be done on the U.S. model leads to inevitable failure; managers who insist upon doing things the way they are done back in the home office in Indiana are often branded in a derisive manner the "ugly American."

PROTECTIONISM AND TRADE BARRIERS

Many countries seek to protect their local industries against the threat of foreign business. Sometimes these local industries are aged and cannot compete against other companies. Sometimes these industries are young and still developing but also cannot compete against more established industrialized nations. This protectionism of local industry can take the following forms:

- A *tariff* is a tax levied against an import that raises its price so that it is equal or higher than the locally produced goods. For example, the Japanese originally placed a small tariff on U.S. tomato paste, but when it became popular with Japanese housewives and made significant inroads into the local market, it was suddenly classified as a "confectionary" and tariffed at the 35 percent level, significantly raising its local price.

- With a *quota*, the government limits the quantity of foreign goods allowed to enter the country, in order to protect local industry. For example, Volkswagen has voluntarily agreed to a quota for automobile importation so as not to provoke U.S. governmental protectionism. It should be noted, however, that this German company has also established a domestic automobile factory and that these cars are not counted against the voluntary quota.

- An *embargo* is a government prohibition against the entry of foreign goods into the country. For example, some medicines from foreign countries are not allowed to be sold in the United States.

An embargo may have as its function not only the protection of local industry but also protection of the population since it will keep out inferior goods that do not meet local health and testing standards. For example, if the United States does not believe that beef produced in Argentina meets local USDA standards, its importation can and has been embargoed.

Management must be aware of protectionist sentiments in terms of importing to a country. The establishment of a foreign production subsidiary is often a way to get around such protectionist sentiments, but as we have stated, there is often a local requirement to have a foreign national (or sometimes the government itself) as a partner.

Furthermore, protectionism often leads to retaliation in the form of counter-protectionism. In an attempt to keep nations from being at each others' throats in terms of protectionist actions, the WTO was created. The WTO **(World Trade Organization)** is an international treaty among the leading industrial nations that is administered through a permanent organization called a *secretariat*. It is through this permanent organization that member nations act jointly to reduce tariff and trading barriers. Constant negotiations take place between trading nations, and business executives who seek to enter the international arena need to be aware of the nature and status of such negotiations. The outcome of these negotiations can and often does impact the way in which international business is done.

YOU SHOULD REMEMBER

Managers should be aware of trends in trade protectionism in both the parent and host countries. Host country protectionism impacts the nature of importing and ability to secure resources from outside the country, and protectionist activity back home in the parent country may provoke a reaction in the other countries in the world. Governments often consider the **tariff, quota,** and **embargo** as foreign policy tools, but business must always view them as significant influences upon potential commercial success.

CONTROL AND ACCOUNTING STANDARDS

The issue of control is frequently a major difficulty confronting the international manager. Foreign business activities are far from the home office and often involve local partners. If local managers do not share the same goals and strategic concerns as the home office, there can be a great deal of friction. There may be disagreement about quality control standards, performance expectations, and acceptable courses of action.

Control as a management issue is highlighted by the differences between markets. What is done and accepted in one country may not be so in a different country, yet the same product may be sold in both. The data from one country will not be comparable to the data from the other country, and management must be aware of the differences and lack of comparable data. For example, the NAVISTAR Corporation (formerly International Harvester) produces tractors in its U.S. factories with highly automated equipment. It produces the same tractors in a foreign plant, however, using much more manual labor. The performance data on each kind of plant cannot and should not be compared with each other since the fundamental production conditions are different. The lack of comparability of data from country to country creates control problems for the international manager. **GAAP (generally accepted accounting principles)** are standards of accounting practice developed in an individual country. They furnish a standard by which the worth of accounting statements in a country may be evaluated. They are highly individualistic to specific countries and vary greatly from country to country.

The issue of control is often accentuated by the fact that the home office will depend upon accounting data to evaluate local performance. The problem arises when accounting standards and practices vary greatly between countries. For example, an English firm called the British Oxygen Company had a 1983 income of £55 million, but by U.S. standards this same company's income was £93 million. The difference between these income figures is due to the differences in accounting procedures and standards (actually in this case, the difference is to be found in different depreciation procedures).

In 1973, the *International Accounting Standards Committee (IASC)* created a common language for accountants so that the GAAP for each country could be made comparable. The end result would be to produce comparable financial statements, but these common terms have not found wide use. There are no universal accounting rules, and the difficulties of understanding and making comparable accounting data remain a significant problem for the international business executive. One of the ways in which the U.S. accounting profession has tried to deal with this problem is to establish local subsidiaries. In this way, U.S. accountants can provide data for managerial control by the home office.

With the emergence of the **European Union (the EU)** and adoption of a common currency **(the euro)** on New Year's Day 1999, businesses were given until December 31, 2001, to make necessary changes to accommodate the new money. By mid-2002, the goal of the EU is to replace individual national currencies with the euro. Anyone doing business with European Union companies must likewise be prepared to switch over to the new currency. Many American countries are, during the 1999–2002 time period, keeping two financial accounting books—one for euro transactions and one for all other transactions.

It should also be noted that often foreign business practices necessitate the payment of bribes, often euphemistically called consulting fees, charitable donations, or commissions, to ensure favorable governmental or business treatment. The Foreign Corrupt Practices Act of 1977 outlawed such practices.

HUMAN RESOURCES: ACQUISITION AND TRAINING

A company seeking to establish a foreign presence, from a local sales representative to a full-scale manufacturing subsidiary, faces the problem of acquiring the necessary human resources. As we have seen, if personnel are to be sent from the home office, they should be carefully selected, trained, and aided during their time overseas. These expatriate managers should ideally know the local language and be intimately familiar with local customs and traditions. The differences in customs may present problems of socialization for not only the manager but also the accompanying family. There may be different standards of education for children, and in many cultures women occupy a far different and less liberated role than in the United States. Given the difficulties of an overseas management assignment, the U.S. government has sought to encourage such expatriate managerial activity. The U.S. Tax Code exempts much of the salary and benefits earned overseas from taxation as a form of encouragement.

A more difficult problem may be found in acquiring local human resources. Local personnel imply local customs that may be quite different from those to which the U.S. manager is accustomed. U.S. managers take for granted a superior managerial position of power that allows personnel assignment, performance appraisal, and employee discipline. Furthermore, U.S. standards of employee attendance and acceptance of absenteeism are not universal norms; many foreign cultures have different standards in these areas, and it is the burden of the U.S. manager to adapt to local custom. In many cultures the manager may not even have the power to terminate a poor employee. Local custom assures the employee a job because job security is considered more a social benefit than individual job performance.

The company may be faced with the seemingly impossible task of recruiting a local workforce. If the level of technology in the manufacturing plant is too high, the local workers may not possess the necessary technological skills. Management is then faced with two possibilities: (1) lower the employee skill level needed by using a reduced technology level or (2) train the local workers. The latter alternative is often very attractive to the host country since it facilitates skill acquisition by local workers and raises the local industrial capacity.

YOU SHOULD REMEMBER

A major problem confronting the company seeking to do manufacturing overseas is the availability of a suitably skilled labor force. If such a labor force is not readily available, the company may have to create an extensive training effort to raise the skill levels of the local workers. Even given the expense of this training effort, the resulting labor costs may still be less than in the home country and lead to substantial savings. Such training also benefits the host country in that the skills level of local employees is raised.

PIRACY

One of the major problems increasingly encountered in the international realm is that of **piracy.** This is the willful violation of copyrights, patents, and trademarks and is possible because many of the less developed countries do not have the same levels of legal protection for these forms of intellectual property.

Generally, trademark and patent (intellectual property) rights, guaranteed under local law, are described as *territorial*—protection ends at the border. While over 200 countries have some form of trademark registration systems or a way of protecting patents, procedures and protections vary from country to country. A company with intellectual property is well advised to seek such protection in every country where it is likely to encounter piracy. This assembly of country-specific protection is referred to as a *portfolio approach*.

The largest losers in the United States are the drug companies, record and entertainment companies, high-technology companies, and fashion companies. Drugs are routinely counterfeited, as are blue jeans, computers, records and videotapes, and just about anything else that can be copied.

For example, Apple was faced with the importation of a cheap copy made in the Far East called, somewhat ironically, the Pineapple. It looked the same as the comparable Apple computer and performed the same but lacked the quality components and had no guarantee. Certified Apple dealers would not repair this illegal copy, and its owners had difficulty in getting it repaired when it inevitably broke down. Additionally, Argentineans seeking Feldene, an antiarthritis drug, had a 90 percent chance of getting a local copy that may or may not have met the original drug manufacturer's standards of purity and effectiveness.

Piracy, it is estimated, costs U.S. manufacturers over $25 billion a year. This amounts to a significant handicap for companies entering into the international arena and may actually force local U.S. companies into combat with the offending companies. It is not strictly a U.S. problem but impacts upon every industrialized country. Recently, IBM, Pfizer, General Electric, Monsanto, and several other large U.S. companies banded together into an informal intellectual property committee to oppose international piracy. This group has attempted to enlist international support by contacting the Siemens and Hoechst companies in Germany and beginning discussion with several large Japanese industrial companies. This informal committee has also lobbied Congress to seek a diplomatic accord with countries that allow and even encourage piracy.

Intellectual property is protected under the international conventions signed in Paris and Bern in the late 1800s, but these conventions have no enforcement power. Now companies and even governments are recognizing that such piracy harms not only specific companies but the industrial efforts of all countries as well. The less-developed countries, in support of piracy, often claim that patents, copyrights, and trademarks are part of the common heritage of all peoples and should therefore be universally available. The more radical of the third world powers go so far as to assert that these trademarks, patents, and copyrights are the "shackles of imperialism" and an attempt on the part of the industrialized nations to control the flow of ideas. One of the trends emerging in the realm of international business is toward greater protection for individual effort. Even those countries, such as Brazil, India, Taiwan, and Argentina, that have evidenced the most support for piracy are feeling the international influence of the more developed countries. The message is clear: allow and encourage piracy, and other countries will limit the ability of their companies to export technology to you. This area continues to be one of great concern, a trend of which U.S. managers must be aware.

INTERNATIONAL BUSINESS: MANAGERIAL CONCERNS

Companies may choose to enter the international arena for either offensive or defensive reasons. A business may seek to expand aggressively into new markets (offensive) or to establish a more stable base market or base of operations (defensive). In either case, management is confronted with the same problems as on the local level but in a more diverse and highly complex arrangement.

In all organizations, managers are confronted with the need to acquire and effectively make use of scarce resources. This is no different in the international realm but often more complicated because the resource markets are foreign. Such issues as the political and economic stability of the resource source, its reliability, style of business, and currency fluctuation must be taken into account by the international manager.

As we have seen, the acquisition and effective use of human resources often present the international manager with his or her biggest challenge. The traditions of worker-manager relations may vary greatly from that of the manager's home country experience. Skill levels and commitment to a traditional work ethic may vary between countries, and management cannot assume that such problems can be solved either by throwing money into worker training or insisting that workers conform to a different philosophy of work. Such insistence will merely infuriate local workers and waste valuable training funds. International management must be aware of local customs and human resource traditions and plan accordingly. In areas of the world in which there is a less sophisticated workforce, international managers may have to make use of suitable technologies that can be efficiently utilized by local workforces.

The concepts of control previously discussed (input, process, and output controls) are applicable in international management, but it should be recognized that there may be local variations. Some cultures may not be as committed to each of these control mechanisms, and the standards applied in each country may differ. For example, Americans place great value upon yearly performance appraisals, but there are countries committed to a socialist ideal in which, since the goal is to have maximal employment, performance appraisals have very little importance.

Additionally, every culture has its own unique leadership styles and motivational techniques, and international managers must adapt their own styles and techniques to what is effective in the host country. In general, the keys to managerial success in the international realm are *awareness* and flexibility. Managers must be aware of regional variations and allow for them. The same management problems of goal definition, planning, organizational design, supervision and control, and task evaluation exist in the international business venture just as in every U.S. company. The international arena complicates the task, but awareness and flexibility facilitate international success.

INTERNATIONAL BUSINESS SUCCESS: AN EXAMPLE

Makudonarudo and Den Fujita are not names readily known or understood by U.S. businesses, but they should be. Both are connected with an unlikely success of U.S. business in a foreign country that defied the odds and should be studied in every business school in the United States. Makudonarudo is the Japanese pronunciation of McDonald's and the architect of its unlikely commercial success in the Land of the Rising Sun is **Mr. Den Fujita.**

Japan would seem one of the least likely countries for a successful McDonald's operation. Consider the cultural facts. Because of the lack of pastureland, meat is very expensive, not a normal part of the daily diet; Japan is the land of fish, sushi and sashimi; the Japanese have developed a substitute for meat protein in the form of bean curd, tofu, that has been part of the national diet for thousands of years; and finally, the U.S. origins of McDonald's is not considered an asset.

When McDonald's planned in the early 1970s to enter the Japanese market, it first sought out a local partner who knew the Japanese culture and character. It found Den Fujita, who has overcome all the disadvantages and made McDonald's the largest fast-food business in Japan. In 15 years, sales had gone from virtually nothing to over $770 million, fully 36 percent of all McDonald's foreign sales. Fujita emphasized the nature of the food, not its U.S. origin, and convinced the Japanese that beef should be more a part of the national diet. This was despite the fact that the national utensil, the chopstick, was inappropriate for eating a hamburger.

Furthermore, Fujita had the courage to insist that McDonald's had to adapt itself to the unique character of the Japanese marketplace. Fast-food outlets were opened in the inner city, not in the suburbs as in the United States. This involved Fujita in a major dispute with the corporate leadership of McDonald's in Oak Brook, Illinois, who wanted to do business just as they do in the United States. Fujita's point was that the pedestrians located in Japan's thriving cities were better potential customers than affluent drivers in the suburbs. He was right and showed McDonald's corporate leadership that such an outlet location could achieve high sales. In fact, the McDonald's located in the popular Tokyo shopping area known as the Ginza set a world record for one day's sales. Corporate leadership learned the lesson; urban outlets could be highly profitable, and now U.S. city locations for McDonald's are common.

Fujita also found that the U.S. formula for expansion—franchising—would not work in Japan. This was not a common or well-received arrangement in Japan. No one wanted to purchase a franchise or share profits with a parent company. So Fujita opened his own franchised outlets and now finds himself in a highly unusual and extremely profitable position. He owned 480 of the 560 McDonald's stores in Japan in 1986 and adds 50–60 new stores each year. He is corporate McDonald's largest franchiser, and in 1984 was the first foreigner named an advisory director of the parent corporation. His personal wealth is estimated at over $1 billion.

All in all, McDonald's triumph in Japan against what must be considered overwhelming odds can serve as a shining example for all international managers. It can be done, as most recently demonstrated in Japan by Toys 'R' Us.

KNOW THE CONCEPTS
DO YOU KNOW THE BASICS?

1. What is an MNC?
2. What is an absolute advantage in marketing?
3. What is a comparative advantage in the marketplace?
4. What is GATT, and why is it important for international business?
5. Define GAAP, and tell why this creates difficulties for international businesses.
6. What are the practical reasons for a company expanding into the world of international business?
7. What are the forms of international business?
8. What is a foreign freight forwarder, and how is this useful for international business?

TERMS FOR STUDY

absolute advantage	IASC
comparative advantage	import duty or tariff
embargo	joint venture
foreign freight forwarder	licensee
foreign licensing	licensor
foreign manufacturing subsidiary	MNC
GAAP	passive or unintentional exporting
GATT	quota
general export license	resident buying office
global marketing	validated export license

ANSWERS
KNOW THE BASICS

1. A multinational company (MNC) is a company established in one country (parent country), doing business in a foreign country (host country). This business may be the marketing or manufacturing of a product or service.
2. Absolute advantage is a concept that asserts that a country that can produce a product exclusively, or nonexclusively but more cheaply than others, possesses an absolute marketing advantage for that product.

3. Comparative advantage is the principle that asserts that countries should specialize in producing those products in which there is the greatest advantage or the least disadvantage *in relationship to other countries.*

4. WTO (World Trade Organization) is an international treaty among the leading industrial nations that is administered through a permanent organization called a secretariat. It is through this permanent organization that member nations act jointly to reduce tariff and trading barriers. It is important for international business in that it is the appropriate forum for individual governments (lobbied by businesses) to seek reductions in protectionist activity and market expansion. Increasingly, it is also the forum in which individual governments can protest international trademark, patent, or copyright piracy.

5. GAAP (generally accepted accounting principles) are standards of accounting practice developed in an individual country. They furnish a standard by which the worth of accounting statements in a country may be evaluated. They are highly individualistic to specific countries and vary greatly from country to country. Because the are individualistic to the country, however, they create problems for management seeking to understand a foreign subsidiary's results and compare those results with other offices. It becomes difficult to compare accounting results across national boundaries.

6. Reasons for going into international business include market expansion, availability of natural resources or a cheap labor supply, the concept of global marketing, and proximity to the final consumer or end user.

7. Forms of international business are exporting, foreign licensing, joint venture, and foreign manufacturing subsidiary.

8. A foreign freight forwarder is a specialized shipper that consolidates many small export loads into one large economical shipment. Such a specialized shipper constitutes a valuable source of expertise for the small exporter since the forwarder possesses the necessary expertise in dealing with foreign governments and with foreign currency systems.

25

CHANGING TRENDS IN MANAGEMENT

If you had lived in northern India 2100 years ago and seen this simple invention, you would not have realized that it was to shape much of the world. Its impact was beyond the power of anyone to predict, yet it helped create and continues to influence the world of everyone reading this book. What is this object of such historic impact and significance? A shoestring.

Ancient Indian illustrations show men riding horses, steadying themselves by placing the big toe in loops of fabric, a shoestring. This method of riding was transmitted to China by Buddhist missionaries, and it appears in the Hunan province by 523 AD. China has a colder climate, however, and the simple toe loop became a stirrup capable of holding the rider's entire foot. The result of a full-foot stirrup is to steady the rider and allow the achievement of greater speed. The horse and rider began to realize greater potential, and this riding system spread to many countries by the late 7th century. No one knows how the stirrup reached Europe, but it had reached the kingdom of the Franks (ancient France, Germany, and Italy) by the 8th century.

This would be a mere historic footnote except that the stirrup not only allowed one to ride faster, it also allowed the effective use of a lance and sword. Before the stirrup the rider could only strike downward by standing up and ran the risk of being thrown off the animal because the platform from which the striking was done was not steady. Once the rider was secure the lance became a terrible weapon since the full power of a large horse could be transmitted along its shaft. This was a shock to the rider but a greater shock to the individual at the other end. The stirrup allowed the rider to concentrate on achieving maximum carnage, secure in the saddle while protected by heavy armor. This created the need for stronger horses, and with selective crossbreeding, the warhorse standing over 7 feet tall became a reality.

All this meant that only someone with a lot of money who could afford a horse, armor, and their upkeep could gain and hold power. Kings, needing such support, granted land to loyal followers so that they could raise horses and tax ordinary people to raise the money necessary to support the horses and maintain armor. This land grant system laid the foundation for the medieval social system and ensured that power would reside in the hands of the wealthy for over 500 years.

On Saturday, October 14, 1066, Harold, the Saxon King of England, battled Duke William of Normandy (later called the Conqueror) for possession of England. As depicted 11 years later in the Bayeux Tapestry, the French soldiers on horseback made extensive use of the stirrup. The English under Harold also had the stirrup but did not make general use of it. The French won, and by 5 PM on that Saturday, King Harold was dead and England had become Norman. Had that event not happened this book might not have been written in English. All from a shoestring!

This final chapter deals with the changing trends and future directions of management and in many ways is the most difficult to write. Management takes place within organizations that exist in rapidly changing environments. These changes have a dramatic impact upon the practice of management. The future directions of management are found in the emerging trends in the environment, but forecasting the future is more art than science and an inexact art at best. It is difficult to know (1) which events will have a significant impact upon management and (2) what that impact will be. No one could have predicted the impact of that ancient Indian shoestring, and it is almost impossible to accurately predict the trends that will be the shoestrings of today.

However, this chapter presents eight emerging trends that have the potential of dramatically impacting U.S. business and the practice of management. They are, to be sure, not the only trends that will influence business, but awareness of such trends allows the *anticipation* of emerging trends rather than a mere reaction. The difference between anticipation and reaction may be nothing less than organizational survival.

CHANGING NATURE OF WORK
THE RISE OF THE INFORMATION ECONOMY

As pointed out by **John Naisbitt** in his blockbuster bestsellers *Megatrends* and *Megatrends 2000,* U.S. business is shifting away from its traditional industrial base to an information-based service economy. The historic industrial base is popularly called *smokestack America*, a term employed to represent the traditional manufacturing core of U.S. industry. Examples of smokestack industries are steel, coal, and automobiles.

This change in the nature of work represents a *structural change* in U.S. industry, a fundamental shift from one kind of productive activity to another. Selling a steel factory and using the money to open a factory to manufacture Teflon-coated pots is not a structural change, merely shifting from one kind of manufacturing activity to another. Selling a steel factory and using the money to create an Internet-based data-processing company represents a structural change, from manufacturing to information processing. This is graphically shown in Figure 25-1.

Structural changes are not new; the United States has seen it before. Originally an agricultural economy, it progressed through mercantilism and manufacturing to services and information processing. In 1979, the occupation employing the greatest number of workers was that of the clerk. Previously this position was held by the laborer, and before that, by the farmer. The fastest growing occupational categories are now to be found in the area of information technology and processing—commonly called *information workers*. Information and service jobs are computer programmers, teachers, secretaries, stockbrokers, researchers, lawyers, bankers, accountants, financial advisors—professionals of all kinds—people who spend their time creating, processing, or distributing information. The growth of information jobs has been one of the most dramatic shifts in the last three decades. This growth is shown in Figure 25-2. As can be seen, only 17 percent of the workforce labored in what could be described as information jobs in 1950, but

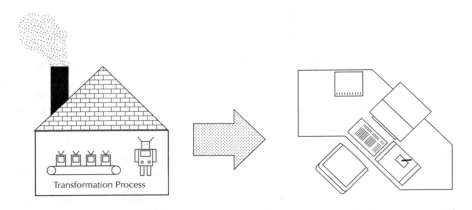

Figure 25-1. The manufacturing ⎯⎯⎯→ information shift.

by 1983 this had increased to 65 percent, and it is projected that the position of systems analyst will show even more explosive growth over the 1996–2006 time frame—increasing by a total of 519,600 jobs. This growth is even more dramatic when you consider that the service economy itself has stayed constant between 10 and 11 percent during the 1950–1995 time frame. This growth of information jobs as a percentage of the total workforce is shown in Figure 25-3. As can be seen, the service sector remained relatively constant at 10–11 percent while the information or knowledge worker segment grew from 17 to 65 percent during the same time frame, and is projected to grow even further.

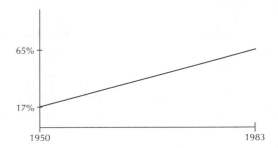

Figure 25-2. Growth of the information career.

These jobs, either in the new Internet-based industries or information jobs within established industries, will impact the practice of management. Productivity will be defined differently than on the assembly line, and managers will have to be even more skilled at motivating employees. Since information workers do not conform to the blue-collar factory worker image, these jobs will be attractive to individuals with higher levels of education.

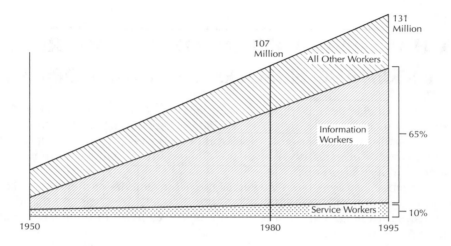

Figure 25–3. Growth of information as a percentage of the workforce.

Even within the manufacturing sector, employment growth will reflect this shift to higher-skilled jobs, and this is the second trend we shall examine.

SHIFT TO HIGHER SKILLED JOBS

The second major change that will impact the practice of management will be the shift from lower skilled to higher skilled jobs. According to the *Monthly Labor Review* (Sept. 99), this will be seen in the projected growth in various job categories over the 1996–2006 time frame. These projected rates of job increase are shown in Table 25-1. The greatest growth in new jobs in the industrial sector will be in the first two categories, systems analyst and general manager. The projected growth in these jobs is far greater than in any other class of jobs. Increasingly, then, managers will be dealing with higher skilled workers with greater levels of formal, informal, and technical education. An additional change in the workforce will be seen in the coming decade—more workers.

Table 25–1 Projected Number of Job Opening Increases by 2006

Position	Increase
Systems Analyst	519,600
General Manager	467,000
Database Administrators, Computer Supply Personnel, Computer Scientists	249,200
Computer Engineers	235,300
Computer Programmers	129,200

CHANGING NATURE OF THE WORKER
INCREASING NUMBERS OF OLDER WORKERS

The third change that will impact the practice of management will be the dramatic increase in the numbers of older workers in the workforce in the next decade. The increase of these workers reflects an ongoing trend and the source of much concern over the ability of this country to emerge as a great industrial power.

U.S. labor history is often viewed as the achievements of the great builders, the moguls of the industrial age, the uniquely American pantheon of industrial royalty, including the oil barons, the captains of commerce, and the princes of industry. The historical reality is that, if the United States has provided the arena for individual accomplishment in the area of industrial achievement, it has also provided the arena for the achievements of the mass of workers. They have, upon their backs and with their hands, with the sweat of their brows and strain of their arms, built this great country. Industrial expansion and growth required and continues to require a source of labor. The U.S. labor force has increased faster than the general population. This is shown in Figure 25-4 (see page 497). As can be seen, the total population in 1980 was 226 million, 47.3 percent of whom (107 million) were workers. The population in 1995 increased to an estimated 260 million, a 15 percent jump from 1980. During the same period, however, the labor population increased from 107 million to an estimated 131 million, a 22 percent increase. U.S. economic prosperity is linked to an increasing labor force. As labor needs continue to increase in the 21st century, where will these workers come from?

Some will come from the baby boom generation who, having moved on in large numbers into the midlevel managerial workforce, are remaining in the labor force longer—hence the "graying of the labor force" discussed earlier. Some will come from where they always have, foreign countries. These so-called undocumented workers already make up a large part of some industries.

- It is estimated that such undocumented workers make up 10–20 percent of all workers in Silicon Valley.

- In Houston, it is estimated that 30 percent of all workers in the construction trades and 70 percent of the highway department workers are undocumented.

As the age of the U.S. labor force increases in the higher skill and technical levels, even more workers will be needed. While illegal workers will help fill out the lower skilled jobs, along with increasing numbers of legal immi-

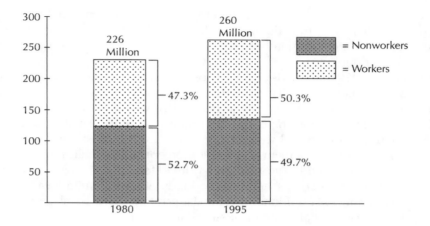

Figure 25–4. Workers and percentage of workers in the population in the 1980–1995 time frame.

grants who seek America as a land of opportunity, the value of an education will increase. It is well documented that each year of education beyond high school pays real dividends in terms of lifetime earnings; the more one learns, the more one earns. Scholars at the University of California, in labor studies, have maintained that such industries as clothing, food processing, and some areas of health care would suffer dramatically if foreign workers were taken out of their employee rosters. Foreign workers bring a more traditional work ethic, solid work habits, and less of an absenteeism rate to the job. They are good employees and, according to some writers, not a threat to the U.S. worker. Foreign workers generally take jobs that U.S. workers spurn and benefit themselves, their employers, and the general economy. Finally, the increasing needs of more workers will be answered by the growing number of women entering the workforce.

WOMEN IN THE WORKFORCE

As both social values and economics have changed over the last four decades, women are entering the workforce in increasing numbers. This has been in response to the demand for workers and the need for women to contribute to the household income. From the 1940s through the 1960s, and for much of U.S. history previous to this period, the model for women was wife-mother-nurturer. This was reflected in the language of the period in which women cited "homemaker" as their primary occupation. It was also reflected in the early television shows that featured families; the man was the breadwinner and the woman was continually portrayed as a housewife. Beginning in the late 1960s and early 1970s, women were shown as workers, but their labor was to support a single-parent family. The woman of the

1980s is shown working not only to support a single-parent family but also to contribute to a partnership or to seek self-fulfillment. Since 1965, the percentage of married women between the ages of 25 and 34 who work has more than doubled.

In fact, by 1998, almost 46 percent of the entire workforce was female, representing almost 60 million full-time women workers, and this trend has continued. Indeed, the percentage of women workers is over 50 percent when the number of part-time female workers is added in. Dual income families where both men and women work now are the most common type, having risen from 10 percent to over 40 percent of all families in America. The most significant thing about this amount of female participation in work is not only the percentage but also the kinds of jobs women have. These jobs are not only the traditional "pink-collar positions" of clerical, secretarial, or staff positions but also the professions and line management. For example, the following increases in female participation in the labor force occurred over the 1970–1998 time frame: architect—4 percent to 18 percent; chemist—12 percent to 33 percent; computer systems analyst or scientist—14 percent to 27 percent; operations or systems researcher or analyst—11 percent to 42 percent; pharmacist—12 percent to 44 percent; physician—10 percent to 27 percent; psychologist—39 percent to 62 percent; public relations specialist—27 percent to 66 percent. (Source: *Women's Figures*, 1999 edition). Many of these jobs, once viewed as almost exclusively male positions, are now increasingly being filled by capable women who are making their presence known.

The most immediate impact of this trend of greater female participation in the workforce will be that (1) more managers will be women and (2) increasingly the employee to be managed will be a woman. Discrimination is legally prohibited in the workplace based upon race, religion, national origin, age, or sex. This means that sexual harassment can be legally punished, and men who are used to having women at home as wives and mothers must get used to having these same women as colleagues, subordinates, superiors, and competitors in the workplace. This generation may be remembered for changing the ideal of woman from wife-mother-nurturer to wife-mother-nurturer-business executive.

The need for women in the workplace will be made even greater by the fact that the number of young people is declining. This is a sign of a significant change in demographics. *Demographics* is the science of measuring and analyzing data about the population. It relies heavily upon survey research and census data. One of its basic measures is the *cohort*, the number of individuals born in any one year. The cohort size for those born in the 1960s was smaller than that of preceding generations, and for each year in the next decade the cohort size continued to decline. As a result of the declining birth rate since the early 1960s, there are fewer young people who are now 18 (as the size of their parent's generation—those born in the early 1960s was smaller). This is the next trend to be examined.

FEWER YOUNG PEOPLE

The number of births per 1000 women declined dramatically between 1960 and 1995. From 118 births per 1000 women in 1960, the rate declined to only 45 in 1995. The effect of this reduced birthrate will be felt for years to come as there are fewer individuals of work age.

This trend continues, although with slight increases on a year-to-year basis. These changes will have dramatic impacts upon those businesses that have traditionally depended upon or employed teenagers. Such businesses as seasonal tourist employment and fast-food restaurants are experiencing difficulty in recruiting needed human resources. The decline in the teenage population will also impact the military, which traditionally recruits from high school graduates, and colleges, which also are dependent upon the teenage market. Indeed, in 1999, the Army proposed offering new recruits a $20,000 sign-on bonus in order to induce young people to enlist.

Management will be challenged to compensate for the loss in teenage labor. Some of this compensation will come from the increased use of robots in industrial areas that lend themselves to mechanization. Robots, looking nothing like the monster on last night's late show, will perform tasks that are either repetitive (and therefore boring to human workers) or extremely hazardous to the human worker. In the late 1990s, Toyota, the most productive automobile manufacturer in the world, produced 3,670,000 vehicles with 23,000 workers. This was 159.5 vehicles per employee. Ford, on the other hand, produced only 3,200,000 vehicles with 37,000 employees, for a production ratio of 86.48 vehicles per employee. One of the reasons that Toyota was almost twice as productive as Ford was the extensive use of industrial robots. In 1981 Toyota used 630 robots; in 1986 the number was 2210, and the number of robots has steadily increased.

Managers in many of the businesses affected by the decline in the youth population cannot make extensive use of mechanization—industries, such as the fast-food business, that are not technology intensive but labor intensive. The management of these businesses faces a different challenge: to acquire the necessary human resources by reaching out to new potential employees. In part this may entail offering jobs to the elderly who wish, because of Social Security restrictions, only to work part-time. In certain areas of the country where there is a severe shortage of young employees, the McMasters program recruits and trains senior citizens for McDonald's employment.

In part, getting necessary workers may entail greater employment of the physically and developmentally challenged, an employment strategy actively endorsed by the Society to Advance Retarded and Handicapped, Inc., a not-for-profit agency of the Association for Retarded Citizens. This organization, currently in Norwalk, Connecticut, places the developmentally challenged in jobs formerly held by high school students and finds employers generally enthusiastic about the worker performance. McDonald's Corporation has started a program called McJobs, an attempt to recruit, train, and employ handicapped and developmentally challenged workers.

The Southland Corporation, parent organization of the nationwide chain of 7-11 stores, has taken yet another approach to acquiring needed human resources. It started innovative advertising to seek out potential employees. Although one might question the taste of having the Lone Ranger, a creature from outer space, and the Queen of England applying for jobs at a 7-11, you cannot doubt the innovation and enthusiasm of this large business as it attempted to hire new workers. Corporations will have to reach out to prospective employees as never before, and the New York-New Jersey-Pennsylvania chain of Abraham and Straus department stores did just that by training inner-city young people and then transporting them on a daily basis to its suburban stores where employees were needed and not available. This is seen as a social action program that benefits all concerned; the company gets needed employees, society gets new tax payers, and the individuals achieve new employment levels otherwise not available.

Management must confront this new reality of labor force scarcity in the teenage ranks. For businesses that have traditionally depended upon this labor pool, the new reality will necessitate creative managerial solutions to the problem of labor acquisition and retention. It is clear that if management seeks out the physically challenged, the aged, and the previously unemployable economically disadvantaged, tomorrow's fast-food restaurant will be considerably different than the store of today. That individual serving you the hamburger and french fries may well be a grandmother, not a fellow classmate from the high school homeroom.

WORKER EDUCATION

As shown in the discussion of the second trend, jobs are becoming more technical and will require more worker skills. Managers have found that workers often lack these requisite skills, particularly in the area of mathematics techniques necessary for the new quality control procedures based upon statistical methodologies. Workers, often safe and secure in their traditional jobs, have been able to get by with minimal reading and mathematics skills in the past because (1) they have acquired the necessary practical knowledge to do their jobs by apprenticeship and (2) the original jobs did not demand the same skill levels as are needed today.

A national survey done in April 1986 and replicated on a regular basis, found that 17–21 million U.S. adults are illiterate. Even more are functionally illiterate, defined as not having sufficient reading skills to cope with everyday tasks. Consider the following results of a study done by the Adult Performance Level project of the University of Texas:

- Of adults 18 years of age or over, 14 percent could not fill out a bank check correctly.

- Of adults 18 or over, 38 percent could not successfully match personal characteristics with those mentioned as job requirements in help-wanted advertisements.

- Of adults in the sample 18 or over, 26 percent could not correctly identify the Social Security deduction on a paycheck stub.

Many personnel managers confirm that the results of this type of study have not only not changed, but have probably become worse. There are large numbers of workers who lack the necessary mathematics and reading skills to perform with maximal efficiency and achieve success in the new jobs. In worker surveys, the employees themselves say that they need training in understanding simple words, labels, and signs; reading basic instructions; and understanding company procedures. As a result, many companies are now entering the education business to upgrade the skills of their workers. This can be done in several ways.

A company may offer a *tuition reimbursement program* that encourages workers to attend local community college remedial adult educational programs. The worker signs up for the program, and the company pays for all or part of the cost. The advantage to the company in this type of program is that it lets the worker choose the most suitable program and makes available the whole range of community resources. The main disadvantage to the company is that the worker's attendance in this program is voluntary, and the worker may elect not to go because of personal embarrassment or inconvenience. As a consequence, some companies, such as Data General and Blue Cross, run their own adult remedial educational programs.

The Continuing Education Institute of Medford, Massachusetts, a nonprofit enterprise engaged in remedial education, finds that it has a thriving business in the Boston area and is increasingly experiencing a national interest with companies that seek to advance the educational levels of employees. Similar enterprises are springing up around the country, and companies are eagerly seeking their services. An educated workforce will be more productive, and such investment often pays for itself. Computer program companies, such as Control Data, are offering self-paced remedial educational programs that allow the worker to study—via computer terminal—at his or her own pace. Also, training courses and even professional certification programs are becoming available via the Internet.

Many lower skilled workers labor in the clerical area or on the factory floor where much activity is routine and requires little in the way of literacy skills. Workers are successful because they learn visually and have been trained by older workers. Computer technology has changed this basic situation. As computer technology has penetrated the factory floor, it is harder for the worker to conceal the lack of literacy skills. Since the next major trend we shall examine is the proliferation of computer technology, it is evident that increasing worker literacy skill levels will continue to be a main managerial concern. Technology creates new literacy demands, and managers, well-trained in motivation and supervisory skills, will find that they need to become part-time educators to meet the challenge of the workforce of tomorrow. The federal government has recognized the crucial need to make information available to managers regarding adult educational programs. It has created the Clearinghouse on Adult Education headquartered in Washington, D.C., as a department of the U.S. Department of Education. Many states have also established directors of adult education within the state educational department, as have some local communities. For example, New York City has created the Business Council for Effective Literacy as an expression of local concern for worker literacy and the viability of metropolitan industry. Without workers, there will be no local industry.

CHANGING NATURE OF THE WORK ENVIRONMENT: GROWTH OF THE COMPUTER

As was noted in Chapter 23, the cost of computing power has fallen dramatically over the last 40 years. Consider the following facts about the first computer, ENIAC:

Its vacuum tubes and structure weighed 60,000 lb.

All this took up two stories of a building and covered over 15,000 ft.

It cost almost $487,000 in 1947 dollars.

As impressive as ENIAC was in its day, further consider that this page you are reading was written on the latest model Apple Macintosh computer, which costs less than $2000 and can perform mathematical functions over 30 times faster than ENIAC. Some computer scientists even estimate that a digital watch, costing only a few dollars, will have as much computing power as the original ENIAC. This is the trend of *technology proliferation*, which describes a condition in which a form of technology, in either theory or application, is widely adapted to new situations.

As the cost of computing power has fallen, it has become widely available. It was estimated that the total computing power sold between 1987 and 1989 equaled all computing power sold in the previous 40 years. This computing power again doubled by 1995. Computer technology is and will continue to be applied to everything from digital watches to supermarket checkout lines and automobiles, in addition to the growing number of computers from the personal to the large mainframe. All this implies that computer technology will play an increasingly important role in the life of the contemporary manager. As was previously pointed out, the computer will be taken for granted in its ability to generate vast amounts of data. Managers will have to know (1) how this information is generated and, of greater importance, (2) how to make effective use of this information.

The computer villain of the cult classic science fiction movie *2001: A Space Odyssey* was HAL, and it was noted that when a letter was added to the computer's name, the following appeared: H + 1 letter = I; A + 1 letter = B; and L + 1 letter = M. HAL was a synonym for IBM and by making it a villain, the film's director Stanley Kubrick related to the unspoken fears of many viewers. The computer was repackaged 9 years later by George Lucas as the manageable, even lovable, R2-D2 and C-3PO, the hero's sidekicks in the monumental original *Star Wars* trilogy. In the interim, programmable hand calculators became common and the first hobby kit home computers were appearing. Since then millions of individuals have purchased personal computers and even the smallest business may now have a computer system to perform bookkeeping and inventory tasks far more accurately than a legion of clerks.

There is no doubt that one of the major challenges to managers has been to learn, adapt to, and become proficient in using the emerging computer technologies. Literacy now includes a knowledge of computer technology and application; a manager must be "computer literate" or risk being left by the wayside. As computers and computer programs become more "user friendly," they will be even more widely applied to basic business problems. In many work situations they are the future, and they work.

By late 1999 Apple G4 desktop computers could perform over one billion operations per second, effectively placing the equivalent of a Cray supercomputer on the manager's desk. The challenge for a manager will be to maximize such processing power, which will surely continue to grow, more effectively. The premium will not be in the power alone but in the use of such power.

CHANGING NATURE OF THE MANAGER: NEED FOR MANAGERIAL AND INTERPERSONAL SKILLS

Viewing the previous seven trends together, it is apparent that there are some seeming contradictions: The workforce will grow and age but the number of young people will decline. Women and foreign workers will enter the labor force in increasing numbers, but not in traditional U.S. manufacturing industries. Computer technology will proliferate even as many workers lack the necessary skills to operate on such a technical level. The one common thread that weaves itself through these seemingly contradictory trends is the need for greater levels of managerial and interpersonal skills.

Increasingly, productivity and employee effectiveness will be the result of good managerial skills, not technology. There will be a continuing need for skilled managers, and those coming to the managerial ranks will be more educated than ever before. Management is an accepted academic discipline and is being seriously studied at major universities. The findings of these academic studies and research are regularly published in scholarly journals and even reported in the popular press. It is not uncommon to find managers with a Master's degree in Business Administration (MBA) who have specialized in the history and practice of management. There will be a premium placed upon managers with good people skills. *People skills* is a popular term used to describe a group of interpersonal relationship skills (as opposed to mechanical or technical skills, which describe a relationship to machinery) generally assumed to relate to managerial success. These include communications skills, knowledge and application of motivational concepts, goal-setting abilities, and performance appraisal skills.

Business organizations recognize that executives will have to be better trained in managerial techniques and such interpersonal skills as communication and motivation. Many companies are encouraging managers to seek advanced training and education outside the workplace by means of tuition reimbursement. Yet other companies hire professional trainers to teach managerial skills, and the field of executive training is thriving. Management education, a response to the emerging trends previously cited, can itself be viewed as an emerging trend.

A final note about future trend forecasting is in order. It can be, as you have seen, a fascinating excursion, going from what is to what might be. It is hardly an exact enterprise, however, it is filled with error. Distrust anyone who claims to know the future, but read widely in the business and popular press. Speak to your fellow managers in your industry and other industries, and participate in trade and industrial associations. Above all, understand that change, however rapid, was the hallmark of the latter half of the 20th century and there is every reason to believe that rapid change in business, and the environments of business, will continue as the hallmark of the 21st century. The successful manager will be the individual who anticipates change and actively plans for it. In change there will be opportunity, and those who are able to anticipate it will be the success stories of tomorrow.

Management is a continually evolving area, and every practicing manager has a potential contribution to the theory and practice of this area. So in a very real sense this is not the end of this book on management—it never ends, merely continues in an action-based format of managerial practice by you, the reader. As you practice management and go from success to even greater success, you will be writing the next chapter. Good luck.

APPENDIX 1
BIBLIOGRAPHY

CHAPTER 1:

Blair, M. Gerard. What Makes a Great Manager? [Online]. Available: *http://www.ee.ed.ac.uk/~gerard/Management/art9.html*. [1999, September 28].

Nelson, Bob. Are you a good manager? [Online]. Available: *http://ivillage.com/TWN/print/0,2707,8674,00.html*. [1999, November 1].

CHAPTER 2:

Barlow, J. (1998, December 8). Improve the firm; listen to workers. *Houston Chronicle*. [Online]. Available: *http://proquest.umi.com*. [1999, February 22].

Chaleff, I. (1998, January/February). Full participation takes courage. *The Journal for Quality and Participation*. [Online]. Available: *http://proquest.umi.com*. [1999, February 26].

Daley, M. D., Patton, R. K. (1998, Spring). Gainsharing in Zebulon. *Public Personnel Management*. [Online]. Available: *http://proquest.umi.com*. [1999, February 2].

Dykeman, B. J. (1998, May). Knowledge management moves from theory toward practice. *Managing Office Technology*. [Online]. Available: *http://proquest.umi.com*. [1999, February 2].

Mayer, C. M. (1998, Fall). Trust an asset in any field. *Baylor Business Review*. [Online]. Available: *http://proquest.umi.com*. [1999, February 26].

Oakland, S., Oakland, S. J. (1998, July). The links between people management, customer satisfaction and business results. *Total Quality Management*. [Online]. Available: *http://proquest.umi.com*. [1999, February 26].

Prasas, S., Tata, J. (1998, December). Cultural and scructural constraints on total quality management implementation. *Total Quality Management*. [Online]. Available: *http://proquest.umi.com*. [1999, February 26].

Sunoo, P. B. (1998, May). Nantucket Nectars' recipe for participation. *Workforce*. [Online]. Available: *http://proquest.umi.com*. [1999, February 22].

Van Winkle, S. (1997, August). Customized management. *PM Public Management*. [Online]. Available: *http://proquest.umi.com*. [1999, March 1].

Weiss, H. W. (1998, October). Improving employee performance: major supervisory responsibility. *Supervision*. [Online]. Available: *http://proquest.umi.com*. [1999, February 22].

CHAPTER 3:

(1998, September 18). Business brief—British Petroleum PLC: carbon-dioxide emissions to be cut 10% by 2010. *The Wall Street Journal*. [Online]. Available: *http://proquest.umi.com*. [1999, March 8].

Daviss, B. (1999, March). Profits from principle. *The Futurist*. [Online]. Available: *http://proquest.umi.com*. [1999, March 5].

Desjardins, J. (1998, January). Corporate environmental responsibility. *Journal of Business Ethics*. [Online]. Available: *http://proquest.umi.com*. [1999, March 5].

Esterson, E. (1998, September). One holdout a white knight who won't quit. *Inc*. [Online]. Available: *http://proquest.umi.com*. [1998, September].

Gallagher, E. (1998, April). Save the earth and make a profit. *Management Today*. [Online]. Available: *http://proquest.umi.com*. [1999, March 12].

(1998, December). GE signs cleanup agreement with U.S. EPA. *Civil Engineering*. [Online]. Available: *http://proquest.umi.com*. [1999, March 12].

Herman, R. (1998, September). It's more than money. *FDM, Furniture Design & Manufacturing*. [Online]. Available: *http://proquest.umi.com*. [1998, September].

Hibbert, L. (1999, January 27). A clean bill of health. *Professional Engineering*. [Online]. Available: *http://proquest.umi.com*. [1999, March 8].

Lermack, B. H. (1998, April). Conrail cuts the risks in risk management. *Railway*. [Online]. Available: *http://proquest.umi.com*. [1999, March 12].

Reed, B. (1998, May/June). The business of social responsibility. *Dollars & Sense*. [Online]. Available: *http://proquest.umi.com*. [1999, March 8].

(1999, January 12). Regulators are set to take legal action against Toyota unit. *The Wall Street Journal*. [Online]. Available: *http://proquest.umi.com*. [1999, March 12].

Romani, N. P. (1998, February). Environmentally responsible business. *Supervision*. [Online]. Available: *http://proquest.umi.com*. [1999, March 8].

Solomon, J. (1998, Spring). Social venture capital. *Whole Earth*. [Online]. Available: *http://proquest.umi.com*. [1999, March 8].

Welles, O. E. (1998, September). Ben's big flop. *Inc*. [Online]. Available: *http://proquest.umi.com*. [1998, September].

Whittaker, E. (1998, December). Are you environmentally challenged? *Chain Store Age*. [Online]. Available: *http://proquest.umi.com*. [1999, March 12].

CHAPTER 4:

Cannon, T. (1998, February). The third industrial revolution. *Director*. [Online]. Available: *http://proquest.umi.com*. [1999, March 19].

Collie, C. (1998, March). The changing face of corporate relocation. *HR Magazine:* 99–102.

Herman, J. (1999, February). Straight to the top: next-gen service management. *Communication Review*. [Online]. Available: *http://proquest.umi.com*. [1999, March 17].

(1999, March). Hot security technologies complement business trends. *Security*. [Online]. Available: *http://proquest.umi.com*. [1999, March 17].

Johnson, L. W. (1998, December). Success in the 21st century. *Executive Excellence*. [Online]. Available: *http://proquest.umi.com*. [1999, March 19].

Knopper, S. Tear up your resume. *Newsday*, 12 September, 1999, pp. A19, A43.

Maiman, J. (1998, October). Trends in human resources. *The CPA Journal*. [Online]. Available: *http://proquest.umi.com*. [1999, March 17].

Matthews, A. (1998, June). Diversity: a principle of human resource management. *Public Personnel Management*. [Online]. Available: *http://nrstg2p.djnr.com*. [1999, March 31].

Mitchell, R. H. III. (1999, January). When a company moves: how to help employees adjust. *HR Magazine*. [Online]. Available: *http://proquest.umi.com*. [1999, March 25].

Steinhauser, S. (1998, July 1). Age bias: is your corporate culture in need of an overhead? *HR Magazine*. [Online]. Available: *http://nrstg2s.djnr.com*. [1999, March 25].

Streeter, A. Fire-wall security: don't leave your LAN without it. *MacWeek*, 8 May, 1995, pp. 18–20.

Weil, M. M, Rosen, D. L. (1999, February). Don't let technology enslave you. *Workforce*. [Online]. Available: *http://proquest.umi.com*. [1999, March 24].

Wood, N. (1998, August 1). The enemy within. *Incentive*. [Online]. Available: *http://nrstg1s.djnr.com*. [1999, March 24].

(1997, October). Working mothers need more than just creches. *Management*. [Online]. Available: *http://proquest.umi.com*. [1999, March 19].

CHAPTER 5:

(1999, November). An intelligent answer. *Insurance & Technology*. [Online]. Available: *http://proquest.umi.com*. [1999, April 1].

Anderson, K. (1999, January). Decision-making traps. *Broadcast Engineering*. [Online]. Available: *http://proquest.umi.com*. [1999, April 1].

Birkner, R. K., Birkner, R. L. (1998, October). Learning organization update. *Occupational Hazards*. [Online]. Available: *http://proquest.umi.com*. [1999, April 1].

Draman, H. R., Boyd, H. L., Spencer, S. M., Cox, F. J. III. (1998, Fourth Quarter). A cause and effect approach to analyzing performance measures: part 2—internal plant operations. *Production and Inventory Management Journal*. [Online]. Available: *http://proquest.umi.com*. [1999, April 1].

Mansdorf, Z. (1998, May). Performance management. *Occupational Hazards*. [Online]. Available: *http://proquest.umi.com*. [1999, April 1].

Neil, D. (1997, October). Managing with systems thinking: making dynamics work for your business decision-making. *Market Research Society*. [Online]. Available: *http://proquest.umi.com*. [1999, April 1].

Pollack, T. (1999, March). How good a problem solver are you? *Supervision*. [Online]. Available: *http://proquest.umi.com*. [1999, April 1].

(1999, March). Sales agency management # 10: a guide to practical decision making. *Agency Sales*. [Online]. Available: *http://proquest.umi.com*. [1999, April 1].

Thomas, H., Plooack, T., Phillip. (1999, February). Global strategic analyses: frameworks and approaches. *The Academy of Management Executive*. [Online]. Available: *http://proquest.umi.com*. [1999, April 1].

CHAPTER 6:

Goff, N. W. Jr. (1999, August 16). Managing field organizations for outstanding results. *National Underwriter*. [Online]. Available: *http://proquest.umi.com*. [1999, October 3].

Moran, J. (1999, September 10). Outsourcing successful if bottom line improves. *Computing Canada*. [Online]. Available: *http://proquest.umi.com*. [1999, October 3].

Tucker, M. J. (1997, January). Hops helps Heineken. *Datamation*. [Online]. Available: *http://proquest.umi.com*. [1999, October 3].

CHAPTER 7:

Mercer, W. M. (1997, May). Making mergers work. *Executive Excellence*. [Online]. Available: *http://proquest.umi.com*. [1999, October 3].

CHAPTER 8:

Collett, S. (1999, July 19). SWOT analysis. *Computerworld*. [Online]. Available: *http://proquest.umi.com*. [1999, November 5].

Connors, J. (1999, January). Maximizing effectiveness through enterprise preformance management solutions. *Business Credit*. [Online]. Available: *http://proquest.umi.com*. [1999, November 5].

CHAPTER 9:

Rolph, P. (1999, July/August). The balanced scorecard: get smart and get control. *Chief Executive*. [Online]. Available: *http://proquest.umi.com*. [1999, November 7].

Stone, F. (1997, January). Who would have thought you were capable of this? *Getting Results*. [Online]. Available: *http://proquest.umi.com*. [1999, November 7].

Wheaton, B. C. (1999, July). Measuring your business. *Catalog Age*. [Online]. Available: *http://proquest.umi.com*. [1999, November 7].

CHAPTER 10:

Sliwa, C. (1999, July 26). Org charts pose problems. *Computerworld*. [Online]. Available: *http://proquest.umi.com*. [1999, November 13].

CHAPTER 11:

Drucker, F. P. (1999, October 5). Management's new paradigms. *Forbes*. [Online]. Available: *http://proquest.umi.com*. [1999, April 5].

Harari, O. (1999, January). The trust factor. *Management Review*. [Online]. Available: *http://proquest.umi.com*. [1999, April 5].

Margaret, M. (1997, February). Preparing organizations to manage the future. *Management Accounting*. [Online]. Available: *http://proquest.umi.com*. [1999, November 3].

Messinger, M. (1998, September). Delegation: your key to time management. *Business Credit*. [Online]. Available: *http://proquest.umi.com*. [1999, April 5].

Metes, G., Grenier, R. (1998, August). Wake up and smell the syzygy. *Business Communications Review*. [Online]. Available: *http://proquest.umi.com*. [1999, April 5].

Ravlin, C. E., Meglino, M. B. (1998, May 1). Individual values in organizations: concepts, controversies, and research. *Journal of Management*. [Online]. Available: *http://nrstg2p.djnr.com*. [1999, April 5].

Rohlander, G. D. (1998, September/October). The value of delegation. *Life & Health Insurance Sales*. [Online]. Available: *http://proquest.umi.com*. [1999, April 5].

Rowe, J. (1998, July/August). Bad company; how to civilize the corporation. *Dollars & Sense*. [Online]. Available. *http://proquest.umi.com*. [1999, April 5].

Schultz, R. (1999, January). Questions they never asked. *Across the Board*. [Online]. Available: *http://proquest.umi.com*. [1999, April 5].

Shelton, K. (1998, November). The burden of business. *Executive Excellence*. [Online] Available: *http://proquest.umi.com*. [1999, April 5].

Tansey, M. M. (1998, October). How delegating authority biases social choices. *Contemporary Economic Policy*. [Online]. Available: *http://proquest.umi.com*. [1999, April 5].

Wren, M. B., Rapert, I. M. (1998, November 1). Reconsidering organizational structure: a dual perspective of frameworks and processes. *Journal of Managerial Issues*. [Online]. Available: *http://nrstg2p.djnr.com*. [1999, April 5].

Yeung, R. (1999, February). Share and share alike. *Accountancy*. [Online]. Available: *http://proquest.umi.com*. [1999, April 5].

CHAPTER 13:

Greaves, S. (1999, July 1). How to keep your staff on message. *Marketing*. [Online]. Available: *http://proquest.umi.com*. [1999, November 14].

McDonald, T. (1999, September). Peerless leaders. *Successful Meetings*. [Online]. Available: *http://proquest.umi.com*. [1999, November 14].

CHAPTER 14:

Beohnke, K., DiStefano, C. A., DiStefano, J. J, Bontis, N. (1997, Summer). Leadership for extraordinary performance. *Ivey Business Quarterly*. [Online]. Available: *http://proquest.umi.com*. [1999, April 8].

Hemsath, D. (1998, January/February). Finding the word on leadership. *The Journal for Quality and Participation*. [Online]. Available: *http://proquest.umi.com*. [1990, April 8].

Laabs, J. (1998, November). Leaving a legacy of trust. *Workforce*. [Online]. Available: *http://proquest.umi.com*. [1999, April 8].

Meyer-Giampetro, A., Brown, T., Browne, N. M. J. S., Kubasek, N. (1998, November). Do we really want more leaders in business? *Journal of Business Ethics*. [Online]. Available: *http://proquest.umi.com*. [1999, April 8].

Schwarts, E. A., Dropop, C. Tools for becoming a successful manager. *Business Credit*. [Online]. Available: *http://proquest.umi.com*. [1999, April 8].

Taillieu, B. C., Tharsi, Roe, A R., De Vries, E. R. (1998, December). Need for supervision: its impact on leadership effectiveness. *The Journal of Applied Behavioral Science*. [Online]. Available: *http://proquest.umi.com*.

CHAPTER 15:

Antrim, D. (1998, July). Managing performance. *Rough Notes*. [Online]. Available: *http://proquest.umi.com*. [1999, April 8].

Berry, K. R. (1998, September). So what does an agent cost? *Best's Review*. [Online] Available: *http://proquest.umi.com*. [1999, April 8].

Bookman, R. (1999, February). Tools for cultivating constructive feedback. *Association Management*. [Online]. Available: *http://proquest.umi.com*. [1999, April 10].

Brandt, R. J. (1999, December 21). Budgeting on faith. *Industry Week*. [Online]. Available: *http://proquest.umi.com*. [1999, April 10].

Greengard, S. (1999, May 15). Fair share. *Industry Week*. [Online]. Available: *http://proquest.umi.com*. [1999, April 10].

Martin, C. D., Bartol, M. K. Performance appraisal: maintaining system effectiveness. *Public Personnel Management*. [Online]. Available: *http://proquest.umi.com*. [1999, April 8].

Miller, W. (1999, January). Basics of association budgeting. *Association Management*. [Online]. Available: *http://proquest.umi.com*. [1999, April 10].

Myers, R. (1998, October). When bigger isn't necessarily better. *Nations' Business*. [Online]. Available: *http://proquest.umi.com*. [1999, April 8].

CHAPTER 16:

Allen, L. R. (1997, October 6). People—the single point of difference—listening to them. *Nation's Restaurant News*. [Online]. Available: *http://proquest.umi.com*. [1999, April 14].

Brown, B. (1998, December). 10 trends for the new year. *Nursing Management*. [Online]. Available: *http://proquest.umi.com*. [1999, April 14].

DeMarie, M. S., Hendrikson, R. A. Virtual teams: technology and the workplace of the future. *Academy of Management Executive*. [Online]. Available: *http://proquest.umi.com*. [1999, April 14].

Klein, J. H. (1998, March 1). The fairness of assigning group members to tasks. *Group & Organization Management*. [Online]. Available: *http://proquest.umi.com*. [1999, April 14].

Nemeth, J. C. (1997, Fall). Managing innovation: when less is more. *California Management*. [Online]. Available: *http://proquest.umi.com*. [1999, April 14].

Ross, N. D. (1999, April 1). Culture as a context for multinational business: a framework for assessing the strategy—culture. *Multinational Business Review*. [Online]. Available: *http://proquest.umi.com*.

Weiss, H. W. (1999, April 14). The science and art of managing. *Supervision*. [Online]. Available: *http://proquest.umi.com*. [1999, April 14].

CHAPTER 17:

Cohen, A. (1999, January). The right stuff. *Sales and Marketing Management*. [Online]. Available: *http://proquest.umi.com*. [1999, April 16].

Fletcher, W. (1998, October). Speak out and remove all doubt. *Management Today*. [Online]. Available: *http://proquest.umi.com*. [1999, April 16].

Handy, Charles. (1997, May). Peel off the label to find a person. *Management*. [Online]. Available: *http://proquest.umi.com*. [1999, April 16].

Kolb, A. J. (1997, August). Are we still stereotyping leadership? A look at gender and other predictors of leader emergence. *Small Group Research*. [Online]. Available: *http://proquest.umi.com*. [1999, April 16].

McPherson, W. (1998, December). Learning business etiquette at dinner. *Business Communication*. [Online]. Available: *http://proquest.umi.com*. [1999, April 16].

Oakland, S., Oakland, S. J. (1998, July). The links between people management, customer satisfaction, and business results. *Total Quality Management*. [Online]. Available: *http://proquest.umi.com*. [1999, April 16].

Pollack, T. (1998, October). Make your criticism pay off. *Supervision*. [Online]. Available: *http://proquest.umi.com*. [1999, April 16].

Saftner, J. T. (1998, January). Talk the talk: how well do you communicate? *Career World* [Online]. Available: *http://proquest.umi.com*. [1999, April 16].

Slipp, S., Blank, R. (1998, July). Managers' diversity workbook. *HR Focus*. [Online]. Available: *http://proquest.umi.com*. [1999, April 16].

Strebler, M. (1997, May 29). Soft skills and hard questions. *People Management*. [Online]. Available: *http://proquest.umi.com*. [1999, April 16].

Taylor, R. (1998, August). Check your cultural competence. *Nursing Management*. [Online]. Available: *http://proquest.umi.com*. [1999, April 16].

CHAPTER 18:

Denison, D. (1999, October). Managing radical organizational change. *Academy of Management. The Academy of Management Review*. [Online]. Available: *http://proquest.umi.com*.

Guido, R. (1998, June). Managing innovation: integrating technological, market and organizational change. *Research Policy*. [Online]. Available: *http://proquest.umi.com*. [1999, December 16].

Kotter, P. J. Leading change: why transformation efforts fail. *Harvard BusinessReview*, March/April, 1999, p. (1).

Neil, D. (1999, April). Managing innovation: integrating technological, market and organizational change. *Market Research Society*. [Online]. Available: *http://proquest.umi.com*. [1999, December 16].

Thomson, T. (1999, Summer). The dynamics of introducing performance metrics into an organization. *National Productivity Review*. [Online]. Available: *http://proquest.umi.com*. [1999, December 16].

CHAPTER 19:

Dutton, G. (1998, April). Caught in the middle. *Management Review*. [Online]. Available: *http://proquest.umi.com*. [1999, April 14].

Gayle, M. B. (1998, November). Assessing emotionality in organizational conflicts. *Management Communication Quarterly*. [Online]. Available: *http://proquest.umi.com*. [1999, April 19].

Lindo. K. D. (1998, June). Are you coaching the bad news bearers? *Supervision*. [Online]. Available: *http://proquest.umi.com*. [1999, April 19].

Miller, Ed. (1998, September). Resolving organizational conflicts. *Computer-Aided Engineering*. [Online]. Available: *http://proquest.umi.com*. [1999, April 19].

Poon, M., Tjosvold, D. (1998, September). Dealing with scarce resources. *Group & Organization Management*. [Online]. Available: *http://proquest.umi.com*. [1999, April 19].

Ross, D., Shaw, M., Mackenzie, S., Wittenberg, C. (1997, September). And justice for all. *HR Magazine*. [Online]. Available: *http://proquest.umi.com*. [1999, April 19].

Schwartz, E. A. (1997, April). How to handle conflict. *The CPA Journal*. [Online]. Available: *http://proquest.umi.com*. [1999, April 19].

CHAPTER 20:

Banks, J., Gibson, R. (1998, November). Simulation evolution. *IIE Solutions*. [Online]. Available: *http://proquest.umi.com*. [1999, May 1].

————. (1997, September). Don't simulate when . . . 10 rules for determining when simulation is not appropriate. *IIE Solutions*. [Online]. Available: *http://proquest.umi.com*. [1999, May 1].

Cammarano, J. (1997, December). Project management: How to make it happen. *IIE Solutions*. [Online]. Available: *http://proquest.umi.com*. [1999, May 1].

Fishwick, A. P. (1998, September). A taxonomy for simulation modeling based on programming language principle. *IIE Transactions*. [Online]. Available: *http://proquest.umi.com*. [1999, May 1].

Fleming, W. Q., Koppelman, M. J. (1997, February). Earned value project management. *Cost Engineering*. [Online]. Available: *http://proquest.umi.com*. [1999, May 1].

Harler, C. (1997, December). How does your faith size up? *Business Communications Review*. [Online]. Available: *http://proquest.umi.com*. [1999, May 1].

Hatfield, A. M. (1998, May). The case for critical path. *Cost Engineering*. [Online]. Available: *http://proquest.umi.com*. [1999, May 1].

Jerry, B., Randall, G. (1997, February). Simulation modeling. *IIE Solutions*. [Online]. Available: *http://proquest.umi.com*. [1999, May 1].

Moizuddin, M., Selim, Z. S. (1999, May 1). Project scheduling under limited resources. *Transactions of Aace International*. [Online]. Available: *http://proquest.umi.com*. [1999, May 1].

West, J. (1998, March/April). Model answers to complex questions. *The British Journal of Administrative Management*. [Online]. Available: *http://proquest.umi.com*. [1999, May 1].

CHAPTER 21:

Goulet, R. L. (1999, August). How managers control employees' time. *The Academy of Management Executive*. [Online]. Available: *http://proquest.umi.com*. [1999, October 3].

Oncken, W. III. (1999, January). Initiative is the key to innovation. *Executive Excellence*. [Online]. Available: *http://proquest.umi.com*. [1999, October 14].

CHAPTER 22:

(1999, January). Tools for exploring careers. *Techniques*. [Online]. Available: *http://proquest.umi.com*. [1999, October 14].

CHAPTER 23:

Dryden, P. (1998, March 9). LAN tools use analysis to find Y2K problems. *Computerworld*. [Online]. Available: *http://proquest.umi.com*. [1999, May 6].

(1998, December). From the ground up. *Risk Management*. [Online]. Available: *http://proquest.umi.com*. [1999, May 6].

Greengard, S. (1998, May). How secure is your data? *Workforce*. [Online]. Available: *http://proquest.umi.com*. [1999, May 6].

Greer, E. (1998, May 25). Network associates puts power on the help desk. *Infoworld*. [Online]. Available: *http://proquest.umi.com*. [1999, May 6].

Knet, A. (1997, November). Internet assurance: a matter of trust. *Australian Accountant*. [Online]. Available: *http://proquest.umi.com*. [1999, May 6].

Leyzorck, M. (1998, October). A missing feature in some records management systems. *ARMA Records Management Quarterly*. [Online]. Available: *http://proquest.umi.com*. [1999, May 6].

McCarthy, P. S. (1998, June). Top secret. *Logistics*. [Online]. Available: *http://proquest.umi.com*. [1999, May 6].

Nelson, M., Vizard, M. (1999, January 18). Internet safety. *Infoworld*. [Online]. Available: *http://proquest.umi.com*. [1999, May 6].

Null, C. (1999, February 8). Unplugging the LAN. *Network World*. [Online]. Available: *http://proquest.umi.com*. [1999, May 6].

Parnell. T. (1999, May 1). ID, please. *Network World*. [Online]. Available: *http://proquest.umi.com*. [1999, May 5].

(1999, February). Remote access control, security a top priority. *Security*. [Online] Available: *http://proquest.umi.com*. [1999, May 6].

Rhodes, L. W. Jr. (1999, February). Network controller provides integrated IP routing. *AS/400 Systems Management*. [Online]. Available: *http://proquest.umi.com*. [1999, May 6].

Sherman, D. (1998, September 7). Tackling the p's and q's of LAN traffic. *Network World*. [Online]. Available: *http://proquest.umi.com*. [1999, May 6].

Strauchs, J. J. (1998, July). Vulnerability of the corporate backbone needs attention. *Security*. [Online]. Available: *http://proquest.umi.com*. [1999, May 6].

Tiazkun, S. (1998, May 25). Keeping networks running smoothly. *Computer Reseller*. [Online]. Available: *http://proquest.umi.com*. [1999, May 6].

CHAPTER 24:

Abrams, N. M. (1998, June). Integrating corporate culture from international M&As. *HR Focus*. [Online]. Available: *http://proquest.umi.com*. [1999, May 13].

Bucholtz, C. (1997, February 17). Masters of their fortune. *Telephony*. [Online]. Available: *http://proquest.umi.com*. [1999, May 13].

Conlin, M. J. (1998, June). The patent files. *Chief Executive*. [Online]. Available: *http://proquest.umi.com*. [1999, May 13].

Joinson, C. (1998, April). Why HR managers need to think globally. *HR Magazine*. [Online]. Available: *http://proquest.umi.com*. [1999, May 13].

Miller, W. H. (1997, March 3). Growing globally, at last. *Industry Week*. [Online]. Available: *http://proquest.umi.com*. [1999, May 13].

Numerof, E. R. (1998, June). Integrating corporate culture from international M&As. *HR Focus*. [Online]. Available: *http://proquest.umi.com*. [1999, May 13].

(1999, March). Thomson & Thomson offers free translations in International Trademark Search reports. *Information Today*. [Online]. Available: *http://proquest.umi.com*. [1999, May 13].

Turton, J. (1999, January). A big year predicted in international mergers. *Corporate Finance*. [Online]. Available: *http://proquest.umi.com*. [1999, May 13].

Van Hoosear, L. J. (1998, December). Protecting your image around the world. *World Trade*. [Online]. Available: *http://proquest.umi.com*. [1999, May 13].

Vinzant, D. (1997, Winter). Five network nightmares you can solve with job scheduling solutions. *The Canadian Magazine*. [Online]. Available: *http://proquest.umi.com*. [1999, May 6].

Westgeest, A. (1999, March). Transitioning to the Euro. *Association Management*. [Online]. Available: *http://proquest.umi.com*. [1999, May 13].

CHAPTER 25:

Cohen, E. J. Now we are six . . . billion. *Newsday*, 10 October, 1999, p. B5.

Frost, B. (1999, May/June). Performance metrics: the new strategic discipline. *Strategy & Leadership*. [Online]. Available: *http://proquest.umi.com*. [1999, May 13].

Fuertes, M. (1999, April). Open resume. *HR Magazine*. [Online]. Available: *http://proquest.umi.com*. [1999, May 13].

Guajardo, S. (1999, Spring). Workforce diversity: monitoring employment trends in public organization. *Public Personnel Management*. [Online]. Available: *http://proquest.umi.com*. [1999, May 13].

Laabs, J. (1999, April). Has downsizing missed its mark? *Workforce*. [Online]. Available: *http://proquest.umi.com*. [1999, May 13].

Preston, R. D. (1999, May). Time for success: a new approach to a familiar challenge. *The American Salesman*. [Online]. Available: *http://proquest.umi.com*. [1999, May 13].

Schutz, J. R. (1998, June). The patent files. *Chief Executive*. [Online]. Available: *http://proquest.umi.com*. [1999, May 13].

Shane, C. (1999, April). The fine arts of corporate management. *Across the Board*. [Online]. Available: *http://proquest.umi.com*. [1999, May 13].

APPENDIX 3:

Ciancarelli, A. (1999, January 14). Certifications advance purchasing careers. *Purchasing.* [Online] Available: *http://proquest.umi.com.* [1999, May 27].

(1999, March 12). Do as I do. *Canadian Business.* [Online]. Available: *http://proquest.umi.com.* [1999, May 27].

Sanders, L. R. (1998, January). Records management returns to the departments: a suggestion for the next century. *ARMA Records Management Quarterly.* [Online]. Available: *http://proquest.umi.com.* [1999, May 27].

Stark, P. (1999, February 13). Mangers bemoan country radio climate. *Billboard.* [Online]. Available: *http://proquest.umi.com.* [1999, May 27].

APPENDIX 5:

Daniels, K. P., Edgar, E. S. *Job seeker's guides to private and public companies.* Gale Research Inc. *Hoover's Master List of Major U.S. Companies.* (1998–1999). Texas: Hoover Business Press.

U.S. Department of Labor (1998). *Occupational Outlook Handbook.* (1998–1999 ed.). Washington, DC: U.S. Depository.

APPENDIX 2
LIFE PLANNING

This series of exercises focuses on your life goals and the plans you may have (or should have) to accomplish those goals. Some typical goals are listed under the phase of adulthood during which they ordinarily occur.

A PERSPECTIVE OF THE ADULT YEARS*

Early adulthood
  Select a mate
  Start an occupation
  Start a family
  Rear children
  Manage a home
  Find a congenial social group
  Take civic responsibility
Middle age
  Relate to one's spouse as a person
  Achieve social and civic responsibility
  Establish and maintain an economic standard of living
  Assist teenage children to become happy and responsible adults
  Reach the top of the vocational ladder
  Adjust to aging parents
  Develop leisure-time activities
Late maturity
  Adjust to decreasing physical strength and health
  Adjust to retirement and reduced income
  Adjust to death of a spouse
  Establish satisfactory living arrangements

EXERCISE 1. VALUES

Values is used here to mean what you consider important *to you*. Something is important to you when you will brave significant risk to attain or protect it. Understanding the priority of your values is basic to setting a priority for your goals, since goals are nothing but values in action, or values made *operational*, in the language of the psychologist.

---

* From material by Robert Havighurst, University of Chicago.

516

• *VALUE DEFINITIONS*

affection Some degree of love and friendship of others in person-to-person relationships and in more remote relationships. The word *degree* is used because affection, like other values, is relative. As members of close groups, we express affection by warm, friendly, and congenial actions toward one another. Loyalty to one's country and a feeling of closeness to one's fellow citizens are expressed more remotely.

enlightenment Knowledge necessary to make important decisions. Information about the past and the present provides a basis for making estimates about the future. Such estimates are of vital importance in making important decisions, for both the individual and the group.

power Some degree of participation in the process of making important decisions. In all societies, decision-making involves power. Helping to make decisions that affect others is a far-reaching exercise of power.

rectitude A sense of right and wrong. Humans have faced differences between right and wrong since our earliest days on earth. Every person needs and wants some degree of moral practice and ethical standards. In a free society, the moral person acts in ways that contribute to the wide sharing of human values. A sampling of verbal equivalents for this value includes honesty, justice, responsibility, trust, and fair play.

respect Some degree of recognition of one's capacity as a human being. The according of respect may range from a simple courtesy to a significant honor. The greeting "Good morning, Bob" recognizes the humanness and the individuality of another person; thus it is a means of according him respect. A sincere compliment for an achievement is another example. An award for an outstanding accomplishment is also a measure of respect.

skill Development of talents. Every individual has potential physical and mental talents to develop.

wealth Access to goods and services. How much we desire wealth is relative to our wants and needs. Money represents a claim against society for goods and services. Property, food, shelter, clothing, and services are a sampling of equivalents of wealth.

well-being Mental and physical health. Each individual's feeling of well-being is largely dependent upon his or her rating of the other values. Deprivation of affection, respect, wealth, or any of the other human values causes a reduction of well-being. If one has a feeling of relatively high status in the other values, one's feeling of well-being is also likely to be high.

Please rank these values in order of their importance to you, giving a rank of 1 to the value you consider most important, 2 to the next, and so on. You should carefully read the definitions on pages 516-517 before proceeding.

Affection _____

Enlightenment _____

Power _____

Rectitude _____

Respect _____

Skill _____

Wealth _____

Well-being _____

EXERCISE 2. ACHIEVEMENTS AND STRENGTHS

Using the chart provided here, break your life to date into three major periods—by years, if you wish, by events, or by a combination of these—for example, from birth through college, from private first class to lieutenant colonel, or from marketing representative to district manager.

Now, list for each age period the three achievements of that period that were most significant to you. Be sure to reflect on all aspects of your life: your family, your career, your society, and so on.

Finally, indicate for each of the nine achievements that personal strength that contributed the most to its accomplishment. A personal strength can be a specific skill, a kind of knowledge, or a personal characteristic, such as initiative, integrity, or courage.

MY LIFE TO DATE

PERIOD 1

From_____

To_____

Achievements	Strengths
1.	
2.	
3.	

PERIOD 2	
From_____	
To_____	
Achievements	*Strengths*
4.	
5.	
6.	

PERIOD 3	
From_____	
To_____	
Achievements	*Strengths*
7.	
8.	
9.	

Chart for examining your achievements through various periods by determining the personal strengths that contributed most to their accomplishment.

EXERCISE 3. LIFE INVENTORY

This next series of exercises is designed to assist you in making your life inventory. You will examine more fully your ambitions, your assets, and your inadequacies. The effort to display all of yourself in terms of your activities and values is hard work. There will be some overlap.

• *PEAK EXPERIENCES*

These are not necessarily the most exquisite moments you have had. These are, or have been, your "kicks," the moments in your life that are remembered as having been really great; the times when you have felt you were really living and enjoying living. These are the moments that have made you feel living is worthwhile, the events that have mattered to you in terms of making you feel you are glad you are a human being and glad you are alive.

_____

_____

_____

_____

_____

_____

• *THINGS I DO WELL*

Some of these are very meaningful to you. There may be duplication with your first list. Some of the things you do well may be things that bore you to death. This is a hard list to compile because it competes with our cultural approval of modesty. Try to overcome this inhibition.

_____

_____

_____

_____

_____

_____

• *THINGS I DO POORLY*

This list should contain things you want to do or that you have to do, but not things in which you have no interest. It should be a list of things that you do poorly that for some reason or another you need to do. You may play the violin poorly, but if you have no desire or need to play well, do not include playing the violin.

_____

_____

_____

_____

_____

• *THINGS I WOULD LIKE TO LEARN TO DO WELL*

This may be a list of desired skills that you would like to include in your personal and potential life. It may be related to an avocational activity or a new skill in your present job.

_____

_____

_____

_____

_____

_____

• *THINGS I WOULD LIKE TO STOP DOING*

This might be something that you have to do but would like to stop doing. Someone else may have suggested things that it would be good for you to stop doing. There may be things you like to do but that you know you do so poorly that you should really stop. There may be things that you hate to do but for some reason feel you have to do—but you would very much like to stop.

_____

_____

_____

_____

_____

_____

Personal Objectives
(Planning *Now* to Reach Goals)

What Do I Want?	Where Am I Now?	When Do I Want It? (When Should It Occur?)	What Will Be Important?	How Can I Get There?
Two-Year Goals				
Five-Year Goals				

APPENDIX 3

CAREERS FOR GENERAL MANAGERS AND TOP EXECUTIVES

The U.S. Bureau of Labor Statistics provides general information on careers in management in its *Occupational Outlook Handbook (1998–1999)*. For your convenience, we reprint some of this information here.

Significant Points

- This group is among the highest paid workers in the Nation, but long hours and substantial travel often are required.

- Competition for top managerial jobs will be keen because of the large number of qualified applicants seeking jobs.

NATURE OF THE WORK

Chief executive officer, president, executive vice president, owner, partner, brokerage office manager, school superintendent, and police chief—each is a general manager or top executive—the individual who formulates the policies and directs the operations of businesses and corporations, nonprofit institutions, and government agencies. (The chief executives who formulate policy in government are discussed in detail in the *Handbook* statement on government chief executives and legislators.)

The fundamental objective of private for-profit companies is to make a profit for their owners, or in corporations, to increase shareholder value. Nonprofit organizations and government agencies implement programs that further their policies within budgetary constraints. General managers and top executives set strategies and try to ensure that their organizations' objectives are met.

A corporation's general goals and policies are established by the chief executive officer in collaboration with other top executives, who are overseen by a board of directors. In a large corporation, the chief executive officer meets frequently with subordinate executives to ensure that operations are being carried out in accordance with these policies. Although the chief executive officer of a corporation retains overall accountability, a chief operating officer may be delegated the authority to oversee the executives who direct the activities of various departments and are responsible for implementing the organization's policies on a day-to-day basis. In publicly-held corporations, it is the board of directors that is ultimately accountable for the success or failure of the enterprise; the chief executive officer reports to the board. In nonprofit corporations, the board of trustees or board of directors fulfills the same role.

The scope of other high level executives' responsibilities depends upon the size of the organization. In large organizations, their duties are highly specialized. Managers of cost and profit centers are responsible for the overall performance of one aspect of the organization, such as manufacturing, marketing, sales, purchasing, finance, personnel, training, administrative services, electronic data processing, property management, transportation, or the legal services department. (Some of these and other managerial occupations are discussed elsewhere in this section of the *Handbook*.) In smaller firms, the chief executive or general manager might be responsible for all or a number of these functions.

Middle managers, in turn, direct their individual departments' activities within the framework of the organization's overall plan with the help of first-line managers and their staffs. First-line managers oversee and motivate the workers to achieve the departments' goals as rapidly and economically as possible. In smaller organizations, such as independent retail stores or small manufacturers, a partner, owner, or general manager may be responsible for all purchasing, hiring, training, quality control, and other day-to-day supervisory duties. (See the *Handbook* statement on retail managers.)

WORKING CONDITIONS

Top executives are generally provided with spacious offices and secretarial and support staff. General managers in large firms or nonprofit organizations are usually provided with comfortable offices close to the top executives to whom they report. Long hours, including evenings and weekends, are the rule for most top executives and general managers, though their schedules may be flexible.

Substantial travel often is required of managers and executives, who may travel between national, regional, and local offices, or overseas, to monitor operations and meet with customers, staff, and other executives. Many managers and executives attend meetings and conferences sponsored by associations. The conferences provide an opportunity to meet with prospective donors, customers, or government officials and contractors, and allow managers and executives to keep abreast of technological and managerial innovations.

In large organizations, frequent job transfers between local offices or subsidiaries are common. General managers and top executives are under intense pressure to earn ever higher profits, provide better service, or attain fundraising and charitable goals. Executives in charge of poorly performing organizations or departments generally find their jobs in jeopardy.

EMPLOYMENT

General managers and top executives held over 3.2 million jobs in 1996. They are found in every industry, but wholesale, retail, and services industries employ over 8 out of 10.

TRAINING, OTHER QUALIFICATIONS, AND ADVANCEMENT

The educational background of managers and top executives varies as widely as the nature of their responsibilities. Many general managers and top executives have a bachelor's degree or higher in liberal arts or business administration. Their major often is related to the departments they direct—for example, accounting for a manager of finance or computer science for a manager of information systems. Graduate and professional degrees are common. Many managers in administrative, marketing, financial, and manufacturing activities have a master's degree in business administration. Managers in highly technical manufacturing and research activities often have a master's degree in engineering or a doctoral degree in a scientific discipline. A law degree is mandatory for managers of legal departments; hospital administrators generally have a master's degree in health services administration or business administration. (For additional information, see the *Handbook* statement on health services managers.) College presidents and school superintendents generally have an advanced degree, the former, a doctorate in the field they originally taught, and the latter, often a masters degree in education administration. (See the *Handbook* statement on education administrators.) On the other hand, in industries such as retail trade or transportation, it is possible for individuals without a college degree to work their way up within the company and become managers.

In the public sector, many managers have liberal arts degrees in public administration or one of the social sciences. Park superintendents, for example, often have liberal arts degrees, while police chiefs are generally graduates of law enforcement academies and hold degrees in criminal justice or a related field.

Since many general manager and top executive positions are filled by promoting experienced, lower level managers when an opening occurs, many are promoted from within the organization. Some companies prefer that their top executives have specialized backgrounds and hire individuals who are managers in other organizations. Qualities critical for success include leadership, self-confidence, motivation, decisiveness, flexibility, the ability to communicate effectively, sound business judgment, and stamina.

Advancement may be accelerated by participation in company training programs to gain a broader knowledge of company policy and operations. Through attendance at national or local training programs sponsored by various industry and trade associations and by continuing their education, normally at company expense, managers can become familiar with the latest developments in management techniques and improve their chances of promotion. Every year thousands of senior managers, who often have experience in a particular field, such as accounting or engineering, attend executive development programs to facilitate their promotion to general managers. Participation in conferences and seminars can expand knowledge of national and international issues influencing the organization and can help develop a network of useful contacts.

General managers and top executives must have highly developed personal skills. An analytical mind able to quickly assess large amounts of information and data is very important, as is the ability to consider and evaluate the interrelationships of numerous factors; they must also be able to communicate clearly and persuasively, and need highly developed interpersonal skills.

General managers may advance to top executive positions, such as executive vice president, in their own firms or they may take a corresponding position in another firm. They may even advance to peak corporate positions such as chief operating officer or chief executive officer. Chief executive officers often become members of the board of directors of one or more firms, typically as a director of their own firm and often as chair of its board of directors. Some general managers and top executives go on to establish their own firms or become independent consultants.

JOB OUTLOOK

Employment of general managers and top executives is expected to grow about as fast as the average for all occupations through the year 2006. Because this is a large occupation, many openings will occur each year as executives transfer to other positions, start their own businesses, or retire. Nonetheless, competition for top managerial jobs will be keen. Many executives who leave their jobs transfer to other executive or managerial positions, limiting openings for new entrants.

Projected employment growth of general managers and top executives varies widely among industries. For example, employment growth is expected to be faster than average in all services industries combined, but only about as fast as average in all finance, insurance, and real estate industry subgroups. Employment of general managers and top executives is projected to decline in manufacturing industries overall.

Experienced managers whose accomplishments reflect strong leadership qualities and the ability to improve the efficiency or competitive position of an organization will have the best opportunities. In an increasingly global economy, certain types of experience, such as international economics, marketing, information systems, and knowledge of several languages, may also help.

EARNINGS

General managers and top executives are among the highest paid workers in the Nation. However, salary levels vary substantially depending upon the level of managerial responsibility, length of service, and type, size, and location of the firm.

At the highest level, chief executive officers (CEOs) of medium and large corporations are extremely well paid. Salaries often are related to the size of the corporation—a top manager in a very large corporation can earn significantly more than a counterpart in a small firm. Total compensation often includes stock options, dividends, and other performance bonuses, in addition to salaries.

Salaries also vary substantially by type and level of responsibilities and by industry. According to a salary survey by Robert Half International, senior vice presidents/heads of lending in banks with $1 billion or more in assets earned about $200,000 to $215,000 in 1997. Executive Compensation Reports, a division of Harcourt Brace & Company, reports that the median salary for CEOs of public companies from the fiscal year 1995 Fortune 500 list was approximately $714,000, with three-quarters making less than about $900,000. In the nonprofit sector, three quarters of the CEOs made under $135,000 in 1996, according to a survey by Abbott, Langer & Associates.

Company-paid insurance premiums and physical examinations, the use of executive dining rooms and company cars, and expense allowances are among benefits commonly enjoyed by general managers and top executives in private industry. CEOs often enjoy company-paid club memberships, a limousine with driver, and other amenities. CEOs of very large corporations may have the use of a private aircraft.

RELATED OCCUPATIONS

General managers and top executives plan, organize, direct, control, and co-ordinate the operations of an organization and its major departments or programs. The members of the board of directors and supervisory managers are also involved in these activities. Related occupations in government with similar functions are President, governor, mayor, commissioner, and legislator.

SOURCES OF ADDITIONAL INFORMATION

For a wide variety of information on general managers and top executives, including educational programs and job listings, contact:

- American Management Association, 1601 Broadway, New York, NY 10019-7420.

- National Management Association, 2210 Arbor Blvd., Dayton, OH 45439.

APPENDIX 4
FIRMS OFFERING EMPLOYMENT SERVICES

Executive Search. These organizations work for the employer looking for an executive to fill a specific position. They are paid by the prospective employer for making the search and for out-of-pocket expenses of advertising, telephone, travel, or testing. They *do not charge the individual executive* who may be placed with the client company.

Executive Job Counseling. These firms work directly for the individual executive. Through counseling sessions (and perhaps with the aid of psychological tests), they help the executive to assess his or her experience, abilities, and interests and/or map out a career plan or job-finding strategy. The executive pays the fee, which applies whether the position is secured or not.

Executive Marketing. These organizations actively help the individual executive to obtain the attention of employers. They may assist in preparing a resume, compile a mailing list of possible employers, and/or send out a quantity of letters and resumes suggesting the executive to employers. The executive pays the fee, which applies whether the position is secured or not.

Licensed Personnel Agency. Agencies serve as intermediaries between employers and job seekers. They interview executives interested in new positions, evaluate their abilities, and classify them according to job specification. Employers contact them when they have openings, and the agency recommends qualifying candidates for interviews. The fee is commonly paid by the individual executive but applies only if he or she actually accepts a position with a company referred by the agency. Some agencies refer candidates only to companies that agree to pay the fee. Check the agreement to see which basis applies.

Job Register. These services maintain a clearinghouse or data bank through which resumes may be channeled to interested employers. Executives send in resumes, which the firms classify. When an employer advises them of a specific opening, their retrieval system locates appropriate resumes, which are forwarded to the employer. They charge the individual executive a fixed amount for entering the resume in the data bank. The fee applies whether the executive secures a position or not.

Internet. Provides access to countless web sites for information on jobs and employment in the new information age.

APPENDIX 5
SOURCES OF USEFUL DATA ON ORGANIZATIONS AND OCCUPATIONS

Dun & Bradstreet Million Dollar Directory

Moody's Industrial Manual

Standard & Poor's Register of Corporations, Directors and Executives

Directory of Washington Representatives of American Associations and Industry, Columbia Books, Inc., Washington, D.C.

Directory of Corporate Affiliations, National Register Publishing Company, Inc., Skokie, IL

National Directory of Addresses and Telephone Numbers, Nicholas Publishing Company, Inc., New York, NY

Federal Yellow Directory, The Washington Monitor, Washington, D.C.

National Trade and Professional Associations of the U.S. and Canada and Labor Unions, Columbia Books, Inc., Washington, D.C.

Directory of Executive Recruiters, Consultant News, Fitzwilliam, NH

Women in Executive Recruiting, Consultant News, Fitzwilliam, NH

International Directory of Executive Recruiters, Consultant News, Fitzwilliam, NH

Firms Doing Executive Search, Association of Consulting Management Engineers, New York, NY

Executive Employment Guide, Management Information Service, American Management Associations, New York, NY

Directory of Private Employment Agencies, National Employment Association, Washington, D.C.

Hoover's Master List of Major U.S. Corporations, Austin, TX

Occupational Outlook Handbook, U.S. Department of Labor, Bureau of Labor Statistics, Washington, D.C.

INDEX

BARRON'S
Business Review

More titles in this series—

Accounting, 5th Ed.
Peter J. Eisen
ISBN 0-7641-3547-3,
408 pp., $16.99, Can$21.50

Finance, 5th Ed.
A. A. Groppelli and E. Nikbakht
ISBN 0-7641-3420-5,
500 pp., $16.99, Can$24.50

Business Law, 4th Ed.
R. W. Emerson
ISBN 0-7641-1984-2,
611 pp., $18.99, Can$25.99

Management, 3rd Ed.
P. J. Montana and B. H. Charnov
ISBN 0-7641-1276-7,
468 pp., $18.99, Can$23.95

Business Statistics, 4th Ed.
D. Downing and J. Clark
ISBN 0-7641-1983-4,
481 pp., $18.99, Can$24.50

Marketing, 3rd Ed.
Richard L. Sandhusen
ISBN 0-7641-1277-5,
464 pp., $16.95, Can$23.95

Economics, 4th Ed.
Walter J. Wessels
ISBN 0-7641-3419-1,
516 pp., $16.99, Can$24.50

Operations Management
J. K. Shim and J. G. Siegel
ISBN 0-7641-0510-8,
624 pp., $16.99, Can$24.50

More selected BARRON'S titles:

Dictionary of Accounting Terms, 4th Ed.
0-7641-2898-1, $13.99, Can $19.99

Dictionary of Banking Terms, 5th Ed.
0-7641-3263-6, $14.99, Can $18.75

Dictionary of Business Terms, 4th Ed.
0-7641-3534-1, $14.99, Can $18.75

Dictionary of Computer and Internet Terms, 9th Ed.
0-7641-3417-5, $12.99, Can $18.99

Dictionary of Finance & Investment Terms, 7th Ed.
0-7641-3416-7, $14.99, Can $21.00

Dictionary of Insurance Terms, 4th Ed.
0-7641-1262-7, $14.95, Can $21.00

Dictionary of International Business Terms, 3rd Ed.
0-7641-2445-5, $14.95, Can $21.95

Dictionary of Marketing Terms, 3rd Ed.
0-7641-1214-7, $14.95, Can $21.95

Dictionary of Real Estate Terms, 6th Ed.
0-7641-2446-3, $13.99, Can $19.95

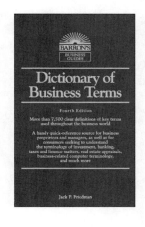

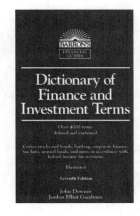

Barron's Educational Series, Inc.
250 Wireless Boulevard, Hauppauge, NY 11788
In Canada: Georgetown Book Warehouse
34 Armstrong Ave., Georgetown, Ontario L7G 4R9

Visit our web site at: www.barronseduc.com

(#12) R 4/07